HOLT McDOUGAL

Europe and Russia

Christopher L. Salter

HISTORY

HOLT McDOUGAL

HOUGHTON MIFFLIN HARCOURT

Author

Dr. Christopher L. Salter

Dr. Christopher L. "Kit" Salter is Professor Emeritus of geography and former Chair of the Department of Geography at the University of Missouri. He did his undergraduate work at Oberlin College and received both his M.A. and Ph.D. degrees in geography from the University of California at Berkeley.

Dr. Salter is one of the country's leading figures in geography education. In the 1980s he helped found the national Geographic Alliance network to promote geography education in all 50 states. In the 1990s Dr. Salter was Co-Chair of the National Geography Standards Project, a group of distinguished geographers who created *Geography for Life* in 1994, the document outlining national standards in geography. In 1990 Dr. Salter received the National Geographic Society's first-ever Distinguished Geography Educator Award. In 1992 he received the George Miller Award for distinguished service in geography education from the National Council for Geographic Education. In 2006 Dr. Salter was awarded Lifetime Achievement Honors by the Association of American Geographers for his transformation of geography education.

Over the years, Dr. Salter has written or edited more than 150 articles and books on cultural geography, China, field work, and geography education. His primary interests lie in the study of the human and physical forces that create the cultural landscape, both nationally and globally.

ISBN-13 978-0-547-48486-0

3 4 5 6 7 8 9 10 0918 19 18 17 16 15 14 13 12

4500369366   B C D E F G

Reviewers

Academic Reviewers

Elizabeth Chako, Ph.D.
Department of Geography
The George Washington
    University

Altha J. Cravey, Ph.D.
Department of Geography
University of North Carolina

Eugene Cruz-Uribe, Ph.D.
Department of History
Northern Arizona University

Toyin Falola, Ph.D.
Department of History
University of Texas

Sandy Freitag, Ph.D.
Director, Monterey Bay History
    and Cultures Project
Division of Social Sciences
University of California,
    Santa Cruz

Oliver Froehling, Ph.D.
Department of Geography
University of Kentucky

Reuel Hanks, Ph.D.
Department of Geography
Oklahoma State University

Phil Klein, Ph.D.
Department of Geography
University of Northern Colorado

B. Ikubolajeh Logan, Ph.D.
Department of Geography
Pennsylvania State University

Marc Van De Mieroop, Ph.D.
Department of History
Columbia University
New York, New York

Christopher Merrett, Ph.D.
Department of History
Western Illinois University

Thomas R. Paradise, Ph.D.
Department of Geosciences
University of Arkansas

Jesse P. H. Poon, Ph.D.
Department of Geography
University at Buffalo–SUNY

Robert Schoch, Ph.D.
CGS Division of Natural Science
Boston University

Derek Shanahan, Ph.D.
Department of Geography
Millersville University
Millersville, Pennsylvania

David Shoenbrun, Ph.D.
Department of History
Northwestern University
Evanston, Illinois

Sean Terry, Ph.D.
Department of Interdisciplinary
    Studies, Geography and
    Environmental Studies
Drury University
Springfield, Missouri

Educational Reviewers

Dennis Neel Durbin
Dyersburg High School
Dyersburg, Tennessee

Carla Freel
Hoover Middle School
Merced, California

Tina Nelson
Deer Park Middle School
Randallstown, Maryland

Don Polston
Lebanon Middle School
Lebanon, Indiana

Robert Valdez
Pioneer Middle School
Tustin, California

Teacher Review Panel

Heather Green
LaVergne Middle School
LaVergne, Tennessee

John Griffin
Wilbur Middle School
Wichita, Kansas

Rosemary Hall
Derby Middle School
Birmingham, Michigan

Rose King
Yeatman-Liddell School
St. Louis, Missouri

Mary Liebl
Wichita Public Schools USD 259
Wichita, Kansas

Jennifer Smith
Lake Wood Middle School
Overland Park, Kansas

Melinda Stephani
Wake County Schools
Raleigh, North Carolina

Contents

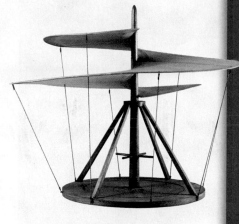

References

Available @

⇗ **hmhsocialstudies.com**

- Facts About the World
- Regions of the World Handbook
- Standardized Test-Taking Strategies
- Economics Handbook

HISTORY
MADE EVERY DAY

HISTORY™ is the leading destination for revealing, award-winning, original non-fiction series and event-driven specials that connect history with viewers in an informative, immersive and entertaining manner across multiple platforms. HISTORY is part of A&E Television Networks (AETN), a joint venture of Hearst Corporation, Disney/ABC Television Group and NBC Universal, an award-winning, international media company that also includes, among others, A&E Network™, BIO™, and History International™.

HISTORY programming greatly appeals to educators and young people who are drawn into the visual stories our documentaries tell. Our Education Department has a long-standing record in providing teachers and students with curriculum resources that bring the past to life in the classroom. Our content covers a diverse variety of subjects, including American and world history, government, economics, the natural and applied sciences, arts, literature and the humanities, health and guidance, and even pop culture.

The HISTORY website, located at **www.history.com**, is the definitive historical online source that delivers entertaining and informative content featuring broadband video, interactive timelines, maps, games, podcasts and more.

"We strive to engage, inspire and encourage the love of learning..."

Since its founding in 1995, HISTORY has demonstrated a commitment to providing the highest quality resources for educators. We develop multimedia resources for K–12 schools, two- and four-year colleges, government agencies, and other organizations by drawing on the award-winning documentary programming of A&E Television Networks. We strive to engage, inspire and encourage the love of learning by connecting with students in an informative and compelling manner. To help achieve this goal, we have formed a partnership with Houghton Mifflin Harcourt.

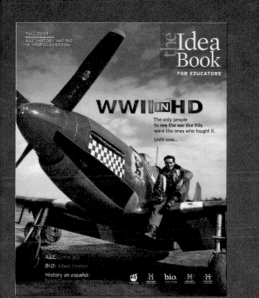
The Idea Book for Educators

Classroom resources that
bring the past to life

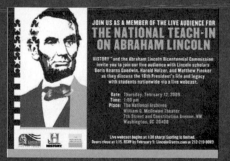
Live webcasts

HISTORY Take a Veteran to School Day

In addition to premium video-based resources, **HISTORY** has extensive offerings for teachers, parents, and students to use in the classroom and in their in-home educational activities, including:

▶ *The Idea Book for Educators* is a biannual teacher's magazine, featuring guides and info on the latest happenings in history education to help keep teachers on the cutting edge.

▶ **HISTORY Classroom (www.history.com/classroom)** is an interactive website that serves as a portal for history educators nationwide. Streaming videos on topics ranging from the Roman aqueducts to the civil rights movement connect with classroom curricula.

▶ **HISTORY email newsletters** feature updates and supplements to our award-winning programming relevant to the classroom with links to teaching guides and video clips on a variety of topics, special offers, and more.

▶ **Live webcasts** are featured each year as schools tune in via streaming video.

▶ **HISTORY Take a Veteran to School Day** connects veterans with young people in our schools and communities nationwide.

In addition to **HOUGHTON MIFFLIN HARCOURT**, our partners include the *Library of Congress*, the *Smithsonian Institution, National History Day, The Gilder Lehrman Institute of American History*, the *Organization of American Historians*, and many more. HISTORY video is also featured in museums throughout America and in over 70 other historic sites worldwide.

Geography and Map Skills Handbook

Contents

Throughout this textbook, you will be studying the world's people, places, and landscapes. One of the main tools you will use is the map—the primary tool of geographers. To help you begin your studies, this Geography and Map Skills Handbook explains some of the basic features of maps. For example, it explains how maps are made, how to read them, and how they can show the round surface of Earth on a flat piece of paper. This handbook will also introduce you to some of the types of maps you will study later in this book. In addition, you will learn about the different kinds of features on Earth and about how geographers use themes and elements to study the world.

↗ **hmhsocialstudies.com** **INTERACTIVE MAPS**

Geography Skills With map zone geography skills, you can go online to find interactive versions of the key maps in this book. Explore these interactive maps to learn and practice important map skills and bring geography to life.

You can access all of the interactive maps in this book through the Interactive Student Edition at

↗ **hmhsocialstudies.com**

Mapping the Earth
Using Latitude and Longitude

A **globe** is a scale model of the Earth. It is useful for showing the entire Earth or studying large areas of Earth's surface.

To study the world, geographers use a pattern of imaginary lines that circles the globe in east-west and north-south directions. It is called a **grid**. The intersection of these imaginary lines helps us find places on Earth.

The east-west lines in the grid are lines of **latitude**, which you can see on the diagram. Lines of latitude are called **parallels** because they are always parallel to each other. These imaginary lines measure distance north and south of the **equator**. The equator is an imaginary line that circles the globe halfway between the North and South Poles. Parallels measure distance from the equator in **degrees**. The symbol for degrees is °. Degrees are further divided into **minutes**. The symbol for minutes is ´. There are 60 minutes in a degree. Parallels north of the equator are labeled with an N. Those south of the equator are labeled with an S.

The north-south imaginary lines are lines of **longitude**. Lines of longitude are called **meridians**. These imaginary lines pass through the poles. They measure distance east and west of the **prime meridian**. The prime meridian is an imaginary line that runs through Greenwich, England. It represents 0° longitude.

Lines of latitude range from 0°, for locations on the equator, to 90°N or 90°S, for locations at the poles. Lines of longitude range from 0° on the prime meridian to 180° on a meridian in the mid-Pacific Ocean. Meridians west of the prime meridian to 180° are labeled with a W. Those east of the prime meridian to 180° are labeled with an E. Using latitude and longitude, geographers can identify the exact location of any place on Earth.

Lines of Latitude

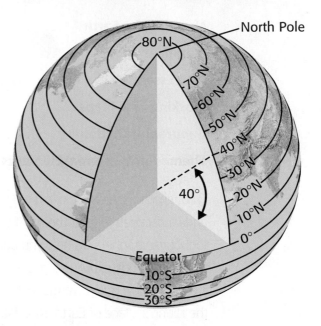

Lines of Longitude

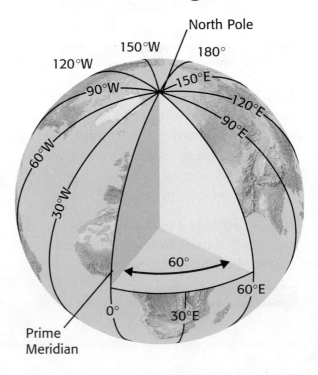

The equator divides the globe into two halves, called **hemispheres**. The half north of the equator is the Northern Hemisphere. The southern half is the Southern Hemisphere. The prime meridian and the 180° meridian divide the world into the Eastern Hemisphere and the Western Hemisphere. Look at the diagrams on this page. They show each of these four hemispheres.

Earth's land surface is divided into seven large landmasses, called **continents**. These continents are also shown on the diagrams on this page. Landmasses smaller than continents and completely surrounded by water are called **islands**.

Geographers organize Earth's water surface into major regions too. The largest is the world ocean. Geographers divide the world ocean into the Pacific Ocean, the Atlantic Ocean, the Indian Ocean, the Arctic Ocean, and the Southern Ocean. Lakes and seas are smaller bodies of water.

Northern Hemisphere

Southern Hemisphere

Western Hemisphere

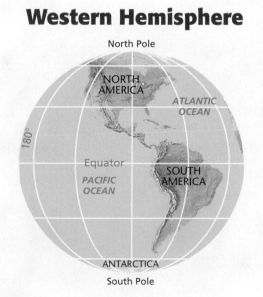

Eastern Hemisphere

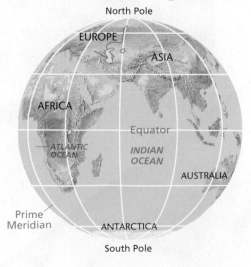

Mapmaking
Understanding Map Projections

A **map** is a flat diagram of all or part of Earth's surface. Mapmakers have created different ways of showing our round planet on flat maps. These different ways are called **map projections**. Because Earth is round, there is no way to show it accurately on a flat map. All flat maps are distorted in some way. Mapmakers must choose the type of map projection that is best for their purposes. Many map projections are one of three kinds: cylindrical, conic, or flat-plane.

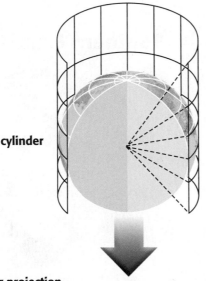

Paper cylinder

Cylindrical Projections

Cylindrical projections are based on a cylinder wrapped around the globe. The cylinder touches the globe only at the equator. The meridians are pulled apart and are parallel to each other instead of meeting at the poles. This causes landmasses near the poles to appear larger than they really are. The map below is a Mercator projection, one type of cylindrical projection. The Mercator projection is useful for navigators because it shows true direction and shape. However, it distorts the size of land areas near the poles.

Mercator projection

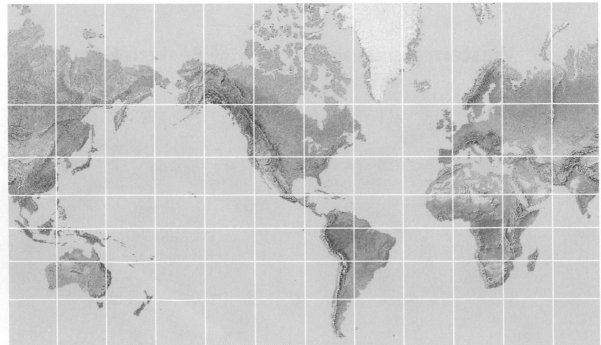

Conic Projections

Conic projections are based on a cone placed over the globe. A conic projection is most accurate along the lines of latitude where it touches the globe. It retains almost true shape and size. Conic projections are most useful for showing areas that have long east-west dimensions, such as the United States.

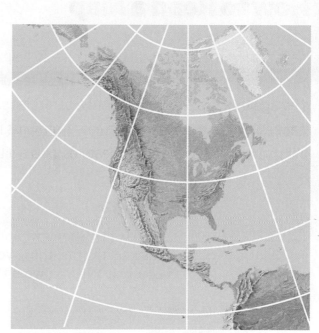

Paper cone

Conic projection

Flat-plane Projections

Flat-plane projections are based on a plane touching the globe at one point, such as at the North Pole or South Pole. A flat-plane projection is useful for showing true direction for airplane pilots and ship navigators. It also shows true area. However, it distorts the true shapes of landmasses.

Flat-plane projection

Flat plane

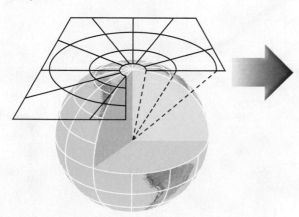

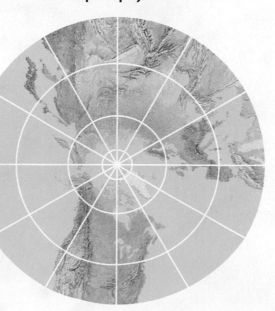

Map Essentials
How to Read a Map

Maps are like messages sent out in code. To help us translate the code, mapmakers provide certain features. These features help us understand the message they are presenting about a particular part of the world. Of these features, almost all maps have a title, a compass rose, a scale, and a legend. The map below has these four features, plus a fifth—a locator map.

❶ Title

A map's **title** shows what the subject of the map is. The map title is usually the first thing you should look at when studying a map, because it tells you what the map is trying to show.

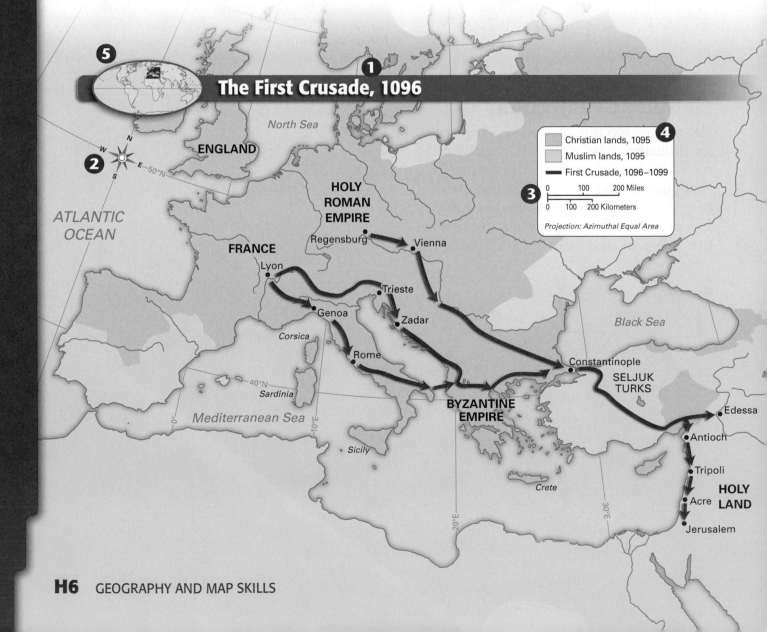

The First Crusade, 1096

North Sea

ENGLAND

ATLANTIC OCEAN

HOLY ROMAN EMPIRE

FRANCE

Regensburg • → • Vienna

Lyon

Trieste

Genoa

Zadar

Corsica

Rome

Sardinia

Mediterranean Sea

Sicily

Crete

BYZANTINE EMPIRE

Black Sea

Constantinople

SELJUK TURKS

Edessa

Antioch

Tripoli

HOLY LAND

Acre

Jerusalem

Legend:
- Christian lands, 1095
- Muslim lands, 1095
- First Crusade, 1096–1099

Scale:
0   100   200 Miles
0   100   200 Kilometers

Projection: Azimuthal Equal Area

❷ Compass Rose

A directional indicator shows which way north, south, east, and west lie on the map. Some mapmakers use a "north arrow," which points toward the North Pole. Remember, "north" is not always at the top of a map. The way a map is drawn and the location of directions on that map depend on the perspective of the mapmaker. Most maps in this textbook indicate direction by using a compass rose. A **compass rose** has arrows that point to all four principal directions.

❸ Scale

Mapmakers use scales to represent the distances between points on a map. Scales may appear on maps in several different forms. The maps in this textbook provide a **bar scale**. Scales give distances in miles and kilometers.

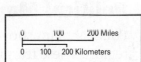

To find the distance between two points on the map, place a piece of paper so that the edge connects the two points. Mark the location of each point on the paper with a line or dot. Then, compare the distance between the two dots with the map's bar scale. The number on the top of the scale gives the distance in miles. The number on the bottom gives the distance in kilometers. Because the distances are given in large intervals, you may have to approximate the actual distance on the scale.

❹ Legend

The **legend**, or key, explains what the symbols on the map represent. Point symbols are used to specify the location of things, such as cities, that do not take up much space on the map. Some legends show colors that represent certain features like empires or other regions. Other maps might have legends with symbols or colors that represent features such as roads. Legends can also show economic resources, land use, population density, and climate.

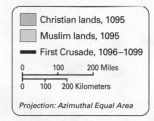

❺ Locator Map

A **locator map** shows where in the world the area on the map is located. The area shown on the main map is shown in red on the locator map. The locator map also shows surrounding areas so the map reader can see how the information on the map relates to neighboring lands.

Working with Maps
Using Different Kinds of Maps

As you study the world's regions and countries, you will use a variety of maps. Political maps and physical maps are two of the most common types of maps you will study. In addition, you will use special-purpose maps. These maps might show climate, population, resources, ancient empires, or other topics.

Political Maps

Political maps show the major political features of a region. These features include country borders, capital cities, and other places. Political maps use different colors to represent countries, and capital cities are often shown with a special star symbol.

Caribbean South America: Political

ATLANTIC OCEAN

Barranquilla
Cartagena
Maracaibo
Caracas
Valencia
Lake Maracaibo
TRINIDAD AND TOBAGO

PANAMA

Orinoco River

Medellín

VENEZUELA

Georgetown

Paramaribo

PACIFIC OCEAN

Bogotá

GUYANA

Cayenne

Cali

SURINAME

FRENCH GUIANA (FRANCE)

COLOMBIA

Orinoco River

ECUADOR

Rio Negro

PERU

Amazon River

Legend	
✪	National capital
★	Other capitals
●	Other cities

0   100   200 Miles
0   100   200 Kilometers
Projection: Azimuthal Equal-Area

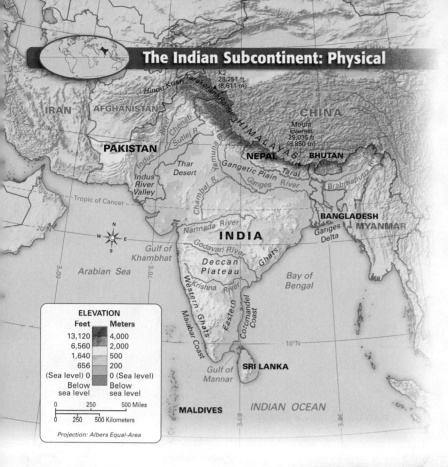

The Indian Subcontinent: Physical

Physical Maps

Physical maps show the major physical features of a region. These features may include mountain ranges, rivers, oceans, islands, deserts, and plains. Often, these maps use different colors to represent different elevations of land. As a result, the map reader can easily see which areas are high elevations, like mountains, and which areas are lower.

Special-Purpose Maps

Special-purpose maps focus on one special topic, such as climate, resources, or population. These maps present information on the topic that is particularly important in the region. Depending on the type of special-purpose map, the information may be shown with different colors, arrows, dots, or other symbols.

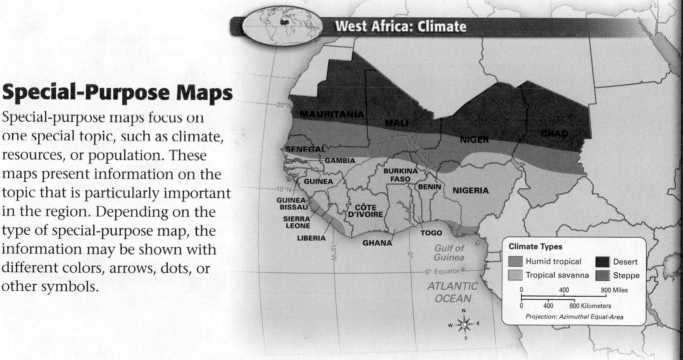

West Africa: Climate

Using Maps in Geography The different kinds of maps in this textbook will help you study and understand geography. By working with these maps, you will see what the physical geography of places is like, where people live, and how the world has changed over time.

Geographic Dictionary

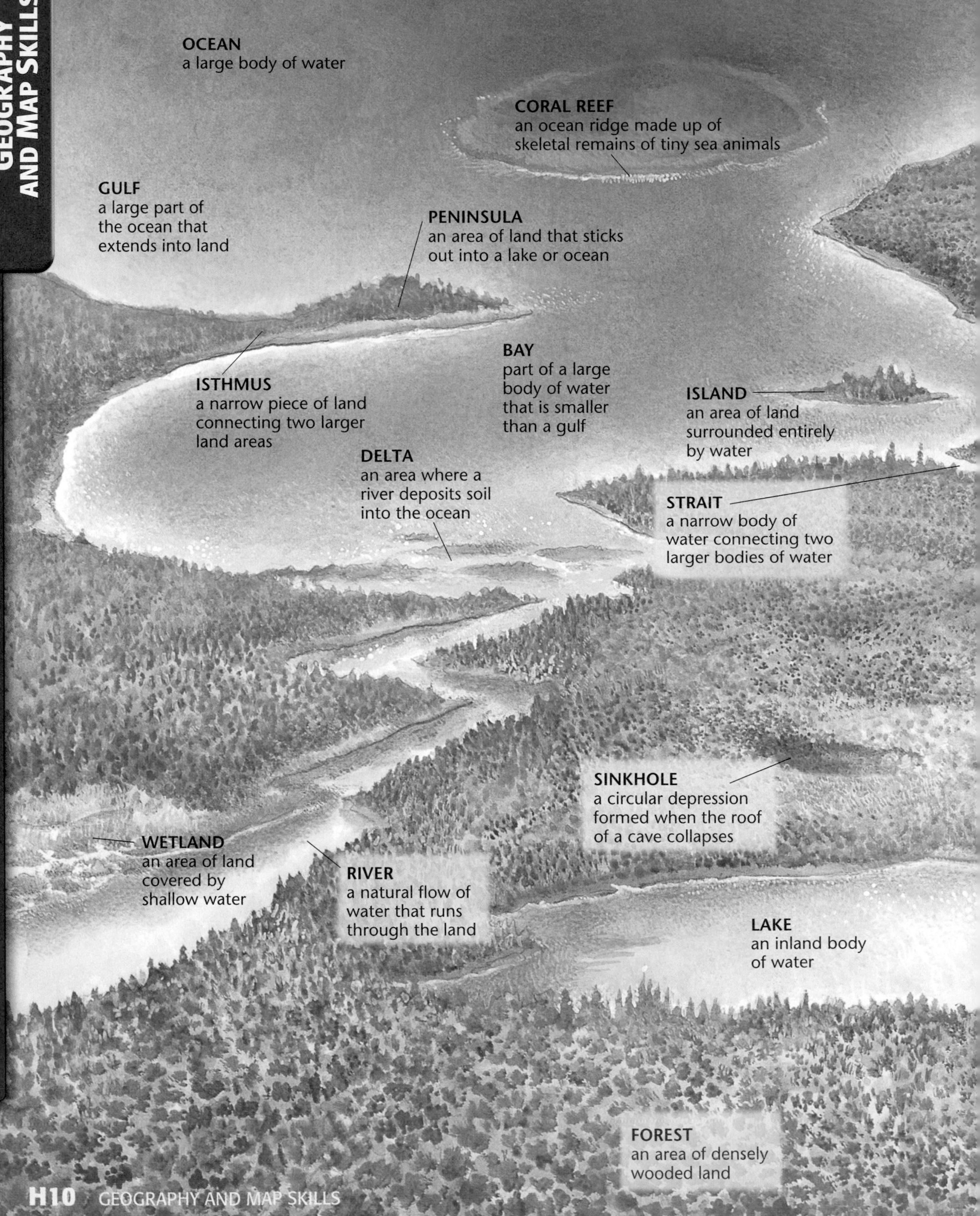

OCEAN
a large body of water

CORAL REEF
an ocean ridge made up of skeletal remains of tiny sea animals

GULF
a large part of the ocean that extends into land

PENINSULA
an area of land that sticks out into a lake or ocean

BAY
part of a large body of water that is smaller than a gulf

ISLAND
an area of land surrounded entirely by water

ISTHMUS
a narrow piece of land connecting two larger land areas

DELTA
an area where a river deposits soil into the ocean

STRAIT
a narrow body of water connecting two larger bodies of water

SINKHOLE
a circular depression formed when the roof of a cave collapses

WETLAND
an area of land covered by shallow water

RIVER
a natural flow of water that runs through the land

LAKE
an inland body of water

FOREST
an area of densely wooded land

COAST
an area of land
near the ocean

MOUNTAIN
an area of rugged
land that generally
rises higher than
2,000 feet

VALLEY
an area of low
land between
hills or mountains

GLACIER
a large area of
slow-moving ice

VOLCANO
an opening in Earth's crust
where lava, ash, and gases erupt

CANYON
a deep, narrow valley
with steep walls

HILL
a rounded, elevated
area of land smaller
than a mountain

PLAIN
a nearly
flat area

DUNE
a hill of sand
shaped by wind

OASIS
an area in the
desert with a
water source

DESERT
an extremely dry area with
little water and few plants

PLATEAU
a large, flat,
elevated
area of land

Themes and Essential Elements of Geography

by Dr. Christopher L. Salter

To study the world, geographers have identified 5 key themes, 6 essential elements, and 18 geography standards.

"How should we teach and learn about geography?" Professional geographers have worked hard over the years to answer this important question.

In 1984 a group of geographers identified the 5 Themes of Geography. These themes did a wonderful job of laying the groundwork for good classroom geography. Teachers used the 5 Themes in class, and geographers taught workshops on how to apply them in the world.

By the early 1990s, however, some geographers felt the 5 Themes were too broad. They created the 18 Geography Standards and the 6 Essential Elements. The 18 Geography Standards include more detailed information about what geography is, and the 6 Essential Elements are like a bridge between the 5 Themes and 18 Standards.

Look at the chart to the right. It shows how each of the 5 Themes connects to the Essential Elements and Standards. For example, the theme of Location is related to The World in Spatial Terms and the first three Standards. Study the chart carefully to see how the other themes, elements, and Standards are related.

The last Essential Element and the last two Standards cover The Uses of Geography. These key parts of geography were not covered by the 5 Themes. They will help you see how geography has influenced the past, present, and future.

5 Themes of Geography

Location The theme of location describes where something is.

Place Place describes the features that make a site unique.

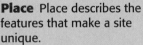

Regions Regions are areas that share common characteristics.

Movement This theme looks at how and why people and things move.

Human-Environment Interaction People interact with their environment in many ways.

Essential Elements

 Geography Standards

I. **The World in Spatial Terms**

1. How to use maps and other tools
2. How to use mental maps to organize information
3. How to analyze the spatial organization of people, places, and environments

II. **Places and Regions**

4. The physical and human characteristics of places
5. How people create regions to interpret Earth
6. How culture and experience influence people's perceptions of places and regions

III. **Physical Systems**

7. The physical processes that shape Earth's surface
8. The distribution of ecosystems on Earth

IV. **Human Systems**

9. The characteristics, distribution, and migration of human populations
10. The complexity of Earth's cultural mosaics
11. The patterns and networks of economic interdependence on Earth
12. The patterns of human settlement
13. The forces of cooperation and conflict

V. **Environment and Society**

14. How human actions modify the physical environment
15. How physical systems affect human systems
16. The distribution and meaning of resources

VI. **The Uses of Geography**

17. How to apply geography to interpret the past
18. How to apply geography to interpret the present and plan for the future

Become an Active Reader

Did you ever think you would begin reading your social studies book by reading about *reading*? Actually, it makes better sense than you might think. You would probably make sure you knew some soccer skills and strategies before playing in a game. Similarly, you need to know something about reading skills and strategies before reading your social studies book. In other words, you need to make sure you know whatever you need to know in order to read this book successfully.

Tip #1
Read Everything on the Page!

You can't follow the directions on the cake-mix box if you don't know where the directions are! Cake-mix boxes always have directions on them telling you how many eggs to add or how long to bake the cake. But, if you can't find that information, it doesn't matter that it is there.

Likewise, this book is filled with information that will help you understand what you are reading. If you don't study that information, however, it might as well not be there. Let's take a look at some of the places where you'll find important information in this book.

The Chapter Opener
The chapter opener gives you a brief overview of what you will learn in the chapter. You can use this information to prepare to read the chapter.

The Section Openers
Before you begin to read each section, preview the information under What You Will Learn. There you'll find the main ideas of the section and key terms that are important in it. Knowing what you are looking for before you start reading can improve your understanding.

Boldfaced Words
Those words are important and are defined somewhere on the page where they appear—either right there in the sentence or over in the side margin.

Maps, Charts, and Artwork
These things are not there just to take up space or look good! Study them and read the information beside them. It will help you understand the information in the chapter.

Questions at the End of Sections
At the end of each section, you will find questions that will help you decide whether you need to go back and re-read any parts before moving on. If you can't answer a question, that is your cue to go back and re-read.

Questions at the End of the Chapter
Answer the questions at the end of each chapter, even if your teacher doesn't ask you to. These questions are there to help you figure out what you need to review.

Tip #2

Use the Reading Skills and Strategies in Your Textbook

Good readers use a number of skills and strategies to make sure they understand what they are reading. In this textbook you will find help with important reading skills and strategies such as "Asking Questions," and "Using Context Clues–Synonyms."

We teach the reading skills and strategies in several ways. Use these activities and lessons and you will become a better reader.

- First, on the opening page of every chapter we identify and explain the reading skill or strategy you will focus on as you work through the chapter. In fact, these activities are called "Focus on Reading."

- Second, as you can see in the example at right, we tell you where to go for more help. The back of the book has a reading handbook with a full-page practice lesson to match the reading skill or strategy in every chapter.

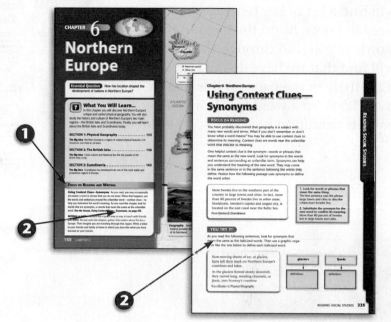

- Third, we give you short practice activities and examples as you read the chapter. These activities and examples show up in the margin of your book. Again, look for the words, "Focus on Reading."

- Finally, we provide another practice activity in the Chapter Review at the end of every chapter. That activity gives you one more chance to make sure you know how to use the reading skill or strategy.

Tip #3

Pay Attention to Vocabulary

It is no fun to read something when you don't know what the words mean, but you can't learn new words if you only use or read the words you already know. In this book, we know we have probably used some words you don't know. But, we have followed a pattern as we have used more difficult words.

- First, at the beginning of each section you will find a list of key terms that you will need to know. Be on the lookout for those words as you read through the section. You will find that we have defined those words right there in the paragraph where they are used. Look for a word that is in boldface with its definition highlighted in yellow.

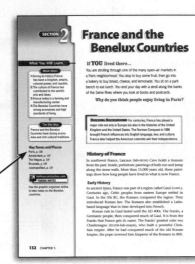

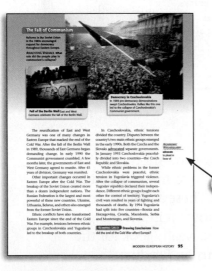

- Second, when we use a word that is important in all classes, not just social studies, we define it in the margin under the heading Academic Vocabulary. You will run into these academic words in other textbooks, so you should learn what they mean while reading this book.

Tip #4

Read Like a Skilled Reader

You won't be able to climb to the top of Mount Everest if you do not train! If you want to make it to the top of Mount Everest then you must start training to climb that huge mountain.

Training is also necessary to become a good reader. You will never get better at reading your social studies book—or any book for that matter—unless you spend some time thinking about how to be a better reader.

Skilled readers do the following:

1. They preview what they are supposed to read before they actually begin reading. When previewing, they look for vocabulary words, titles of sections, information in the margin, or maps or charts they should study.

2. They get ready to take some notes while reading by dividing their notebook paper into two parts. They title one side "Notes from the Chapter" and the other side "Questions or Comments I Have."

3. As they read, they complete their notes.

4. They read like **active readers**. The Active Reading list below shows you what that means.

5. Finally, they use clues in the text to help them figure out where the text is going. The best clues are called signal words. These are words that help you identify chronological order, causes and effects, or comparisons and contrasts.

Chronological Order Signal Words: *first, second, third, before, after, later, next, following that, earlier, subsequently, finally*

Cause and Effect Signal Words: *because of, due to, as a result of, the reason for, therefore, consequently, so, basis for*

Comparison/Contrast Signal Words: *likewise, also, as well as, similarly, on the other hand*

Active Reading

There are three ways to read a book: You can be a turn-the-pages-no-matter-what type of reader. These readers just keep on turning pages whether or not they understand what they are reading. Or, you can be a stop-watch-and-listen kind of reader. These readers know that if they wait long enough, someone will tell them what they need to know. Or, you can be an active reader. These readers know that it is up to them to figure out what the text means. Active readers do the following as they read:

Predict what will happen next based on what has already happened. When your predictions don't match what happens in the text, re-read the confusing parts.

Question what is happening as you read. Constantly ask yourself why things have happened, what things mean, and what caused certain events. Jot down notes about the questions you can't answer.

Summarize what you are reading frequently. Do not try to summarize the entire chapter! Read a bit and then summarize it. Then read on.

Connect what is happening in the section you're reading to what you have already read.

Clarify your understanding. Be sure that you understand what you are reading by stopping occasionally to ask yourself whether you are confused by anything. Sometimes you might need to re-read to clarify. Other times you might need to read further and collect more information before you can understand. Still other times you might need to ask the teacher to help you with what is confusing you.

Visualize what is happening in the text. In other words, try to see the events or places in your mind. It might help you to draw maps, make charts, or jot down notes about what you are reading as you try to visualize the action in the text.

Social Studies Words

As you read this textbook, you will be more successful if you learn the meanings of the words on this page. You will come across these words many times in your social studies classes, like geography and history. Read through these words now to become familiar with them before you begin your studies.

Social Studies Words

WORDS ABOUT TIME

AD	refers to dates after the birth of Jesus
BC	refers to dates before Jesus's birth
BCE	refers to dates before Jesus's birth, stands for "before the common era"
CE	refers to dates after Jesus's birth, stands for "common era"
century	a period of 100 years
decade	a period of 10 years
era	a period of time
millennium	a period of 1,000 years

WORDS ABOUT THE WORLD

climate	the weather conditions in a certain area over a long period of time
geography	the study of the world's people, places, and landscapes
physical features	features on Earth's surface, such as mountains and rivers
region	an area with one or more features that make it different from surrounding areas
resources	materials found on Earth that people need and value

WORDS ABOUT PEOPLE

anthropology	the study of people and cultures
archaeology	the study of the past based on what people left behind
citizen	a person who lives under the control of a government
civilization	the way of life of people in a particular place or time
culture	the knowledge, beliefs, customs, and values of a group of people
custom	a repeated practice or tradition
economics	the study of the production and use of goods and services
economy	any system in which people make and exchange goods and services
government	the body of officials and groups that run an area
history	the study of the past
politics	the process of running a government
religion	a system of beliefs in one or more gods or spirits
society	a group of people who share common traditions
trade	the exchange of goods or services

Academic Words

What are academic words? They are important words used in all of your classes, not just social studies. You will see these words in other textbooks, so you should learn what they mean while reading this book. Review this list now. You will use these words again in the chapters of this book.

Academic Words

Word	Definition	Word	Definition
agreement	a decision reached by two or more people or groups	**logical**	reasoned, well thought out
contemporary	modern	**neutral**	unbiased, not favoring either side in a conflict
contract	a binding legal agreement	**primary**	main, most important
facilitate	to make easier	**purpose**	the reason something is done
features	characteristics	**reaction**	a response to something
function	use or purpose	**strategy**	a plan for fighting a battle or war
implications	consequences		
incentive	something that leads people to follow a certain course of action		

Academic Words features provide definitions for important terms that will help you understand social studies content.

War and Victory

Germany struck the first blow in the war, sending a large army into Belgium and France. Allied troops, however, managed to stop the Germans just outside Paris. In the east, Russia attacked Germany and Austria-Hungary, forcing Germany to fight on two fronts. Hopes on both sides for a quick victory soon disappeared.

ACADEMIC VOCABULARY
strategy a plan for fighting a battle or war

A New Kind of War

A new military **strategy**, trench warfare, was largely responsible for preventing a quick victory. Early in the war both sides turned to trench warfare. **Trench warfare** is a style of fighting in which each side fights from deep ditches, or trenches, dug into the ground.

Both the Allies and the Central Powers dug hundreds of miles of trenches along the front lines. Soldiers in the trenches faced great suffering. Not only did they live in constant danger of attack, but cold, hunger, and disease also plagued them. Sometimes soldiers would "go over the top" of their trenches and fight for a few hours, only to retreat to the same position. Trench warfare cost millions of lives, but neither side could win the war.

To gain an advantage in the trenches, each side developed deadly new weapons. Machine guns cut down soldiers as they tried to move forward. Poison gas, first used by the Germans, blinded soldiers in the trenches. It was later used by both sides. The British introduced another weapon, the tank, to break through enemy lines.

At sea, Britain used its powerful navy to block supplies from reaching Germany. Germany responded by using submarines, called U-boats. German U-boats tried to break the British blockade and sink ships carrying supplies to Great Britain.

The Allies Win

For three years the war was a stalemate—neither side could defeat the other. Slowly, however, the war turned in favor of the Allies. In early 1917 German U-boats began attacking American ships carrying supplies to Britain. When Germany ignored U.S. warnings to stop, the United States entered the war on the side of the Allies.

Help from American forces gave the Allies a fresh advantage. Soon afterward, however, the exhausted Russians pulled out of the war. Germany quickly attacked the Allies, hoping to put an end to the war. Allied troops, however, stopped Germany's attack. The Central Powers had suffered a great blow. In the fall of 1918 the Central Powers surrendered. The Allied Powers were victorious.

READING CHECK Sequencing What events led to the end of World War I?

The War's End

After more than four years of fighting, the war came to an end on November 11, 1918. More than 8.5 million soldiers had been killed, and at least 20 million more were wounded. Millions of civilians had lost their lives as well. The war brought tremendous change to Europe.

Making Peace

Shortly after the end of the war, leaders from the Allied nations met at Versailles (ver-SY), near Paris. There, they debated the terms of peace for the Central Powers.

The United States, led by President Woodrow Wilson, wanted a just peace after the war. He did not want harsh peace terms that might anger the losing countries and lead to future conflict.

Other Allied leaders, however, wanted to punish Germany. They believed that Germany had started the war and should pay for it. They believed that weakening Germany would prevent future wars.

In the end, the Allies forced Germany to sign a treaty. The **Treaty of Versailles** was the final peace settlement of World War I. It forced Germany to accept the blame for starting the war. Germany also had to slash the size of its army and give up its overseas colonies. Additionally, Germany had to pay billions of dollars for damages caused during the war.

FOCUS ON READING What does the term just peace mean? How can you tell?

Close-up
Trench Warfare

Both the Allied Powers and the Central Powers relied on trenches for defense during World War I. As a result, the war dragged on for years with no clear victor. Each side developed new weapons and technology to try to gain an advantage in the trenches.

Each side used airplanes to observe troop movements and other actions behind enemy lines.

Soldiers often threw or fired small bombs known as grenades.

Armored vehicles, or tanks, were used to launch attacks across rough terrain.

Trenches dug in zigzag patterns prevented the enemy from firing down the length of a trench.

Soldiers used gas masks to survive attacks of poison gas.

ANALYSIS SKILL ANALYZING VISUALS
What advantages and disadvantages did trench warfare pose for soldiers?

82 CHAPTER 3

MODERN EUROPEAN HISTORY 83

Making This Book Work for You

Studying geography will be easy for you with this textbook. Take a few minutes now to become familiar with the easy-to-use structure and special features of your book. See how it will make geography come alive for you!

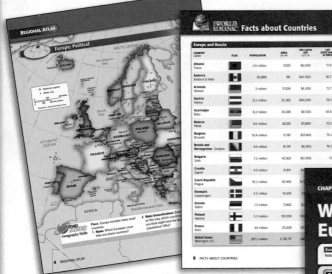

Your book begins with a satellite image, a regional atlas, and a table with facts about each country. Use these pages to get an overview of the region you will study.

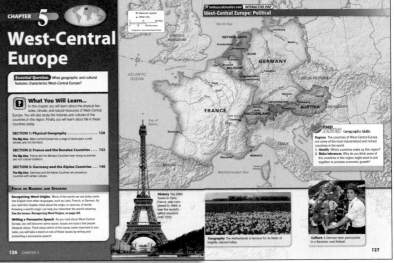

Chapter

Each chapter includes an introduction, a Social Studies Skills activity, Chapter Review pages, and a Standardized Test Practice page.

Reading Social Studies Chapter reading lessons give you skills and practice to help you read the textbook. More help with each lesson can be found in the back of the book. Margin notes and questions in the chapter make sure you understand the reading skill.

Social Studies Skills The Social Studies Skills lessons give you an opportunity to learn, practice, and apply an important skill. Chapter Review questions then follow up on what you learned.

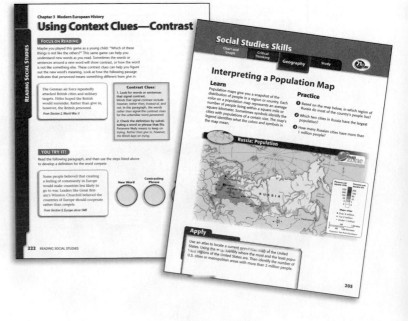

Section

The section opener pages include Main Ideas, an overarching Big Idea, and Key Terms and Places. In addition, each section includes these special features.

If YOU Lived There . . . Each section begins with a situation for you to respond to, placing you in a place that relates to the content you will be studying in the section.

Building Background Building Background connects what will be covered in each section with what you already know.

Short Sections of Content The information in each section is organized into small chunks of text that you can easily understand.

Taking Notes Suggested graphic organizers help you read and take notes on the important ideas in the section.

SECTION 4

The Balkan Countries

What You Will Learn...

Main Ideas

1. The history of the Balkan countries is one of conquest and conflict.
2. The cultures of the Balkan countries are shaped by the many ethnic groups who live there.
3. Civil War and weak economies are major challenges to the region today.

The Big Idea

Life in the Balkans reflects the region's troubled past and its varied ethnic makeup.

Key Terms
ethnic cleansing, p. 186

hmhsocialstudies.com
TAKING NOTES

Use the graphic organizer online to take notes on the Balkan countries.

If YOU lived there...

As part of your summer vacation, you are hiking across the Balkan Peninsula. As you hike through villages in the rugged mountains, you are amazed at the different churches you see. There are small Roman Catholic churches, huge Orthodox churches with onion-shaped domes, and Muslim mosques with tall minarets.

Why are there so many types of churches here?

BUILDING BACKGROUND The Balkan countries are possibly the most diverse area in Europe. In addition to practicing many religions, the people there speak many languages and have different customs. At times, the area's diversity has led to serious problems.

History

Like the rest of Eastern Europe, the Balkan Peninsula has been conquered and ruled by many different groups. The presence of these many groups continues to shape life in the area today.

Early History

By the 600s BC the ancient Greeks had founded colonies on the northern Black Sea coast. The area they settled is now part of Bulgaria and Romania. Later, the Romans conquered most of the area from the Adriatic Sea to the Danube River.

When the Roman Empire divided into west and east in the late AD 300s, the Balkan Peninsula became part of the Eastern, or Byzantine, Empire. Under Byzantine rule, many people of the Balkans became Orthodox Christians. More than 1,000 years later, Muslim Ottoman Turks conquered the Byzantine Empire. Under the Ottomans, many people became Muslims.

The Ottomans ruled the Balkan Peninsula until the 1800s. At that time, the people of the region rose up and drove the Ottomans out. They then created their own kingdoms.

The largest city in the British Isles, London serves as one of Europe's major financial centers.

The Economy

The economies of the United Kingdom and the Republic of Ireland are among Europe's strongest. **London**, the capital of the United Kingdom, is a center for world trade and industry. North Sea energy reserves have made the United Kingdom a major producer of oil and natural gas. In Ireland, computer equipment and software have become major industries, especially near **Dublin**, Ireland's capital. The economies of the United Kingdom and the Republic of Ireland also rely on service industries like banking, tourism, and insurance.

READING CHECK Summarizing What has been the cause of conflict in Northern Ireland?

SUMMARY AND PREVIEW You have learned about the rich history and culture of the British Isles. Next, you will learn about the countries of Scandinavia.

Section 2 Assessment

Reviewing Ideas, Terms, and Places
1. a. **Identify** What peoples invaded the British Isles?
   b. **Make Inferences** How did the Industrial Revolution strengthen the British Empire?
2. a. **Describe** What elements of British culture are found around the world?
   b. **Explain** How did **Magna Carta** affect British government?
3. a. **Define** What does **disarm** mean?
   b. **Analyze** What are the central issues of the conflict in Northern Ireland?
   c. **Elaborate** Why do you think the economy of the British Isles is so strong?

Critical Thinking
4. **Summarizing** Using your notes and a graphic organizer like the one here, summarize the history and culture of the British Isles in your own words.

History

Culture

hmhsocialstudies.com
ONLINE QUIZ

FOCUS ON WRITING

5. **Writing about the British Isles** What information about the British Isles do you think is most interesting? Take notes on what you could include in a letter to someone who has never visited the area.

160 CHAPTER 6

Reading Check Questions end each section of content so you can check to make sure you understand what you just studied.

Summary and Preview The Summary and Preview connects what you studied in the section to what you will study in the next section.

Section Assessment Finally, the section assessment boxes make sure that you understand the main ideas of the section. We also provide assessment practice online!

Scavenger Hunt

Are you ready to explore the world of geography? *Holt McDougal: Europe and Russia* is your ticket to this exciting world. Before you begin your journey, complete this scavenger hunt to get to know your book and discover what's inside.

On a separate sheet of paper, fill in the blanks to complete each sentence below. In each answer, one letter will be in a yellow box. When you have answered every question, copy these letters in order to reveal the answer to the question at the bottom of the page.

1 According to the Table of Contents, Section 2 of Chapter 6 is called The ☐☐☐☐☐☐☐ Isles. On what page does that section start?

2 The first word listed in the English and Spanish Glossary is ☐☐☐☐☐☐☐☐. What does this word mean?

3 The last word of The Big Idea on page 184 is ☐☐☐☐☐☐.

4 The Close-up feature on page 182 is called ☐☐☐☐☐☐☐☐.

5 Page 68 includes an overview of the entire preceding section called ☐☐☐☐☐☐☐ and Preview.

6 On page 89, there is a Primary Source feature titled The Diary of ☐☐☐☐ ☐☐☐☐☐.

7 The Social Studies Skills lesson on page 146 will teach you to analyze a ☐☐☐☐☐☐ ☐☐☐☐☐.

Fact!

One of the most popular foods in the United States was named after a German city. What city was it?

☐☐☐☐☐☐☐

Europe and Russia

The Alps

The Alps, one of Europe's major mountain ranges, stretch across the heart of central Europe.

Islands and Peninsulas

Islands and peninsulas surround the edges of Europe, drawing people to the sea to work, travel, and trade.

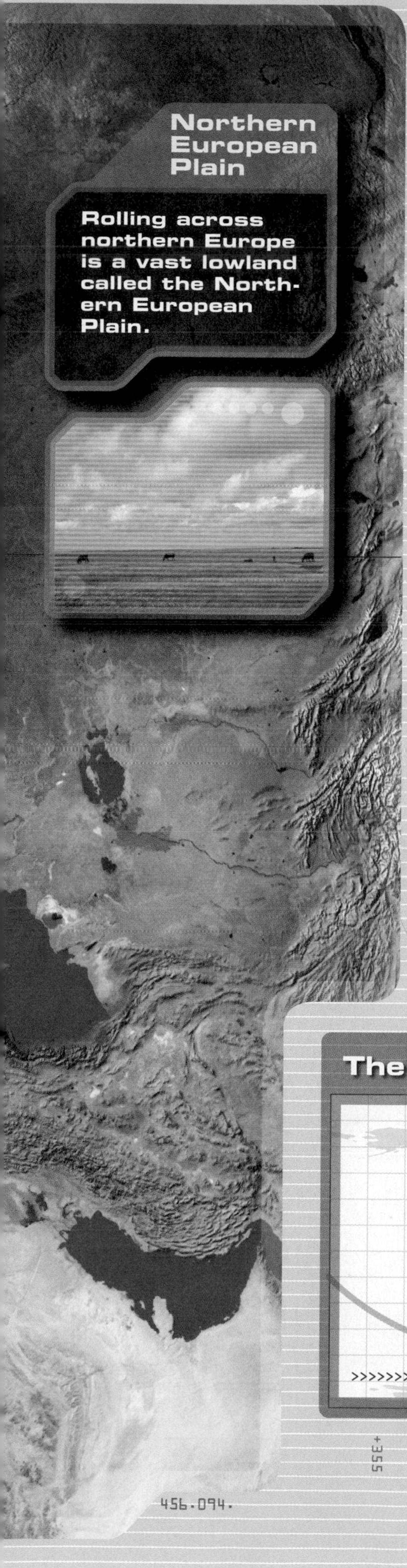

Northern European Plain

Rolling across northern Europe is a vast lowland called the Northern European Plain.

Europe and Russia

Explore the Satellite Image
Land and sea are always close together in Europe. Islands and peninsulas are key features of this region. What can you learn about Europe's geography from this satellite image?

The Satellite's Path

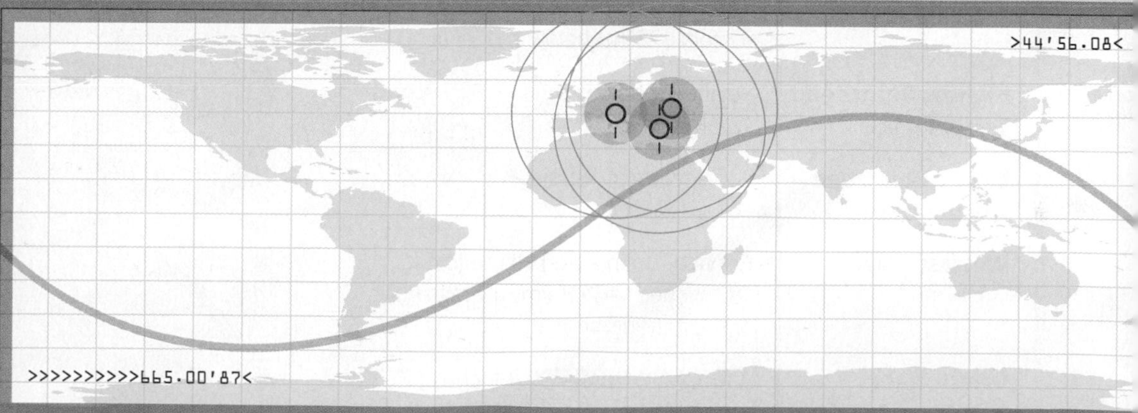

>44'56.08<

>>>>>>>>>>665.00'87<

+355

567.476.348

+799

+808
+996

456.094.

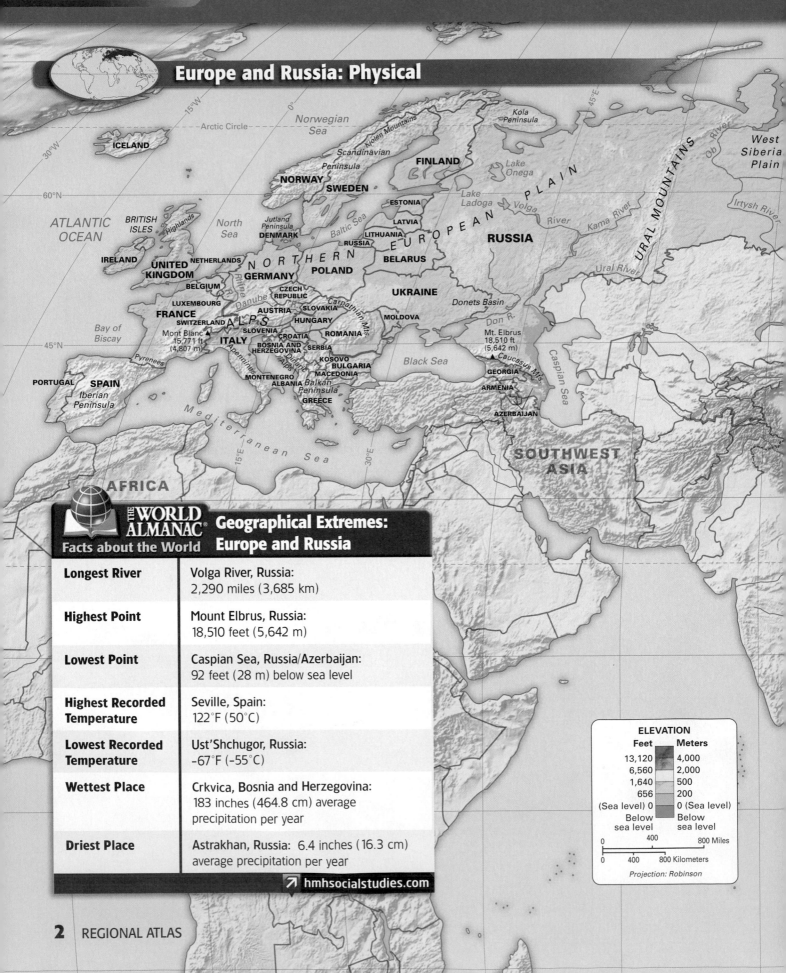

Europe and Russia: Physical

Arctic Circle

Norwegian Sea

Kola Peninsula

ICELAND

Kjolen Mountains

West Siberia Plain

Scandinavian Peninsula

FINLAND

Lake Onega

Ob River

Irtysh River

NORWAY

SWEDEN

Lake Ladoga

Volga

RUSSIA

ATLANTIC OCEAN

BRITISH ISLES

Highlands

North Sea

Jutland Peninsula

ESTONIA

LATVIA

LITHUANIA

Baltic Sea

RUSSIA

River

Kama River

URAL MOUNTAINS

IRELAND

UNITED KINGDOM

NETHERLANDS

DENMARK

E U R O P E A N   P L A I N

N O R T H E R N

GERMANY

POLAND

BELARUS

Ural River

BELGIUM

Rhine R.

CZECH REPUBLIC

UKRAINE

Donets Basin

LUXEMBOURG

Danube

AUSTRIA

SLOVAKIA

HUNGARY

Carpathian Mts.

MOLDOVA

Don R.

FRANCE

SWITZERLAND

A L P S

SLOVENIA

ROMANIA

Mt. Elbrus 18,510 ft (5,642 m)

Bay of Biscay

Mont Blanc 15,771 ft (4,807 m)

ITALY

Apennines

CROATIA

BOSNIA AND HERZEGOVINA

Dinaric Alps

SERBIA

KOSOVO

Caucasus Mts.

Caspian Sea

Pyrenees

MONTENEGRO

BULGARIA

MACEDONIA

Black Sea

GEORGIA

PORTUGAL

SPAIN

Iberian Peninsula

ALBANIA

Balkan Peninsula

GREECE

ARMENIA

AZERBAIJAN

M e d i t e r r a n e a n   S e a

SOUTHWEST ASIA

AFRICA

THE WORLD ALMANAC
Facts about the World
Geographical Extremes: Europe and Russia

Longest River	Volga River, Russia: 2,290 miles (3,685 km)
Highest Point	Mount Elbrus, Russia: 18,510 feet (5,642 m)
Lowest Point	Caspian Sea, Russia/Azerbaijan: 92 feet (28 m) below sea level
Highest Recorded Temperature	Seville, Spain: 122°F (50°C)
Lowest Recorded Temperature	Ust'Shchugor, Russia: –67°F (–55°C)
Wettest Place	Crkvica, Bosnia and Herzegovina: 183 inches (464.8 cm) average precipitation per year
Driest Place	Astrakhan, Russia: 6.4 inches (16.3 cm) average precipitation per year

↗ hmhsocialstudies.com

ELEVATION

Feet	Meters
13,120	4,000
6,560	2,000
1,640	500
656	200
(Sea level) 0	0 (Sea level)
Below sea level	Below sea level

0   400   800 Miles

0   400   800 Kilometers

Projection: Robinson

Europe and Russia

Taymyr Peninsula

Laptev Sea

New Siberian Islands

ARCTIC OCEAN

75°N

165°W

East Siberian Sea

Central Siberian Plateau

RUSSIA

S I B E R I A

Yenisey River

Lena River

Kolyma R.

Kolyma Mountains

Bering Strait

60°N

Kuznetsk Basin

Angara River

Stanovoy Mts.

Sayan Mts.

Lake Baikal

Yablonovy Range

Amur River

Bering Sea

180°

Kamchatka Peninsula

Sea of Okhotsk

Sakhalin Island

Kuril Islands

EAST ASIA

Sea of Japan (East Sea)

PACIFIC OCEAN

45°N

165°E

Size Comparison: The United States and Europe and Russia

N
W · E
S

map Zone
Geography Skills

Place Europe is a small continent. Russia stretches from Eastern Europe across northern Asia.

1. Name What is the large region located in eastern Russia called?

2. Make Inferences Based on its latitude, what do you think the environment of Siberia is like?

Europe: Political

ARCTIC OCEAN

Denmark Strait

70°N

Norwegian Sea

Reykjavik ✪ **ICELAND**

Arctic Circle

Faeroe Islands
(DENMARK)

Shetland
Islands
(U.K.)

60°N

NORWAY   **SWEDEN**   **FINLAND**

RUSSIA

Oslo ✪   Helsinki ✪

Stockholm ✪   Tallinn ✪

ESTONIA

North Sea

IRELAND

Dublin ✪

DENMARK   Riga ✪
Copenhagen ✪   **LATVIA**

Baltic Sea

Kaliningrad
(RUSSIA)   **LITHUANIA**
Vilnius ✪

Minsk ✪

**UNITED
KINGDOM**

50°N

London ✪   **NETHERLANDS**
Amsterdam ✪

Berlin ✪   **POLAND**
Warsaw ✪   **BELARUS**

**ATLANTIC
OCEAN**

Brussels ✪
BELGIUM

Rhine R.   **GERMANY**

Kiev ✪   *Dnieper River*

LUXEMBOURG
Luxembourg ✪

Prague ✪   **UKRAINE**

Paris ✪   **CZECH
REPUBLIC**

Danube R.   **SLOVAKIA**   Bratislava ✪   **MOLDOVA**

FRANCE   **LIECHTENSTEIN**
Bern ✪   Vienna ✪   Budapest ✪   Chişinău ✪

SWITZERLAND   **AUSTRIA**   **HUNGARY**   **ROMANIA**

Ljubljana ✪ **SLOVENIA**   Belgrade ✪   Bucharest ✪   *Black Sea*

40°N

CROATIA   Zagreb ✪

ANDORRA   **SAN
MARINO**   **BOSNIA AND
HERZEGOVINA**   **SERBIA**

PORTUGAL   Madrid ✪   **MONACO**   Sarajevo ✪   **KOSOVO**   **BULGARIA**

Lisbon ✪   **ITALY**   Podgorica ✪   Pristina ✪
Sofia ✪

SPAIN   *Corsica
(FRANCE)*   **MONTENEGRO**   Skopje ✪

**VATICAN
CITY** Rome ✪   Tirane ✪   **MACEDONIA**

ASIA

*Balearic
Islands
(SPAIN)*   *Sardinia
(ITALY)*   **ALBANIA**   *Aegean
Sea*

Strait of
Gilbraltar   Gibraltar
(U.K.)   **GREECE**

*Sicily
(ITALY)*   Athens ✪

AFRICA   **MALTA** ✪ Valletta   *Crete
(GREECE)*

Mediterranean Sea

Legend

✪ National capital

● Other city

0   200   400 Miles

0   200   400 Kilometers

Projection: Azimuthal Equal-Area

map zone

Geography Skills

Place Europe includes many small countries.

1. Name Which European countries are island countries?

2. Make Generalizations Based on this map, which countries do you think might have the largest populations? Why?

Europe and Russia

ATLANTIC OCEAN

Arctic Circle

North Sea

Baltic Sea

60°N

80°W

100°W

120°W

140°W

160°W

40°W

20°W

0°

180°

20°E

ARCTIC OCEAN

160°E

40°E

140°E

60°E

80°N

120°E

80°E

100°E

Bering Strait

Bering Sea

60°N

Barents Sea

Kaliningrad

St. Petersburg

EUROPE

Moscow

Nizhniy Novgorod

Volga River

Samara

Yekaterinburg

Ob River

Yenisey River

R U S S I A

Lena River

Sea of Okhotsk

Black Sea

GEORGIA

Tbilisi

ARMENIA

Yerevan

Baku

AZERBAIJAN

Caspian Sea

KAZAKHSTAN

Novosibirsk

MONGOLIA

CHINA

Vladivostok

40°N

JAPAN

PACIFIC OCEAN

Tropic of Cancer

20°N

✪ National capital

● Other city

0   300   600 Miles

0   300   600 Kilometers

Projection: Two-Point Equidistant

map zone
Geography Skills

Place Russia is the largest country in the world.

1. Use the Map About how many miles is Russia from west to east?

2. Analyze Where does Russia have access to the ocean? How do you think that affects trade?

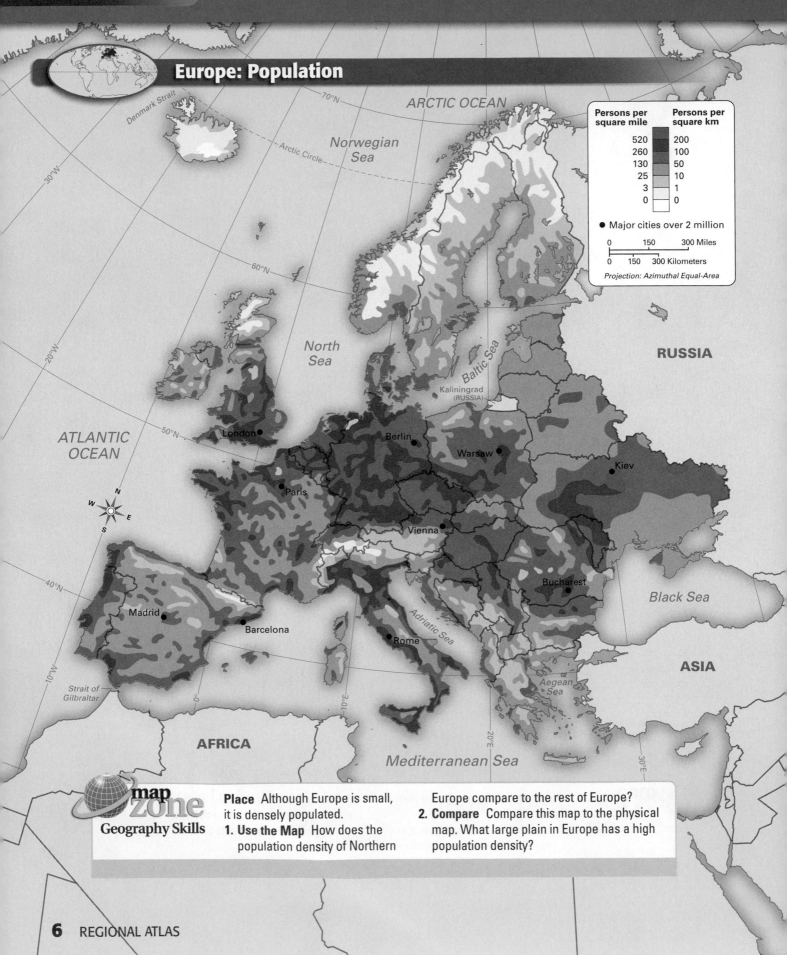

Europe: Population

Denmark Strait

70°N

ARCTIC OCEAN

Norwegian
Sea

Arctic Circle

30°W

60°N

20°W

North
Sea

Kaliningrad
(RUSSIA)

Baltic Sea

RUSSIA

ATLANTIC
OCEAN

50°N

London

Berlin

Warsaw

Kiev

Paris

Vienna

Bucharest

Black Sea

40°N

Madrid

Barcelona

Rome

Adriatic Sea

ASIA

10°W

Strait of
Gilbraltar

Aegean
Sea

AFRICA

Mediterranean Sea

10°E

20°E

30°E

**Persons per
square mile**

520
260
130
25
3
0

**Persons per
square km**

200
100
50
10
1
0

● Major cities over 2 million

0   150   300 Miles
0   150   300 Kilometers

Projection: Azimuthal Equal-Area

N
W   E
S

map zone
Geography Skills

Place Although Europe is small, it is densely populated.

1. Use the Map How does the population density of Northern

Europe compare to the rest of Europe?

2. Compare Compare this map to the physical map. What large plain in Europe has a high population density?

Europe and Russia

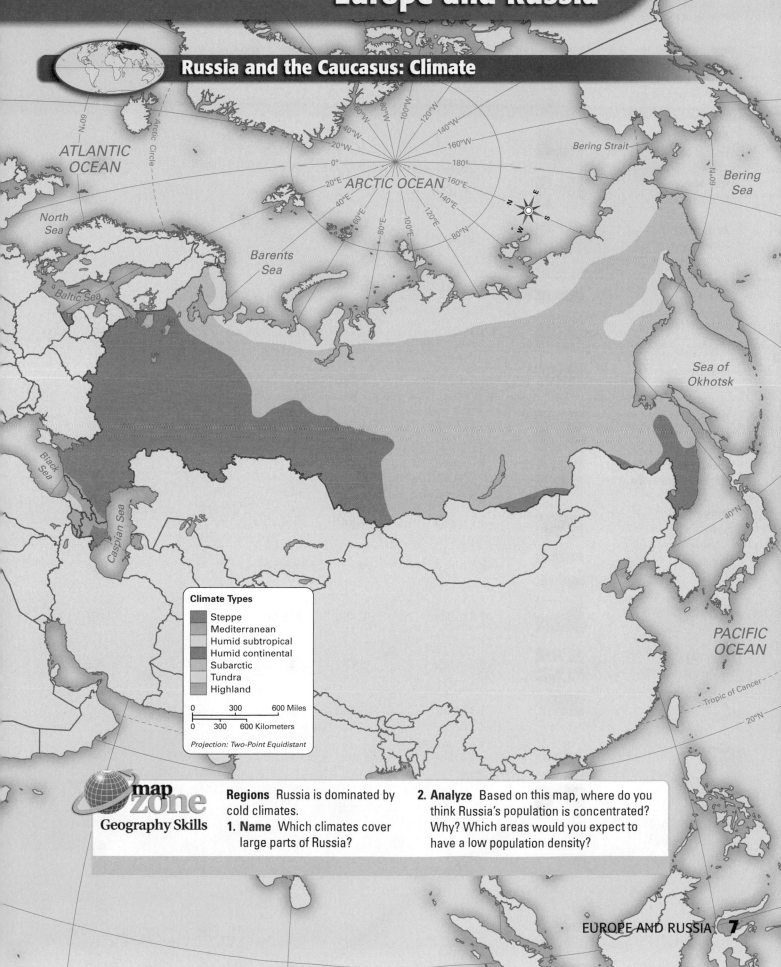

ATLANTIC
OCEAN

Arctic Circle

ARCTIC OCEAN

Bering Strait

Bering
Sea

North
Sea

Barents
Sea

Baltic Sea

Sea of
Okhotsk

Black
Sea

Caspian Sea

PACIFIC
OCEAN

Tropic of Cancer

Climate Types

- Steppe
- Mediterranean
- Humid subtropical
- Humid continental
- Subarctic
- Tundra
- Highland

0   300   600 Miles
0   300   600 Kilometers

Projection: Two-Point Equidistant

map zone

Geography Skills

Regions Russia is dominated by cold climates.

1. Name Which climates cover large parts of Russia?

2. Analyze Based on this map, where do you think Russia's population is concentrated? Why? Which areas would you expect to have a low population density?

Europe and Russia

COUNTRY Capital	FLAG	POPULATION	AREA (sq mi)	PER CAPITA GDP (U.S. $)	LIFE EXPECTANCY AT BIRTH	TVS PER 1,000 PEOPLE
Albania Tirana		3.6 million	11,100	$6,000	77.9	146
Andorra Andorra la Vella		83,888	181	$42,500	82.7	440
Armenia Yerevan		3 million	11,506	$6,300	72.7	241
Austria Vienna		8.2 million	32,382	$40,200	79.5	526
Azerbaijan Baku		8.2 million	33,436	$9,500	66.6	257
Belarus Minsk		9.6 million	80,155	$11,800	70.5	331
Belgium Brussels		10.4 million	11,787	$37,400	79.2	532
Bosnia and Herzegovina: Sarajevo		4.6 million	19,741	$6,500	78.5	112
Bulgaria Sofia		7.2 million	42,823	$12,900	73	429
Croatia Zagreb		4.5 million	21,831	$18,300	75.3	286
Czech Republic Prague		10.2 million	30,450	$25,900	76.7	487
Denmark Copenhagen		5.5 million	16,639	$37,100	78.2	776
Estonia Tallinn		1.3 million	17,462	$21,000	72.8	567
Finland Helsinki		5.3 million	130,559	$36,900	78.9	643
France Paris		64 million	211,209	$33,200	81	620
United States Washington, D.C.		307.2 million	3,718,711	$46,900	78.2	844

COUNTRY Capital	FLAG	POPULATION	AREA (sq mi)	PER CAPITA GDP (U.S. $)	LIFE EXPECTANCY AT BIRTH	TVS PER 1,000 PEOPLE
Georgia T'bilisi		4.6 million	26,911	$4,600	76.8	516
Germany Berlin		82.3 million	137,847	$35,400	79.2	581
Greece Athens		10.7 million	50,942	$32,000	79.6	480
Hungary Budapest		9.9 million	35,919	$19,800	73.3	447
Iceland Reykjavik		306,694	39,769	$41,800	80.6	505
Ireland Dublin		4.2 million	27,135	$45,300	78.2	406
Italy Rome		58.1 million	116,306	$31,300	80.2	492
Kosovo Pristina		1.8 million	4,203	$2,300	69.5	Not available
Latvia Riga		2.2 million	24,938	$17,300	72	757
Liechtenstein Vaduz		34,761	62	$118,000	80	469
Lithuania Vilnius		3.6 million	25,174	$17,800	74.8	422
Luxembourg Luxembourg		491,775	998	$81,000	79.3	599
Macedonia Skopje		2 million	9,781	$9,100	74.6	273
Malta Valletta		405,165	122	$24,700	79.4	549
Moldova Chişinau		4.3 million	13,067	$2,500	70.6	297
United States Washington, D.C.		307.2 million	3,718,711	$46,900	78.2	844

COUNTRY Capital	FLAG	POPULATION	AREA (sq mi)	PER CAPITA GDP (U.S. $)	LIFE EXPECTANCY AT BIRTH	TVS PER 1,000 PEOPLE
Monaco Monaco		32,965	1	$30,000	80.1	758
Montenegro Cetinje, Podgorica		672,180	5,415	$10,100	77.3	Not available
Netherlands Amsterdam		16.7 million	16,033	$40,400	79.4	540
Norway Oslo		4.7 million	125,182	$59,300	79.9	653
Poland Warsaw		38.5 million	120,728	$17,300	75.6	387
Portugal Lisbon		10.7 million	35,672	$22,200	78.2	567
Romania Bucharest		22.2 million	91,699	$12,200	72.3	312
Russia Moscow		140 million	6,592,772	$16,100	66.2	421
San Marino San Marino		30,324	24	$41,900	82	875
Serbia Belgrade		7.4 million	39,518	$10,800	75.4	277
Slovakia Bratislava		5.5 million	18,859	$21,900	75.3	418
Slovenia Ljubljana		2 million	7,827	$29,600	76.9	362
Spain Madrid		40.5 million	194,897	$34,700	80.1	555
Sweden Stockholm		9 million	173,732	$38,100	80.8	551
Switzerland Bern		7.6 million	15,942	$41,800	80.8	457
United States Washington, D.C.		307.2 million	3,718,711	$46,900	78.2	844

COUNTRY Capital	FLAG	POPULATION	AREA (sq mi)	PER CAPITA GDP (U.S. $)	LIFE EXPECTANCY AT BIRTH	TVS PER 1,000 PEOPLE
Ukraine Kiev		45.7 million	233,090	$7,400	68.2	433
United Kingdom London		61.1 million	94,526	$36,500	79	661
Vatican City Vatican City		826	0.17	Not available	Not available	Not available
United States Washington, D.C.		307.2 million	3,718,711	$46,900	78.2	844

World's Highest Per Capita GDPs

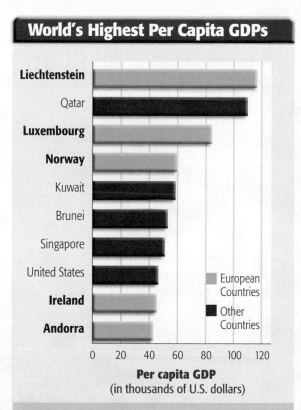

Per capita GDP (in thousands of U.S. dollars)

- Liechtenstein
- Qatar
- Luxembourg
- Norway
- Kuwait
- Brunei
- Singapore
- United States
- Ireland
- Andorra

0 20 40 60 80 100 120

■ European Countries
■ Other Countries

Europe includes some of the wealthiest countries in the world. In fact, five of the ten countries with the highest per capita GDPs are in Europe.

Densely Populated Countries: Europe

Country	Population Density (per square mile)
Netherlands	1,278
Belgium	891
United Kingdom	655
Germany	611
Italy	512
Switzerland	495
Denmark	336
Poland	327
United States	87

Many European countries are densely populated, especially when compared to the United States.

ANALYSIS SKILL **ANALYZING INFORMATION**

1. In the chart above, what three European countries are the most densely populated? How do their densities compare to that of the United States?
2. Which countries in Europe seem to have the lowest per capita GDPs? Look at the atlas political map. Where are these countries located in Europe?

Early History of Europe

2000 BC–AD 1500

> **Essential Question** What are the major political and cultural legacies from Europe's early history?

What You Will Learn...

In this chapter you will learn about three major periods in the early history of Europe. First you will learn about ancient Greece, a culture whose ideas still shape the world. Then you will learn about Rome, one of the most powerful civilizations in all of world history. Finally, you will read about the Middle Ages, a time of great changes in Europe.

FOCUS ON READING AND WRITING

Re-reading Sometimes a single reading is not enough to fully understand a passage of text. If you feel like you do not fully understand a passage after you read it, it may help to re-read the passage more slowly. **See the lesson, Re-reading, on page 220.**

Writing a Myth A myth is a story that tries to explain why something happened. Throughout history, people have used myths to explain natural and historical events. After you read this chapter, you will write a myth that people might have used to explain a major event in European history.

map zone
Geography Skills

Place Europe was home to some of the world's great civilizations.

1. **Locate** In what city was the Colosseum built?
2. **Analyze** Which of the buildings pictured on this map do you think is most impressive? Why?

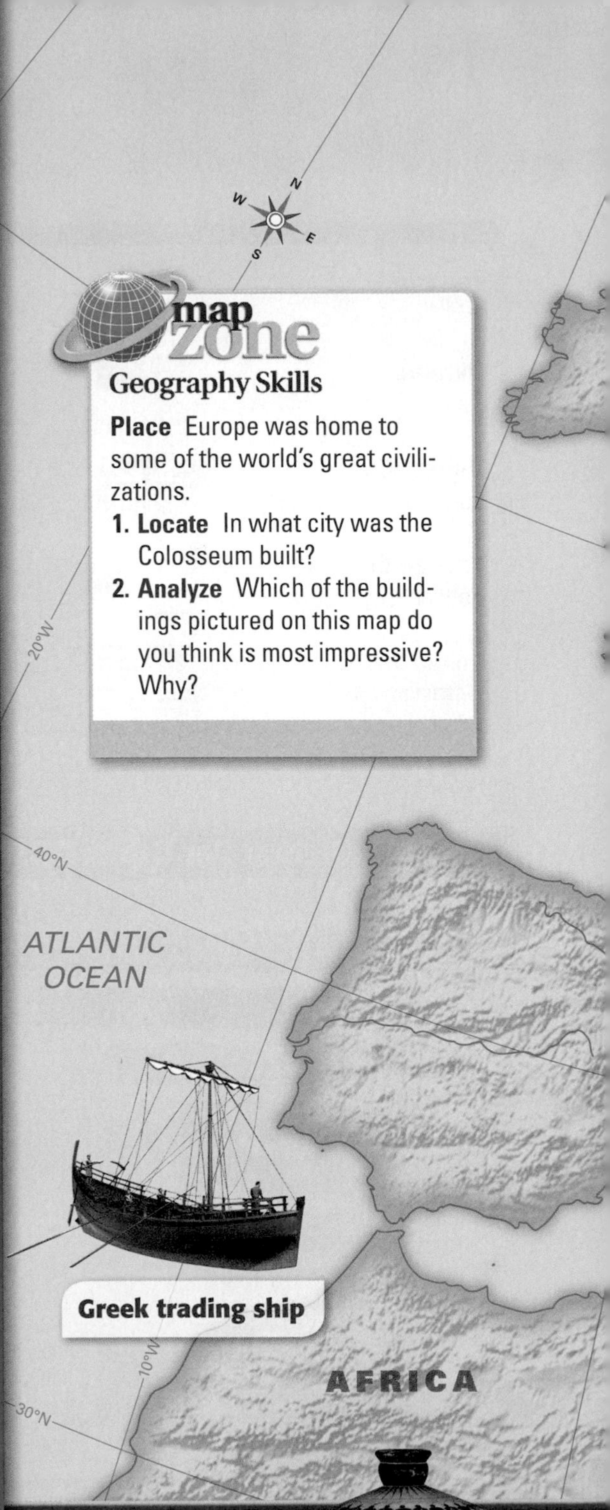

ATLANTIC OCEAN

Greek trading ship

AFRICA

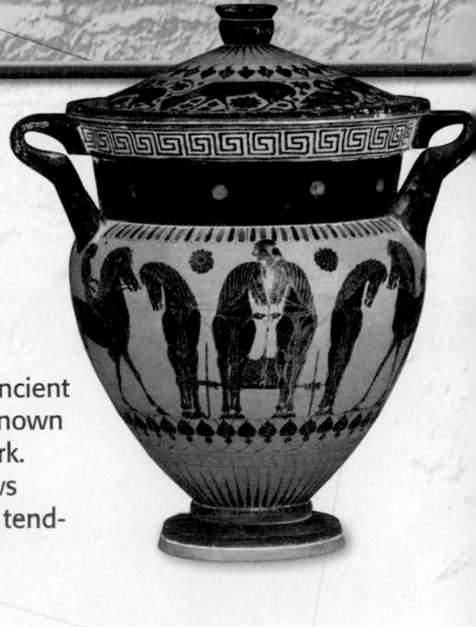

Greece The ancient Greeks were known for their artwork. This vase shows Greek soldiers tending to horses.

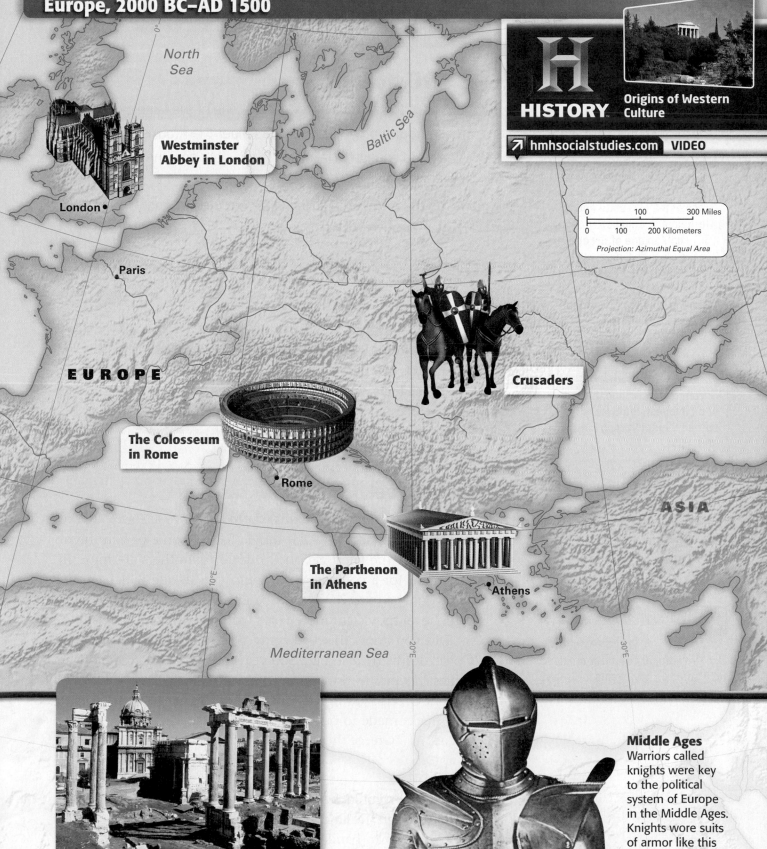

Europe, 2000 BC–AD 1500

North Sea

Baltic Sea

Westminster Abbey in London

London

Paris

HISTORY. Origins of Western Culture

hmhsocialstudies.com VIDEO

0   100   300 Miles
0 100 200 Kilometers
Projection: Azimuthal Equal Area

E U R O P E

Crusaders

The Colosseum in Rome

Rome

10°E

The Parthenon in Athens

Athens

20°E

A S I A

Mediterranean Sea

30°E

Rome The forum, or town square, was central to life in ancient Rome. The ruins of the forum can still be seen in Rome.

Middle Ages
Warriors called knights were key to the political system of Europe in the Middle Ages. Knights wore suits of armor like this one into battle.

Ancient Greece

If **YOU** lived there...

You live in the ancient city of Athens, one of the largest cities in Greece. Your brother, just two years older than you, is excited. He is finally old enough to take part in the city's government. He and your father, along with the other free men in the city, will meet to vote on the city's laws and leaders. Your mother and your sisters, however, cannot take part in the process.

Why is your brother excited about voting?

What You Will Learn...

Main Ideas

1. Early Greek culture saw the rise of the city-state and the creation of colonies.
2. The golden age of Greece saw advances in government, art, and philosophy.
3. Alexander the Great formed a huge empire and spread Greek culture into new areas.

The Big Idea

Through colonization, trade, and conquest, the Greeks spread their culture in Europe and Asia.

Key Terms and Places

city-states, p. 14
golden age, p. 16
Athens, p. 17
Sparta, p. 19
Hellenistic, p. 20

> hmhsocialstudies.com
> **TAKING NOTES**

Use the graphic organizer online to take notes on key events in Greek history.

BUILDING BACKGROUND In ancient times, people in most cultures lived under the rule of a king. In Greece, however, life was different. There was no ruler who held power over all of Greece. Instead, people lived in independent cities. Each of these cities had its own government, culture, and way of life.

Early Greek Culture

Suppose you and some friends wanted to go to the movies, but you could not decide which movie to see. Some of you might want to see the latest action thriller, while others are more in the mood for a comedy. How could you decide which movie you would go to see? One way to decide would be to take a vote. Whichever movie got more votes would be the one you saw.

Did you know that by voting you would be taking part in a process invented some 2,500 years ago? It is true. One of the earliest peoples to use voting to make major decisions was the ancient Greeks. Voting was only one of the many contributions the Greeks made to our culture, though. In fact, many people call ancient Greece the birthplace of modern civilization.

City-States

Early Greece could be a dangerous place. Waves of invaders swept through the land, and violence was common. Eventually, people began to band together in groups for protection. Over time, these groups developed into **city-states**, or political units made up of a city and all the surrounding lands.

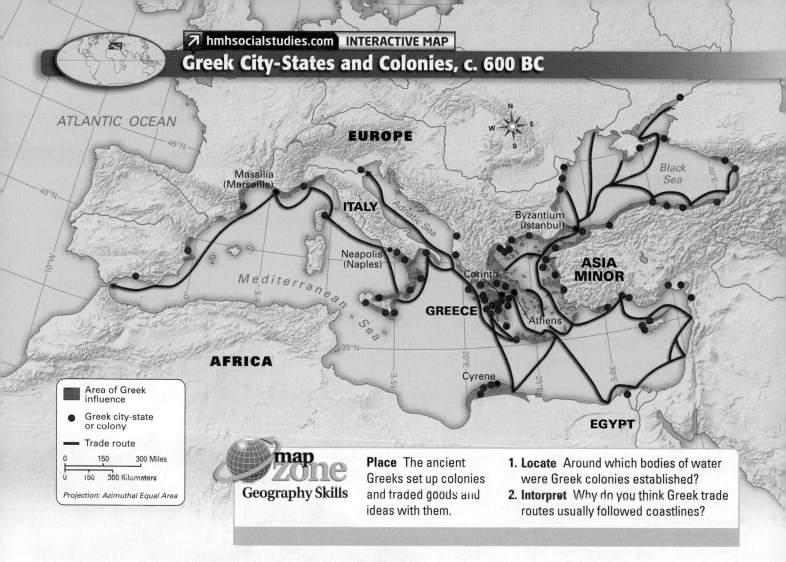

Greek City-States and Colonies, c. 600 BC

ATLANTIC OCEAN

EUROPE

Massilia
(Marseille)

ITALY

Adriatic Sea

Neapolis
(Naples)

Mediterranean Sea

Byzantium
(Istanbul)

Black
Sea

ASIA
MINOR

Corinth

GREECE

Athens

AFRICA

Cyrene

EGYPT

■ Area of Greek
influence

● Greek city-state
or colony

— Trade route

0   150   300 Miles
0   150   300 Kilometers

Projection: Azimuthal Equal Area

map zone
Geography Skills

Place The ancient Greeks set up colonies and traded goods and ideas with them.

1. **Locate** Around which bodies of water were Greek colonies established?
2. **Interpret** Why do you think Greek trade routes usually followed coastlines?

In the center of most city-states was a fortress on a hill. This hill was called the acropolis (uh-KRAH-puh-luhs), which is Greek for "top city." In addition to the fortress, many city-states built temples and other public buildings on the acropolis.

Around the acropolis was the rest of the city, including houses and markets. High walls usually surrounded the city for protection. In wartime, farmers who lived outside the walls could seek safety inside.

Living in city-states provided many advantages for the Greeks. The city was a place where people could meet and trade. In addition, the city-state gave people a new sense of identity. People thought of themselves as residents of a particular city-state, not as Greeks.

Colonies

In time, some city-states established new outposts, or colonies, around the Black and Mediterranean seas. You can see these colonies on the map above. Some of them still exist today as modern cities, such as Naples, Italy, and Marseille, France.

Although they were independent, most colonies kept ties with the older cities of Greece. They traded goods and shared ideas. These ties helped strengthen the economies of both cities and colonies, and they kept Greek culture strong. Because they stayed in contact, Greek cities all over Europe shared a common culture.

READING CHECK **Summarizing** Where did the ancient Greeks establish colonies?

The Golden Age of Greece

When most people think of ancient Greek culture today, certain images come to mind. They think of the ruins of stately temples and of realistic statues. They also think of great writers, philosophers, and scientists whose ideas changed the world.

These images represent some of the many contributions the Greeks made to world history. Remarkably, most of these contributions were developed during a relatively short time, between 500 and 300 BC. For that reason, this period is often called a **golden age**, a period in a society's history marked by great achievements.

HISTORY

VIDEO
Mysteries and Discoveries

hmhsocialstudies.com

The Growth of Greek Power

Early in Greece's history, city-states remained fiercely independent. Each city-state focused on its own concerns and did not interfere in the others' affairs.

Around 500 BC, however, an invading army caused the Greeks to band together against a common enemy. That invasion came from Persia, a powerful empire in central Asia. The Persian army was huge, well-trained, and experienced. Greece, on the other hand, had no single army. Each city-state had an army, but none was as large as Persia's. As a result, the Persians expected a quick victory.

Close-up

The Parthenon

The Parthenon is often seen as a symbol of ancient Athens. It was a beautiful temple to the goddess Athena, whom the people of Athens considered their protector. The temple is now in ruins, but this illustration shows how it may have looked when it was built around 440 BC.

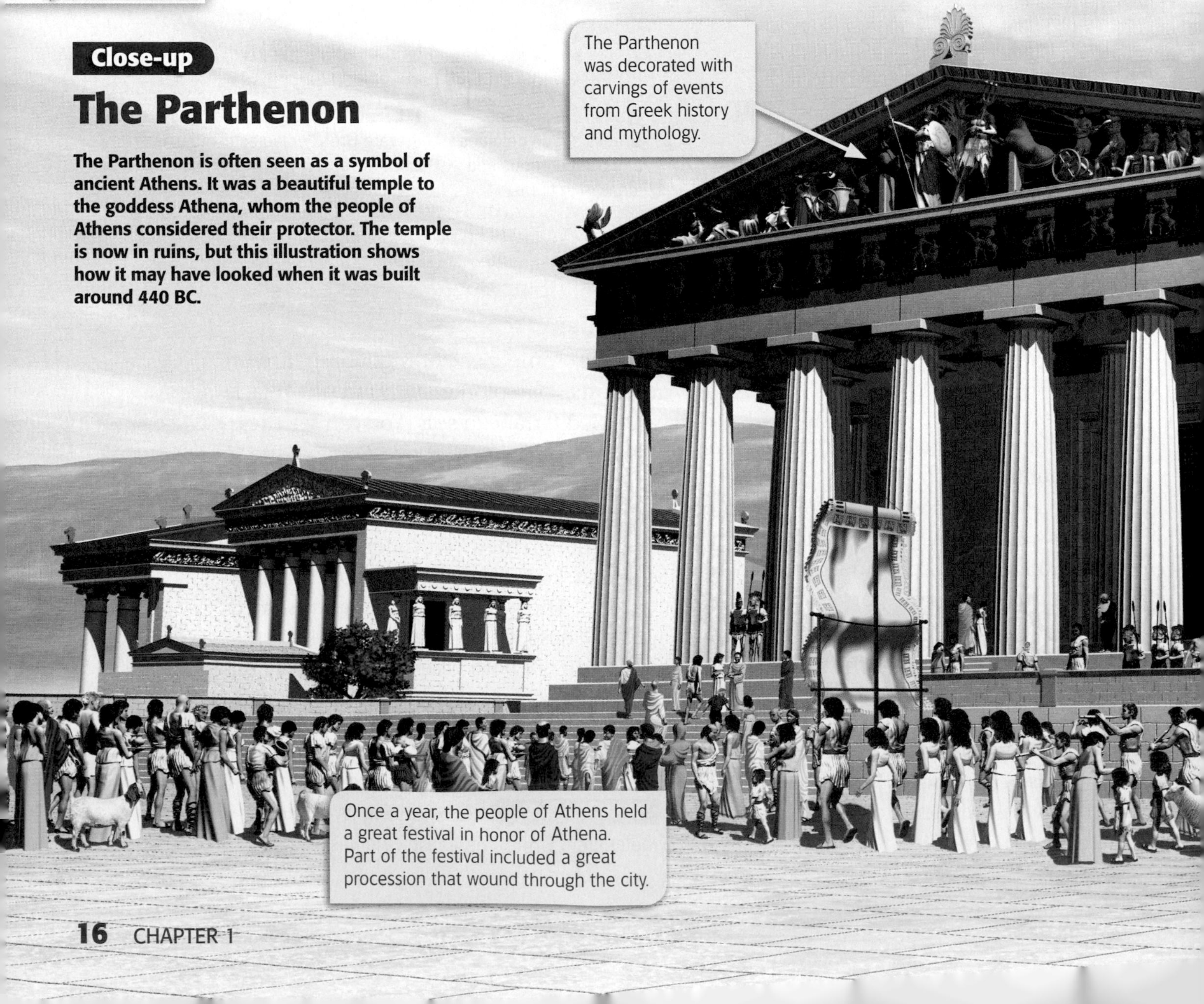
The Parthenon was decorated with carvings of events from Greek history and mythology.
Once a year, the people of Athens held a great festival in honor of Athena. Part of the festival included a great procession that wound through the city.

Nevertheless, the Greeks took up arms against the Persians. Led by **Athens**, a city-state in eastern Greece, the Greeks were able to defeat the Persians and keep Greece from being conquered. When the Persians invaded again 10 years later, the Athenians once again helped defeat them.

The victory over the Persians increased the confidence of people all over Greece. They realized that they were capable of great achievements. In the period after the Persian invasion, the people of Greece made amazing advances in art, writing, and thinking. Many of these advances were made by the people of Athens.

Athenian Culture

In the century after the defeat of Persia, Athens was the cultural center of Greece. Some of history's most famous politicians, artists, and thinkers lived in Athens during this time.

One reason for the great advances the Athenians made during this time was their city's leadership. Leaders such as Pericles (PER-uh-kleez), who ruled Athens in the 400s BC, supported the arts and encouraged the creation of great works. For example, Pericles hired great architects and artists to construct and decorate the Parthenon, the temple shown below.

Inside the Parthenon was a magnificent statue of Athena by the sculptor Phidias. Many people consider him the greatest sculptor in all of Greece.

Like most Greek temples, the Parthenon had huge marble columns to support its roof.

ANALYSIS
SKILL **ANALYZING VISUALS**

Why do you think people consider the Parthenon to be a symbol of ancient Athens?

Athens was governed as a democracy. Once a month, all adult men in the city gathered together in an assembly to make the city's laws.

Men spoke in the assembly to support or argue against ideas. Sometimes, people in the crowd argued with them.

Voting was done either by show of hands or by secret ballot. The ballots used were broken pieces of pottery.

BIOGRAPHY

Pericles
(c. 495–429 BC)

Pericles, the most famous leader in all of Athenian history, wanted the city's people to be proud of their city. In his speeches, he emphasized the greatness of Athenian democracy and encouraged everyone to take part. He also worked to make the city beautiful. He hired the city's best architects to build monuments, such as the Parthenon, and hired great artists to decorate them. He also supported the work of writers and poets in order to make Athens the cultural center of all Greece.

Athenian Democracy

Leaders like Pericles had great power in Athens, but they did not rule alone. The city of Athens was a democracy, and its leaders were elected. In fact, Athens was the world's first democracy. No one else in history had created a government in which people ruled themselves.

In Athens most power was in the hands of the people. All the city's leaders could do was suggest ideas. Those ideas had to be approved by an assembly made up of the city's free men before they were enacted. As a result, it was vital that all the men of Athens took part in making government decisions.

The people of Athens were very proud of their democracy, and also of their city in general. This pride was reflected in their city's buildings and art.

Turn back to the previous page and look at the picture of the Parthenon again. Why do you think the temple was so large and so elaborately decorated? Like many Greek buildings, it was designed to be a symbol of the city. It was supposed to make people see Athens as a great and glorious city.

Architecture and Art

The Parthenon may be the most famous building from ancient Greece, but it is only one of many magnificent structures built by the Greeks. All over Greece, builders created beautiful marble temples. These temples were symbols of the glory of the cities in which they were built.

Greek temples and other buildings were often decorated with statues and carvings. These works by Greek artists are still admired by people today.

Greek art is so admired because of the skill and careful preparation of ancient Greek artists. These artists wanted their works to look realistic. To achieve their goals, they watched people as they stood and moved. They wanted to learn exactly what the human body looked like while it was in motion. The artists then used what they learned from their observations to make their statues as lifelike as possible.

Science, Philosophy, and Literature

Artists were not the only people in ancient Greece to study other people. Scientists, for example, studied people to learn how the body worked. Through these studies, the Greeks learned a great deal about medicine and biology. Other Greek scholars made great advances in math, astronomy, and other areas of science.

Greek philosophers, or thinkers, also studied people. They wanted to figure out how people could be happy. Three of the world's most influential philosophers—Socrates, Plato, and Aristotle—lived and taught in Athens during this time. Their ideas continue to shape how we live and think even today.

The ancient Greeks also made huge contributions to world literature. Some of the world's timeless classics were written in ancient Greece. They include stories of Greek heroes and their daring adventures, poems about love and friendship, and myths meant to teach lessons about life. Chances are that you have read a book, seen a film, or watched a play inspired by— or even written by—the ancient Greeks.

Actually, if you have ever seen a play at all then you have the Greeks to thank. The ancient Greeks were the first people to write and perform drama, or plays. Once a part of certain religious ceremonies, plays became one of the most popular forms of entertainment in Greece.

The Decline of the City-States

As great as it was, the Greek golden age could not last forever. In the end, Greece was torn apart by a war between Athens and its rival city-state, **Sparta**.

Sparta was a military city with one of the strongest armies in Greece. Jealous of the influence Athens had over other city-states, the Spartans attacked Athens.

The war between these two powerful city-states devastated Greece. Other city-states joined the war, supporting one side or the other. For years the war went on. In the end, Sparta won, but Greece was in shambles. Thousands of people had been killed and whole cities had been destroyed. Weakened, Greece lay open for a foreign conqueror to swoop in and take over.

READING CHECK **Analyzing** Why is the period between 500 and 300 BC called a golden age in Greece?

Greek Art

The ancient Greeks took great care to make their art lifelike. This statue shows Athena, a goddess from Greek mythology.

ANALYZING VISUALS What details make this statue lifelike?

The Empire of Alexander

In fact, a conqueror did take over all of Greece in the 330s BC. For the first time in its history, all of Greece was unified under a single ruler. He was from an area called Macedonia just north of Greece, an area that many Greeks considered uncivilized. He was known as Alexander the Great.

Alexander's Conquests

Alexander swept into Greece with a strong, well-trained army in 336 BC. In just a few years, he had conquered all of Greece.

Alexander, however, was not satisfied to rule only Greece. He wanted to create a huge empire. In 334 BC he set out to do just that. As you can see on the map, he was quite successful.

At its greatest extent, Alexander's empire stretched from Greece in the west all the way to India in the east. It included nearly all of central Asia—including what had been the Persian Empire—and Egypt. Alexander had dreams of extending his empire even farther east, but his troops refused to keep fighting. Tired and far from home, they demanded that Alexander turn back. He did, turning back toward home in 325 BC. On his way back home, however, Alexander became ill and died. He was 33.

The Spread of Greek Culture

FOCUS ON READING

After you read this passage, reread it to make sure you understand all the details.

During his life, Alexander wanted Greek culture to spread throughout his empire. To help the culture spread, he built cities in the lands he conquered and urged Greek people to move there. He named many of the cities Alexandria after himself.

As Greek people moved to these cities, however, they mingled with the people and cultures in the area. As a result, Greek culture blended with other cultures. The result was a new type of culture that mixed elements from many people and places.

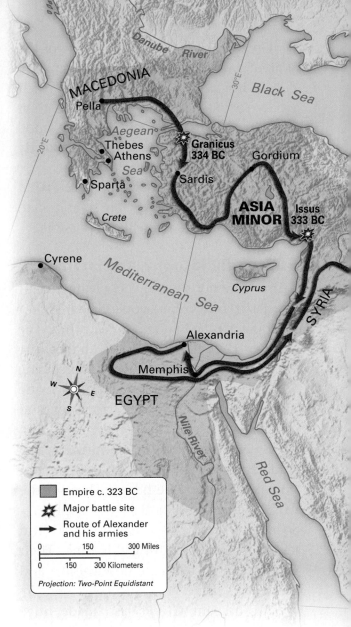

Because the Greek word for Greek is Hellenic, historians often refer to these blended cultures as **Hellenistic**, or Greek-like. Hellenistic culture helped shape life in Egypt, central Asia, and other parts of the world for many years.

READING CHECK Finding Main Ideas What lands were included in Alexander's empire?

SUMMARY AND PREVIEW Greece was the location of the first great civilization in Europe. In time, though, it was defeated by a new power, the Roman Empire.

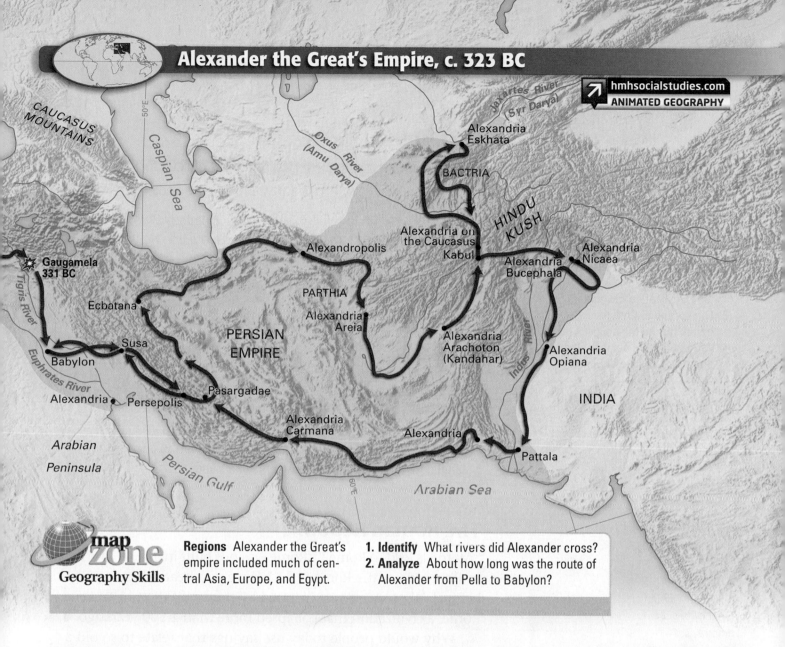

Alexander the Great's Empire, c. 323 BC

hmhsocialstudies.com
ANIMATED GEOGRAPHY

CAUCASUS MOUNTAINS

Caspian Sea

Jaxartes River (Syr Darya)

Oxus River (Amu Darya)

Alexandria Eskhata

BACTRIA

HINDU KUSH

Alexandria on the Caucasus

Kabul

Alexandria Bucephala

Alexandria Nicaea

Gaugamela 331 BC

Tigris River

Ecbatana

Alexandropolis

PARTHIA

Alexandria Areia

PERSIAN EMPIRE

Alexandria Arachoton (Kandahar)

Indus River

Alexandria Opiana

INDIA

Susa

Euphrates River

Babylon

Alexandria

Persepolis

Pasargadae

Alexandria Carmana

Alexandria

Arabian Peninsula

Persian Gulf

Pattala

Arabian Sea

map zone
Geography Skills

Regions Alexander the Great's empire included much of central Asia, Europe, and Egypt.

1. **Identify** What rivers did Alexander cross?
2. **Analyze** About how long was the route of Alexander from Pella to Babylon?

Section 1 Assessment

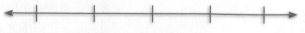

hmhsocialstudies.com
ONLINE QUIZ

Reviewing Ideas, Terms, and Places

1. **a. Describe** What did an ancient Greek **city-state** include?
   b. Explain Why did the Greeks form city-states?
2. **a. Identify** What were some major achievements in Greece between 500 and 300 BC?
   b. Summarize What was the government of ancient Athens like?
   c. Evaluate Would you have liked living in ancient Greece? Why or why not?
3. **a. Describe** How did Alexander the Great try to spread Greek culture in his empire?
   b. Drawing Conclusions How might Greek history have been different if Alexander had not existed?

Critical Thinking

4. **Analyzing** Using your notes, draw a time line of major events in Greek history. For each event you list on your time line, write a sentence explaining why it was important.

FOCUS ON WRITING

5. **Choosing Characters** Many ancient myths focused on the deeds of heroes or other great figures. What people from ancient Greece might feature in such a myth? Write some ideas in your notebook.

The Roman World

What You Will Learn...

Main Ideas

1. The Roman Republic was governed by elected leaders.
2. The Roman Empire was a time of great achievements.
3. The spread of Christianity began during the empire.
4. Various factors helped bring about the decline of Rome.

The Big Idea

The Romans unified parts of Europe, Africa, and Asia in one of the ancient world's greatest civilizations.

Key Terms and Places

Rome, *p. 22*
republic, *p. 23*
Senate, *p. 23*
citizens, *p. 23*
Carthage, *p. 24*
empire, *p. 24*
aqueducts, *p. 26*

hmhsocialstudies.com
TAKING NOTES

Use the graphic organizer online to take notes on Roman history and culture.

If YOU lived there...

You live in Rome in about 50 BC. Times are difficult for ordinary Romans. Bread is scarce in the city, and you are finding it hard to find work. Now a popular general is mounting a campaign to cross the mountains into a territory called Gaul. He wants to try to conquer the barbarians who live there. It might be dangerous, but being a soldier guarantees work and a chance to make money.

Will you join the army? Why or why not?

BUILDING BACKGROUND Rome's well-trained army helped it conquer large parts of Europe, Africa, and Asia. Through these conquests, Rome built a long-lasting empire that left its mark on the languages, cultures, and governments of Europe.

The Roman Republic

"All roads lead to Rome." "Rome was not built in a day." "When in Rome, do as the Romans do." Have you heard these sayings before? All of them were inspired by the civilization of ancient Rome, a civilization that collapsed more than 1,500 years ago.

Why would people today use sayings that relate to so old a culture? They refer to Rome because it was one of the greatest and most influential civilizations in history. In fact, we can still see the influence of ancient Rome in our lives.

Rome's Early History

Rome was not always so influential, however. At first it was just a small city in Italy. According to legend, the city of **Rome** was established in the year 753 BC by a group called the Latins.

For many years, the Romans were ruled by kings. Not all of these kings were Latin, though. For many years the Romans were ruled by a group called the Etruscans. The Romans learned a great deal from the Etruscans. For example, they learned about written language and how to build paved roads and sewers. Building on what they learned from the Etruscans, the Romans made Rome into a large and successful city.

The Beginning of the Republic

Not all of Rome's kings were good leaders, or good people. Some were cruel, harsh, and unfair. The last king of Rome was so unpopular that he was overthrown. In 509 BC a group of Roman nobles forced the king to flee the city.

In place of the king the people of Rome created a new type of government. They formed a **republic**, a type of government in which people elect leaders to make laws for them. Once elected, these leaders made all government decisions.

To help make some decisions, Rome's leaders looked to the **Senate**, a council of rich and powerful Romans who helped run the city. By advising the city's leaders, the Senate gained much influence in Rome.

For Rome's republican government to succeed, **citizens**, or people who could take part in the government, needed to be active. Rome's leaders encouraged citizens to vote and to run for office. As a result, speeches and debates were common in the city. One popular place for these activities was in the forum, the city's public square.

HISTORY

VIDEO
The Glory of
Rome's Forum

↗ hmhsocialstudies.com

Close-up

The Roman Forum

The forum was a large public square that stood in the center of the city. Roman citizens often met in the forum to discuss city affairs and politics.

Government buildings and temples stood on the hills around the forum.

Only citizens, or people who could vote, were allowed to wear this article of clothing, called a toga.

Many people met in the forum to discuss politics, current affairs, and other issues.

ANALYSIS SKILL **ANALYZING VISUALS**

What are some places in your local community that serve the same function as the forum did?

23

Growth and Conquest

FOCUS ON READING
After you read this passage, re-read it. Make a list of details you did not notice in your first reading.

After the creation of the republic, the Romans began to expand their territory. They started this expansion in Italy. As the map at right shows, however, the republic kept growing. By 100 BC the Romans ruled much of the Mediterranean world.

The Romans were able to take so much land because of their strong, organized army. They used this army to conquer their rivals. For example, the Romans fought the people of **Carthage**, a city in North Africa, and took over their lands.

Rome's expansion did not stop in 100 BC. In the 40s BC a general named Julius Caesar conquered many new lands for Rome. Caesar's conquests made him very powerful and very popular in Rome. Afraid of Caesar's power, a group of Senators decided to put an end to it. They banded together and killed Caesar in 44 BC.

READING CHECK **Summarizing** How did the Romans expand their territory?

The Roman Empire

The murder of Julius Caesar changed Roman society completely. The Romans were shocked and horrified by his death, and they wanted Caesar's murderers to be punished. One of the people they called on to punish the murderers was Caesar's adopted son, Octavian. Octavian's actions would reshape the Roman world. Under his leadership, Rome changed from a republic to an **empire**, a government that includes many different peoples and lands under a single rule.

The First Emperor

Octavian moved quickly to punish his uncle's murderers. He led an army against them and, before long, defeated them all.

After defeating his enemies, Octavian became more powerful. One by one, he eliminated his rivals for power. Eventually, Octavian alone ruled the entire Roman world as Rome's first emperor.

Roman Conquests

The Roman army was both powerful and flexible, which allowed it to take on and defeat many foes. Even the huge elephants ridden by the soldiers of Carthage were no match for the Romans' bravery and cleverness.

ANALYZING VISUALS What kind of equipment did the Roman army use?

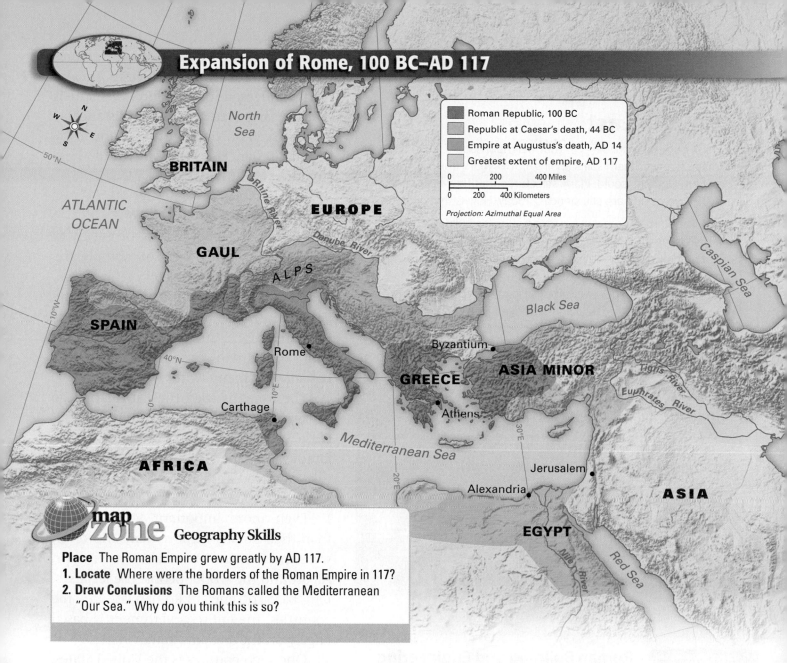

Expansion of Rome, 100 BC–AD 117

Roman Republic, 100 BC

Republic at Caesar's death, 44 BC

Empire at Augustus's death, AD 14

Greatest extent of empire, AD 117

0   200   400 Miles

0   200   400 Kilometers

Projection: Azimuthal Equal Area

North Sea

BRITAIN

ATLANTIC OCEAN

EUROPE

GAUL

ALPS

Rhine River

Danube River

SPAIN

Rome

Carthage

AFRICA

Mediterranean Sea

GREECE

Athens

Byzantium

ASIA MINOR

Black Sea

Caspian Sea

Tigris River

Euphrates River

Jerusalem

Alexandria

ASIA

EGYPT

Nile River

Red Sea

map zone Geography Skills

Place The Roman Empire grew greatly by AD 117.
1. **Locate** Where were the borders of the Roman Empire in 117?
2. **Draw Conclusions** The Romans called the Mediterranean "Our Sea." Why do you think this is so?

As emperor, Octavian was given a new name, Augustus, which means "honored one." The people of Rome respected and admired Augustus. This respect was mainly the result of his many accomplishments. As the map above shows, Augustus added a great deal of territory to the empire. He also made many improvements to lands already in the empire. For example, he built monuments and public buildings in the city of Rome. He also improved and expanded Rome's network of roads, which **facilitated** both travel and trade.

The Pax Romana

The emperors who ruled after Augustus tried to follow his example. Some of them worked to add even more land to the empire. Others focused their attentions on improving Roman society.

Because of these emperors' efforts, Rome experienced a long period of peace and achievement. There were no major wars or rebellions within the empire, and trade increased. This period, which lasted for about 200 years, was called the Pax Romana, or the Roman Peace.

ACADEMIC VOCABULARY

facilitate (fuh-SI-luh-tayt) to make easier

Built to Last

Think about the buildings in your neighborhood. Can you imagine any of them still standing 1,000 years from now? The ancient Romans could. Many structures that they built nearly 2,000 years ago are still standing today. How is that possible?

The Romans knew many techniques for building strong, long-lasting structures. Look at the Colosseum, pictured here. Notice how many arches were used in its design. Arches are one of the strongest shapes you can use in construction, a fact the Romans knew well. They also invented materials like cement to make their buildings stronger.

Making Generalizations How did technology help the Romans build strong and lasting structures?

hmhsocialstudies.com
ANIMATED GEOGRAPHY
Roman Aqueduct

Roman Building and Engineering

Because the Pax Romana was a time of stability, the Romans were able to make great cultural achievements. Some of the advances made during this time continue to affect our lives even today.

One of the areas in which the Romans made visible advances was architecture. The Romans were great builders, and many of their structures have stood for centuries. In fact, you can still see Roman buildings in Europe today, almost 2,000 years after they were built. This is because the Romans were skilled engineers who knew how to make their buildings strong.

Buildings are not the only structures that the Romans built to last. Ancient roads, bridges, and **aqueducts** —channels used to carry water over long distances— are still seen all over Europe. Planned by skilled Roman engineers, many of these structures are still in use.

Roman Language and Law

Not all Roman achievements are as easy to see as buildings, however. For example, the Romans greatly influenced how we speak, write, and think even today. Many of the languages spoken in Europe today, such as Spanish, French, and Italian, are based on Latin, the Romans' language. English, too, has adopted many words from Latin.

The Romans used the Latin language to create great works of literature. Among these works were some of the world's most famous plays, poems, and stories. Many of them are read and enjoyed by millions of people around the world today.

Even more important to the world than their literary achievements, however, were the Romans' political contributions. All around the world, people use legal systems based on ancient Roman law. In some countries, the entire government is based largely on the ancient Roman system.

One such country is the United States. The founders of our country admired the Roman government and used it as a model for our government. Like ancient Rome, the United States is a republic. We elect our leaders and trust them to make our laws. Also like the Romans, we require all people to obey a set of basic written laws. In ancient Rome, these laws were carved on stone tablets and kept on display. In the United States, they are written down in a document, the Constitution.

READING CHECK Finding Main Ideas What were some of the Romans' main achievements?

The Spread of Christianity

In addition to art and law, the ancient Romans also had a tremendous influence on religion. One of the world's major religions, Christianity, first appeared and spread in the Roman world.

The Beginnings of Christianity

Christianity is based on the life, actions, and teachings of Jesus of Nazareth. He and his early followers lived in the Roman territory of Judea in southwest Asia. They converted many people in Jerusalem and other cities in Judea to Christianity.

However, Christianity quickly spread far beyond the borders of Judea. Jesus's followers traveled widely, preaching and spreading his teachings. Through their efforts, communities of Christians began to appear in cities throughout the Roman world. Christian ideas spread quickly through these cities, as more and more people converted to Christianity.

Persecution and Acceptance

The rapid spread of Christianity worried some Roman leaders. They feared that Christianity would soon grow larger than all other religions in the empire. If that ever happened, they feared, the Christians might rebel and take over Rome.

To prevent a rebellion, some emperors began to persecute, or punish, Christians. They arrested, fined, or even killed any Christians they found.

The persecution did not cause people to abandon Christianity, however. Instead, Christians began to meet in secret, hiding their religion from the government.

Eventually, the persecution was ended. In the 300s a powerful emperor named Constantine became a Christian himself. Once the emperor had converted, the Christian faith was openly accepted even more widely in the empire. Look at the map below to see how Christianity spread between 300 and 400.

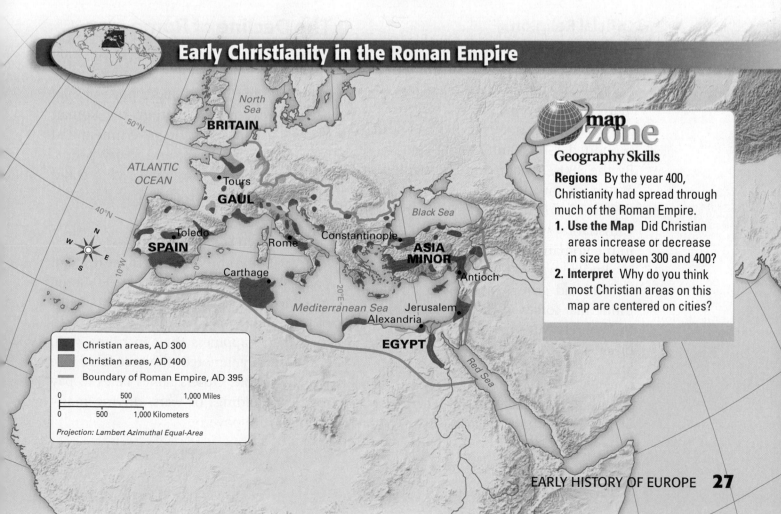

Early Christianity in the Roman Empire

North Sea
50°N
BRITAIN
ATLANTIC OCEAN
Tours
40°N
GAUL
Toledo
SPAIN
Rome
Carthage
Black Sea
Constantinople
ASIA MINOR
Antioch
Mediterranean Sea
Jerusalem
Alexandria
EGYPT
Red Sea

Christian areas, AD 300
Christian areas, AD 400
Boundary of Roman Empire, AD 395

0   500   1,000 Miles
0   500   1,000 Kilometers
Projection: Lambert Azimuthal Equal-Area

map zone

Geography Skills

Regions By the year 400, Christianity had spread through much of the Roman Empire.

1. **Use the Map** Did Christian areas increase or decrease in size between 300 and 400?
2. **Interpret** Why do you think most Christian areas on this map are centered on cities?

The Decline of Rome

Beginning around 200, the once-mighty Roman Empire began to weaken. Factors from inside and outside the empire caused many problems for Rome's leaders and led to the empire's collapse in the late 400s.

Barbarian invaders

Which factors in Rome's decline were internal? Which came from outside the empire?

Reasons for the Decline of Rome

- Poor leaders cared less for the people of Rome than they did for their own happiness.
- Taxes and prices rose, increasing poverty.
- People became less loyal to Rome.
- Military leaders fought each other for power.
- The empire was too large for a single person to govern well.
- Barbarians invaded the empire from outside.

Official Religion

Even after Constantine became Christian, many people in the Roman Empire did not convert. Romans continued to practice many different religions.

Over time, however, Rome's leaders supported Christianity more and more. By the 380s, support for Christianity had grown so much that an emperor chose to ban all other religions. With that ban, Christianity was the only religion allowed in the Roman Empire.

By the end of the 300s, the Christian church had grown into one of the most influential forces in the Roman world. As the church was growing, however, many other parts of Roman society were falling apart. The Roman Empire was ending.

READING CHECK Sequencing How did the Christian church gain influence in Rome?

The Decline of Rome

Rome's problems had actually started long before 300. For about a century, crime rates had been rising and poverty had been increasing. In addition, the Roman systems of education and government had begun breaking down, and many people no longer felt loyal to Rome. What could have happened to cause these problems?

Problems in the Government

Many of Rome's problems were the result of poor government. After about 200, Rome was ruled by a series of bad emperors. Most of these emperors were more interested in their own happiness than in ruling well. Some simply ignored the needs of the Roman people. Others raised taxes to pay for new buildings or wars, driving many Romans into poverty.

Frustrated by these bad emperors, some military leaders tried to take over and rule Rome in their place. In most cases, though, these military leaders were no better than the emperors they replaced. Most of them were poor leaders. In addition, fighting between rival military leaders almost led to civil war on many occasions.

Rome did have a few good emperors who worked furiously to save the empire. One emperor feared that the empire had grown too large for one person to rule. To correct this problem, he divided the empire in half and named a co-ruler to help govern. Later, the emperor Constantine built a new capital, Constantinople, in what is now Turkey, nearer to the center of the Roman Empire. He thought that ruling from a central location would help keep the empire together. These measures helped restore order for a time, but they were not enough to save the Roman Empire.

Invasions

Although internal problems weakened the empire, they alone probably would not have destroyed it. However, as the empire was getting weaker from within, invaders from outside also began to attack in the late 300s and 400s. Already suffering from their own problems, the Romans could not fight off these invasions.

Most Roman people considered the various groups who invaded their empire barbarians, uncivilized and backward. In truth, however, some of these so-called barbarian groups had their own complex societies and strong, capable leaders. As a result, they were able to defeat Roman armies and take lands away from the empire. In the end, the barbarians were even able to attack and destroy the city of Rome itself. In 476 the last emperor of Rome was overthrown and replaced by the leader of an invading group.

Most historians consider the capture of the Roman emperor in 476 the end of the Roman Empire in western Europe. Although people continued to think of themselves as Romans, there was no empire to tie them together. As a result, European society slowly broke apart.

READING CHECK **Generalizing** Why did the Roman Empire decline?

SUMMARY AND PREVIEW In this section you learned that the Romans brought a vast territory under one government. Next, you will learn what happened after that government collapsed, in a period called the Middle Ages.

Section 2 Assessment

hmhsocialstudies.com
ONLINE QUIZ

Reviewing Ideas, Terms, and Places

1. **a. Describe** What was the government of the Roman **Republic** like?
   b. Contrast How was **Rome**'s government in the republic unlike the government under kings?
2. **a. Identify** Who was Augustus?
   b. Explain How did the Pax Romana help the Romans make great achievements?
3. **Generalize** How did Rome's emperors affect the spread of Christianity?
4. **a. Identify** What threats to the Roman Empire appeared in the 200s, 300s, and 400s?
   b. Evaluate Do you think internal problems or invasions were more responsible for Rome's fall? Why?

Critical Thinking

5. **Identifying Causes** Draw a graph like the one at right. On the left side, list the main causes of Rome's growth. On the right, list the main causes of its decline.

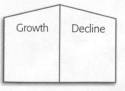

Growth | Decline

FOCUS ON WRITING

6. **Finding a Setting** Where will your myth be set? Think back over this section and the previous one to find an appropriate location for your myth.

Roman Roads

The Romans are famous for their roads. They built a road network so large and well constructed that parts of it remain today, roughly 2,000 years later. Roads helped the Romans run their empire. Armies, travelers, messengers, and merchants all used the roads to get around. They stretched to every corner of the empire in a network so vast that people even today say that "all roads lead to Rome."

Roman roads reached as far north as Scotland.

The Romans built about 50,000 miles of roads. That's enough to circle Earth—twice!

EUROPE

PYRENEES

In the west, roads crisscrossed Spain.

ITALY

Rome

Roman roads in the south connected different parts of northern Africa.

Mediterranean Sea

N
W E
S

AFRICA

Paving stones

Drainage ditch

Curbstones

Sand, clay, and gravel

Stone chips

Gravel concrete

Roman roads were built to last. They were constructed of layers of sand, concrete, rock, and stone. Drainage ditches let water drain off, preventing water damage.

The roads were built by and for the military. The main purpose of the roads was to allow Rome's armies to travel quickly throughout the empire.

In the east, Roman roads stretched into Southwest Asia.

The Romans built tall "milestones" along their roads to mark distances. Just like modern highway signs, the markers told travelers how far it was to the next town.

ANALYSIS
SKILL **ANALYZING VISUALS**

1. **Movement** Why did the Romans build their roads?
2. **Location** How does the map show that "all roads lead to Rome"?

31

The Middle Ages

What You Will Learn...

Main Ideas

1. The Christian church influenced nearly every aspect of society in the Middle Ages.
2. Complicated political and economic systems governed life in the Middle Ages.
3. The period after 1000 was a time of great changes in medieval society.

The Big Idea

Christianity and social systems influenced life in Europe in the Middle Ages.

Key Terms and Places

Middle Ages, *p. 32*
pope, *p. 33*
Crusade, *p. 33*
Holy Land, *p. 33*
Gothic architecture, *p. 34*
feudal system, *p. 35*
manor, *p. 36*
nation-state, *p. 39*

hmhsocialstudies.com
TAKING NOTES

Use the graphic organizer online to take notes on medieval society.

If YOU lived there...

You are the youngest child of a noble family in medieval France. One day your father tells you that you are being sent to the court of another noble family. There you will learn fine manners and proper behavior. You will also learn music and drawing. You know it is a great honor, but you will miss your own home.

How do you feel about this change in your life?

BUILDING BACKGROUND When people think of the Middle Ages today, they usually think of castles, princesses, and knights in shining armor. Although these were all part of the Middle Ages, they do not tell the whole story. The Middle Ages was a time of great change in Europe, as the influence of the ancient world faded away.

The Christian Church and Society

When historians talk about the past, they often divide it into three long periods. The first period is the ancient world, the time of the world's earliest civilizations, such as Egypt, China, Greece, and Rome. The last period historians call the modern world, the world since about 1500. Since that time, new ideas and contacts between civilizations changed the world completely.

What happened between ancient and modern times? We call this period, which lasted from about 500 until about 1500, the **Middle Ages**. We also call it the medieval (mee-DEE-vuhl) period. The word *medieval* comes from two Latin words that mean "middle age." It was a time of great changes in Europe, many of them inspired by the Christian church.

The Importance of the Church

When the Roman Empire fell apart in the late 400s, the people of Europe were left without a single dominant government to unite them. In the absence of strong leaders, Europe broke into many small kingdoms. Each of these kingdoms had its own laws, customs, and language. Europe was no longer the same place it had been under the Romans.

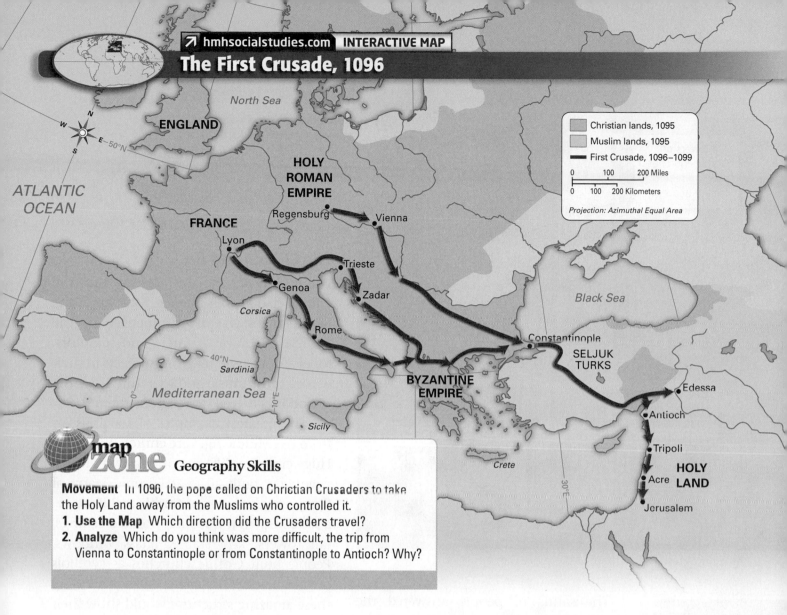

The First Crusade, 1096

hmhsocialstudies.com **INTERACTIVE MAP**

North Sea

ENGLAND

ATLANTIC OCEAN

HOLY ROMAN EMPIRE

Regensburg — Vienna

FRANCE

Lyon

Trieste

Genoa

Zadar

Corsica

Rome

Sardinia

Mediterranean Sea

Sicily

Black Sea

Constantinople

SELJUK TURKS

BYZANTINE EMPIRE

Crete

Edessa

Antioch

Tripoli

Acre

HOLY LAND

Jerusalem

Christian lands, 1095
Muslim lands, 1095
First Crusade, 1096–1099

0   100   200 Miles
0   100   200 Kilometers

Projection: Azimuthal Equal Area

map zone Geography Skills

Movement In 1090, the pope called on Christian Crusaders to take the Holy Land away from the Muslims who controlled it.
1. **Use the Map** Which direction did the Crusaders travel?
2. **Analyze** Which do you think was more difficult, the trip from Vienna to Constantinople or from Constantinople to Antioch? Why?

One factor, however, continued to tie the people of Europe together—religion. Nearly everyone in Europe was Christian, and so most Europeans felt tied together by their beliefs. Over time, the number of Christians in Europe increased. People came to feel more and more like part of a single religious community.

Because Christianity was so important in Europe, the Christian church gained a great deal of influence. In time, the church began to influence the politics, art, and daily lives of people all over the continent. In fact, almost no part of life in Europe in the Middle Ages was unaffected by the church and its teachings.

The Christian Church and Politics

As the Christian church gained influence in Europe, some church leaders became powerful. They gained political power in addition to their religious authority.

The most powerful religious leader was the **pope**, the head of the Christian church. The pope's decisions could have huge effects on people's lives. For example, one pope decided to start a religious war, or **Crusade**, against the church's enemies in Southwest Asia. He wanted Europeans to take over the **Holy Land**, the region in which Jesus had lived. For many years, the region had been in the hands of another religious group, the Muslims.

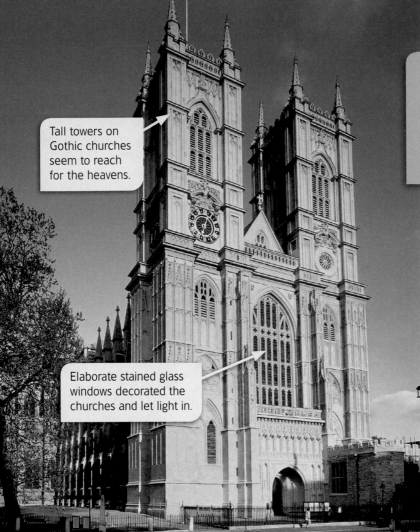

Tall towers on Gothic churches seem to reach for the heavens.

Elaborate stained glass windows decorated the churches and let light in.

Gothic Architecture

Gothic churches were designed to tower over medieval cities as symbols of the church's greatness. This cathedral, Westminster Abbey, stands in London, England.

The Church and Art

Politics was not the only area in which the church had great influence. Most art of the Middle Ages was also influenced by the church. Medieval painters and sculptors, for example, used religious subjects in their works. Most music and literature from the period is centered on religious themes.

The greatest examples of religious art from the Middle Ages are church buildings. Huge churches like the one shown on this page were built all over Europe. Many of them are examples of **Gothic architecture**, a style known for its high pointed ceilings, tall towers, and stained glass windows. People built Gothic churches as symbols of their faith. They believed that building these amazing structures would show their love for God. The insides of such churches are as elaborate and ornate as the outsides.

The Church and Daily Life

Most people in Europe never saw a Gothic church, especially not the inside. Instead they worshipped at small local churches. In fact, people's lives often centered around their local church. Markets, festivals, and religious ceremonies all took place there. Local priests advised people on how to live and act. In addition, because most people could not read or write, they depended on the church to keep records for them.

READING CHECK Summarizing How did the Christian church shape life in the Middle Ages?

VIDEO
The Crusades' Aftermath

hmhsocialstudies.com

Thousands of people answered the pope's call for a Crusade. As the map on the previous page shows, they traveled thousands of miles to fight the church's enemies. This Crusade was the first of eight attempts by Christians over two centuries to win back the Holy Land.

In the end, the Crusades did not drive the Muslims from the Holy Land. They did, however, lead to sweeping changes in Europe. Crusaders brought new goods and ideas back to Europe with them. Europeans began to want more of these goods, so trade between Europe and Asia increased. At the same time, though, relations between Christians and Muslims grew worse. For years to come, followers of the religions distrusted and resented each other.

Life in the Middle Ages

Christianity was a major influence on people's lives in the Middle Ages, but it was not the only one. Much of European society was controlled by two systems of relationships. They were the feudal (FYOO-duhl) system and the manor system.

The Feudal System

Medieval Europe was divided into many small kingdoms. In most kingdoms, the king owned all the land. Sometimes, kings gave parts of their land to nobles—people born into wealthy, powerful families. In turn, these nobles gave land to knights, or trained warriors, who promised to help them defend both their lands and the king. This system of exchanging land for military service is called the **feudal system**, or feudalism (FYOO-duh-li-zuhm).

Everyone involved in the feudal system had certain duties to perform. The kings and nobles provided land and promised to protect the people who served them and to treat everyone fairly. In return, the knights who received land promised to serve the nobles dutifully, especially in times of war. The set of relationships between knights and nobles was the heart of Europe's feudal system.

The feudal system was very complex. Its rules varied from kingdom to kingdom and changed constantly. Feudal duties in France, for example, were not the same as those in Germany or England. Also, it was possible for one knight to owe service to more than one noble. If the two nobles he served went to war, the poor knight would be torn between them. In such situations, feudal relationships could be confusing or even dangerous.

FOCUS ON READING

After you read this passage, reread it. Make a list of details you did not notice in your first reading.

Feudal Relationships

Europe's feudal system was based on relationships between knights and nobles. Each had certain duties that he or she had to perform.

ANALYZING VISUALS Who had to provide military service as one of his duties?

hmhsocialstudies.com
ANIMATED GEOGRAPHY

Noble's duties
- Provide knight with land
- Treat knights fairly and honestly

Knight's duties
- Provide military service
- Supply food and shelter for noble during visits

The Manor System

The feudal system was only one set of guidelines that governed life in the Middle Ages. Another system, the manor system, controlled most economic activities in Europe during this period.

At the center of the manor system was the **manor**, a large estate owned by a noble or knight. Every manor was different, but most included a large house or castle, fields, pastures, and forests. A manor also had a village where workers lived. They traveled back and forth to the fields each day.

The owner of a manor did not farm his own land. Instead, he had workers to farm it for him. Most of the crops grown on the manor went to the owner. In exchange for their work, the workers got a place to live and a small piece of land on which they could grow their own food.

The workers on most manors included either free peasants or serfs. Peasants were free farmers. Serfs, on the other hand, were not free. Although they were not slaves, they were not allowed to leave the land on which they worked.

Life on a Manor

Manors were large estates that developed during the Middle Ages. Many manors were largely self-sufficient, producing most of the food and goods they needed. This picture shows what a manor in England might have looked like.

The owner of the manor lived in a large stone house called the manor house.

Peasants grew vegetables in small gardens located near their houses.

In late spring, peasants harvested crops like wheat.

Towns and Trade

Not everyone in the Middle Ages lived on manors. Some people chose to live in towns and cities like Paris or London. Compared to our cities today, most of these medieval cities were small, dirty, and dark.

Many of the people who lived in cities were traders. They bought and sold goods from all over Europe and other parts of the world. Most of their goods were sold at trade fairs. Every year, merchants from many places in Europe would meet at these large fairs to sell their wares.

Before the year 1000, trade was not very common in Europe. After that year, however, trade increased. As it did, more people began to move to cities. Once small, these cities began to grow. As cities grew, trade increased even more, and the people who lived in them became wealthier. By the end of the Middle Ages, cities had become the centers of European culture and wealth.

READING CHECK **Finding Main Ideas** What were two systems that governed life in Europe during the Middle Ages? How did they differ?

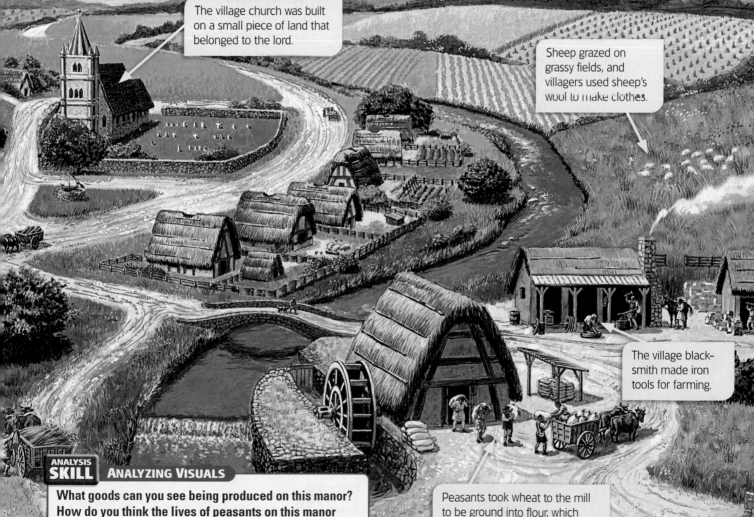

The village church was built on a small piece of land that belonged to the lord.

Sheep grazed on grassy fields, and villagers used sheep's wool to make clothes.

The village black-smith made iron tools for farming.

Peasants took wheat to the mill to be ground into flour, which they used to make bread.

ANALYSIS SKILL **ANALYZING VISUALS**

What goods can you see being produced on this manor? How do you think the lives of peasants on this manor differed from the life of the owner?

Changes in Medieval Society

Life in the Middle Ages changed greatly after the year 1000. You have already seen how cities grew and trade increased. Even as these changes were taking place, bigger changes were sweeping through Europe.

Political Changes in England

One of the countries most affected by change in the Middle Ages was England. In the year 1066 a noble from northern France, William the Conqueror, sailed to England and overthrew the old king. He declared himself the new king of England.

William built a strong government in England, something the English had not had before. Later kings of England built on William's example. For more than a century, these kings increased their power. By the late 1100s England's king was one of the most powerful men in Europe.

When William's descendant John took the throne, however, he angered many nobles by raising taxes. John believed that the king had the right to do whatever he wanted. England's nobles disagreed.

In 1215 a group of nobles forced King John to sign Magna Carta, one of the most important documents in English history. Magna Carta stated that the law, not the king, was the supreme power in England. The king had to obey the law. He could not raise taxes without the nobles' permission.

Many people consider Magna Carta to be one of the first steps toward democracy in modern Europe and one of history's most important documents. By stating that the king was not above the law, Magna Carta set limits on his power. In addition, it gave a council of nobles the power to advise the king. In time, that council developed into Parliament (PAHR-luh-muhnt), the elected body that governs England today.

Primary Source

HISTORIC DOCUMENT
Magna Carta

Magna Carta was one of the first documents to protect the rights of the people. Magna Carta was so influential that the British still consider it part of their constitution. Some of its ideas are also in the U.S. Constitution. Included in Magna Carta were 63 demands that English nobles made King John agree to follow. A few of these demands are listed here.

Demand number 31 defended people's right to property, not just wood.

Magna Carta guaranteed that free men had the right to a fair trial.

To all free men of our kingdom we have also granted, for us and our heirs for ever, all the liberties written out below, to have and to keep for them and their heirs, of us and our heirs.

(16) No man shall be forced to perform more service for a knight's 'fee,' or other free holding of land, than is due from it.

(31) Neither we nor any royal official will take wood for our castle, or for any other purpose, without the consent [permission] of the owner.

(38) In future no official shall place a man on trial upon his own unsupported statement, without producing credible [believable] witnesses to the truth of it.

—Magna Carta, from a translation by the British Library

ANALYSIS SKILL ANALYZING PRIMARY SOURCES

In what ways do you think the ideas listed above influenced modern democracy?

The Black Death

Not all of the changes that struck medieval Europe had such positive results. In 1347 a disease called the Black Death swept through Europe. Up to a third of Europe's people died from the disease. Even such a disaster, however, had some positive effects. With the decrease in population came a labor shortage. As a result, people could demand higher wages for their work.

The Fight for Power

Even as the Black Death was sweeping across Europe, kings fought for power. In 1337 the Hundred Years' War broke out between England and France. As its name suggests, the war lasted more than 100 years. In the end, the French won.

Inspired by the victory, France's kings worked to increase their power. They took land away from nobles to rule themselves. France became a **nation-state**, a country united under a single strong government.

Around Europe, other rulers followed the French example. As nation-states arose around Europe, feudalism disappeared, and the Middle Ages came to an end.

> **READING CHECK** **Finding Main Ideas** What changes occurred in Europe after 1000?

BIOGRAPHY

Joan of Arc
(c. 1412–1431)

One of the most famous war leaders in all of European history was a teenage girl. Joan of Arc, a leader of French troops during the Hundred Years' War, was only 16 when she first led troops into battle. She won many battles against the English but was captured in battle in 1430, tried, and executed. Nevertheless, her courage inspired the French, who went on to win the war. Today Joan is considered a national hero in France.

Make Inferences Why do you think Joan is considered a hero in France?

> **SUMMARY AND PREVIEW** In this chapter you read about early Europe, a time that still influences how we live today. From the earliest civilizations of Greece and Rome to the Middle Ages, the people of Europe helped shape Western society. Next, you will learn about later periods that also affect our lives.

Section 3 Assessment

Reviewing Ideas, Terms, and Places

1. **a. Recall** Why did the **pope** call for a **Crusade**?
   b. Generalize How did the Christian church affect art in the Middle Ages?
2. **a. Define** What was the **feudal system**?
   b. Explain How did the **manor** system work?
   c. Elaborate What made the feudal system so complex?
3. **a. Describe** How did the Black Death affect Europe?
   b. Explain How did England's government change after 1000?

Critical Thinking

4. **Analyzing** Use your notes to complete a table like the one on the right. List ways the Church shaped medieval politics, life, and art.

```
      The Christian
         Church
        /        \
   Politics        Art
        \        /
       Daily
       Life
```

FOCUS ON WRITING

5. **Selecting a Topic** Now you have read about events and people in the Middle Ages. Choose one that could be the subject of your myth.

Geography and History

The Black Death

"And they died by the hundreds," wrote one man who saw the horror, "both day and night." The Black Death had arrived. The Black Death was a series of deadly plagues that hit Europe between 1347 and 1351, killing millions. People didn't know what caused the plague. They also didn't know that geography played a key role in its spread—as people traveled to trade, they unwittingly carried the disease with them to new places.

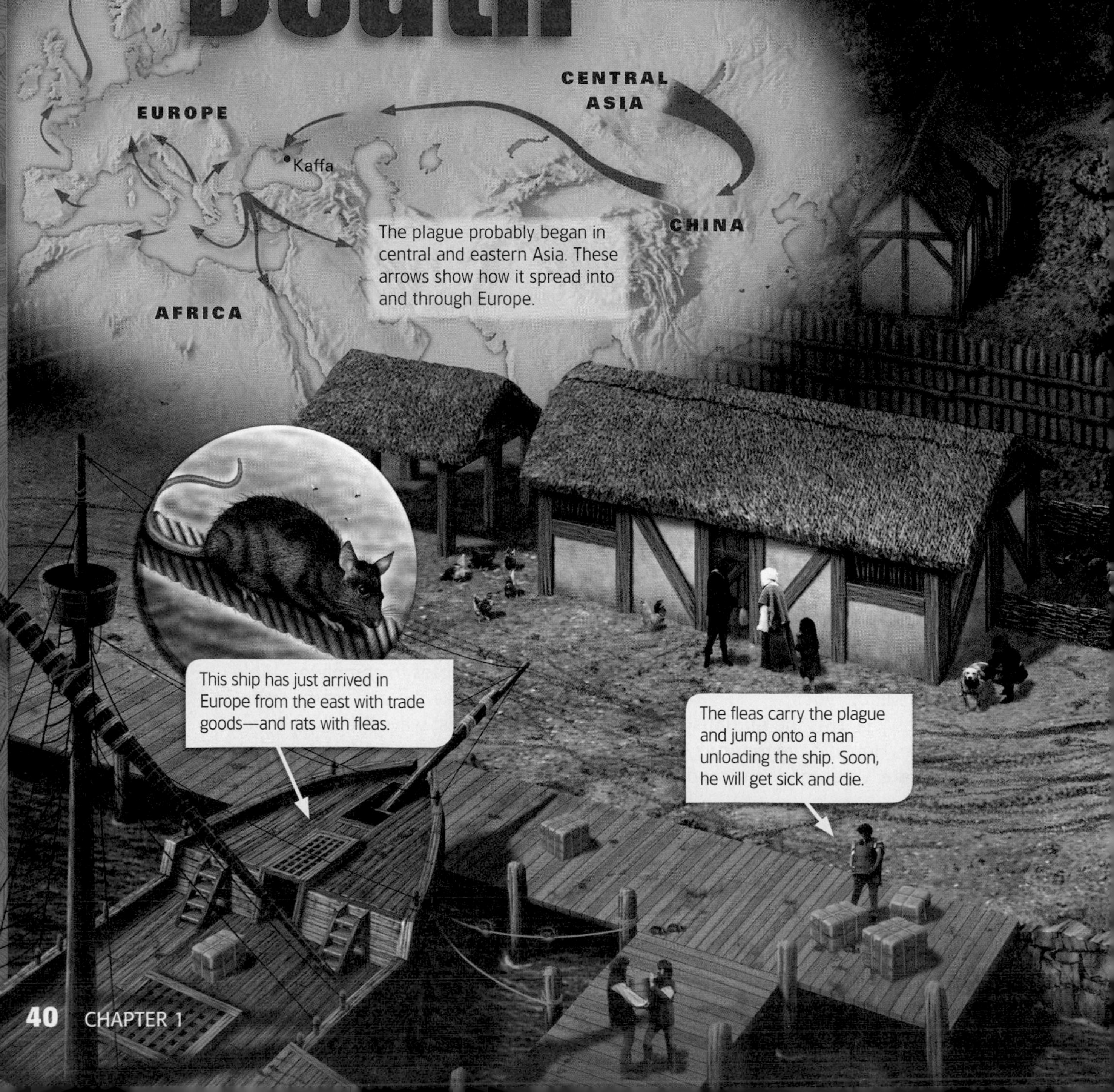
CENTRAL ASIA
EUROPE
Kaffa
CHINA
AFRICA
The plague probably began in central and eastern Asia. These arrows show how it spread into and through Europe.
This ship has just arrived in Europe from the east with trade goods—and rats with fleas.
The fleas carry the plague and jump onto a man unloading the ship. Soon, he will get sick and die.

VIDEO
The Black
Death

↗ hmhsocialstudies.com

The plague is so terrifying that many people think it's the end of the world. They leave town for the country, spreading the Black Death even further.

People dig mass graves to bury the dead. But often, so many victims are infected that there is no one left to bury them.

The garbage and dirty conditions in the town provide food and a home for the rats, allowing the disease to spread even more.

So many people die so quickly that special carts are sent through the streets to gather the bodies.

ANALYSIS SKILL ANALYZING VISUALS

1. **Movement** How did the Black Death reach Europe from Asia?
2. **Place** What helped spread the plague within Europe?

Interpreting a Historical Map

Learn

History and geography are closely related. You cannot truly understand the history of a place without knowing where it is and what it is like. For that reason, historical maps are important in the study of history. A historical map is a map that shows what a place was like at a particular time in the past.

Like other maps, historical maps use colors and symbols to represent information. One color, for example, might represent the lands controlled by a certain kingdom or the areas in which a particular religion or type of government was common. Symbols might identify key cities, battle sites, or other major locations.

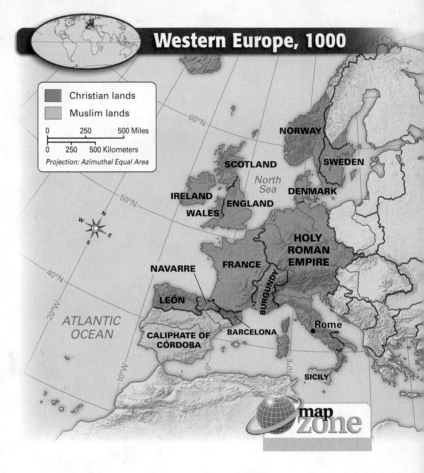

Western Europe, 1000

Christian lands
Muslim lands

0   250   500 Miles
0   250   500 Kilometers
Projection: Azimuthal Equal Area

NORWAY
SCOTLAND
SWEDEN
North Sea
IRELAND   DENMARK
WALES   ENGLAND
NAVARRE   FRANCE   HOLY ROMAN EMPIRE
BURGUNDY
LEÓN
ATLANTIC OCEAN   CALIPHATE OF CÓRDOBA   BARCELONA   Rome
SICILY

map zone

Practice

Use the map on this page to answer the following questions.

1 Read the map's title. What area does this map show? What time period?

2 Check the map's legend. What does the color purple represent on this map?

3 According to the map, what territory lay between France and the Holy Roman Empire at this time?

4 What parts of Europe were Muslim in the year 1000?

Apply

Look back at the map called Early Christianity in the Roman Empire in Section 2 of this chapter. Study the map, and then write five questions that you might see about such a map on a test. Make sure that the questions you ask can be answered with just the information on the map.

Geography's Impact
video series
Review the video to answer the closing question:
What are three ways in which Greek scholars have influenced education in America?

Visual Summary

Use the visual summary below to help you review the main ideas of the chapter.

QUICK FACTS

Ancient Greece was the birthplace of democracy, theater, and many other advances of Western society.

The Romans were master builders who created one of the largest empires in world history.

During the Middle Ages, new political and economic systems took hold in Europe, and religion dominated society.

Reviewing Vocabulary, Terms, and Places

For each group of terms below, write the letter of the term that does not relate to the others. Then write a sentence that explains how the other two terms are related.

1. **a.** Athens
   b. Sparta
   c. Rome
2. **a.** feudal system
   b. aqueduct
   c. manor
3. **a.** Crusade
   b. republic
   c. empire
4. **a.** Senate
   b. citizen
   c. colony

Comprehension and Critical Thinking

SECTION 1 *(Pages 14–21)*

5. **a. Identify** What was the basic political unit in ancient Greece? What is one example?

   b. Contrast How was life in Greece different under Alexander than it had been during the golden age?

   c. Evaluate What do you think was the greatest achievement of the ancient Greeks? Why?

SECTION 2 *(Pages 22–29)*

6. **a. Define** What was the Pax Romana? What happened during that time?

   b. Summarize How did Rome's government change after the republic fell apart?

   c. Elaborate What role did Rome's leaders play in the spread of Christianity?

SECTION 3 (Pages 32–39)

7. a. Describe What were two changes that affected Europe in the late Middle Ages?

b. Explain What duties did knights have under the feudal system?

c. Develop Why do you think so much of the art created in the Middle Ages was religious?

Using the Internet

8. Activity: Exploring Ancient Greece The golden age of Greece was an amazing time—the Greeks helped shape our government, art, philosophy, writing, and more! Through your online textbook, learn more about the ancient Greek world. Imagine you have traveled through time, back to ancient Greece. What are the people doing? What kinds of buildings do you see? What is the area like? Draw a picture or make a collage to record your observations.

↗ hmhsocialstudies.com

Social Studies Skills

Interpreting a Historical Map *Use the map on the Expansion of Rome in Section 2 of this chapter to answer the following questions.*

9. What time period is shown on this map?

10. What does the orange color on this map represent?

11. Did the areas shown on the map in gold become part of Rome before or after the areas shown in light green?

12. Which was conquered by the Romans first— Spain or Gaul?

13. Between which two years did Egypt become a Roman territory?

Map Activity

14. Europe, 2000 BC–AD 1500 On a separate sheet of paper, match the letters on the map with their correct labels.

Athens	Carthage	Rome
Gaul	Holy Land	Alexandria

↗ hmhsocialstudies.com **INTERACTIVE MAP**

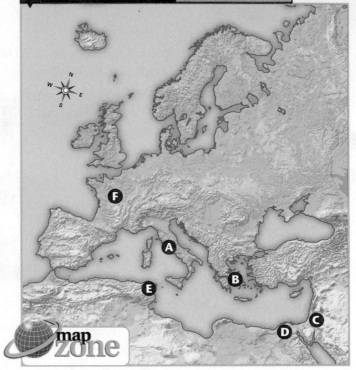

FOCUS ON READING AND WRITING

15. Re-Reading Read the passage titled The Manor System in Section 3. After you read, write down the main ideas of the passage. Then go back and re-read the passage carefully. Add to your list of main ideas anything more that you noticed in your second reading. How much more did you learn from the passage when you re-read it?

16. Writing Your Myth Now that you have learned about the events and people of ancient and medieval Europe, you can write a myth about one of them. Remember that your myth should try to explain the person or the event in a way that people of the time might have. For example, they might have thought that Caesar was the son of a goddess or that the Black Death was caused by a terrible unknown monster. Try to include descriptive details that will help bring your myth to life for the people who read it.

Standardized Test Prep

DIRECTIONS: Read questions 1 through 7 and write the letter of the best response. Then read question 8 and write your own well-constructed response.

1 **Democracy was first practiced in which city-state of ancient Greece?**

A Athens

B Carthage

C Rome

D Sparta

2 **A large estate owned by a noble or knight in the Middle Ages was called a**

A city-state.

B republic.

C empire.

D manor.

3 **The first Roman emperor to become a Christian was named**

A Julius Caesar.

B Augustus.

C Constantine.

D Jesus of Nazareth.

4 **Which of the following was first created in the Middle Ages?**

A aqueducts

B Gothic architecture

C drama

D democracy

5 **The blended culture that was created in Alexander the Great's empire is called**

A Greek

B Hellenistic

C Roman

D Medieval

Europe, AD 117

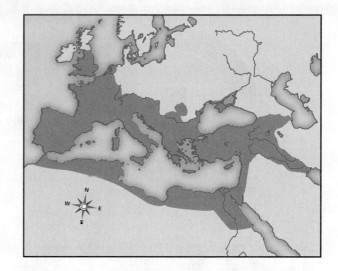

6 **Study the map above. The area shown in orange on this map was ruled by the**

A Greeks

B Etruscans

C Romans

D French

7 **Which document limited the powers of the king of England?**

A Black Death

B Crusade

C Feudal system

D Magna Carta

8 **Extended Response** As the map above shows, much of Europe was unified under a single government in 117. By the Middle Ages, though, that government had fallen apart. Write a brief paragraph in which you explain two ways in which European society was different in the Middle Ages than it had been in earlier times.

ANCIENT GREECE

The Acropolis of Athens symbolizes the city and represents the architectural and artistic legacy of ancient Greece. *Acropolis* means "highest city" in Greek, and there are many such sites in Greece. Historically, an acropolis provided shelter and defense against a city's enemies. The Acropolis of Athens—the best known of them all—contained temples, monuments, and artwork dedicated to the Greek gods. Archaeological evidence indicates that the Acropolis was an important place to inhabitants from much earlier eras. However, the structures that we see today on the site were largely conceived by the statesman Pericles during the Golden Age of Athens in the 5th century B.C.

Explore the Acropolis of ancient Greece and learn about the legacy of Greek civilization. You can find a wealth of information, video clips, primary sources, activities, and more at 🡕 hmhsocialstudies.com .

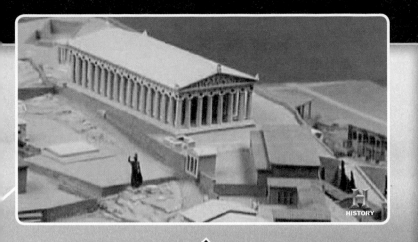

The Parthenon

Watch the video to see what the Parthenon, one of the most important temples on the Acropolis, might have looked like after it was completed.

The Persian Wars

Watch the video to find out how Athens emerged as the principal Greek city-state at the conclusion of the Persian Wars.

The Goddess Athena

Watch the video to learn how, according to Greek mythology, Athena became the protector of Athens.

Legacy of Greece

Watch the video to analyze *The School of Athens*, a painting by the Italian Renaissance artist Raphael, which pays tribute to the legacy of ancient Greece in philosophy and science.

CHAPTER 2

History of Early Modern Europe

Essential Question What important events shaped Europe from the Middle Ages to modern times?

What You Will Learn...

In this chapter you will learn about European history from the end of the Middle Ages to 1900. During this period new ideas and innovations changed life and expanded knowledge across Europe.

FOCUS ON READING AND WRITING

Understanding Chronological Order Chronological means "related to time." Many of the events in this chapter are described in sequence, or in the order in which they occurred. Words such as first, before, next, and later can signal chronological order. **See the lesson, Understanding Chronological Order, on page 221.**

Creating a Travel Brochure Your job is to encourage people to visit a time from Europe's exciting past. Read about Europe's history from the Renaissance through the Industrial Revolution. Then choose one time period and create a travel brochure to convince others to visit Europe during that period. What exciting changes might visitors see? What experiences might they have? Describe it all in your brochure.

ATLANTIC OCEAN

Explorer's ship

Madrid

AFRICA

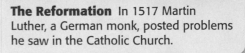

The Reformation In 1517 Martin Luther, a German monk, posted problems he saw in the Catholic Church.

Europe, 1500–1900

HISTORY. Da Vinci Tech

hmhsocialstudies.com VIDEO

0   100   300 Miles
0   100   200 Kilometers
Projection: Azimuthal Equal Area

Steam train

North Sea

Baltic Sea

Printing press

Wittenberg

Paris

French Revolution

EUROPE

Milan

Venice

Florence

Rome

Duomo, a cathedral in Florence

Mediterranean Sea

10°E   20°E   30°E

map zone Geography Skills

Place The nations and kingdoms of Europe underwent many changes during this period.

1. **Identify** What city is connected with the French Revolution?
2. **Analyze** Based on the images on the map, what types of changes do you think occurred during this period of Europe's history?

The Age of Exploration Italian sailor Christopher Columbus led a voyage that reached the Americas in 1492.

The Industrial Revolution First used in factories, the steam engine later powered trains and ships. Inventions such as the steam engine changed life in Europe during the 1700s and 1800s.

The Renaissance and Reformation

What You Will Learn...

Main Ideas

1. The Renaissance was a period of new learning, new ideas, and new advances in art, literature, and science.
2. The Reformation changed the religious map of Europe.

The Big Idea

The periods of the Renaissance and the Reformation introduced new ideas and new ways of thinking into Europe.

Key Terms and Places

Renaissance, *p. 48*
Florence, *p. 48*
Venice, *p. 48*
humanism, *p. 49*
Reformation, *p. 52*
Protestants, *p. 53*
Catholic Reformation, *p. 53*

hmhsocialstudies.com
TAKING NOTES

Use the graphic organizer online to take notes on the Renaissance and the Reformation.

If YOU lived there...

You live in Florence, Italy, in the 1400s. Your father, a merchant, has just hired a tutor from Asia Minor to teach you and your sisters and brothers. Your new teacher starts by stating, "Nothing good has been written in a thousand years." He insists that you learn to read Latin and Greek so that you can study Roman and Greek books that were written long ago.

What can you learn from these ancient books?

BUILDING BACKGROUND The end of the Middle Ages brought important changes to European politics and society. These changes set the stage for an exciting new period of learning and creativity. During this period, new ideas influenced the arts, science, and attitudes toward religion.

The Renaissance

Do you ever get the urge to do something creative? If so, how do you express your creativity? Do you like to draw or paint? Maybe you prefer to write stories or poems or create music.

At the end of the Middle Ages, people across Europe found the urge to be creative. Their creativity was sparked by new ideas and discoveries that were sweeping through Europe at the time. This period of creativity, of new ideas and inspirations, is called the **Renaissance** (REN-uh-sahns). It lasted from about 1350 through the 1500s. *Renaissance* is French for "rebirth." The people who named this period believed it represented a new beginning, or rebirth, in Europe's history and culture.

New Ideas

The Renaissance started in Italy. During and after the Crusades, Italian cities such as **Florence** and **Venice** became rich through trade. Goods from faraway Asia moved through these cities.

These goods made the people who lived there curious about the larger world. At the same time, scholars from other parts of the world came to Italy. They brought books written by ancient Greeks and Romans.

Inspired by these books and by the ancient ruins around them, some people in Italy became interested in ancient cultures. These people began reading works in Greek and Latin and studying subjects that had been taught in Greek and Roman schools.

These subjects, known as the humanities, included history, poetry, and grammar. Increased study of the humanities led to a new way of thinking and learning known as humanism.

Humanism emphasized the abilities and accomplishments of human beings. The humanists believed that people were capable of great things. As a result, they admired artists, architects, leaders, writers, scientists, and other talented individuals.

THE IMPACT TODAY

American universities grant degrees in the humanities. You might one day get a degree in a humanities field.

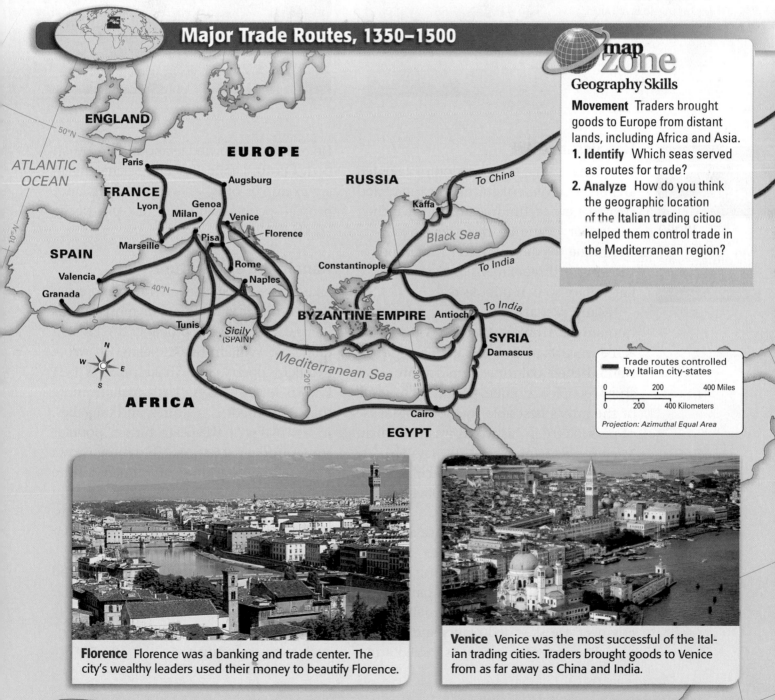

Major Trade Routes, 1350–1500

map zone

Geography Skills

Movement Traders brought goods to Europe from distant lands, including Africa and Asia.
1. **Identify** Which seas served as routes for trade?
2. **Analyze** How do you think the geographic location of the Italian trading cities helped them control trade in the Mediterranean region?

ENGLAND
50°N
ATLANTIC OCEAN
EUROPE
Paris
FRANCE
Lyon
Augsburg
RUSSIA
Genoa
Milan
Venice
Florence
Pisa
Marseille
SPAIN
Rome
Valencia
40°N
Naples
Granada
Tunis
Sicily (SPAIN)
Kaffa
Black Sea
Constantinople
To China
To India
BYZANTINE EMPIRE
Antioch
To India
SYRIA
Damascus
Mediterranean Sea
AFRICA
Cairo
EGYPT

Trade routes controlled by Italian city-states
0   200   400 Miles
0   200   400 Kilometers
Projection: Azimuthal Equal Area

Florence Florence was a banking and trade center. The city's wealthy leaders used their money to beautify Florence.

Venice Venice was the most successful of the Italian trading cities. Traders brought goods to Venice from as far away as China and India.

The Renaissance

The Renaissance was a period of great creativity and advances in art, literature, and science.

Renaissance sculptors were careful to show the tiniest details in their works. This statue by Michelangelo is of David, a king of ancient Israel.

Painters like Hans Holbein the Younger wanted to show what real life was like for people in Europe.

HISTORY

VIDEO
Humanism Triggers the Renaissance

hmhsocialstudies.com

Renaissance Art

The Renaissance was a period of talented artistic achievements. Artists of the period created new techniques to improve their work. For example, they developed the technique of perspective, a method of showing a three-dimensional scene on a flat surface so that it looks real.

Many Renaissance artists were also humanists. Humanist artists valued the achievements of individuals. These artists wanted their paintings and sculptures to show people's unique personalities. One of the artists best able to show this sense of personality in his works was the Italian Michelangelo (mee-kay-LAHN-jay-loh). He was both a great painter and sculptor. His statues, like the one of King David above, seem almost to be alive.

Another famous Renaissance artist was Leonardo da Vinci. Leonardo achieved the Renaissance goal of excelling in many areas. He was not only a great painter and sculptor but also an architect, scientist, and engineer. He sketched plants and animals as well as inventions such as a submarine.

He collected knowledge about the human body. Both Leonardo and Michelangelo are examples of what we call Renaissance people—people who can do practically anything well.

Renaissance Literature

Like artists, Renaissance writers expressed the attitudes of the time. The most famous Renaissance writer is probably the English dramatist William Shakespeare. He wrote excellent poetry, but Shakespeare is best known for his plays. They include more than 30 comedies, histories, and tragedies. In his plays, Shakespeare turned popular stories into great drama. His writing shows a deep understanding of human nature and skillfully expresses the thoughts and feelings of his characters. For these reasons, Shakespeare's plays are still highly popular in many parts of the world.

Renaissance writings were read and enjoyed by a larger audience than earlier writings had been. This change was largely due to advances in science and technology, such as the printing press.

William Shakespeare is considered the greatest of all Renaissance writers. His plays are still read and performed today.

Leonardo da Vinci drew sketches of many devices that were not invented until centuries after his death. This model of a type of helicopter was based on the sketch by Leonardo shown below.

Renaissance Science

Some of the ancient works rediscovered during the Renaissance dealt with science. For the first time in centuries, Europeans could read about early Greek and Roman scientific advances. Inspired by what they read, some people began to study math, astronomy, and other fields of science.

Using this new scientific knowledge, Europeans developed new inventions and techniques. For example, they learned how to build enormous domes that could rise higher than earlier buildings.

Another invention of the Renaissance was the movable type printing press. A German named Johann Gutenberg built the first movable type printing press in the mid-1400s. This type of printing press could print books quickly and cheaply. For the first time, people could easily share ideas with others in distant areas. The printing press helped the ideas of the Renaissance spread beyond Italy.

READING CHECK **Summarizing** How did life in Europe change during the Renaissance?

CONNECTING TO Technology

The Printing Press

Printing was not a new idea in Renaissance Europe. What was new was the method of printing. Johann Gutenberg designed a printing system called movable type. It used a set of tiny lead blocks, each carved with a letter of the alphabet. These blocks could then be used to spell out an entire page of text for printing. Once copies of the page were made, the printer could reuse the blocks to spell out another page. This was much faster and easier than earlier systems had been.

Generalizing How did movable type improve printing?

The Reformation

By the early 1500s some Europeans had begun to complain about problems they saw in the Roman Catholic Church. For example, they thought the church had become corrupt. In time, their complaints led to a religious reform movement called the **Reformation** (re-fuhr-MAY-shuhn).

The Protestant Reformation

Although people called for church reform in other places, the Reformation began in what is now Germany. This area was part of the Holy Roman Empire. Some people there thought church officials were too focused on their own power and had lost sight of their religious duties.

↗ hmhsocialstudies.com **INTERACTIVE MAP**

Religion in Europe, 1600

ICELAND

SWEDEN

NORWAY

SCOTLAND

North Sea

DENMARK

Baltic Sea

RUSSIA

IRELAND

ENGLAND

London

Wittenberg

ATLANTIC OCEAN

Paris

POLAND

FRANCE

Geneva

HUNGARY

O T T O M A N

PORTUGAL

Madrid

PAPAL STATES

Rome

Black Sea

SPAIN

E M P I R E

Mediterranean Sea

OTTOMAN EMPIRE

Legend:
- Protestant
- Roman Catholic
- Roman Catholic with Protestant minorities
- Eastern Orthodox
- Muslim
- Boundary of the Holy Roman Empire

0   250   500 Miles
0   250   500 Kilometers

Projection: Lambert Azimuthal Equal-Area

map zone
Geography Skills

Regions By the Reformation's end, parts of Europe were still Catholic, while others had become mostly Protestant.

1. **Locate** In which part of Europe were most people Protestant?
2. **Analyze** How were religious areas spread across the Holy Roman Empire?

One of the first people to express protests against the Catholic Church was a German monk named Martin Luther. In 1517 Luther nailed a list of complaints to a church door in the town of Wittenberg. Luther's protests angered church officials, who soon expelled him from the church. In response, Luther's followers formed a separate church. They became the first **Protestants**, Christians who broke from the Catholic Church over religious issues.

Other reformers who followed Luther began creating churches of their own as well. The Roman Catholic Church was no longer the only church in Western Europe. As you can see on the map, many areas of Europe had become Protestant by 1600.

The Catholic Reformation

Protestants were not the only ones who called for reform in the Roman Catholic Church. Many Catholic officials wanted to reform the church as well. Even as the first Protestants were breaking away from the church, Catholic officials were launching a series of reforms that became known as the **Catholic Reformation**.

As part of the Catholic Reformation, church leaders began focusing more on spiritual concerns and less on political power. They also worked to make church teachings easier for people to understand. To tell people about the changes, church leaders sent priests and teachers all over Europe. Church leaders also worked to spread Catholic teachings into Asia, Africa, and other parts of the world.

Religious Wars

The Reformation caused major changes to the religious map of Europe. Catholicism, once the main religion in most of Europe, was no longer so dominant. In many areas, especially in the north, Protestants now outnumbered Catholics.

In some parts of Europe, Catholics and Protestants lived together in peace. In some other places, however, this was not the case. Bloody religious wars broke out in France, Germany, the Netherlands, and Switzerland. Wars between religious groups left parts of Europe in ruins.

These religious wars led to political and social changes in Europe. For example, many people began relying less on what church leaders and other authority figures told them. Instead, people raised questions and began looking to science for answers.

READING CHECK **Finding Main Ideas** How did Europe change after the Reformation?

FOCUS ON READING

Dates in a text, such as the dates 1517 and 1600 in the text at left, help you keep events in order in your mind.

SUMMARY AND PREVIEW In the 1300s through the 1500s, new ideas changed Europe. Next, you will learn about other ideas and events that brought changes.

Section 1 Assessment

hmhsocialstudies.com
ONLINE QUIZ

Reviewing Ideas, Terms, and Places

1. a. **Define** What was the **Renaissance**?
   b. **Summarize** What were some changes made in art during the Renaissance?
   c. **Elaborate** How did the printing press help spread Renaissance ideas?
2. a. **Describe** What led to the **Reformation**?
   b. **Explain** Why did church leaders launch the series of reforms known as the **Catholic Reformation**?

Critical Thinking

3. **Finding Main Ideas** Draw a chart like the one shown. Use your notes to describe new ideas of the Renaissance and the Reformation. Add rows as needed.

Idea	Description

FOCUS ON WRITING

4. **Describing the Renaissance and the Reformation** Note things about these two periods that might interest visitors. For example, visitors might want to see Renaissance art.

Science and Exploration

What You Will Learn...

Main Ideas

1. During the Scientific Revolution, discoveries and inventions expanded knowledge and changed life in Europe.
2. In the 1400s and 1500s, Europeans led voyages of discovery and exploration.
3. As Europeans discovered new lands, they created colonies and new empires all over the world.

The Big Idea

New inventions and knowledge led to European exploration and empires around the world.

Key Terms

Scientific Revolution, *p. 55*
New World, *p. 59*
circumnavigate, *p. 59*

⬈ hmhsocialstudies.com
TAKING NOTES

Use the graphic organizer online to take notes on science and exploration.

If **YOU** lived there...

You are an adviser to a European king in the 1500s. The rulers of several other countries have sent explorers to search for new trade routes. Your king does not want to fall behind. Now a young sea captain has come to the royal court with a daring plan. The king is interested, but funding such a voyage could be costly.

What will you advise the king to do?

BUILDING BACKGROUND The Renaissance made Europeans more curious about science and the world. This curiosity led to new inventions and technologies that helped people explore the world. As a result, a spirit of adventure swept across Europe.

The Scientific Revolution

Can you imagine what your life would be like without science? Think of all the things that science has provided in our daily lives. Without it, we would have no electricity, no automobiles, no plastic. Our lives would be totally different.

Scientific Advances and Exploration

Several inventions and technical advances enabled people to explore the world and to study the heavens.

ANALYZING VISUALS Why do you think these inventions and advances contributed to increased exploration of the world?

Astrolabe With an astrolabe, sailors could use the stars to calculate a ship's exact location.

Did you know that there was a time when people lived without the benefits of modern science? In fact, it was not until the 1500s and 1600s that most people in Europe began to appreciate what science and technology could do to improve life.

A New View of Science

Before the 1500s, most educated people who studied the world relied on authorities such as ancient Greek writers and church officials. People thought these authorities could tell them all they needed to know. Europeans had little need for science.

Between about 1540 and 1700, though, European views about how to study the world changed. This widespread change in views was part of the **Scientific Revolution**, the series of events that led to the birth of modern science. People began placing more importance on what they observed and less on what they were told. They used their observations to come up with **logical** explanations for how the world worked. This new focus on observation marked the start of modern science.

Why is the birth of modern science called a revolution? The new approach to science was a radical idea. In the same way a political revolution changes a country, this new view of science changed society.

Science and Religion

Not everyone was happy with the new role of science in society. Some people feared that scientific ideas would eventually lead to the breakdown of European society.

Many of the people who most feared the increasing influence of science were church officials. They tended to oppose science when it went against the teachings of the church. For example, the church taught that Earth was at the center of the universe. Some scientists, though, had observed through telescopes that Earth orbited the sun. This observation went against the church's teaching.

This growing tension between religion and science came to a head in 1632. That year, an Italian scientist named Galileo (gal-uh-LEE-oh) published a book in which he stated that Earth orbited the sun. He was arrested and put on trial. Afraid that the church would expel him, Galileo publicly stated that his writings were wrong. Privately, though, he held to his beliefs.

Despite conflicts such as these, science and religion were able to exist together in Europe. In fact, many scientists saw a connection between science and religion. These scientists believed that science could better explain church teachings. Science continued developing rapidly as a result.

ACADEMIC VOCABULARY
logical
reasoned, well thought out

Compass The compass, which always points north, helped sailors find their way at sea.

Telescope With the telescope, scientists could study the heavens like never before.

Close-up

A Caravel

Many of the explorers who set out from Europe in the 1400s and 1500s did so in a new type of ship, the caravel. These ships could sail across huge distances because of some important advances in shipbuilding technology.

Triangular sails enabled the caravel to sail into the wind.

The caravel's smooth, rounded hull, or frame, could stand up to even rough seas.

A large center rudder made the ship easier to move and enabled quick turns.

ANALYSIS SKILL **ANALYZING VISUALS**

What features made the caravel an excellent ship for sailing across long distances?

VIDEO
Sir Isaac Newton: The Gravity of Genius

↗ hmhsocialstudies.com

Discoveries and Inventions

The Scientific Revolution was a period of great advances in many fields of science. With increased interest in science came discoveries in astronomy, biology, physics, and other fields. For example, astronomers discovered how the stars and the planets move in the sky. Biologists learned how blood circulates throughout the human body. Physicists figured out how mirrors and pendulums worked.

Some of the greatest advances of the Scientific Revolution were made by one man, Sir Isaac Newton. He made exciting contributions to both math and physics.

Newton is probably best known today for his observations about gravity, the force that attracts objects to each other. Before his observations, scientists knew very little about how gravity works.

Many of the discoveries of the Scientific Revolution were possible because of new inventions. Devices such as the telescope, the microscope, and the thermometer were invented at this time. Some of these new inventions helped contribute to another exciting time—the Age of Exploration.

READING CHECK **Summarizing** What happened during the Scientific Revolution?

The Voyages of Discovery

Some advances in science and technology enabled people to make longer, safer sea voyages. New compasses and astrolabes helped sailors figure out where they were even when far from land. Improvements in mapmaking helped people plan safer routes for their journeys. In addition, new ships, such as the caravel, made sea travel safer. The caravel could sail farther than earlier ships could.

Equipped with these new advances, many Europeans set out on great voyages of discovery. They sailed into unknown waters hoping to find new trade routes to faraway places. They would succeed in their quest, and their discoveries would change the world.

The Drive to Discover

Why were Europeans so eager to explore? They had many reasons. Some explorers were curious about the unknown. They hoped to find out what lay beyond the horizon. Others sought adventure and the excitement of life at sea. Still others had religious reasons. These explorers wanted to spread the Christian faith.

Another reason to explore was the desire to get rich. Some explorers wanted to find new lands that had products they could sell in Europe. The explorers hoped to sell these goods for lots of money and to become rich.

In addition, some European leaders promoted exploration in hope it would benefit their countries. Prince Henry, a member of the Portuguese royal family, encouraged explorers to find a route to India's rich spice trade. Queen Isabella of Spain also promoted exploration. She paid for explorers to seek out new lands and claim them for Spain. She hoped these lands would bring Spain wealth.

Voyages to the East

In the mid-1400s, explorers from Europe began searching for an all-water route to Asia. They wanted to reach Asia to get goods from China and India. During the Middle Ages, Europeans had discovered the exotic goods available in Asia. Many of them, such as silk and spices, were not found in Europe. These Asian goods were costly, because traders had to bring them long distances over land. Further, Italian traders controlled the sale of such goods in Europe—and these Italian traders had become very rich.

Other European countries wanted to break the hold the Italians had on trade with Asia. The Italians controlled all the trade routes in the eastern Mediterranean. If other countries could find an all-water route to Asia, they would not have to pay Italian traders to get exotic Asian goods.

BIOGRAPHY

Queen Isabella
(1451–1504)

Christopher Columbus's voyage to the Americas would not have been possible without the support of Queen Isabella of Spain. In 1492 Columbus approached the queen in search of money to pay for his voyage. He had already been turned down by the king of Portugal, who thought Columbus's plan was foolhardy. Isabella liked his plan, however. She gave Columbus money and ships to help make his voyage. With the support of the queen and others, he was able to complete his journey. It would change the history of Europe, the Americas, and the world forever.

Analyzing How did Isabella make Columbus's voyage possible?

European Exploration, 1487–1580

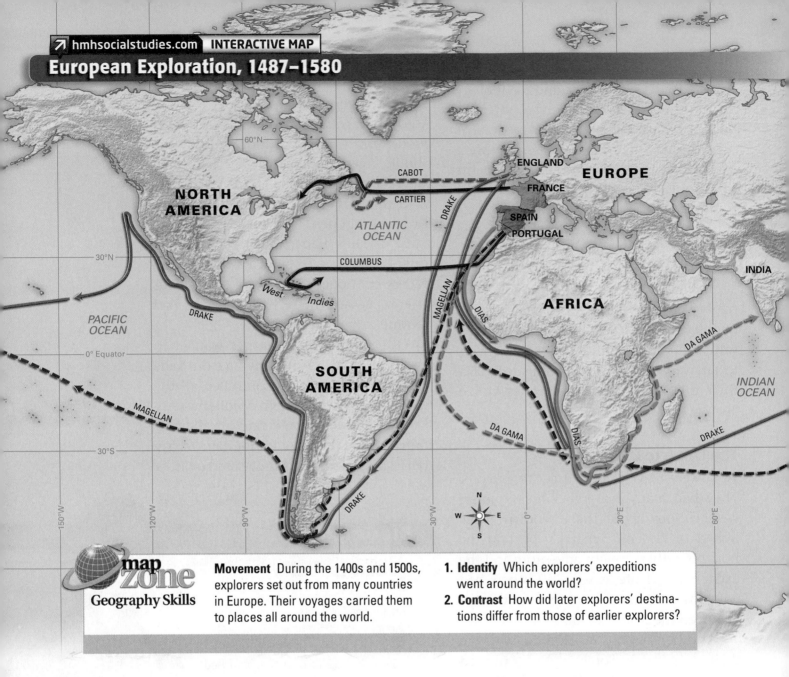

map zone

Geography Skills

Movement During the 1400s and 1500s, explorers set out from many countries in Europe. Their voyages carried them to places all around the world.

1. **Identify** Which explorers' expeditions went around the world?
2. **Contrast** How did later explorers' destinations differ from those of earlier explorers?

FOCUS ON READING

What signal words on this page give you clues about the chronological order of events?

The first explorers to search for a sea route to Asia were from Portugal. Under the direction of Prince Henry, they sailed south along Africa's west coast. As they went, they set up trading posts along the Atlantic coast of Africa. In time, explorers sailed farther south.

In 1497–1498 a Portuguese explorer named Vasco da Gama sailed around the southern tip of Africa and on to the west coast of India. You can see his route on the map above. Portugal had found a new sea route to Asia.

Voyages to America

Meanwhile, other countries had also been sending explorers out to find new routes to Asia. The most important expedition came from Spain. In 1492 Queen Isabella of Spain helped pay for a voyage led by Christopher Columbus, an Italian sailor. Columbus hoped to reach Asia by sailing west across the Atlantic. The voyage was long and difficult, but he finally reached land after several months at sea. He landed on an island in what is now the Bahamas. Columbus had reached a new land.

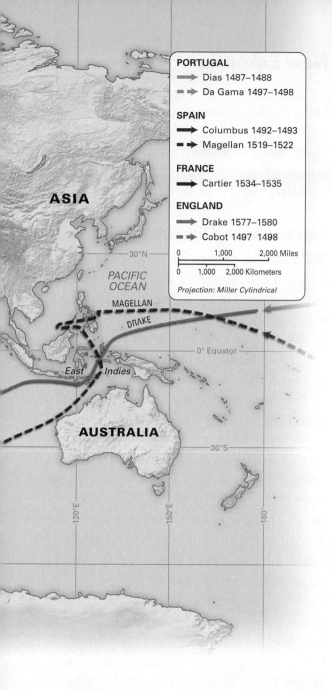

PORTUGAL
→ Dias 1487–1488
⇢ Da Gama 1497–1498

SPAIN
→ Columbus 1492–1493
⇢ Magellan 1519–1522

FRANCE
→ Cartier 1534–1535

ENGLAND
→ Drake 1577–1580
⇢ Cabot 1497 1498

0   1,000   2,000 Miles
0   1,000   2,000 Kilometers

Projection: Miller Cylindrical

ASIA

30°N

PACIFIC
OCEAN

MAGELLAN

DRAKE

0° Equator

East   Indies

AUSTRALIA

30°S

120°E   150°E   180°

This wave of European exploration of the Americas had many different causes. Some explorers were still looking for the best water route to Asia. They hoped to find a passage through the Americas by which ships could sail to India or China.

Other explorers led voyages in search of riches. These explorers had heard that the native people of the Americas had lots of gold—more gold than most Europeans had ever seen. These explorers dreamed of the glory and riches they hoped to gain from conquering the lands and people of the Americas.

Voyages around the World

For some Europeans, their new knowledge of the Americas made them more curious about the world. Since they had not known about the Americas, they wondered what else about the world they did not know. One way to learn more about the world, they decided, would be to **circumnavigate**, or travel all the way around, Earth.

The first person to try such a journey was Ferdinand Magellan (muh-JEHL-uhn), a Portuguese sailor. Magellan sailed west from Spain around the southern tip of South America. From there he continued into the Pacific Ocean, where no European had sailed before. Magellan made it as far as the Philippines, where he was killed in a conflict with natives. His crew pushed on, however, and finally reached Spain to complete their trip around the world.

The voyages of explorers like Magellan taught Europeans much about the world. In time, they even achieved the goal of Christopher Columbus—to reach Asia by sailing west from Europe. In addition, they paved the way for European settlement and colonization of the Americas.

Columbus thought he had found a route to Asia, which Europeans called the Indies. Europeans came to realize that he had reached a land unknown to them. They called this land, which in time came to be known as America, the **New World**.

Excited by the new discovery, explorers set out from Europe to learn more about the new land. Led by Spain, explorers from Portugal, France, England, and the Netherlands set sail for North and South America. Before long, little of the Americas would remain unexplored.

READING CHECK **Identifying Cause and Effect** What were two causes of exploration?

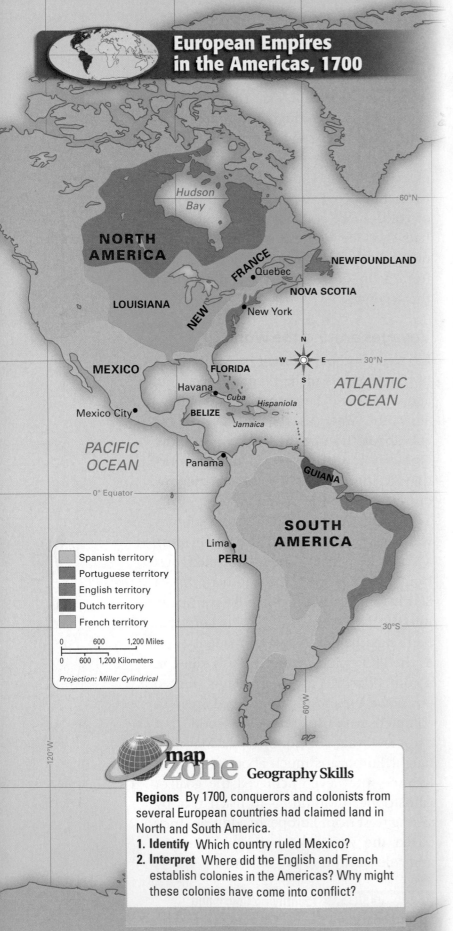

European Empires in the Americas, 1700

Hudson Bay

NORTH AMERICA

NEWFOUNDLAND

NEW FRANCE
Quebec

NOVA SCOTIA

LOUISIANA

New York

MEXICO

FLORIDA

Havana
Cuba
Hispaniola

Mexico City
BELIZE

Jamaica

ATLANTIC OCEAN

PACIFIC OCEAN

Panama

GUIANA

0° Equator

SOUTH AMERICA

Lima
PERU

60°N

30°N

30°S

Spanish territory
Portuguese territory
English territory
Dutch territory
French territory

0   600   1,200 Miles
0   600 1,200 Kilometers

Projection: Miller Cylindrical

map zone Geography Skills

Regions By 1700, conquerors and colonists from several European countries had claimed land in North and South America.

1. **Identify** Which country ruled Mexico?
2. **Interpret** Where did the English and French establish colonies in the Americas? Why might these colonies have come into conflict?

New Empires

As European explorers discovered new lands in the Americas and elsewhere, they claimed these lands for their countries. These land claims formed the basis for new European empires that stretched across the sea into lands far from Europe.

Conquests and Empires

The Spanish, who were the first Europeans to reach the Americas, claimed large areas of land there. In some places, the Spanish met powerful native empires. These native people fought to defend their lands.

Before long, though, the Spanish had defeated the two most powerful empires in the Americas. These empires were the Aztecs in what is now Mexico and the Incas in what is now Peru. The Spanish had steel swords, firearms, and horses—all unknown in the Americas. This advantage helped the Spanish defeat the Aztec and Inca armies. In addition, diseases that the Spanish carried killed many thousands of Native Americans. By the mid-1500s, Spain ruled a huge area in the Americas.

One of Spain's central goals in the Americas was to gain wealth. The Spanish wanted the gold and silver that could be found in Mexico and some other places. To get these riches, the Spanish enslaved Native Americans and forced them to work in mines. In addition, the Spanish brought African slaves to the Americas to work in the mines. Soon, ships full of gold and silver from these mines were crossing the Atlantic Ocean back to Spain.

Riches from the Americas made Spain the wealthiest country in Europe. Spain's rulers used this money to buy equipment for its armies and to produce ships for its navy. With this powerful military, Spain became Europe's mightiest country, the center of a huge empire.

Other Colonies

Other European countries envied Spain's wealth and power. They wanted a share of the wealth that Spain was finding in the Americas. In hope of finding similar wealth, these countries began to establish colonies in the lands they explored. As the map shows, colonists from England, France, the Netherlands, and Portugal had settled in the Americas by 1700.

Like the Spanish, these colonists found Native Americans living in the places they settled. In some cases, new colonists lived peacefully with Native Americans. In other cases, conflict occurred, and colonists and Native Americans fought bloody wars.

Unlike the Spanish, other European colonists in the Americas did not find huge deposits of gold or silver. They did find other valuable resources, though. Among these resources were wood, furs, rich soil, and different foods. These resources helped the countries of England, France, Portugal, and the Netherlands grow wealthy.

READING CHECK **Analyzing** How did the Spanish create an empire in the Americas?

Conquest of Mexico
The Spanish soldiers who conquered Mexico had better armor and more advanced weapons than the Aztecs.

SUMMARY AND PREVIEW The Scientific Revolution and the Age of Exploration expanded knowledge and led to changes around the world. Next, you will read about another time of great change. Called the Enlightenment, this period led to major political changes in Europe.

Section 2 Assessment

hmhsocialstudies.com
ONLINE QUIZ

Reviewing Ideas, Terms, and Places

1. **a. Describe** How did European attitudes toward science change in the 1500s and 1600s?
   b. Evaluate What do you think is the greatest advance of the **Scientific Revolution**? Why?
2. **a. Identify** Who was Christopher Columbus?
   b. Explain What drove Europeans to launch the voyages of discovery?
   c. Elaborate What challenges do you think made it difficult for explorers to **circumnavigate** the world for the first time?
3. **a. Describe** What enabled Spain to create a huge, powerful empire in the Americas?
   b. Contrast How did other countries' American colonies differ from Spain's?

Critical Thinking

4. **Identifying Cause and Effect** Draw a diagram like the one shown. Using your notes for information, on the left list the causes of European exploration. On the right, list the effects of that exploration.

   Causes → European Exploration → Effects

FOCUS ON WRITING

5. **Describing the Scientific Revolution and the Age of Exploration** What were Europeans discovering and inventing? Where were Europeans traveling? How did these events change Europe? Take notes on events and changes that might interest visitors.

Political Change in Europe

What You Will Learn...

Main Ideas

1. During the Enlightenment, new ideas about government took hold in Europe.
2. The 1600s and 1700s were an Age of Revolution in Europe.
3. Napoleon Bonaparte conquered much of Europe after the French Revolution.

The Big Idea

Ideas of the Enlightenment inspired revolutions and new governments in Europe.

Key Terms

Enlightenment, *p. 62*
English Bill of Rights, *p. 64*
Declaration of Independence, *p. 65*
Declaration of the Rights of Man and of the Citizen, *p. 66*
Reign of Terror, *p. 66*

hmhsocialstudies.com
TAKING NOTES

Use the graphic organizer online to take notes on Enlightenment ideas and the events they inspired.

If YOU lived there...

You live in a village in northern France in the 1700s. Your father is a baker, and your mother is a seamstress. Like most people in your village, your family struggles to make ends meet. All your life you have been taught that the nobility has a right to rule over you. Today, though, a man made an angry speech in the village market. He said that the common people should demand more rights.

How do you think your village will react?

BUILDING BACKGROUND The Scientific Revolution and the Age of Exploration expanded Europeans' knowledge and changed life in many ways. The 1600s and 1700s brought still more changes. Some people began to use reason to improve government and society.

The Enlightenment

Think about the last time you faced a problem that required careful thought. Perhaps you were working a complex math problem or trying to figure out how to win a game. Whatever the problem, when you thought carefully about how to solve it, you were using your power to reason, or to think logically.

The Age of Reason

During the 1600s and 1700s a number of people began to put great importance on reason, or logical thought. They started using reason to challenge long-held beliefs about education, government, law, and religion. By using reason, these people hoped to solve problems such as poverty and war. They believed the use of reason could achieve three great goals—knowledge, freedom, and happiness—and thereby improve society. The use of reason in shaping people's ideas about society and politics defined a period called the **Enlightenment**. Because of its focus on reason, this period is also known as the Age of Reason.

The Enlightenment

This 1764 painting shows a salon, a social gathering where people met to discuss Enlightenment ideas. The artist is Michel-Barthelemy Ollivier.

INTERPRETING CHARTS What were the key Enlightenment ideas about natural laws?

Key Enlightenment Ideas

- The ability to reason is unique to humans.
- Reason can be used to solve problems and to improve people's lives.
- Reason can free people from ignorance.
- The natural world is governed by laws that can be discovered through reason.
- Natural laws also govern human behavior.
- Governments should reflect natural laws and encourage education and debate.

New Ideas about Government

During the Enlightenment, some people used reason to examine government. They questioned how governments worked and what the purpose of government should be. In doing so, these people developed completely new ideas about government. These ideas would help lead to the creation of modern democracy.

At the time of the Enlightenment, monarchs, or kings and queens, ruled in most of Europe. Many of these monarchs believed they ruled through divine right. That is, they thought God gave them the right to rule however they chose.

Some people challenged rule by divine right. They thought rulers' powers should be limited to protect people's freedoms. These people said government's purpose was to protect and to serve the people.

John Locke, an English philosopher, had a major influence on Enlightenment thinking about the role of government.

Locke thought government should be a **contract** between a ruler and the people. A contract binds both sides, so it would limit the ruler's power. Locke also believed that all people had certain natural rights, such as life, liberty, and property. If a ruler did not protect these natural rights, people had the right to change rulers.

Other scholars built on Locke's ideas. One was Jean-Jacques Rousseau (roo-SOH). He said government should express the will, or desire, of the people. According to Rousseau, citizens give the government the power to make and enforce laws. But if these laws do not serve the people, the government should give up its power.

These Enlightenment ideas spread far and wide. In time, they would inspire some Europeans to rise up against their rulers.

READING CHECK **Contrasting** How did Enlightenment ideas about government differ from the views of most monarchs?

ACADEMIC VOCABULARY

contract
a binding legal agreement

The Age of Revolution

The 1600s and 1700s were a time of great change in Europe. Some changes were peaceful, such as those in science. Other changes were more violent. In England, North America, and France, new ideas about government led to war and the Age of Revolution.

Civil War and Reform in England

In England, Enlightenment ideas led to conflict between the monarchs, or rulers, and Parliament, the lawmaking body. For many years England's rulers had shared power with Parliament. The relationship was an uneasy one, however. As rulers and Parliament fought for power, the situation grew worse.

In 1642 the power struggle erupted in civil war. Supporters of Parliament forced King Charles I from power. He was later tried and beheaded. A new government then formed, but it was unstable.

By 1660 many of the English were tired of instability. They wanted to restore the monarchy. They asked the former king's son to rule England as Charles II. However, Charles had to agree to let Parliament keep powers it had gained during the civil war.

In 1689 Parliament further limited the monarch's power. That year, it approved the **English Bill of Rights**. This document listed rights for Parliament and the English people. For example, it gave Parliament the power to pass laws and to raise taxes.

In addition, Parliament made the king promise to honor Magna Carta. Signed in 1215, this document limited the English ruler's power and protected some rights of the people. However, few monarchs had honored it during the previous 400 years. Parliament wanted to be sure future rulers honored Magna Carta.

By 1700 Parliament held most of the political power in England. Divine right to rule had ended for England's monarchy.

FOCUS ON READING

Read the paragraph about Magna Carta. What date and signal words help you tell that this document was written long before the English Bill of Rights?

Documents of Democracy

The key documents shown here greatly influenced the growth of modern democracy.

ANALYZING VISUALS Which two of the documents at right contain some of John Locke's ideas?

Magna Carta (1215)
- Limited the power of the monarchy
- Identified people's rights to property
- Established people's rights to trial by a jury

The English Bill of Rights (1689)
- Outlawed cruel and unusual punishment
- Guaranteed free speech for members of Parliament

The American Revolution

In time, Enlightenment ideas spread to the British colonies in North America. There, the British ruler's power was not limited as it was in England. For this reason, many colonists had grown unhappy with British rule. These colonists began to protest the British laws that they thought were unfair.

In 1775 the protests turned to violence, starting the Revolutionary War. Colonial leaders, influenced by the ideas of Locke and Rousseau, claimed Great Britain had denied their rights. In July 1776 they signed the **Declaration of Independence**. Largely written by Thomas Jefferson, this document declared the American colonies' independence from Britain. A new nation, the United States of America, was born.

In 1783 the United States officially won its independence. The colonists had successfully put Enlightenment ideas into practice. Their success would inspire many other people, particularly in France.

The French Revolution

The people of France closely watched the events of the American Revolution. Soon, they grew inspired to fight for their own rights in the French Revolution.

A major cause of the French Revolution was anger over the differences between social classes. In France, the king ruled over a society split into three classes called estates. The Catholic clergy made up the First Estate. They enjoyed many benefits. Nobles belonged to the Second Estate. These people held important positions in military, government, and the courts. The majority of the French people were members of the Third Estate. This group included peasants, craftworkers, and shopkeepers.

Many Third Estate members thought France's classes were unfair. These people were poor and often hungry. Yet, they paid the highest taxes. While they suffered, King Louis XVI held fancy parties, and Queen Marie-Antoinette wore costly clothes.

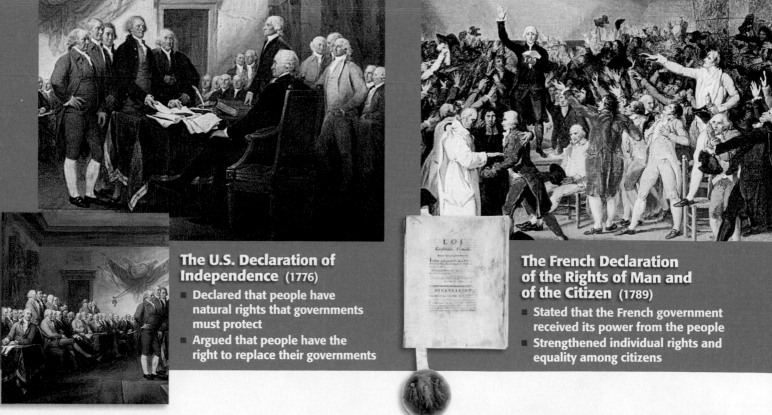

The U.S. Declaration of Independence (1776)
- Declared that people have natural rights that governments must protect
- Argued that people have the right to replace their governments

The French Declaration of the Rights of Man and of the Citizen (1789)
- Stated that the French government received its power from the people
- Strengthened individual rights and equality among citizens

Meanwhile, France's government was deeply in debt. To raise money, Louis XVI wanted to tax the wealthy. He called a meeting of the representatives of the three estates to discuss a tax increase.

The meeting did not go smoothly. Some members of the Third Estate were familiar with Enlightenment ideas. These members demanded a greater voice in the meeting's decisions. Eventually, the Third Estate members formed a separate group called the National Assembly. This group demanded that the French king accept a constitution limiting his powers.

Louis XVI refused, which angered the common people of Paris. On July 14, 1789, this anger led a mob to storm the Bastille, a prison in Paris. The mob released the prisoners and destroyed the building. The French Revolution had begun.

The French Revolution quickly spread to the countryside. In events called the Great Fear, peasants took revenge on landlords and other nobles for long years of poor treatment. In their rage, the peasants burned down houses and monasteries.

At the same time, other leaders of the revolution were taking peaceful steps. The National Assembly wrote and approved the **Declaration of the Rights of Man and of the Citizen**. This 1789 French constitution guaranteed French citizens some rights and made taxes fairer. Among the freedoms the constitution supported were the freedoms of speech, of the press, and of religion.

The French Republic

In time, revolutionary leaders created a French republic. The new republic did not end France's many growing problems, however. Unrest soon returned.

In 1793 the revolutionaries executed Louis XVI. His execution was the first of many as the government began arresting anyone who questioned its rule. The result was the **Reign of Terror**, a bloody period of the French Revolution during which the government executed thousands of its opponents and others at the guillotine (GEE-uh-teen). This device beheaded victims with a large, heavy blade. The Reign of Terror finally ended when one of its own leaders was executed in 1794.

Although a violent period, the French Revolution did achieve some of its goals. French peasants and workers gained new political rights. The government opened new schools and improved wages. In addition, it ended slavery in France's colonies.

The French republic's leaders struggled, though. As problems grew worse, a strong leader rose up to take control.

READING CHECK Analyzing Why did many members of the Third Estate support revolution?

The Storming of the Bastille

On July 14, 1789, a mob stormed and destroyed the Bastille, a prison in Paris. To many French people, this prison symbolized the king's harsh rule.

ANALYZING VISUALS What were some weapons used in the French Revolution?

Napoleon Bonaparte

Jacques-Louis David painted this scene of Napoleon crowning his wife, Josephine, empress after crowning himself emperor. The coronation took place in 1804 in Notre Dame Cathedral in Paris, France.

ANALYZING VISUALS How does the event show Napoleon's power?

Napoleonic Empire, 1812

North Sea

ATLANTIC OCEAN

Paris

Vienna

Madrid

Rome

Mediterranean Sea

Napoleon Bonaparte

In 1799 France was ripe for a change in leadership. That year, Napoleon Bonaparte, a 30-year-old general, took control. Many French people welcomed him because he seemed to support the Revolution's goals. His popularity grew quickly, and in 1804 Napoleon crowned himself emperor.

Military Conquests and Rule

Napoleon was a brilliant military leader. Under his command, the French army won a series of dazzling victories. By 1810 France's empire stretched across Europe.

In France, Napoleon restored order. He created an efficient government, made taxes fairer, and formed a system of public education. Perhaps his most important accomplishment was the creation of a new French legal system, the Napoleonic Code.

This legal code reflected the ideals of the French Revolution, such as equality before the law and equal civil rights.

With these many accomplishments, Napoleon sounds like a perfect leader. But he was not. He harshly punished anyone who opposed or questioned his rule.

Napoleon's Defeat

In the end, bad weather contributed to Napoleon's downfall. In 1812 he led an invasion of Russia. The invasion was a disaster. Bitterly cold weather and smart Russian tactics forced Napoleon's army to retreat. Many French soldiers died.

Great Britain, Prussia, and Russia then joined forces and in 1814 defeated Napoleon's weakened army. He returned a year later with a new army, but was again defeated. The British then exiled him to an island, where he died in 1821.

Europe after the Congress of Vienna, 1815

map zone

Geography Skills

Regions After the defeat of Napoleon in 1814, the Congress of Vienna reorganized Europe.

1. **Name** What were Europe's largest empires in 1815?
2. **Analyze** How might France's location have contributed to Napoleon's rise and fall?

In 1814 European leaders met at the Congress of Vienna. There, they redrew the map of Europe. Their goal was to keep any country from ever becoming powerful enough to threaten Europe again.

READING CHECK **Drawing Inferences** Why did other countries want to defeat Napoleon?

SUMMARY AND PREVIEW You have read how new ideas about government arose out of the Enlightenment. These ideas led to revolutions and political change in Europe and elsewhere. Next, you will read about the growth of industry and how it changed European society.

Section 3 Assessment

hmhsocialstudies.com
ONLINE QUIZ

Reviewing Ideas, Terms, and Places

1. **a. Define** What does divine right mean?
   b. Explain What did **Enlightenment** thinkers believe the purpose of government should be?
2. **a. Describe** What was the significance of the **English Bill of Rights**?
   b. Make Inferences Why do you think many Americans consider Thomas Jefferson a hero?
   c. Evaluate How successful do you think the French Revolution was? Explain your answer.
3. **a. Identify** Who was Napoleon Bonaparte, and what were his main accomplishments?
   b. Analyze How were Napoleon's forces weakened and then defeated?

Critical Thinking

4. **Sequencing** Review your notes. Then use a time line like the one here to list the main events of the Age of Revolution. List the events in the order in which they occurred.

↔ ┬──────┬──────┬──────┬──────┬

FOCUS ON WRITING

5. **Describing Political Change in Europe** Take notes on the political changes that occurred during this period. What exciting and dramatic events might interest visitors? For example, visitors might want to see the American Revolution firsthand.

Social Studies Skills

Making Economic Choices

Learn

The economic choices that people make are a part of geography. For example, consider an economic choice you might make. You have a certain amount of spending money. You can either go to a movie with a friend or buy a CD. You cannot afford to do both, so you must make a choice.

Countries also must make economic choices. For example, a country might face a choice about whether to spend government money on improving defense, education, or health care.

Making economic choices involves sacrifices, or trade-offs. If you choose to spend your money on a movie, the trade-offs are the other things you want but cannot buy. By considering trade-offs, you can make better economic choices.

Practice

You are on the school dance committee. The committee has enough money to upgrade one item for the dance. As the diagram below shows, the committee can spend the money on fancy decorations, a live band, or a ballroom. The committee votes and chooses the fancy decorations.

❶ Based on the diagram below, what are the trade-offs of the committee's choice?

❷ What would have been the trade-offs if the committee had voted to spend the money on a ballroom instead?

❸ How do you think creating a diagram like the one below might have helped the committee make its economic choice?

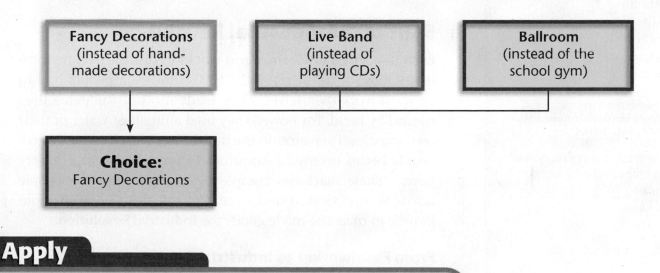

Fancy Decorations (instead of hand-made decorations)

Live Band (instead of playing CDs)

Ballroom (instead of the school gym)

Choice: Fancy Decorations

Apply

1. Describe an example of an economic choice you might face that has three possible trade-offs.

2. For each possible economic choice, identify what the trade-offs are if you make that choice.

3. What final choice will you make? Why?

4. How did considering trade-offs help you make your choice?

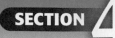
The Industrial Revolution

What You Will Learn...

Main Ideas

1. Britain's large labor force, raw materials, and money to invest led to the start of the Industrial Revolution.
2. Industrial growth began in Great Britain and then spread to other parts of Europe.
3. The Industrial Revolution led to both positive and negative changes in society.

The Big Idea

Driven by new ideas and technologies, much of Europe developed industrial societies in the 1700s and 1800s.

Key Terms

Industrial Revolution, *p. 70*
textiles, *p. 72*
capitalism, *p. 72*
suffragettes, *p. 74*

TAKING NOTES

Use the graphic organizer online to take notes on the Industrial Revolution.

If YOU lived there...

You live in Lancashire, England, in 1815. You and your family are weavers. You spin sheep's wool into thread. Then you weave the thread into fine woolen cloth to sell to local merchants. Now a mill is being built nearby. It will have large machines that weave cloth. The mill owner is looking for workers to run the machines. Some of your friends are going to work in the mill to earn more money.

What do you think about working in the mill?

BUILDING BACKGROUND In the mid-1700s great changes in industry revolutionized life in Europe. Like some earlier revolutions, the growth of industry was driven by new inventions and technology. This industrial growth would have far-reaching effects on society.

Start of the Industrial Revolution

Each day, machines from alarm clocks to dishwashers perform many jobs for us. In the early 1700s, however, people had to do most work themselves. They made most of the items they needed by hand. For power, they used animals or water or their own muscles. Then around the mid-1700s, everything changed. People began inventing machines to make goods and supply power. These machines completely changed the way people across Europe worked and lived. We call this period of rapid growth in machine-made goods the **Industrial Revolution**.

From Farmworker to Industrial Laborer

Changes in farming helped pave the way for industrial growth. Since the Middle Ages, farming in Europe had been changing. Wealthy farmers had started buying up land and creating larger farms. These large farms were more efficient. For this reason, many people who owned small farms lost their land. They then had to work for other farmers or move to cities.

At the same time, Europe's growing population was creating a need for more food. To meet this need, farmers began looking for ways to grow more and better crops. Farmers began to experiment with new methods. They also began improving farm technology. Englishman Jethro Tull, for example, invented a seed drill. This device made it possible to plant seeds in straight rows and at certain depths. As a result, more seeds grew into plants.

Better farming methods and technology had several effects. For one, farmers could grow more crops with less labor. With more crops available for food, the population grew even more. With less need for labor, however, many farmworkers lost their jobs. These workers then moved to cities. There, they created a large labor force for the coming industrial growth.

Great Britain's Resources

Great Britain provided the setting for the Industrial Revolution's start. Britain and its colonies had the resources needed for industrial growth. These resources included labor, raw materials, and money to invest. For example, Britain had a large workforce, rich supplies of coal, and many rivers for waterpower.

In addition, Great Britain's colonial markets and its growing population were increasing the demand for manufactured goods. Increased demand led people to look for ways to make goods faster or more easily. In Britain all these things came together to start the Industrial Revolution.

READING CHECK **Identifying Cause and Effect** How did new technology and better farming methods affect agriculture in Europe?

Inventions of the Industrial Revolution

Starting in the mid-1700s, inventions changed the way goods were made. James Hargreaves's spinning jenny, above, made thread quickly. The Bessemer furnace, at left, was an invention of the late Industrial Revolution. The furnace made steel from molten iron.

ANALYZING VISUALS What do you think operating a Bessemer furnace was like?

Industrial Growth

Industrial growth began with **textiles**, or cloth products. In the early 1700s people made cloth by hand. They used spinning wheels to make thread and looms to weave it into cloth. Given the time and effort this took, it is not surprising that people would want a way to make cloth quickly.

New inventions continue to make communication faster and easier. Cell phones and e-mail are just two examples.

FOCUS ON READING

Which came first, Arkwright's invention or Bessemer's? How can you tell?

The Textile Industry

A big step toward manufactured clothing came in 1769. That year, an Englishman, named Richard Arkwright invented a waterpowered spinning machine. Called a water frame, this machine could produce dozens of threads at one time. In contrast, a person using a traditional spinning wheel could produce only one thread at a time.

Other machines sped up production even more. With these new machines, workers could produce large amounts of cloth quickly. As a result, the price of cloth fell. Soon, the British were using machines to make many types of goods. People housed these machines in buildings called factories, and the factories needed power.

Other Inventions

Most early machines ran on waterpower. Thus, factories had to be located by rivers. Although Britain had many rivers, they were not always in desirable locations.

Steam power provided a solution. In the 1760s James Watt, a Scot, built the first modern steam engine. Soon, steam powered most machines. Factories could now be built in better places, such as in cities.

Steam power increased the demand for coal and iron, which were needed to make machinery. Iron can be a brittle metal, though, and iron parts often broke. Then in 1855 Englishman Henry Bessemer developed a cheap way to convert iron into steel, which is stronger. This invention led to the growth of the steel industry.

In addition, new inventions improved transportation and communication. Steam engines powered riverboats and trains, speeding up transportation. The telegraph made communication faster. Instead of sending a note by boat or train, people could go to a telegraph office and instantly send a message over a long distance.

The Factory System

Industrial growth led to major changes in the way people worked and lived. Before, most people had worked on farms or in their homes. Now, more people were going to work in factories. Many of these workers were young women and children, whom owners paid lower wages.

Factory work was long, tiring, and dangerous. Factory workers did the same tasks for 12 hours or more a day, six days a week. Breaks were few, and rules were strict. Although people made more than on farms, wages were still low.

To add to the toil, factory conditions were miserable and unsafe. Year-round, the air was thick with dust, which could harm workers' lungs. In addition, the large machines were dangerous and caused many injuries. Even so, factory jobs were desirable to people with few alternatives.

Spread of Industry

In time, the Industrial Revolution spread from Great Britain to other parts of Europe. By the late 1800s, factories were making goods across much of Western Europe.

The growth of industry helped lead to a new economic system, **capitalism**. In this system, individuals own most businesses and resources. People invest money in businesses in the hope of making a profit.

READING CHECK Evaluating If you had lived at this time, would you have left a farm to work in a factory for more money? Why, or why not?

A British Textile Factory

In early textile factories, workers ran machines in a large room. A supervisor kept a watchful eye. Conditions in factories were poor, and the work was long, tiring, and dangerous. Even so, young women and children as young as six worked in many early factories.

Factory owners keep windows shut to prevent air from blowing the threads. This creates a hot, stuffy room.

Dust and cotton fibers fill the air, causing breathing problems.

One task is to straighten threads as they come out of the machines. This task can cut workers' hands.

Machines are loud. Workers must shout to be heard over the deafening roar.

To avoid being injured or killed, girls must tie back their hair to keep it from getting caught in the machines.

ANALYSIS SKILL **ANALYZING VISUALS**

Why do you think the machines in early textile factories caused so many injuries?

Reform efforts addressed the workplace, society, and government. Here, British suffragettes campaign for the right to vote.

At the same time, industrial growth made life worse in other ways. Cities grew rapidly. They became dirty, noisy, and crowded. Many workers remained poor. They often had to live crammed together in shabby, unsafe apartments. In these conditions, diseases spread rapidly as well.

Such problems led to efforts to reform society and politics. People worked to have laws passed improving wages and factory conditions. Others worked to make cities cleaner and safer. Efforts to gain political power were led by **suffragettes**, women who campaigned to gain the right to vote. In 1928 British suffragettes won the right to vote for women in Great Britain. Changes like these helped usher in the modern age.

READING CHECK **Summarizing** How did the Industrial Revolution affect cities in Europe?

Changes in Society

The Industrial Revolution improved life in Europe in many ways. Manufactured goods became cheaper and more available. Inventions made life easier. More people grew wealthier and joined the middle class. These people could afford to live well.

SUMMARY AND PREVIEW As you have read, industrial growth greatly changed how many Europeans lived and worked. In the next chapter you will learn about Europe's modern history.

Section 4 Assessment

hmhsocialstudies.com
ONLINE QUIZ

Reviewing Ideas, Terms, and Places

1. **a. Recall** In which country did the start of the **Industrial Revolution** take place?
   b. Draw Conclusions How did changes in farming help pave the way for industrial growth?
   c. Develop Write a few sentences defending the idea that Great Britain was ready for industrial growth in the early 1700s.
2. **a. Identify** What were two inventions that contributed to industrial growth during this period?
   b. Make Inferences How do you think work in a factory differed from that on a farm?
3. **a. Recall** What did the **suffragettes** achieve?
   b. Summarize What problems did industry create? How did people work to solve these problems?

Critical Thinking

4. **Identifying Cause and Effect** Review your notes. Then use a diagram like the one shown to explain how each change in society led to the next.

Changes in Farming → New Inventions → Factory System → New Ways of Life

FOCUS ON WRITING

5. **Describing the Industrial Revolution** What might encourage people to visit Europe during the Industrial Revolution? Jot down some ideas in your notes. For example, people might want to see what it was like to work in an early factory.

Chapter Review

Geography's Impact
video series
Review the video to answer the closing question:
How did the Renaissance and Reformation change Europe?

Visual Summary

Use the visual summary below to help you review the main ideas of the chapter.

QUICK FACTS

The Renaissance and the Reformation introduced new ideas, art, and ways of thinking into Europe.

Advances of the Scientific Revolution, such as the astrolabe, led to European exploration and empires.

The new ideas of the Enlightenment led to European revolutions, such as the French Revolution.

Driven by new technologies, much of Europe developed industrial societies in the 1700s and 1800s.

Reviewing Vocabulary, Terms, and Places

Copy each sentence onto your own paper and fill in the blank with the word or place in the pair that best completes each sentence.

1. Two important Italian trading cities were Venice and _____ (Florence/Wittenberg).

2. A way of thinking and learning that stresses the importance of human abilities is called _____ (humanism/perspective).

3. The _____ (Renaissance/Reformation) was a movement to reform the Catholic Church.

4. Magellan led a voyage that became the first to _____ (circumnavigate/navigate) Earth.

5. The first European country to build an American empire was _____ (Spain/Portugal).

6. The _____ (Renaissance/Enlightenment) is the period during which people used reason to examine society and politics.

7. John Locke thought government should be a _____ (contract/divine right) between the ruler and the people.

8. The Industrial Revolution began in _____ (steel/textiles).

9. Industrial growth led to a new economic system called _____ (capitalism/communism).

10. British women called _____ (suffragettes/reformers) campaigned for the right to vote.

Comprehension and Critical Thinking

SECTION 1 *(Pages 48–53)*

11. **a. Describe** What was the Reformation?

    b. Summarize How did the Renaissance affect art, literature, and science?

    c. Evaluate Do you think the Renaissance was truly a rebirth of Europe? Why, or why not?

SECTION 2 (Pages 54–61)

12. **a. Identify** What did Christopher Columbus and Ferdinand Magellan achieve?

b. Identify Cause and Effect How did the Scientific Revolution help contribute to the Age of Exploration?

c. Elaborate How did European colonization of the Americas affect European society?

SECTION 3 (Pages 62–68)

13. **a. Recall** What three goals did Enlightenment thinkers believe the use of reason could achieve?

b. Compare What ideas did John Locke and Jean-Jacques Rousseau share?

c. Elaborate How did the English Bill of Rights and the Declaration of the Rights of Man and of the Citizen change the power of monarchs?

SECTION 4 (Pages 70–74)

14. **a. Recall** In which country did the Industrial Revolution start?

b. Identify Cause and Effect How did industrial growth lead to improvements in society?

c. Evaluate Which Industrial Revolution invention do you think was most significant? Why?

Using the Internet

15. **Activity: Creating a Biography** The period of the Renaissance saw many advances in art and literature. Through your online textbook, learn about some of the artists and writers of the Renaissance. Then choose one artist or writer to learn more about and write a brief biography of his or her life. Be sure to include information on the person's accomplishments and significance.

↗ hmhsocialstudies.com

Social Studies Skills

Making Economic Choices *You have enough money to buy one of the following items: shoes, a DVD, or a book.*

16. What are the trade-offs if you buy the DVD?

17. What are the trade-offs if you buy the book?

Map Activity

18. **Europe, 1500–1900** On a separate sheet of paper, match the letters on the map with their correct labels.

Florence	Madrid	Venice
London	Paris	Wittenberg

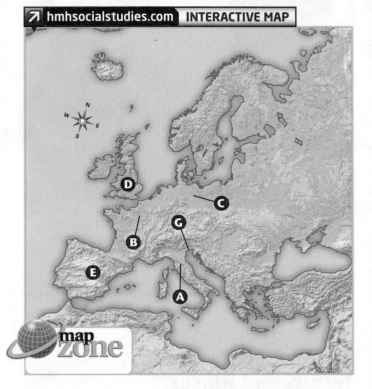

↗ hmhsocialstudies.com **INTERACTIVE MAP**

FOCUS ON READING AND WRITING

19. **Understanding Chronological Order** Create a time line that lists 10 significant events covered in this chapter. List the events in the order in which they occurred and provide a date and label for each event.

20. **Creating a Travel Brochure** By now you should know which time period you want to cover. Create a travel brochure to encourage people to visit Europe during that time period. Use images and descriptive language to convince your readers to travel to the period. In your brochure, highlight interesting historical events that visitors might witness, interesting people they might meet, or new ideas they might learn.

Standardized Test Prep

DIRECTIONS: Read questions 1 through 7 and write the letter of the best response. Then read question 8 and write your own well-constructed response.

1 Which person played an important role in spreading the ideas of the Renaissance beyond Italy?

A Johann Gutenberg

B Leonardo da Vinci

C Martin Luther

D William Shakespeare

2 What land did Christopher Columbus reach on his voyage in 1492?

A America

B China

C India

D Spain

3 Which event marked the beginning of the French Revolution?

A Congress of Vienna

B Great Fear

C Reign of Terror

D Storming of the Bastille

4 The Industrial Revolution began in which of the following countries?

A France

B Germany

C Great Britain

D Spain

5 A period of rapid growth in machine-made goods during the 1700s and 1800s is the

A American Revolution.

B French Revolution.

C Industrial Revolution.

D Scientific Revolution.

Religions in Europe, 1600

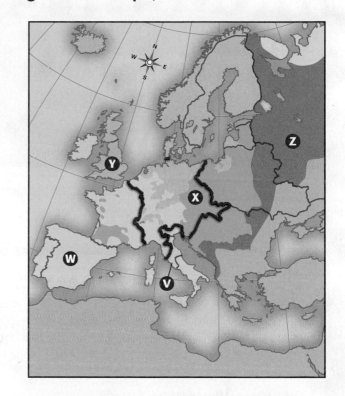

6 On the map above, which letter marks a Protestant area?

A V

B W

C Y

D Z

7 On the map, which letter indicates Rome?

A V

B W

C X

D Y

8 **Extended Response** Examine the Section 2 map European Exploration, 1487–1580. Select the two voyages that you think are most significant in European history. Describe each voyage, identify who led it, and explain its significance.

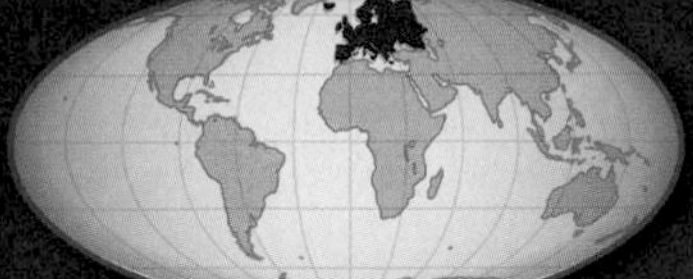

Modern European History

1900–Today

> **Essential Question** How have major conflicts shaped the history of modern Europe?

What You Will Learn...

In this chapter you will learn about Europe since 1900. You will study the causes and effects of World Wars I and II. You will also learn about the Cold War and how it divided Europe. Finally, you will discover how Europe was reunited at the end of the Cold War.

FOCUS ON READING AND WRITING

Using Context Clues—Contrast As you read, you may come across words you do not understand. When that happens, use context clues— words and sentences around the word—to guess at its meaning. Sometimes the clue to a word's meaning is a contrast clue. It tells you how the unknown word is different from a word you already know. **See the lesson, Using Context Clues—Contrast, on page 222.**

Writing a Diary Entry In this chapter you will read about European history since 1900. As you read, think about what it would have been like to live during this period. Later you will write a diary entry from the point of view of someone who lived during these times.

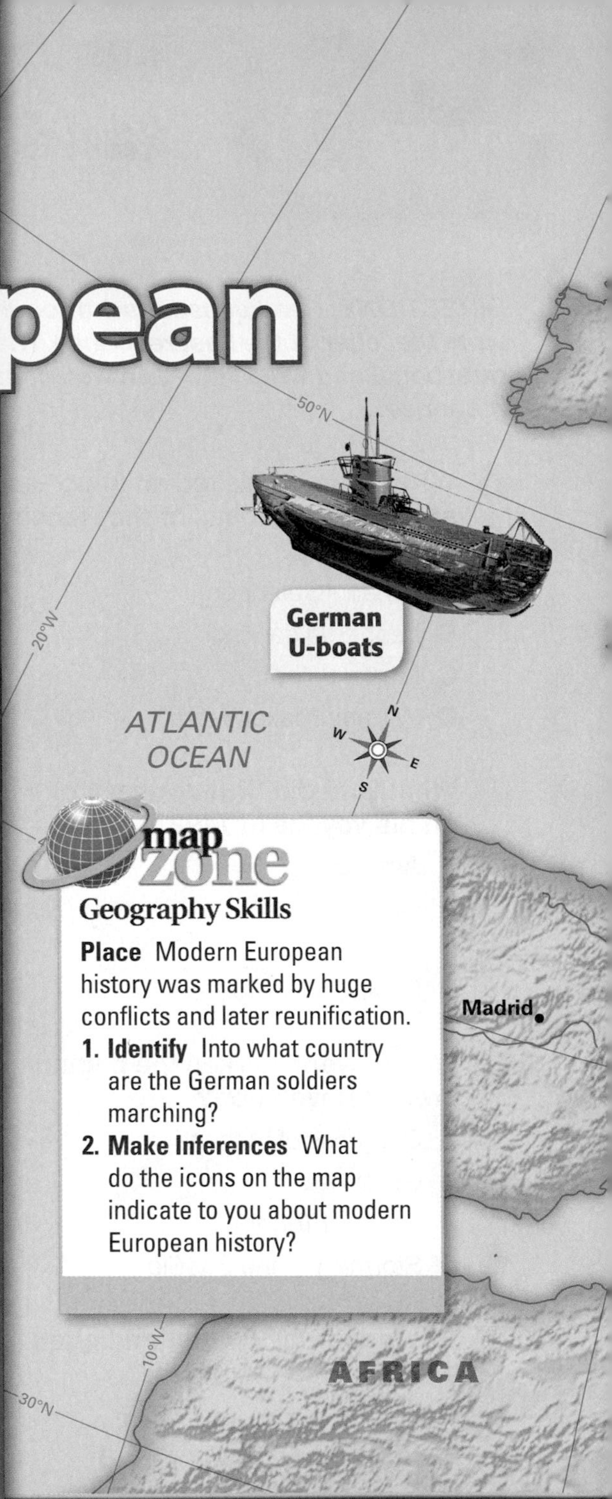

German U-boats

ATLANTIC OCEAN

Geography Skills

Place Modern European history was marked by huge conflicts and later reunification.

Madrid

1. **Identify** Into what country are the German soldiers marching?
2. **Make Inferences** What do the icons on the map indicate to you about modern European history?

AFRICA

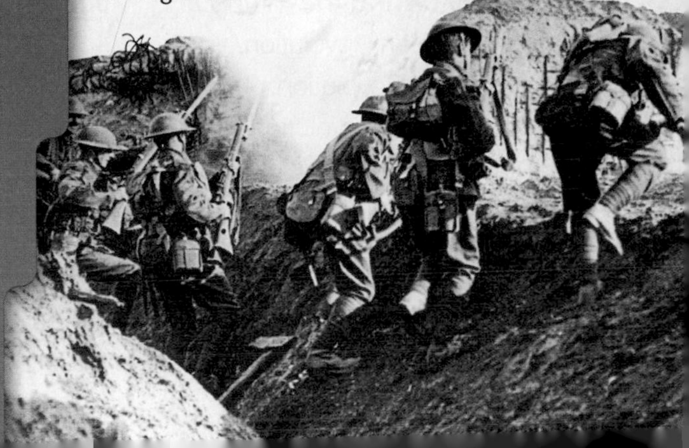

World War I Soldiers from Europe's most powerful countries engaged in trench warfare during World War I.

Europe, 1900–Today

North Sea

Baltic Sea

European Union

London

Berlin

HISTORY Battle of Britain

⬈ hmhsocialstudies.com VIDEO

Vladimir Lenin

Paris

German troops invade France

EUROPE

Bombing damage in Warsaw

Rome

Black Sea

0   100   300 Miles
0   100   200 Kilometers
Projection: Azimuthal Equal Area

10°E   20°E   30°E

ASIA

Mediterranean Sea

World War II The rise of strong dictators, like Germany's Adolf Hitler, led to the outbreak of the Second World War.

Europe since 1945 The end of the Cold War and the fall of the Berlin Wall helped to reunite Europe by the end of the 1900s.

79

World War I

What You Will Learn...

Main Ideas

1. Rivalries in Europe led to the outbreak of World War I.
2. After a long, devastating war, the Allies claimed victory.
3. The war's end brought great political and territorial changes to Europe.

The Big Idea

World War I and the peace treaty that followed brought tremendous change to Europe.

Key Terms

nationalism, *p. 80*
alliance, *p. 81*
trench warfare, *p. 82*
Treaty of Versailles, *p. 83*
communism, *p. 84*

hmhsocialstudies.com
TAKING NOTES

Use the graphic organizer online to take notes on the causes and effects of World War I.

If YOU lived there...

It is 1914, and you live in London. For years you have heard about an important alliance between Great Britain, France, and Russia. Each country has promised to protect the others. Just days ago, you learned that war has broken out in Eastern Europe. Russia and France are preparing for war. People are saying that Britain will fight to protect its allies. If that happens, Europe's most powerful countries will be at war.

How do you feel about the possibility of war?

BUILDING BACKGROUND The 1800s were a time of rapid change in Europe. Industries grew quickly. Cities expanded. The countries of Europe raced to build empires and gain power. As each country tried to outdo the others, conflicts emerged. Europe was poised for war.

The Outbreak of War

In the early 1900s Europe was on the brink of war. Rivalries were building among Europe's strongest nations. One small spark would be enough to start World War I.

Causes of the War

During the 1800s nationalism changed Europe. **Nationalism** is devotion and loyalty to one's country. Some groups that were ruled by powerful empires wanted to build their own nation-states. For example, nationalism led some people in Bosnia and Herzegovina, a region in southeastern Europe, to demand their independence from the Austro-Hungarian Empire. Nationalism also created rivalries among many nations. By the early 1900s nationalism had grown so strong that countries were willing to go to war to prove their superiority over their rivals. A fierce competition emerged among the countries of Europe.

This competition for land, resources, and power drove many European countries to strengthen their armed forces. They built powerful armies and created stockpiles of new weapons. Each country wanted to show its strength and intimidate its rivals.

European Alliances, 1914

NORWAY
SWEDEN
North Sea
DENMARK
Baltic Sea
GREAT BRITAIN
NETHERLANDS
GERMAN EMPIRE
RUSSIA
BELGIUM
LUXEMBOURG
FRANCE
AUSTRIA-HUNGARY
SWITZERLAND
ROMANIA
Black Sea
SERBIA
BULGARIA
PORTUGAL
SPAIN
Corsica
ITALY
MONTENEGRO
Sardinia
ALBANIA
OTTOMAN EMPIRE
GREECE
ATLANTIC OCEAN
Mediterranean Sea
Sicily

Triple Alliance
Triple Entente

0   200   400 Miles
0   200   400 Kilometers
Projection: Azimuthal Equal-Area

map zone   Geography Skills

Regions Rivalries split Europe into two opposing alliances—the Triple Alliance and the Triple Entente.
1. Locate Which alliance controlled central Europe?
2. Draw Conclusions Why do you think the location of the Triple Entente might have threatened the Triple Alliance?

Both Great Britain and Germany, for example, competed to build strong navies and powerful new battleships.

As tensions and suspicions grew, some European leaders hoped to protect their countries by creating alliances. An **alliance** is an agreement between countries. If one country is attacked, its allies—members of the alliance—help defend it. In 1882 Italy, Germany, and Austria-Hungary formed the Triple Alliance. In response, France, Great Britain, and Russia created their own alliance, the Triple Entente (ahn-TAHNT). As you can see in the map, these alliances divided Europe.

The Spark for War

By the summer of 1914, war in Europe seemed certain. Tensions between Austria-Hungary and Serbia arose over the control of Bosnia and Herzegovina, a province of Austria-Hungary and Serbia's neighbor. On June 28, 1914, a Serbian assassin shot and killed Archduke Francis Ferdinand, the heir to the throne of Austria-Hungary. Seeking revenge, Austria-Hungary declared war on Serbia. After Serbia turned to Russia for help, the alliance system quickly split Europe into two warring sides. On one side was Austria-Hungary and Germany, known as the Central Powers. The Allied Powers—Serbia, Russia, Great Britain, and France—were on the other side.

READING CHECK   Finding Main Ideas What were the causes of World War I?

War and Victory

Germany struck the first blow in the war, sending a large army into Belgium and France. Allied troops, however, managed to stop the Germans just outside Paris. In the east, Russia attacked Germany and Austria-Hungary, forcing Germany to fight on two fronts. Hopes on both sides for a quick victory soon disappeared.

A New Kind of War

ACADEMIC VOCABULARY

strategy a plan for fighting a battle or war

A new military **strategy**, trench warfare, was largely responsible for preventing a quick victory. Early in the war both sides turned to trench warfare. **Trench warfare** is a style of fighting in which each side fights from deep ditches, or trenches, dug into the ground.

Both the Allies and the Central Powers dug hundreds of miles of trenches along the front lines. Soldiers in the trenches faced great suffering. Not only did they live in constant danger of attack, but cold, hunger, and disease also plagued them. Sometimes soldiers would "go over the top" of their trenches and fight for a few hours, only to retreat to the same position. Trench warfare cost millions of lives, but neither side could win the war.

To gain an advantage in the trenches, each side developed deadly new weapons. Machine guns cut down soldiers as they tried to move forward. Poison gas, first used by the Germans, blinded soldiers in the trenches. It was later used by both sides. The British introduced another weapon, the tank, to break through enemy lines.

Close-up

Trench Warfare

Both the Allied Powers and the Central Powers relied on trenches for defense during World War I. As a result, the war dragged on for years with no clear victor. Each side developed new weapons and technology to try to gain an advantage in the trenches.

Soldiers often threw or fired small bombs known as grenades.

Soldiers used gas masks to survive attacks of poison gas.

Trenches dug in zigzag patterns prevented the enemy from firing down the length of a trench.

At sea, Britain used its powerful navy to block supplies from reaching Germany. Germany responded by using submarines, called U-boats. German U-boats tried to break the British blockade and sink ships carrying supplies to Great Britain.

The Allies Win

For three years the war was a stalemate—neither side could defeat the other. Slowly, however, the war turned in favor of the Allies. In early 1917 German U-boats began attacking American ships carrying supplies to Britain. When Germany ignored U.S. warnings to stop, the United States entered the war on the side of the Allies.

Help from American forces gave the Allies a fresh advantage. Soon afterward, however, the exhausted Russians pulled out of the war. Germany quickly attacked the Allies, hoping to put an end to the war. Allied troops, however, stopped Germany's attack. The Central Powers had suffered a great blow. In the fall of 1918 the Central Powers surrendered. The Allied Powers were victorious.

READING CHECK **Sequencing** What events led to the end of World War I?

The War's End

After more than four years of fighting, the war came to an end on November 11, 1918. More than 8.5 million soldiers had been killed, and at least 20 million more were wounded. Millions of civilians had lost their lives as well. The war brought tremendous change to Europe.

Making Peace

Shortly after the end of the war, leaders from the Allied nations met at Versailles (ver-SY), near Paris. There, they debated the terms of peace for the Central Powers.

The United States, led by President Woodrow Wilson, wanted a just peace after the war. He did not want harsh peace terms that might anger the losing countries and lead to future conflict.

Other Allied leaders, however, wanted to punish Germany. They believed that Germany had started the war and should pay for it. They believed that weakening Germany would prevent future wars.

In the end, the Allies forced Germany to sign a treaty. The **Treaty of Versailles** was the final peace settlement of World War I. It forced Germany to accept the blame for starting the war. Germany also had to slash the size of its army and give up its overseas colonies. Additionally, Germany had to pay billions of dollars for damages caused during the war.

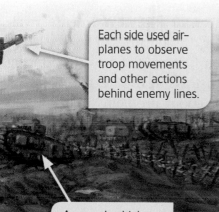

Each side used airplanes to observe troop movements and other actions behind enemy lines.

Armored vehicles, or tanks, were used to launch attacks across rough terrain.

ANALYSIS SKILL **ANALYZING VISUALS**

What advantages and disadvantages did trench warfare pose for soldiers?

FOCUS ON READING
What does the term *just peace* mean? How can you tell?

Vladimir Lenin encouraged Russian workers to support his new Communist government.

over Russia's government and established a Communist government. **Communism** is a political system in which the government owns all property and controls all aspects of life in a country. An uprising toward the end of the war also forced the German emperor from power. A fragile republic replaced the German Empire.

World War I also altered the borders of many European countries. Austria and Hungary became separate countries. Poland and Czechoslovakia each gained their independence. Serbia, Bosnia and Herzegovina, and other Balkan states were combined to create Yugoslavia. Finland, Estonia, Latvia, and Lithuania, which had been part of Russia, became independent.

READING CHECK **Summarizing** How did World War I change Europe?

A New Europe

World War I had a tremendous effect on the countries of Europe. It changed the governments of some European countries and the borders of others. For example, in Russia the war had caused great hardship for the people. A revolution then forced the Russian czar, or emperor, to give up power. Shortly after, Vladimir Lenin took

SUMMARY AND PREVIEW Intense rivalries among the countries of Europe led to World War I, one of the most devastating wars in history. In the next section you will learn about problems that plagued Europe and led to World War II.

Section 1 Assessment

hmhsocialstudies.com
ONLINE QUIZ

Reviewing Ideas, Terms, and Places

1. **a. Identify** What event triggered World War I?
   b. Analyze How did **nationalism** cause rivalries between some European countries?
   c. Evaluate Do you think **alliances** helped or hurt most countries? Explain your answer.
2. **a. Describe** What was **trench warfare** like?
   b. Draw Conclusions What difficulties did soldiers face as a result of trench warfare?
   c. Predict How might the war have been different if the United States had not entered it?
3. **a. Recall** How did the **Treaty of Versailles** punish Germany for its role in the war?
   b. Contrast How did the Allied leaders' ideas for peace with Germany differ?
   c. Elaborate Why do you think the war caused changes in government in Russia and Germany?

Critical Thinking

4. **Categorizing** Draw a chart like the one here. Use your notes to list the results of World War I in the appropriate category.

Political	Economic

FOCUS ON WRITING

5. **Writing about World War I** Think about the events of World War I. Imagine that you were present at one or more events during or after the war. What might you write about in your diary?

from
All Quiet on the Western Front

by Erich Maria Remarque

About the Reading *In* All Quiet on the Western Front, *author Erich Maria Remarque provides a fictional account of the lives of soldiers during World War I. The book is considered one of the most realistic accounts of the war. In this selection, the book's narrator, twenty-year-old German soldier Paul Bäumer, describes a battle between German and British forces.*

AS YOU READ Note the words the speaker uses to describe the battle.

Our trenches have now for some time been shot to pieces, and we have an elastic line, so that there is practically no longer any proper trench warfare. ❶ When attack and counter-attack have waged backwards and forwards there remains a broken line and a bitter struggle from crater to crater. The front-line has been penetrated, and everywhere small groups have established themselves, the fight is carried on from clusters of shell-holes.

We are buried in a crater, the English are coming down obliquely, they are turning our flank and working in behind us. ❷ We are surrounded. It is not easy to surrender, fog and smoke hang over us, no one would recognize that we wanted to give ourselves up, and perhaps we don't want to, a man doesn't even know himself at such moments. We hear the explosions of the hand-grenades coming towards us. Our machine-gun sweeps over the semicircle in front of us . . . Behind us the attack crashes ever nearer.

Soldiers prepare to rush over the top of a trench during a battle in World War I.

GUIDED READING

WORD HELP

crater a hole in the ground made by the explosion of a bomb or choll

penetrated passed into or through

obliquely indirectly or underhandedly

❶ An elastic line describes a battle line that is pushed back and forth by enemy forces.

❷ "Turning our flank" refers to a tactic in which one military force moves around the side of the opposing force in order to surround them.

Connecting Literature to Geography

1. **Describing** What details in the first paragraph show that the technique of trench warfare is no longer working?

2. **Making Inferences** Why do you think the location of this trench is so important to the war and the people fighting in it?

World War II

If YOU lived there...

It is 1922, and you are part of a huge crowd in one of Rome's public squares. Everyone is listening to the fiery speech of a dynamic new leader. He promises to make Italy great again, as it was in the days of ancient Rome. You know that your parents and some of your teachers are excited about his ideas. Others are concerned that he may be too forceful.

What do you think of this new leader's message?

BUILDING BACKGROUND Many countries faced deep economic and political problems as a result of World War I. Dictators rose to power in a number of countries, but did not bring solutions. Instead, they attacked their neighbors and plunged the world back into war.

Problems Trouble Europe

After World War I, Europeans began rebuilding their countries. Just as they had started to recover, however, many economic and political problems emerged. These problems threatened the peace and security of Europe.

The Great Depression

World War I left much of Europe in shambles. Factories and farmland had been destroyed, and economies were in ruins. Countries that had lost the war, like Germany and Austria, owed billions in war damages. Many countries turned to the United States for help. During the 1920s the U.S. economy was booming. Loans from American banks and businesses helped many European nations recover and rebuild after World War I.

In 1929, however, the recovery fell apart. A stock market crash in the United States triggered a global economic crisis in the 1930s known as the **Great Depression**. As the U.S. economy faltered, American banks stopped lending to Europe. Without U.S. loans and investments, European economies declined. Unemployment skyrocketed as businesses and farms, as well as banks, went bankrupt.

What You Will Learn...

Main Ideas

1. Economic and political problems troubled Europe in the years after World War I.
2. World War II broke out when Germany invaded Poland.
3. Nazi Germany targeted the Jews during the Holocaust.
4. Allied victories in Europe and Japan brought the end of World War II.

The Big Idea

Problems in Europe led to World War II, the deadliest war in history.

Key Terms

Great Depression, *p. 86*
dictator, *p. 87*
Axis Powers, *p. 89*
Allies, *p. 89*
Holocaust, *p. 89*

hmhsocialstudies.com
TAKING NOTES

Use the graphic organizer online to take notes on the important dates and events of World War II.

The Rise of Dictators

The Great Depression added to Europe's problems. Blaming weak governments for the hard times, some Europeans turned to dictators to strengthen their countries and improve their lives. A **dictator** is a ruler who has total control. Dictators rose to power in Russia, Italy, and Germany.

One of the first dictators in Europe was Russia's Vladimir Lenin. Lenin gained power as a result of a 1917 revolution. He formed the first Communist government and took control of businesses and private property. He also united Russia and other republics to create the Soviet Union. After Lenin's death in 1924, Joseph Stalin took power. As dictator, he made all economic decisions, restricted religious worship, and used secret police to spy on citizens.

Benito Mussolini of Italy was another powerful dictator during this period. In the 1920s Mussolini won control of the Italian government and made himself dictator. He promised to make Italy stronger and to revive the economy. He even spoke of restoring the glory of the former Roman Empire. As dictator, however, Mussolini suspended basic rights like freedom of speech and trial by jury.

By the 1930s many Germans had lost faith in their government. They turned to a new political party, the Nazi Party. The party's leader, Adolf Hitler, promised to strengthen Germany. He vowed to rebuild Germany's military and economy. After years of struggle, many Germans listened eagerly to his message. In 1933 Hitler rose to power and soon became dictator. He banned all parties except the Nazi Party. He also began discriminating against so-called inferior races, particularly Germany's Jews.

READING CHECK **Generalizing** Why did some people support the rise of dictators?

European Dictators

Popular dictators rose to power in Europe in the 1920s and 1930s. Adolf Hitler in Germany and Benito Mussolini in Italy gained public support with promises to make life better and to strengthen their countries.

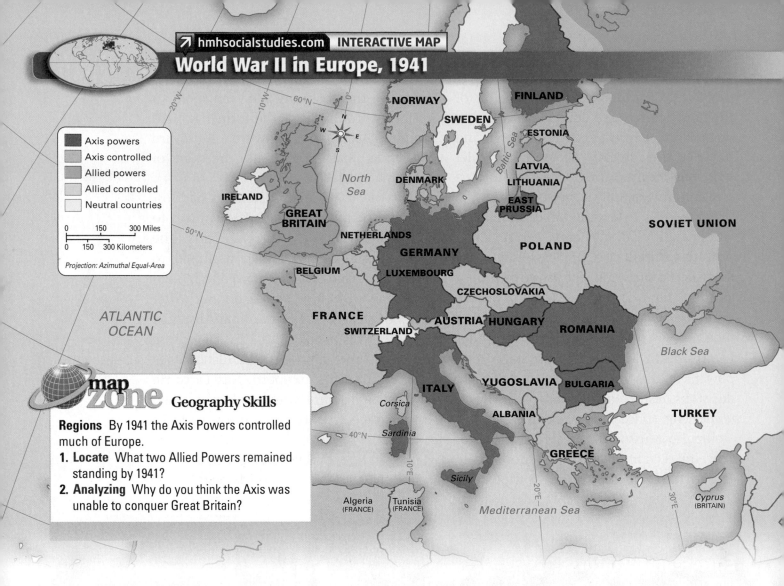

Axis powers
Axis controlled
Allied powers
Allied controlled
Neutral countries

0   150   300 Miles
0   150   300 Kilometers

Projection: Azimuthal Equal-Area

map zone Geography Skills

Regions By 1941 the Axis Powers controlled much of Europe.
1. **Locate** What two Allied Powers remained standing by 1941?
2. **Analyzing** Why do you think the Axis was unable to conquer Great Britain?

War Breaks Out

As dictators, Hitler and Mussolini were determined to strengthen their countries at any cost. Their actions led to history's deadliest war—World War II.

Threats to Peace

After World War I, European countries wanted peace. Many countries hoped to prevent another deadly war. By the late 1930s, however, attempts at peace had failed. Instead of peace, Italian and German aggression forced Europe into a second world war.

In 1935 Benito Mussolini ordered his Italian troops to invade Ethiopia, a country in East Africa. Other nations were shocked

FOCUS ON READING

How do contrast clues help you understand the meaning of the word *aggression*?

by his actions, but none tried to turn back the invasion. Meanwhile, the Italian leader and Germany's Adolf Hitler joined together to form an alliance known as the Rome-Berlin Axis.

Hitler was next to act. In 1938 he broke the Treaty of Versailles when he annexed, or added, Austria to Germany's territory. Although Britain and France protested, they did not attempt to stop Germany.

Later that year, Hitler announced his plan to take Czechoslovakia as well. Many European leaders were worried, but they still hoped to avoid a war. They allowed Hitler to annex part of Czechoslovakia in return for his promise of peace. By the spring of 1939, however, Germany had conquered the rest of Czechoslovakia.

Italy quickly moved to occupy Albania in the Balkans. Attempts to keep the peace had failed.

Eventually, Great Britain and France realized they could not ignore Hitler's actions. When Germany threatened to take Polish territory, the Allies vowed to protect Poland at all costs. On September 1, 1939, German forces launched an all-out attack on Poland. Two days later, Great Britain and France responded by declaring war on Germany. World War II had begun.

Allies Lose Ground

Germany's invasion of Poland triggered the Second World War. Germany, Italy, and Japan formed an alliance called the **Axis Powers**. Against them stood the **Allies** —France, Great Britain, and other countries that opposed the Axis.

Germany struck first. After defeating Poland, Germany moved on to a series of quick victories in Western Europe. One by one, countries fell to German forces. In June 1940 Germany invaded and quickly defeated one of Europe's greatest powers, France. In less than a year, Hitler had gained control of almost all of Western Europe.

Next, Germany set its sights on Britain. The German air force repeatedly attacked British cities and military targets. Hitler hoped the British would surrender. Rather than give in, however, the British persevered.

Unable to defeat Great Britain, the Axis Powers turned their attention elsewhere. As German troops marched into Eastern Europe, Italian forces invaded North Africa. By the end of 1941 Germany had invaded the Soviet Union, and Japan had attacked the United States at Pearl Harbor, Hawaii. The Allies were losing ground in the war.

READING CHECK **Drawing Inferences** Why do you think the Axis Powers easily gained the advantage in the early years of the war?

The Holocaust

One of the most horrifying aspects of the war was the Holocaust (HOH-luh-kawst). The **Holocaust** was the attempt by the Nazi government during World War II to eliminate Europe's Jews. Believing that the Germans were a superior race, the Nazis tried to destroy people who they believed were inferior, especially the Jews.

Even before the war began, the Nazi government began restricting the rights of Jews and others in Germany. For example, laws restricted Jews from holding government jobs or attending German schools. Nazis imprisoned countless Jews in camps.

Primary Source

JOURNAL ENTRY
The Diary of Anne Frank

Anne Frank and her family fled to Amsterdam to escape Nazi persecution of Jews in Germany. In 1942, when Nazis began rounding up Jews in the Netherlands, the Franks were forced to hide. Anne kept a diary of her time in hiding.

" Countless friends and acquaintances have gone to a terrible fate. Evening after evening the green and gray army lorries [trucks] trundle past. The Germans ring at every front door to inquire if there are any Jews living in the house. If there are, then the whole family has to go at once. If they don't find any, they go on to the next house. No one has a chance of evading them unless one goes into hiding. "

—from *The Diary of a Young Girl*

ANALYSIS SKILL **ANALYZING PRIMARY SOURCES**

What likely happened to the Jews that were rounded up by German officials?

World War II

September 1–3, 1939
German forces invade Poland; Britain and France declare war.

June 22, 1941
Germany launches invasion of the Soviet Union.

1940   1941   1942   1943

June 22, 1940
France falls to German forces.

July–September 1940
Germany bombs London during the Battle of Britain.

Thousands of Jews fled Germany to escape persecution, but many had to remain behind because they were not allowed into other countries.

Germany's expansion into Eastern Europe brought millions more Jews under Hitler's control. In 1942 the Nazi government ordered the destruction of Europe's entire Jewish population. The Nazis used mass executions and concentration camps, like Auschwitz in Poland, to murder 6 million Jews.

The Nazis did face resistance. Some Jews fought back. For example, Jews in Warsaw, Poland, staged an uprising. Some non-Jewish Europeans tried to save Jews from the Nazis. German businessman Oskar Schindler, for example, saved Jews by employing them in his factories. By the time the Nazis were defeated, they had killed about two-thirds of Europe's Jews and several million non-Jews.

READING CHECK **Analyzing** Why did Hitler's Nazi government attempt to destroy the Jews?

End of the War

The Allies did not fare well in the early years of the war. Victories in 1943 and 1944, though, helped them end World War II.

Allies Are Victorious

In early 1943 U.S. and British forces gained control of North Africa and Italy, forcing Mussolini to surrender. That same year, the Allies defeated the Japanese in several key battles. In the east, Soviet troops forced Germany to retreat.

In June 1944 Allied forces landed on the beaches of Normandy, France. The invasion, or D-Day as it was called, dealt a serious blow to the Axis. It paved the way for Allied forces to advance on Germany.

By the spring of 1945 Allied troops had crossed into German territory. In May 1945 Germany surrendered. In August 1945 the United States used a powerful new weapon, the atomic bomb, to bring the war with Japan to an end. After almost six years of fighting, World War II was over.

February 1945
Allied leaders plan the final defeat of the Axis Powers.

April 1945
Allied troops begin liberation of Nazi concentration camps.

1944

1945

1946

June 6, 1944
Allied forces launch D-Day invasion in Normandy, France.

May 7, 1945
Germany surrenders to Allied Powers.

HISTORY

VIDEO
BBC Report on D-Day
↗ hmhsocialstudies.com

ANALYSIS SKILL **READING TIME LINES**

About how long after the beginning of the war did Germany invade the Soviet Union?

Results of the War

The war had a huge impact on the world. It resulted in millions of deaths, tensions between the Allies, and the creation of the United Nations.

World War II was the deadliest conflict in history. More than 50 million people lost their lives. Millions more were wounded.

The United States and the Soviet Union emerged from the war as the most powerful countries in the world. An intense rivalry developed between the two countries.

After the war, people hoped to prevent another deadly conflict. In 1945 some 50 nations formed the United Nations, an international peacekeeping organization.

READING CHECK **Summarizing** What were the main results of World War II?

SUMMARY AND PREVIEW World War II was the deadliest war in history. Next, you will learn about developments in Europe during the postwar period.

Section 2 Assessment ↗ hmhsocialstudies.com
ONLINE QUIZ

Reviewing Ideas, Terms, and Places

1. **a. Define** What was the **Great Depression**?
   b. Explain How did economic problems in the United States lead to the Great Depression?
2. **a. Describe** What led to the outbreak of World War II?
   b. Predict What might have happened if Great Britain had fallen to Germany?
3. **a. Identify** What was the **Holocaust**?
   b. Draw Inferences Why did the Nazis target certain groups for elimination?
4. **a. Recall** What events led to Germany's surrender?
   b. Analyze How did World War II change Europe?

Critical Thinking

5. **Sequencing** Draw a time line like this one. Using your notes on important events, place the main events and their dates on the time line.

   1917   1945

FOCUS ON WRITING

6. **Telling about World War II** Imagine that you are an adult during the Second World War. Where might you have lived? What might you have seen and done there? Write down some ideas in your notebook.

SECTION 3

Europe since 1945

If YOU lived there...

It is November 1989, and you live on the East German side of Berlin. For years the Berlin Wall has divided your city in two. The government has carefully controlled who could cross the border. One night, you hear an exciting rumor—the gate through the Wall is open. People in East and West Berlin can now travel back and forth freely. Young Berliners are celebrating in the streets.

What will this change mean for your country?

What You Will Learn...

Main Ideas

1. The Cold War divided Europe between democratic and Communist nations.
2. Many Eastern European countries changed boundaries and forms of government at the end of the Cold War.
3. European cooperation has brought economic and political change to Europe.

The Big Idea

After years of division during the Cold War, today Europe is working toward unity.

Key Terms

superpowers, *p. 92*
Cold War, *p. 92*
arms race, *p. 94*
common market, *p. 96*
European Union (EU), *p. 96*

hmhsocialstudies.com
TAKING NOTES

Use the graphic organizer online to take notes on events in Europe since 1945.

BUILDING BACKGROUND In the years after World War II, tensions between the Western Allies and the Soviet Union divided Europe into East and West. By the late 1980s, those tensions were at last coming to an end. Europe could finally work toward unity.

The Cold War

Although Europeans were relieved when World War II ended, new problems soon arose. Countries whose governments and economies had been weakened during the war had to work to strengthen them. Entire cities had to be rebuilt. Most importantly, postwar tensions between the Allies divided Europe.

Superpowers Face Off

The United States and the Soviet Union emerged from World War II as the world's most powerful nations. Allies during the war, the two **superpowers**, or strong and influential countries, now distrusted each other. Growing hostility between the superpowers led to the **Cold War**, a period of tense rivalry between the United States and the Soviet Union.

Much of the hostility between the Soviet Union and the United States focused on political and economic differences. The United States is a democracy with an economy based on free enterprise. The Soviet Union was a Communist country, in which individual freedoms were limited. Its leaders exerted strict control over the political system and the economy. These basic differences separated the two countries.

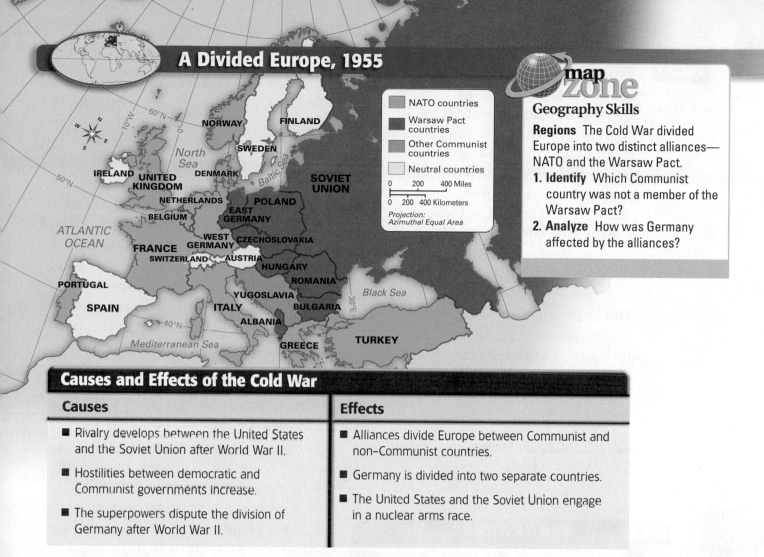

A Divided Europe, 1955

map zone

Geography Skills

Regions The Cold War divided Europe into two distinct alliances—NATO and the Warsaw Pact.
1. **Identify** Which Communist country was not a member of the Warsaw Pact?
2. **Analyze** How was Germany affected by the alliances?

Map legend:
- NATO countries
- Warsaw Pact countries
- Other Communist countries
- Neutral countries

0   200   400 Miles
0   200   400 Kilometers
Projection: Azimuthal Equal Area

Causes and Effects of the Cold War

Causes	Effects
■ Rivalry develops between the United States and the Soviet Union after World War II.	■ Alliances divide Europe between Communist and non-Communist countries.
■ Hostilities between democratic and Communist governments increase.	■ Germany is divided into two separate countries.
■ The superpowers dispute the division of Germany after World War II.	■ The United States and the Soviet Union engage in a nuclear arms race.

A Divided Europe

The Cold War divided Europe into non-Communist and Communist countries. Most of Western Europe supported democracy and the United States. Much of Eastern Europe practiced Soviet-style communism. British prime minister Winston Churchill described the split that existed in Europe:

" …an iron curtain has descended across the Continent. Behind that line lie all the capitals of the ancient states of Central and Eastern Europe. …all are subject…not only to Soviet influence but to…control from Moscow. "

—from Winston Churchill's 1946 speech at Westminster College in Fulton, Missouri

Within this divided Europe was a divided Germany. After World War II, the Allies had separated Germany into four zones. By 1948 the Western Allies were ready to reunite their zones. However, the Soviet government feared the threat that a united Germany might pose. The next year, the Western zones were joined to form the Federal Republic of Germany, or West Germany. The Soviets helped to establish the German Democratic Republic, or East Germany. The city of Berlin, located within East Germany, was itself divided into East and West. In 1961 Communist leaders built the Berlin Wall to prevent any East Germans from fleeing to the West.

New alliances divided Europe even further. In 1949 the United States joined with several Western nations to create a powerful new alliance known as NATO, or the North Atlantic Treaty Organization.

THE IMPACT
TODAY

NATO is still a powerful alliance today with 26 member nations in Europe and North America.

The members of NATO agreed to protect each other if attacked. In response, the Soviet Union formed its own alliance, the Warsaw Pact. Most Eastern European countries joined the Warsaw Pact. The two alliances used the threat of nuclear war to defend themselves. By the 1960s the United States, the Soviet Union, Britain, and France all had nuclear weapons.

The postwar division of Europe into East and West had a lasting effect on both sides. With U.S. assistance, many Western countries experienced economic growth. The economies of Communist Eastern Europe, however, failed to develop. Due to their lack of a market economy and strong industries, they suffered many shortages. They often lacked enough food, clothing, and automobiles to meet demand.

READING CHECK Summarizing How did the Cold War affect Europe?

BIOGRAPHY

Mikhail Gorbachev
(1931–   )

Mikhail Gorbachev was a key figure in bringing the Cold War to an end. In 1985 Communist officials appointed Gorbachev the leader of the Soviet Union. He quickly enacted reforms to modernize his country. He expanded basic freedoms, such as freedom of speech and freedom of the press. His democratic reforms helped bring an end to communism in the Soviet Union. In 1990 Mikhail Gorbachev won the Nobel Peace Prize for his efforts to end the Cold War and promote peace.

Evaluating Do you think Gorbachev was a popular ruler? Why or why not?

The End of the Cold War

In the late 1980s tensions between East and West finally came to an end. The collapse of communism and the end of the Cold War brought great changes to Europe.

Triumph of Democracy

During the Cold War the United States and the Soviet Union competed against each other in an arms race. An **arms race** is a competition between countries to build superior weapons. Each country tried to create more-advanced weapons and to have more nuclear missiles than the other. This arms race was incredibly expensive. The high cost of the arms race eventually damaged the Soviet economy.

By the 1980s the Soviet economy was in serious trouble. Soviet leader Mikhail Gorbachev (GAWR-buh-chawf) hoped to solve the many problems his country faced. He reduced government control of the economy and introduced democratic elections. He improved relations with the United States. Along with U.S. president Ronald Reagan, Gorbachev took steps to slow the arms race.

In part because of these new policies, reform movements soon spread. Beginning in 1989, democratic movements swept through the East. For example, Poland and Czechoslovakia threw off Communist rule. Joyful Germans tore down the Berlin Wall that separated East and West. Several Soviet republics began to demand their independence. Finally, in December 1991 the Soviet Union broke apart.

Changes in Eastern Europe

The end of the Cold War brought many changes to Eastern Europe. These changes resulted from Germany's reunification, the creation of new countries, and rising ethnic tensions in southeastern Europe.

The Fall of Communism

Reforms in the Soviet Union in the 1980s encouraged support for democracy throughout Eastern Europe.

ANALYZING VISUALS What role did the people play in communism's collapse?

Fall of the Berlin Wall East and West Germans celebrate the fall of the Berlin Wall.

Democracy in Czechoslovakia
In 1989 pro-democracy demonstrations swept Czechoslovakia. Rallies like this one led to the collapse of Czechoslovakia's Communist government.

The reunification of East and West Germany was one of many changes in Eastern Europe that marked the end of the Cold War. After the fall of the Berlin Wall in 1989, thousands of East Germans began demanding change. In early 1990 the Communist government crumbled. A few months later, the governments of East and West Germany agreed to reunite. After 45 years of division, Germany was reunited.

Other important changes occurred in Eastern Europe after the Cold War. The breakup of the Soviet Union created more than a dozen independent nations. The Russian Federation is the largest and most powerful of these new countries. Ukraine, Lithuania, Belarus, and others also emerged from the former Soviet Union.

Ethnic conflicts have also transformed Eastern Europe since the end of the Cold War. For example, tensions between ethnic groups in Czechoslovakia and Yugoslavia led to the breakup of both countries.

In Czechoslovakia, ethnic tensions divided the country. Disputes between the country's two main ethnic groups emerged in the early 1990s. Both the Czechs and the Slovaks **advocated** separate governments. In January 1993 Czechoslovakia peacefully divided into two countries—the Czech Republic and Slovakia.

While ethnic problems in the former Czechoslovakia were peaceful, ethnic tension in Yugoslavia triggered violence. After the collapse of communism, several Yugoslav republics declared their independence. Different ethnic groups fought each other for control of territory. Yugoslavia's civil wars resulted in years of fighting and thousands of deaths. By 1994 Yugoslavia had split into five countries—Bosnia and Herzegovina, Croatia, Macedonia, Serbia and Montenegro, and Slovenia.

ACADEMIC VOCABULARY
advocate
to plead in favor of

READING CHECK **Drawing Conclusions** How did the end of the Cold War affect Europe?

Country	Year Admitted	Monetary Unit	Representatives in the European Parliament
Austria	1995	Euro	17
Belgium	1952	Euro	22
Bulgaria	2007	Lev	17
Cyprus	2004	Pound	6
Czech Republic	2004	Koruna	22
Denmark	1973	Krone	13
Estonia	2004	Kroon	6
Finland	1995	Euro	13
France	1952	Euro	72
Germany	1952	Euro	99
Greece	1979	Euro	22
Hungary	2004	Forint	22
Ireland	1973	Euro	12
Italy	1952	Euro	72
Latvia	2004	Lats	8
Lithuania	2004	Litas	12
Luxembourg	1952	Euro	6
Malta	2004	Lira	5
The Netherlands	1952	Euro	25
Poland	2004	Zloty	50
Portugal	1986	Euro	22
Romania	2007	Leu	33
Slovakia	2004	Koruna	13
Slovenia	2004	Euro	7
Spain	1986	Euro	50
Sweden	1995	Krona	18
United Kingdom	1973	Pound	72

Drawing Conclusions What are the most powerful countries in the European Parliament?

hmhsocialstudies.com

European Cooperation

Many changes shaped postwar Europe. One of the most important of those changes was the creation of an organization that now joins together most of the countries of Europe.

A European Community

Two world wars tore Europe apart in the 1900s. After World War II many of Europe's leaders began to look for ways to prevent another deadly war. Some people believed that creating a feeling of community in Europe would make countries less likely to go to war. Leaders like Great Britain's Winston Churchill believed the countries of Europe should cooperate rather than compete. They believed strong economic and political ties were the key.

Six countries—Belgium, France, Italy, Luxembourg, the Netherlands, and West Germany—took the first steps toward European unity. In the early 1950s these six countries joined to create a united economic community. The organization's goal was to form a **common market**, a group of nations that cooperates to make trade among members easier. This European common market, created in 1957, made trade easier among member countries. Over time, other nations joined. Europeans had begun to create a new sense of unity.

The European Union

Since its beginning in the 1950s, many new nations have become members of this European community, now known as the European Union. The **European Union (EU)** is an organization that promotes political and economic cooperation in Europe. Today the European Union has more than 25 members. Together, they deal with a wide range of issues, including trade, the environment, and migration.

The European Union has executive, legislative, and judicial branches. The EU is run by a commission made up of one representative from each member nation. Two legislative groups, the Council of the European Union and the European Parliament, debate and make laws. Finally, the Court of Justice resolves disputes and enforces EU laws.

Through the European Union, the countries of Europe work together toward common economic goals. The EU helps its member nations compete with economic powers like the United States and Japan. In 1999 the EU introduced a common currency, the euro, which many member countries now use. The euro has made trade much easier.

The European Union has helped unify Europe. In recent years many countries from Eastern Europe have joined the EU. Other countries hope to join in the future. Despite difficulties, EU leaders hope to continue their goal to bring the nations of Europe closer together.

READING CHECK Finding Main Ideas How has cooperation in Europe affected the region?

In 2005 French and Dutch voters rejected a proposed constitution for the European Union. Here, voters in France demand that their vote be upheld.

SUMMARY AND PREVIEW In this section you learned how the European Union helped unify much of Europe after years of division during the Cold War. In the next chapter, you will learn about Southern Europe's physical geography and culture.

Section 3 Assessment

Reviewing Ideas, Terms, and Places

1. **a. Recall** What was the **Cold War**?
   b. Analyze Why was Europe divided during the Cold War?
2. **a. Identify** What new countries were formed after the end of the Cold War?
   b. Compare and Contrast How were ethnic tensions in Czechoslovakia and Yugoslavia similar and different?
   c. Evaluate Do you think the end of the Cold War helped or hurt the nations of Eastern Europe?
3. **a. Define** What is a **common market**?
   b. Make Inferences Why did some Europeans believe stronger economic and political ties could prevent war in Europe?

Critical Thinking

4. **Summarizing** Use your notes and the chart below to summarize the effect that each event had on the different regions of Europe. Write a sentence that summarizes the effect of each event.

	Cold War	End of Cold War	European Union
Western Europe			
Eastern Europe			

FOCUS ON WRITING

5. **Thinking about Europe since 1945** You are now in your mid-80s. How might events during and after the Cold War have affected your life?

Interpreting Political Cartoons

Learn

Political cartoons are drawings that express views on important political or social issues. The ability to interpret political cartoons will help you understand issues and people's attitudes about them.

Political cartoons use images and words to convey a message about a particular event, person, or issue in the news. Most political cartoons use symbols to represent those ideas. For example, political cartoonists often use Uncle Sam to represent the United States. They also use titles and captions to express their point of view.

Practice

Examine the cartoon on this page. Then, answer the following questions to interpret the message of the cartoon.

❶ Read any title, labels, or captions to identify the subject of the cartoon. What information does the caption for this cartoon give you? To what event does this cartoon refer?

❷ Identify the people and symbols in the cartoon. What person is pictured in this cartoon? What does the crushed hammer and sickle represent?

❸ What message is the cartoonist trying to convey?

Soviet leader Mikhail Gorbachev examines a broken hammer and sickle.

Apply

Use your new skills to interpret a recent political cartoon. Locate a political cartoon that deals with an issue or event that has been in the news recently. Then answer the questions below.

1. What issue or event does the cartoon address?

2. What people or symbols are represented in the cartoon?

3. What point is the cartoon attempting to make?

Chapter Review

Geography's Impact
video series
Review the video to answer the closing question:
Why do you think the creation of the European Union was important to many Europeans?

Visual Summary

Use the visual summary below to help you review the main ideas of the chapter.

QUICK FACTS

World War I introduced many changes to Europe, including a new type of fighting called trench warfare.

The Allied and Axis powers faced off in World War II, the deadliest war in the world's history.

After years of division, the end of the Cold War finally reunited the nations of Europe.

Reviewing Vocabulary, Terms, and Places

Match the words or names with their definitions or descriptions.

1. arms race
2. Axis Powers
3. dictator
4. nationalism
5. strategy
6. trench warfare

a. a powerful ruler that exerts complete control and often rules by force

b. a style of fighting in which each side fights from deep ditches dug into the ground

c. a plan for fighting a battle or war

d. the alliance of Germany, Italy, and Japan in World War II

e. devotion and loyalty to one's country

f. a competition between countries for superior weapons

Comprehension and Critical Thinking

SECTION 1 *(Pages 80–84)*

7. **a. Recall** What causes led to the outbreak of World War I?

   b. Draw Conclusions How did the U.S. entry into World War I affect the war's outcome?

   c. Elaborate Why do you think World War I led to revolutions in some countries?

SECTION 2 *(Pages 86–91)*

8. **a. Identify** What two alliances fought in World War II? What countries belonged to each?

   b. Compare In what ways were Joseph Stalin, Benito Mussolini, and Adolf Hitler similar?

   c. Elaborate In your opinion, how were the Allies able to win World War II?

SECTION 3 *(Pages 92–97)*

9. **a. Identify** Into what alliances was Europe divided during the Cold War?

b. Analyze How did the Cold War come to an end?

c. Predict Do you think that the European Union will hurt or help Europe? Explain.

Using the Internet

10. Activity: Creating a Poster The D-Day invasion of Normandy was crucial to the Allies' victory in World War II. Through your online textbook, find out more about D-Day. Then create a poster that celebrates the anniversary of the D-Day invasion. Be sure to include a short statement explaining why the invasion was important and images that grab your audience's attention.

↗ **hmhsocialstudies.com**

Social Studies Skills

Interpreting Political Cartoons *Examine the political cartoon below, then answer the questions that follow.*

11. What event does the cartoon depict?

12. What symbols does the cartoon use? To what do those symbols refer?

13. What point is the artist trying to make?

Map Activity

14. Europe, 1989 On a separate sheet of paper, match the letters on the map with their correct labels.

Berlin	Poland	West Germany
London	Moscow	Yugoslavia
Paris		

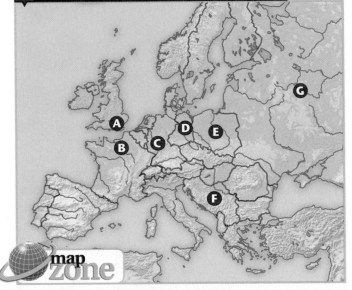

↗ **hmhsocialstudies.com** **INTERACTIVE MAP**

FOCUS ON READING AND WRITING

Using Context Clues—Contrast *Use context clues to determine the meaning of the underlined words in the sentences below.*

15. During World War II, people who aided Jews were often <u>detained</u> rather than set free.

16. Many celebrations at the end of the Cold War were <u>frenzied</u>, not calm and orderly.

17. European dictators who rose to power were <u>ruthless</u> as opposed to kind.

Writing a Diary Entry Use your notes and the directions below to write a diary entry.

18. Review your notes to organize the diary of your imaginary person. Divide your diary into three periods—World War I, World War II, and 1945–today. Describe the events your imaginary person experienced from his or her point of view. Remember to describe his or her thoughts and feelings about each event.

Standardized Test Prep

DIRECTIONS: Read questions 1 through 7 and write the letter of the best response. Question 8 will require a brief essay.

1 Which world leader was *most* involved in the end of the Cold War?

A Francis Ferdinand

B Joseph Stalin

C Mikhail Gorbachev

D Winston Churchill

2 The fall of the Berlin Wall is an important symbol of

A the Communist revolution in Russia.

B the Allied victory in World War II.

C the collapse of communism in Europe.

D the formation of the European Union.

3 Which of the following was a result of World War II?

A The United Nations was formed.

B Adolf Hitler was charged with war crimes.

C A Communist revolution took place in Russia.

D The U.S. economy collapsed.

4 Which of the following was a key cause of World War I?

A The United Nations failed to negotiate a peaceful settlement between East and West.

B Germany and Italy launched invasions.

C Competition between the countries of Europe created fierce rivalries.

D Countries feared that communism would spread throughout Europe.

5 Who was the first leader of Communist Russia?

A Benito Mussolini

B Joseph Stalin

C Mikhail Gorbachev

D Vladimir Lenin

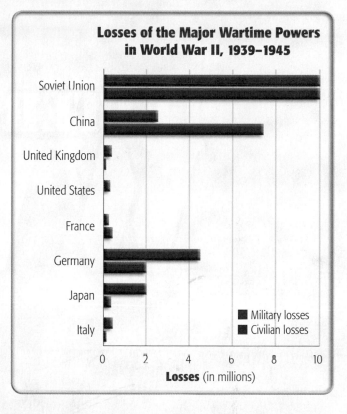

Losses of the Major Wartime Powers in World War II, 1939–1945

Losses (in millions)

- Military losses
- Civilian losses

6 Based on the information in the chart above, which Allied power lost the *fewest* civilians in World War II?

A France

B United Kingdom

C Italy

D United States

7 Ethnic tensions at the end of the Cold War divided which of the following countries?

A France

B Germany

C United States

D Yugoslavia

8 **Extended Response** Tensions after World War II led to the Cold War between the United States and the Soviet Union. Use the map in Section 3 to explain how the Cold War affected Europe.

Dear home: LETTERS FROM WWI

When U.S. troops arrived in Europe in 1917 to fight in World War I, the war had been dragging on for nearly three years. The American soldiers suddenly found themselves in the midst of chaos. Each day, they faced the threats of machine gun fire, poison gas, and aerial attacks. Still, the arrival of American reinforcements had sparked a new zeal among the Allies, who believed the new forces could finally turn the tide in their favor. The letters soldiers wrote to their families back home reveal the many emotions they felt on the battlefield: confusion about their surroundings, fear for their own safety, concern for friends and loved ones, and hope that the war would soon be over.

Explore World War I online through the eyes of the soldiers who fought in it. You can find a wealth of information, video clips, primary sources, activities, and more at ↗ hmhsocialstudies.com.

"I have been on every front in France. You cant imagine how torn up this country really is. Every where there are wire entanglements and trenches and dugouts. Even out of the war zone there are entanglements and dugouts to protect the civilians from air raids."

-Corp. Albert Smith, U.S. soldier

Letter from France
Read the document to learn about one soldier's observations of wartime life.

Over There
Watch the video to learn about the experiences of American soldiers on the way to Europe and upon their arrival.

War on the Western Front
Watch the video to hear one soldier's vivid account of battle and its aftermath.

Surrender!
Watch the video to experience soldiers' reactions to the news that the war was finally over.

Southern Europe

Essential Question How has climate influenced the land and people of Southern Europe?

What You Will Learn...

In this chapter you will learn about four large countries located in Southern Europe—Greece, Italy, Spain, and Portugal. You will learn about the countries' long histories and the many groups that have influenced their societies. Finally, you will see how the countries' histories still affect their cultures and governments.

FOCUS ON READING AND WRITING

Asking Questions As you read a text, it can be helpful to ask yourself questions about what you are reading to be sure you understand it. One set of questions that you can use to test your understanding of a passage is the five Ws—who, what, when, where, and why. **See the lesson, Asking Questions, on page 223.**

Writing a News Report You are a newspaper reporter on special assignment in Southern Europe. Your editor has told you that many readers know about Southern Europe's past but not about the region today. After you read this chapter, you will write a news report about an imaginary event in a Southern European country today.

Geography Mountains cover large areas of Southern Europe. The Dolomites, shown here, are in northern Italy.

GERMANY

FRANCE

SWITZERLAND

AUSTRIA

Milan

Venice

Po River

Genoa

ITALY

SAN MARINO

Florence

ANDORRA

Tiber River

Adriatic Sea

Barcelona

VATICAN CITY

Rome

Balearic Islands

Naples

Sardinia

Thessaloniki

Tyrrhenian Sea

GREECE

TURKEY

Aegean Sea

Ionian Sea

Palermo

Athens

ALGERIA

Sicily

MALTA

Crete

TUNISIA

Mediterranean Sea

HISTORY Humanism Triggers the Renaissance

↗ hmhsocialstudies.com **VIDEO**

map zone Geography Skills

Place Southern Europe occupies three large peninsulas and thousands of small islands in the Mediterranean Sea.
1. **Identify** What is the capital of Greece?
2. **Interpret** Why is Southern Europe also called Mediterranean Europe?

History Greece was the home of Europe's first great civilization. The ruins in Delphi are more than 2,300 years old.

Culture Bullfights are popular events in parts of Spain. Bullfighters, called matadors, are honored members of society.

103

Physical Geography

If YOU lived there...

You are in a busy fish market in a small town on the coast of Italy, near the Mediterranean Sea. It is early morning. Colorful fishing boats have just pulled into shore with their catch of fresh fish and seafood. They unload their nets of slippery octopus and wriggling shrimp. Others bring silvery sea bass. You are looking forward to lunch—perhaps a tasty fish soup or pasta dish.

How does the Mediterranean affect your life?

BUILDING BACKGROUND The Mediterranean Sea has shaped the geography, climate, and culture of Southern Europe. All of these countries have long coastlines, with good harbors and beautiful beaches. Because much of the interior is rugged and mountainous, the sea has also been a highway for trade and travel.

Physical Features

The continent of Europe has often been called a peninsula of peninsulas. Why do you think this is so? Look at the map of Europe in this book's Atlas to find out. Notice how Europe juts out from Asia like one big peninsula. Also, notice how smaller peninsulas extend into the many bodies of water that surround the continent.

Look at the map of Europe again. Do you see the three large peninsulas that extend south from Europe? From west to east, these are the Iberian Peninsula, the Italian Peninsula, and the Balkan Peninsula. Together with some large islands, they form the region of Southern Europe.

Southern Europe is also known as Mediterranean Europe. All of the countries of Southern Europe have long coastlines on the **Mediterranean Sea**. In addition to this common location on the Mediterranean, the countries of Southern Europe share many common physical features.

What You Will Learn...

Main Ideas

1. Southern Europe's physical features include rugged mountains and narrow coastal plains.
2. The region's climate and resources support such industries as agriculture, fishing, and tourism.

The Big Idea

The peninsulas of Southern Europe have rocky terrains and sunny, mild climates.

Key Terms and Places

Mediterranean Sea, *p. 104*
Pyrenees, *p. 105*
Apennines, *p. 105*
Alps, *p. 105*
Mediterranean climate, *p. 106*

hmhsocialstudies.com
TAKING NOTES

Use the graphic organizer online to take notes on the physical geography of Southern Europe.

Landforms

The three peninsulas of Southern Europe are largely covered with rugged mountains. In Greece, for example, about three-fourths of the land is mountainous. Because much of the land is so rugged, farming and travel in Southern Europe can be a challenge.

The mountains of Southern Europe form several large ranges. On the Iberian Peninsula, the **Pyrenees** (PIR-uh-neez) form a boundary between Spain and France to the north. Italy has two major ranges. The **Apennines** (A-puh-nynz) run along the whole peninsula, and the **Alps**—Europe's highest mountains—are in the north. The Pindus Mountains cover much of Greece.

Southern Europe's mountains extend into the sea as well, where they rise above the water to form islands. The Aegean Sea east of Greece is home to more than 2,000 such islands. Southern Europe also has many larger islands formed by undersea mountains. These include Crete, which is south of Greece; Sicily, at the southern tip of Italy; and many others.

Not all of Southern Europe is rocky and mountainous, though. Some flat plains lie in the region. Most of these plains are along the coast and in the valleys of major rivers. It is here that most farming in Southern Europe takes place. It is also here that most of the region's people live.

FOCUS ON READING

As you read, ask yourself this question: Where are the Pyrenees?

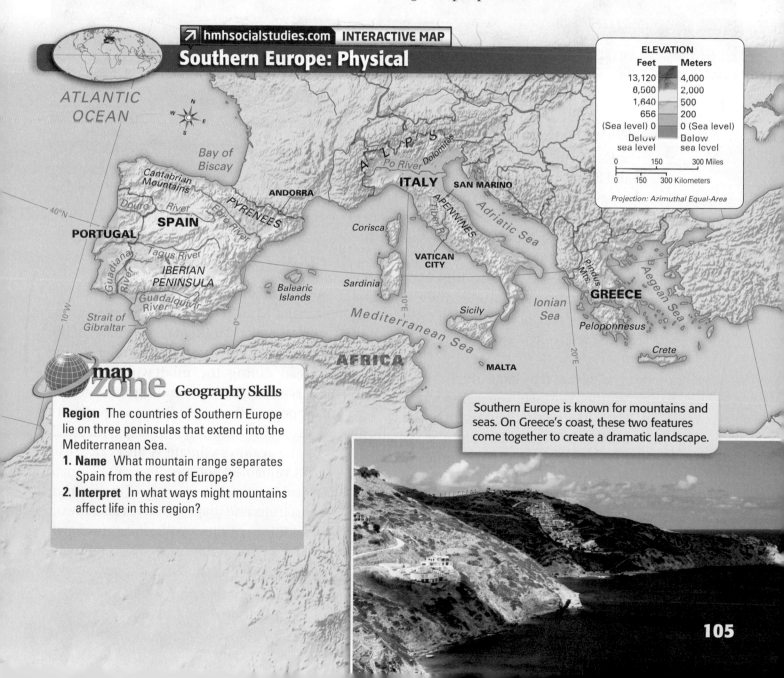

↗ hmhsocialstudies.com **INTERACTIVE MAP**

Southern Europe: Physical

ELEVATION

Feet		Meters
13,120		4,000
6,500		2,000
1,640		500
656		200
(Sea level) 0		0 (Sea level)
Below sea level		Below sea level

0   150   300 Miles
0   150   300 Kilometers

Projection: Azimuthal Equal-Area

ATLANTIC OCEAN

Bay of Biscay

Cantabrian Mountains

Douro River
Ebro River
PYRENEES
ANDORRA

40°N

SPAIN

PORTUGAL

Tagus River

IBERIAN PENINSULA

Guadiana River

Guadalquivir River

Strait of Gibraltar

Balearic Islands

Corsica

Sardinia

ALPS
Po River
Dolomites
ITALY
SAN MARINO
APENNINES
Tiber R.
Adriatic Sea

VATICAN CITY

Mediterranean Sea

Sicily

Ionian Sea

Pindus Mts.

GREECE

Aegean Sea

Peloponnesus

Crete

AFRICA

MALTA

map zone Geography Skills

Region The countries of Southern Europe lie on three peninsulas that extend into the Mediterranean Sea.

1. Name What mountain range separates Spain from the rest of Europe?

2. Interpret In what ways might mountains affect life in this region?

Southern Europe is known for mountains and seas. On Greece's coast, these two features come together to create a dramatic landscape.

Mediterranean Climate

Southern Europe is known for its Mediterranean climate, which features warm, dry summers and mild, wet winters. This climate affects nearly every aspect of life in the region.

1 Agriculture The climate of Southern Europe is ideal for growing many crops. Here, Portuguese farmers harvest grapes.

2 Tourism The region's mild and sunny climate draws millions of tourists to places like this beach in Ibiza, Spain.

Water Features

Since Southern Europe is mostly peninsulas and islands, water is central to the region's geography. No place in Southern Europe is very far from a major body of water. The largest of these bodies of water is the Mediterranean, but the Adriatic, Aegean, and Ionian seas are also important to the region. For many centuries, these seas have given the people of Southern Europe food and a relatively easy way to travel around the region.

Only a few large rivers run through Southern Europe. The region's longest river is the Tagus (TAY-guhs), which flows across the Iberian Peninsula. In northern Italy, the Po runs through one of Southern Europe's most fertile and densely populated areas. Other rivers run out of the mountains and into the many surrounding seas.

READING CHECK Finding Main Ideas What are the region's major features?

Climate and Resources

Southern Europe is famous for its pleasant climate. Most of the region enjoys warm, sunny days and mild nights for most of the year. Little rain falls in the summer, falling instead during the mild winter. In fact, the type of climate found across Southern Europe is called a **Mediterranean climate** because it is common in this region.

The region's climate is also one of its most valuable resources. The mild climate is ideal for growing a variety of crops, from citrus fruits and grapes to olives and wheat. In addition, millions of tourists are drawn to the region each year by its climate, beaches, and breathtaking scenery.

ITALY

3

GREECE

4

4 **Architecture** Climate also affects architecture in Southern Europe. Buildings, like these in Greece, are airy and made of light materials to reflect sunlight and heat.

ANALYSIS SKILL **ANALYZING VISUALS**

What are four ways in which the Mediterranean climate affects life in Southern Europe?

3 **Vegetation** This field in Tuscany, a region of Italy, shows the variety of plants that thrive in Southern Europe's climate.

The sea is also an important resource in Southern Europe. Many of the region's largest cities are ports, which ship goods all over the world. In addition, the nearby seas are full of fish and shellfish, which provide the basis for profitable fishing industries.

READING CHECK **Generalizing** How is a mild climate important to Southern Europe?

SUMMARY AND PREVIEW In this section you learned about the physical features of Southern Europe. In the next section you will learn how those features affect life in one country—Greece.

Section 1 Assessment

hmhsocialstudies.com
ONLINE QUIZ

Reviewing Ideas, Terms, and Places

1. **a. Recall** Which three peninsulas are in Southern Europe?
   b. Explain Why is the sea important to Southern Europe?
   c. Elaborate Why do you think most people in Southern Europe live on coastal plains or in river valleys?
2. **a. Describe** What is the **Mediterranean climate** like?
   b. Generalize How is climate an important resource for the region?

Critical Thinking

3. **Finding Main Ideas**
   Draw a diagram like the one shown here.

   Landforms   Climate

   In the left oval, use your notes to explain how landforms affect life in Southern Europe. In the right oval, explain how climate affects life in the region.

FOCUS ON WRITING

4. **Describing the Setting** Your news report will be about an imaginary event someplace in Southern Europe. That event might happen on a beach, in the mountains, or on a farm. Write some ideas in your notebook.

Social Studies Skills

Reading a Climate Map

Learn

Geographers use many different types of maps to study a region. One type that can be very useful is a climate map. Because climate affects so many aspects of people's lives, it is important to know which climates are found in a region.

Practice

Use the climate map of Europe below to answer the following questions.

1 What does orange mean on this map?

2 What city has a highland climate?

3 What is the dominant climate in the countries of Southern Europe?

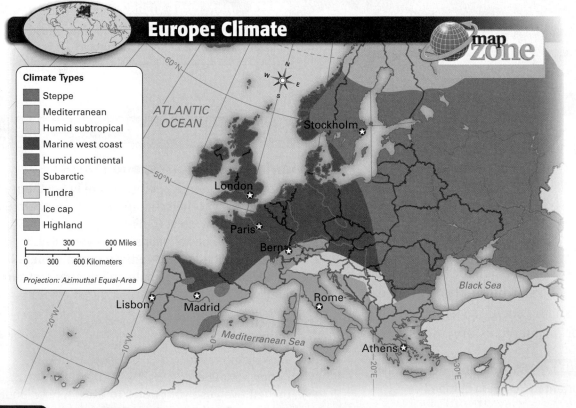

Europe: Climate

map zone

Climate Types
- Steppe
- Mediterranean
- Humid subtropical
- Marine west coast
- Humid continental
- Subarctic
- Tundra
- Ice cap
- Highland

0   300   600 Miles
0   300   600 Kilometers

Projection: Azimuthal Equal-Area

ATLANTIC OCEAN

Stockholm

London

Paris

Bern

Lisbon   Madrid

Rome

Black Sea

Mediterranean Sea

Athens

Apply

Choose one of the cities shown on the map above. Imagine that you are planning a trip to that city and need to know what the climate is like so you can prepare. Use the map to identify the type of climate found in your chosen city. Then use the library or the Internet to find out more about that type of climate. Write a short description of the climate and how you could prepare for it.

Greece

If YOU lived there...

You live in a small town on one of the many Greek islands. White houses perch on steep streets leading down to the sea. Many tourists come here by boat after visiting the busy capital city of Athens. They tell you about the beautiful ancient buildings they saw there. But your island has ancient statues and temple sites too. Still, some of your friends talk about moving to the city.

What might make people move to the city?

> **BUILDING BACKGROUND** In recent years, many people have moved out of Greece's small towns and villages into cities, especially Athens. Now the capital of Greece, Athens is an ancient city. It was home to one of Europe's greatest civilizations, one whose influence is still felt today all around the world.

History

Greece is a country steeped in history. Home to one of the world's oldest civilizations, it has been called the birthplace of Western culture. Even today, remnants of ancient Greece can be found all over the country, and ideas from ancient thinkers continue to affect people's lives today.

Ancient Greece

Theater. Philosophy. Democracy. These are just a few of the ideas that the modern world owes to ancient Greece. The Greeks were pioneers in many fields, and their contributions still affect how we live and think.

In art, the Greeks created lifelike paintings and statues that served as examples for later artists to imitate. In architecture, they built stately temples of marble that continue to inspire architects around the world.

An ancient Greek jar

What You Will Learn...

Main Ideas
1. Early in its history, Greece was the home of a great civilization, but it was later ruled by foreign powers.
2. The Greek language, the Orthodox Church, and varied customs have helped shape Greece's culture.
3. In Greece today, many people are looking for new economic opportunities.

The Big Idea

The home of one of the Western world's oldest civilizations, Greece is trying to reclaim its place as a leading country in Europe.

Key Terms and Places
Orthodox Church, *p. 111*
Athens, *p. 112*

hmhsocialstudies.com
TAKING NOTES

Use the graphic organizer online to take notes on Greek history and culture.

Proportion

The ancient Greeks were great admirers of mathematics. They thought math could be used in many areas of their lives. For example, they used it to design temples and other buildings.

Greek builders believed in a concept called the Golden Mean. This concept said that the height of a building should be a particular fraction of the building's width. If the building were too tall, they thought it would look flimsy. If it were too wide, it would look squat and ugly. As a result, these builders were very careful in planning their buildings. The Parthenon, the temple pictured below, was built using the Golden Mean. Many consider it to be the greatest of all Greek temples.

Generalizing How did mathematical ideas influence ancient Greek architecture?

They invented new forms of literature, including history and drama, and made advances in geometry and other branches of math that we still study. In philosophy, they created a system of reasoning that is the foundation for modern science. In government, they created democracy, which inspired the government embraced by most people around the world today.

No ancient civilization lasted forever, though. In the 300s BC Greece became a part of Alexander the Great's empire, which also included Egypt and much of Southwest Asia. Under Alexander, Greek culture spread throughout his empire.

The Romans and the Turks

Alexander's empire did not last very long. When it broke up, Greece became part of another empire, the Roman Empire. For about 300 years, the Greeks lived under Roman rule.

After about AD 400 the Roman Empire was divided into two parts. Greece became part of the Eastern, or Byzantine, Empire. The rulers of the Byzantine Empire admired Greek culture and encouraged people to adopt the Greek language and customs. They also encouraged people to adopt their religion, Christianity.

Greece was part of the Byzantine Empire for about 1,000 years. In the 1300s and 1400s, however, Greece was taken over by the Ottoman Turks from central Asia. The Turks were Muslim, but they allowed the people of Greece to remain Christian. Some elements of Greek culture, though, began to fade. For example, many people began speaking Turkish instead of Greek.

Independent Greece

Many Greeks were not happy under Turkish rule. They wanted to be free of foreign influences. In the early 1800s, they rose up against the Turks. The rebellion seemed likely to fail, but the Greeks received help from other European countries and drove the Turks out. After the rebellion, Greece became a monarchy.

Greece's government has changed many times since independence. The country's first kings took steps toward restoring democracy, but for most of the 1900s the nation experienced instability. A military dictatorship ruled from 1967 to 1974. More recently, democracy has once again taken root in the country where it was born nearly 2,500 years ago.

READING CHECK **Sequencing** What groups have ruled Greece throughout history?

Culture

Over the course of its history, many factors have combined to shape Greece's culture. These factors include the Greek language, Christianity, and customs adopted from the many groups who have ruled Greece.

Language and Religion

The people of Greece today speak a form of the same language their ancestors spoke long ago. In fact, Greek is one of the oldest languages still spoken in Europe today. The language has changed greatly over time, but it was never lost.

Although the Greeks maintained their language, their ancient religions have long since disappeared. Today nearly everyone in Greece belongs to the **Orthodox Church**, a branch of Christianity that dates to the Byzantine Empire. Religion is important to the Greeks, and holidays such as Easter are popular times for celebration.

Customs

Greek customs reflect the country's long history and its physical geography. Greek food, for example, is influenced both by products native to Greece and by groups who have ruled Greece over time.

Ingredients such as lamb, olives, and vegetables are easily available in Greece because they grow well there. As a result, the Greeks use lots of these ingredients in their cooking. Greek cuisine was later enhanced with ideas borrowed from other people. From the Turks, the Greeks learned to cook with yogurt and honey, and from the Italians they learned about pasta.

Greek meals are often eaten at family gatherings. For centuries, family has been central to Greek culture. Even as Greece is becoming more modernized, the family has remained the cornerstone of society.

READING CHECK **Summarizing** What are two dominant elements of Greek culture?

Easter in Greece

Easter is one of the most sacred days of the year for Orthodox Christians. All over Greece, people celebrate Easter with festivals, feasts, and special rituals.

ANALYZING VISUALS What evidence in this photo suggests that Easter is a major celebration?

The priests carry containers of holy water. Later, they will sprinkle this holy water on crowds as part of a blessing.

Priests wear richly decorated robes as part of their Easter celebration.

Many Easter ceremonies are led by an archbishop, a high-ranking official in the Orthodox Church.

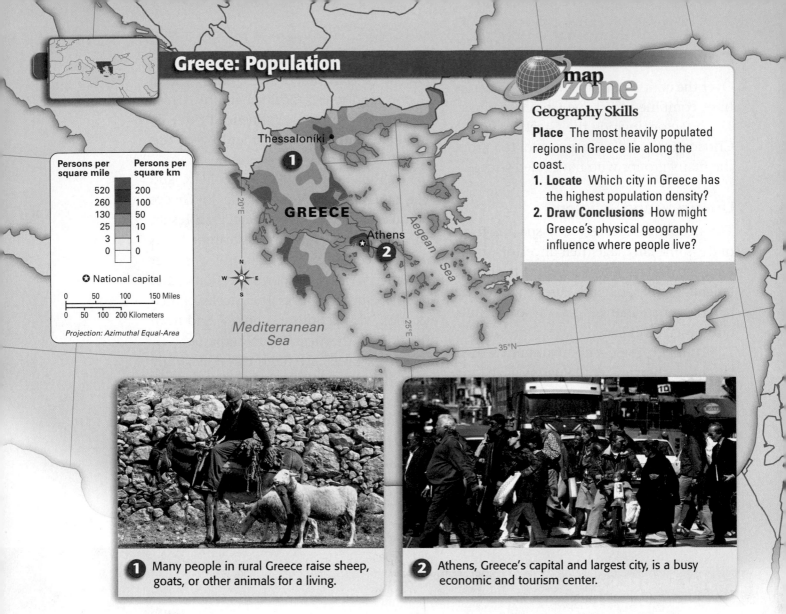

map Zone

Geography Skills

Place The most heavily populated regions in Greece lie along the coast.

1. **Locate** Which city in Greece has the highest population density?
2. **Draw Conclusions** How might Greece's physical geography influence where people live?

Persons per square mile	Persons per square km
520	200
260	100
130	50
25	10
3	1
0	0

⊛ National capital

0   50   100   150 Miles
0   50   100   200 Kilometers

Projection: Azimuthal Equal-Area

Thessaloníki

GREECE

Athens

Aegean Sea

Mediterranean Sea

① Many people in rural Greece raise sheep, goats, or other animals for a living.

② Athens, Greece's capital and largest city, is a busy economic and tourism center.

Greece Today

When many people think of Greece now, they think about the country's history. In fact, Greece's past often overshadows its present. Today, though, Greece is a largely urbanized society with a diverse economy.

Urban and Rural Greece

About three-fifths of all people in Greece today live in cities. Of these cities, **Athens**—the nation's capital—is by far the largest. In fact, almost one-third of the country's entire population lives in or around the city of Athens.

Athens is a huge city where old and new mix. Modern skyscrapers rise high above the ancient ruins of Greek temples. Most of the country's industry is centered there. However, this industry has resulted in air pollution, which damages the ancient ruins and causes health problems.

Outside of the city, Greek life is very different. People in rural areas still live largely as people have lived for centuries. Many live in isolated mountain villages, where they grow crops and raise sheep and goats. Village life often centers around the village square. People meet there to discuss local events and make decisions.

Greece's Economy

Although Greece has experienced rapid economic growth, it lags behind most other European nations. Greece's economy has been hurt by a huge level of government debt. Greece has few mineral resources, and only about one-fifth of its land can be farmed. The rest of the land is too rugged.

One industry in which Greece excels is shipping. Greece has one of the largest shipping fleets in the world. Greek ships can be found in ports all around the world, loaded with cargo from countries in Europe and other parts of the world.

Another profitable industry in Greece is tourism. Millions of people from around the world visit every year. Some are drawn to ancient ruins in Athens and other parts of the country. Others prefer the sunny, sandy beaches of Greece's many islands. The Greek government actively promotes this tourism, and more people visit the country every year. Despite the boost that tourism provides, the country's debt crisis has slowed the economy.

READING CHECK Finding Main Ideas What are the most important industries in Greece?

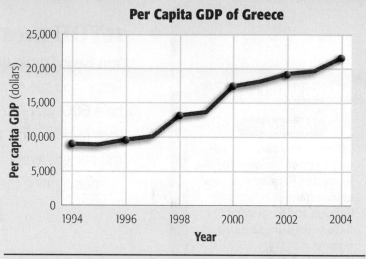

Per Capita GDP of Greece

Interpreting Graphs What was Greece's per capita GDP in 1994? What was it in 2004?

↗ **hmhsocialstudies.com**

SUMMARY AND PREVIEW In this section you learned about Greece, a country with a long and varied history that still shapes its culture and economy today. In the next section you will learn about Italy, another country in the region that has been shaped by history.

Section 2 Assessment

↗ **hmhsocialstudies.com**
ONLINE QUIZ

Reviewing Ideas, Terms, and Places

1. **a. Identify** What were two major achievements of the ancient Greeks?
   b. Sequence What steps did the Greeks take to gain their independence?
2. **a. Define** What is the **Orthodox Church**?
   b. Generalize What is one way in which Greece's history affects its culture today?
3. **a. Describe** What is life like in **Athens** today?
   b. Explain Why is manufacturing not a major industry in Greece?
   c. Evaluate Would you rather live in Athens or in rural Greece? Why?

Critical Thinking

4. **Categorizing** Draw a table like the one here. Use the table to organize your notes into columns about Greece's history, its culture, and Greece today.

Greece		
History	Culture	Today

FOCUS ON WRITING

5. **Introducing Greece** If you choose Greece for the site of your news report, what would be a good topic? The movement of people to the cities? An event at a historic site? Jot down your ideas.

Italy

What You Will Learn...

Main Ideas

1. Italian history can be divided into three periods: ancient Rome, the Renaissance, and unified Italy.
2. Religion and local traditions have helped shape Italy's culture.
3. Italy today has two distinct economic regions—northern Italy and southern Italy.

The Big Idea

Once the center of a huge empire, Italy grew to become a prosperous European country.

Key Terms and Places

pope, *p. 116*
Vatican City, *p. 116*
Sicily, *p. 117*
Naples, *p. 117*
Milan, *p. 117*
Rome, *p. 118*

hmhsocialstudies.com
TAKING NOTES

Use the graphic organizer online to take notes on Italian history, life, and culture.

If YOU lived there...

You live in Rome, the historic heart of Italy. Wherever you walk in Rome, you see reminders of the city's long and rich history. It may be a 600-year-old church or a 2,000-year-old market. One of your favorite spots to visit is the Colosseum. When you sit inside this ancient arena, you can imagine fierce gladiators and wild animals fighting there long ago.

How does history affect life in Italy?

BUILDING BACKGROUND Italian history continues to affect life in Italy today, but its influence extends far beyond that one country. All around the world, people owe their ideas about art, government, law, and language to Italy and its people. Many of these ideas are ancient, but even today Italians help shape the world's culture.

History

Greece may have been the birthplace of the first civilization in Europe, but Italy was the home of the continent's greatest empire. For centuries, Italy was the heart of one of the largest and most powerful states the world has ever seen. Even after that state collapsed, Italy remained a major influence on Europe and other parts of the world.

Ancient Rome

The great civilization that developed in Italy was Rome. Built in the 700s BC as a tiny village, Rome grew to control nearly all the land around the Mediterranean Sea. At the height of the Roman Empire, the Romans controlled an empire that stretched from Britain in the northwest to the Persian Gulf. It included most of Europe as well as parts of southwest Asia and northern Africa.

Roman influences in the world can still be seen today. The Romans' art, architecture, and literature are still admired. Their laws and political ideas have influenced the governments and legal systems of many countries. In addition, the Romans helped spread Christianity, one of the world's major religions.

The Renaissance

The Roman Empire collapsed in the AD 400s, largely due to weak leadership and invasions from outside. With no central government to unite them, Italy's cities formed their own states. Each had its own laws, its own government, and its own army. Wars between them were common.

As time passed, the cities of Italy became major centers of trade. Merchants from these cities traveled to far-off places like China to bring goods back to Europe.

Many merchants became very rich from this trade. With the money they made, these merchants sponsored artists and architects. Their support of the arts helped lead to the Renaissance, a period of great creativity in Europe. It lasted from about 1350 through the 1500s. During the Renaissance artists and writers—many of them Italian—created some of the world's greatest works of art and literature.

Unified Italy

Italy remained divided into small states until the mid-1800s. At that time, a rise in nationalism, or strong patriotic feelings for a country, led people across Italy to fight for unification. As a result of their efforts, Italy became a unified kingdom in 1861.

In the 1920s a new government came to power. Under Benito Mussolini, Italy became a dictatorship. That dictatorship was short-lived, however. Mussolini joined Hitler to fight other countries of Europe in World War II. In 1945 Italy was defeated.

After World War II, Italy became a democracy. Since that time, power has rested in an elected Parliament and prime minister. Also since the end of the war, Italy has developed one of the strongest economies in Europe.

READING CHECK **Summarizing** What are some key periods in the history of Italy?

Italian History

The history of Italy stretches back nearly 3,000 years. This long span includes several key periods.

Ancient Rome

- According to legend, the city of Rome was built in the 700s BC.
- The Romans created a huge empire. At its height, the empire included parts of Europe, Southwest Asia, and northern Africa.
- Roman art, architecture, literature, and law still influence people today.
- Christianity arose and spread in the Roman Empire.

Roman statue

The Renaissance

- The Renaissance was a period of great advances in art, architecture, and literature.
- The Renaissance began in the 1300s in cities like Florence.
- From Italy, the Renaissance spread to other parts of Europe.
- Some of the world's greatest works of art were created at this time.

Leonardo da Vinci's *Mona Lisa*

Unified Italy

- Since the Middle Ages, Italy had been divided into small states.
- In the mid-1800s, increased feelings of nationalism led people across Italy to fight for unification.
- The fight for unification was led by Giuseppe Garibaldi.
- Italy was officially unified in 1861.

Giuseppe Garibaldi

Culture

For centuries, people around the world have admired and borrowed from Italian culture. Italy's culture has been shaped by many factors. Among these factors are the Roman Catholic Church, local traditions, and regional geography.

Religion

Most people in Italy belong to the Roman Catholic Church. Historically, the church has been the single strongest influence on Italian culture. This influence is strong in part because the **pope**, the spiritual head of the Roman Catholic Church, lives on the Italian Peninsula. He resides in **Vatican City**, an independent state located within the city of Rome.

The lasting importance of the church can be seen in many ways in Italy. For example, the city of Rome alone is home to hundreds of Catholic churches from all periods of history. In addition, religious holidays and festivals are major events.

ACADEMIC VOCABULARY
contemporary
modern

Local Traditions

In addition to religion, local traditions have influenced Italian culture. Italian food, for example, varies widely from region to region. These variations are based on local preferences and products. All over Italy, people eat many of the same foods—olives, tomatoes, rice, pasta. However, the ways in which people prepare this food differ. In the south, for example, people often serve pasta with tomato sauces. In the north, creamy sauces are much more common.

Other traditions reflect Italy's past. For example, Italy has always been known as a center of the arts. The people of Italy have long been trendsetters, shaping styles that are later adopted by other people. As a result, the Italians are leaders in many **contemporary** art forms. For example, Italy has produced some of the world's greatest painters, sculptors, authors, composers, fashion designers, and filmmakers.

READING CHECK **Finding Main Ideas** What are two major influences on Italian culture?

Major Cities of Italy

Milan, Rome, and Naples are the three largest cities in Italy. Because of their varied histories and locations, each city has a distinct landscape and culture.

ANALYZING VISUALS Which city would you most like to visit?

ITALY

Milan
Venice
Florence
Rome
Naples

Milan Milan, the largest city in Italy, is a global fashion capital. The clothes created there influence fashion designers around the world.

Italy Today

A shared language, the Roman Catholic Church, and strong family ties help bind Italians together. At the same time, though, major differences exist in the northern and southern parts of the country.

Southern Italy

Southern Italy is the country's poorer half. Its economy has less industry than the north and depends heavily on agriculture. Farming is especially important in **Sicily**, an island at the peninsula's tip. Tourism is also vital to the south's economy. Among the region's attractions are its dazzling beaches and ancient Roman ruins.

In recent decades, Italy's government has tried to promote industry in the south. It has offered **incentives**, such as lower taxes, to private companies that will build factories there. Many of these government efforts center on the city of **Naples**, a busy port and the largest city in southern Italy. Thanks to government programs, Naples is now also an industrial center.

Northern Italy

In contrast to southern Italy, the northern part of the country has a strong economy. Northern Italy includes the country's most fertile farmlands, its major trade centers, and its most popular tourist destinations.

The Po River valley in northern Italy has the country's most productive farmland. For decades, the Po valley has been called the breadbasket of Italy because most of the country's crops are grown there. Despite its fertile soils, farmers cannot grow enough to support Italy's population. Italy has to import much of its food.

The north is also home to Italy's major industrial centers. Busy factories in such cities as Turin and Genoa make appliances, automobiles, and other goods for export. **Milan** is also a major industrial center as well as a worldwide center for fashion design. The location of these cities near central Europe helps companies sell their goods to foreign customers. Railroads, highways, and tunnels make the shipment of goods through the Alps easy.

ACADEMIC VOCABULARY

incentive something that leads people to follow a certain course of action

Rome Rome, the capital of Italy, is in the central part of the country. A major center of banking and industry, Rome is also one of the world's most popular tourist sites.

Naples Naples is the most important city in southern Italy. Less glamorous than many northern cities, it is a port and manufacturing center.

Satellite View

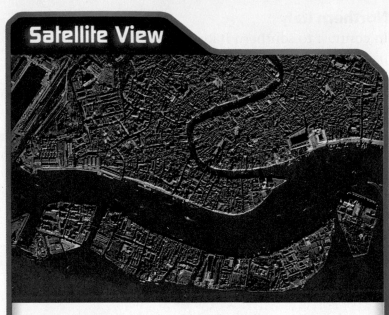

Venice

Venice, in northeastern Italy, is one of the country's most visited tourist attractions. Look at the image of Venice above, taken by an orbiting satellite. Does it look like other cities you have seen? What may not be obvious is that the paths that wind their way through the city are not roads, but canals. In fact, Venice has very few roads. This is because the city was built on islands—118 of them! People move about the city on boats that navigate along the canals. Every year, millions of tourists travel to Venice to see the sights as they are rowed along the scenic waterways.

Contrasting How is Venice unlike other cities you have studied?

Tens of millions of tourists visit the cities of northern Italy every year. They are drawn by the cities' rich histories and unique cultural features. Florence, for example, is a center of Italian art and culture. It was there that the Renaissance began in the 1300s. To the west of Florence is Pisa, famous for its Leaning Tower—the bell tower of the city's church. On the coast of the Adriatic Sea lies the city of Venice. Tourists are lured there by the romantic canals that serve as roads through the city.

Nestled in the center of the country is Italy's capital, **Rome**. With ties to both north and south, Rome does not fully belong to either region. From there, the country's leaders attempt to bring all the people of Italy together as one nation.

READING CHECK **Contrast** How are northern and southern Italy different?

SUMMARY AND PREVIEW In this section you read about Italy. The country's long history continues to affect life in Italy even today. Next, you will study two other countries whose pasts still affect life there—Spain and Portugal.

Section 3 Assessment

hmhsocialstudies.com
ONLINE QUIZ

Reviewing Ideas, Terms, and Places

1. **a. Describe** What was Renaissance Italy like?
   b. Interpret How did nationalism influence Italian history?
2. **a. Identify** What religion has had a major impact on Italian culture?
   b. Explain How have local traditions helped shape Italian culture?
3. **a. Recall** What is the main economic activity of southern Italy?
   b. Contrast How are the economies of **Milan**, **Rome**, and **Naples** different?
   c. Rate If you could visit any one city in Italy, which would it be? Why?

Critical Thinking

4. **Comparing and Contrasting** Draw two circles like the ones here. Using your notes, list details about southern Italy in the left circle and about northern Italy in the right circle. Where the circles overlap, list common features of the two.

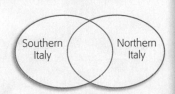

FOCUS ON WRITING

5. **Investigating Italy** What Italian event could you report on? Perhaps it could be a fashion show or a religious service at the Vatican. Make a list of events that could make an interesting report.

Spain and Portugal

If **YOU** lived there...

You have just moved to southern Spain from a town in the far north. You cannot help noticing that many of the buildings here look different from those in your hometown. Many of the buildings here have rounded arches over the doorways and tall towers in front of them. In addition, some are decorated with ornate tiles.

Why do you think the buildings look different?

BUILDING BACKGROUND Throughout history, many different groups have ruled parts of Spain and Portugal. Each group brought elements of its own culture to the region. As a result, parts of the two countries have cultures unlike those found anywhere else.

History

The countries of Spain and Portugal share the Iberian Peninsula, or **Iberia**, the westernmost peninsula in Europe. Although the two are different in many ways, they share a common history.

Across the centuries, several powerful empires controlled all or part of the Iberian Peninsula. By 700 BC, the Phoenicians, from the eastern Mediterranean, had colonized coastal areas of what is now Spain. After the Phoenicians came the Greeks. A few centuries later, all of Iberia became part of the Roman Empire.

After the Roman Empire fell apart, Iberia was invaded by the Moors, a group of Muslims from North Africa. For about 600 years, much of the Iberian Peninsula was under Muslim rule.

Moorish structures, such as this tower outside of Lisbon, Portugal, can still be seen all over Iberia.

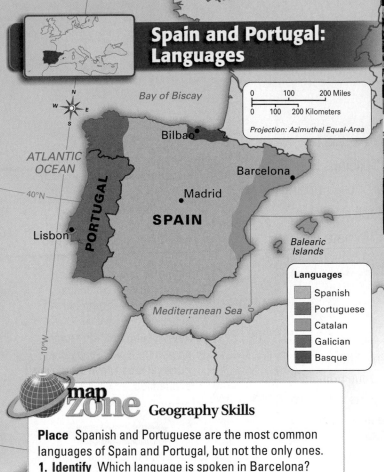

Spain and Portugal: Languages

Bay of Biscay

ATLANTIC OCEAN

Bilbao

Barcelona

Madrid

SPAIN

Lisbon

PORTUGAL

Balearic Islands

Mediterranean Sea

40°N

10°W

| 0 | 100 | 200 Miles |
| 0 | 100 | 200 Kilometers |

Projection: Azimuthal Equal-Area

Languages
- Spanish
- Portuguese
- Catalan
- Galician
- Basque

map zone Geography Skills

Place Spanish and Portuguese are the most common languages of Spain and Portugal, but not the only ones.
1. **Identify** Which language is spoken in Barcelona?
2. **Draw Conclusions** Based on this map, which country do you think has a more unified culture? Why?

Many Basque speakers take part in rallies like this one in support of independence. The banner in this photo reads "Basque Nation Arise" in the Basque language.

By the end of the 1400s, however, the Muslims were driven out of Iberia. The rulers of the Christian kingdoms of Spain and Portugal banded together to force non-Christians to leave Iberia. Those who refused to leave were made to convert or face severe punishments.

Spain and Portugal went on to build large empires that spanned the oceans. Both countries ruled huge territories in the Americas as well as smaller areas in Africa and Asia. These territories made the two kingdoms rich and powerful until most of their colonies broke away and became independent in the 1800s and 1900s.

READING CHECK **Summarizing** What empires have ruled Spain and Portugal?

Culture

In some ways, the cultures of Spain and Portugal are like those of other southern European countries. For example, the Spanish, Portuguese, Greeks, and Italians all cook with many of the same ingredients. The Catholic Church is very influential in Italy as well as Spain and Portugal. In other ways, Iberian cultures are unique.

Language

The most spoken languages in Iberia are, of course, Spanish and Portuguese. Various dialects of these languages are spoken in different parts of the peninsula. In addition, other languages are also spoken by many people in Iberia. The Catalan language of eastern Spain is similar to Spanish. Galician, which is spoken in northwest Spain, is more closely related to Portuguese.

In addition, the Basque (BASK) people of the Pyrenees have their own language, which is not related to either Spanish or Portuguese. The Basques also have their own customs and traditions, unlike those of the rest of Spain. As a result, many Basques have long wanted to form their own independent country.

Religion

Most people in both Spain and Portugal are Roman Catholic. People in both countries celebrate Christian holidays like Christmas and Easter. In addition, many towns hold fiestas, or festivals, in honor of their patron saints. At these festivals, people may gather to dance or to watch a bullfight.

Music and Art

Music and art have been central to Iberian culture for centuries. The Portuguese are famous for sad folk songs called fados. The Spanish are known for a style of song and dance called flamenco.

Many elements of Iberia's art and architecture reflect its Muslim past. Many buildings in the peninsula have elements of Muslim design, such as round arches and elaborate tilework.

READING CHECK **Comparing** What is one culture element that Spain and Portugal share?

Spain and Portugal Today

Compared to most other countries in Western Europe, Spain's and Portugal's economies are struggling. Their economic problems were brought on both by recent hardships and by past events.

Challenge of the Past

Spain and Portugal were once Europe's richest countries. Their wealth came from gold and silver found in their colonies.

When other countries in Europe began to build industrial economies, Spain and Portugal continued to rely on gold from their colonies. As those colonies became independent, that source of income was lost. As a result, Spain and Portugal were late in developing manufacturing.

Spain and Portugal are still poorer than other countries in Western Europe. Despite recent economic growth and vibrant industries such as tourism, their economies are struggling.

FOCUS ON READING

As you read, ask yourself this question: Why did Spain and Portugal fall behind other countries economically?

FOCUS ON CULTURE

Flamenco

Complex guitar rhythms, a heavy beat, and whirling dancers—these are all part of the traditional Spanish art form known as flamenco. The word *flamenco* refers both to a style of music and a style of dance. The most important instrument in the music is the guitar, which was itself a Spanish invention. Most of the time, the guitar is accompanied by other musical instruments and by singers.

When most people think of flamenco, however, they picture dancers. Flamenco dancers perform alone, in pairs, or in large groups. They wear brightly colored costumes as they perform complex steps. It is not unusual for dancers to clap their hands or snap their fingers to the beat or to play castanets as they dance. Castanets are small, hinged wooden instruments. The dancers clap the castanets together to make a clicking noise.

Finding Main Ideas What are the major elements of flamenco music and dancing?

Spanish culture blends old and new ideas. Here, modern vehicles drive by historic buildings in Barcelona.

In other ways, Spain has become a more modern country. Agriculture was once the major economic activity, but factories now create automobiles and other high-tech products. Cities such as **Madrid**—the capital—and **Barcelona** are centers of industry, tourism, and culture.

Portugal Today

Unlike Spain, Portugal is not a monarchy. It is a republic with elected leaders. As in Spain, the economy is based largely on industries centered in large cities, especially **Lisbon**. In many rural areas, though, people depend on agriculture. Farmers there grow many crops but are most famous for grapes and cork. Farmers harvest cork from the bark of a particular type of oak tree. Once it is dried, the cork is used to make bottle stoppers and other products.

READING CHECK **Contrasting** How are Spain and Portugal's governments different?

SUMMARY AND PREVIEW You have just learned about the countries of Southern Europe. Next, you will move north to study West-Central Europe.

Spain Today

The people of Spain have kept many aspects of their history alive. For example, Spain is still governed by a king, a descendant of the kings who ruled the country long ago. Unlike in the past, however, Spain today is a **parliamentary monarchy**, which means that the king shares power with an elected parliament and a prime minister.

Section 4 Assessment

hmhsocialstudies.com
ONLINE QUIZ

Reviewing Ideas, Terms, and Places

1. **a. Recall** What is **Iberia**? What two countries are located there?
   b. Sequence What people have ruled Iberia, and in what order did they rule it?
2. **a. Identify** What is the most common religion in Spain and Portugal?
   b. Generalize How is Spain's history reflected in its architecture?
   c. Elaborate Why do you think many Basques want to become independent from Spain?
3. **a. Identify** What are two crops grown in Portugal?
   b. Analyze What is Spain's government like?

Critical Thinking

4. **Categorizing** Draw a diagram like the one here. Using your notes, record information about the cultures and economies of Spain and Portugal.

	Spain	Portugal
Culture		
Economy		

FOCUS ON WRITING

5. **Writing about Spain and Portugal** What details about Spain and Portugal will grab your readers' attention? Look back through your notes to choose the topic for your article.

Geography's Impact
video series
Review the video to answer the closing question:
Why did the 2004 Olympics have so great an impact on Athens?

Visual Summary

Use the visual summary below to help you review the main ideas of the chapter.

QUICK FACTS

Greece
The birthplace of democracy, Greece is working to improve its economy.

Italy
Italy is one of Europe's leading cultural and economic countries.

Spain and Portugal
The rich cultures of Spain and Portugal are shaped by their histories.

Reviewing Vocabulary, Terms, and Places

Fill in the blanks with the correct term or location from this chapter.

1. The climate found in most of Southern Europe is the _____.

2. The _____ is the head of the Roman Catholic Church.

3. The highest mountains in Europe are the _____.

4. _____ is the capital of Greece.

5. A _____ is a government in which a king rules with the help of an elected body.

6. Italy's capital, _____, was the birthplace of an ancient civilization.

7. _____ is an independent state located within the city of Rome.

8. Spain and Portugal are located on a peninsula known as _____.

Comprehension and Critical Thinking

SECTION 1 *(Pages 104–107)*

9. **a. Describe** What are two physical features that all the countries of Southern Europe have in common?

   b. Draw Conclusions Why has Southern Europe's climate been called its most valuable resource?

   c. Predict How would daily life in Southern Europe be different if it were not a coastal region?

SECTION 2 *(Pages 109–113)*

10. **a. Identify** What is the largest city in Greece? How would you describe the city?

   b. Generalize How has Greece's economy changed in the last decade? What is largely responsible for this change?

   c. Elaborate How does Greek history still affect the country today?

SECTION 3 (Pages 114–118)

11. a. Recall Which region of Italy has the stronger economy? Why?

b. Sequence What periods followed the Roman Empire in Italy? What happened during those periods?

c. Elaborate What are some ways in which the Italians have influenced world culture?

SECTION 4 (Pages 119–122)

12. a. Identify Who are the Basques?

b. Compare and Contrast How are Spain and Portugal alike? How are they different?

c. Elaborate How do you think Iberia's history makes it different from other places in Europe?

Social Studies Skills

Reading a Climate Map *Use the climate map from the Social Studies Skills lesson of this chapter to answer the following questions.*

13. What type of climate does London have?

14. What climate is found only in the far north?

15. Where in Europe would you find a humid subtropical climate?

Using the Internet

16. Activity: Exploring Italian Cuisine Pizza. Pasta. Mozzarella. Olive oil. These are some of the most popular elements of Italian food, one of the world's favorites. Through your online textbook, learn more about the history and variety of Italian cooking. Then test your knowledge with the interactive activity.

Map Activity

17. Southern Europe On a separate sheet of paper, match the letters on the map with their correct labels.

Mediterranean Sea	Lisbon, Portugal
Athens, Greece	Po River
Sicily	Rome, Italy
Spain	Aegean Sea

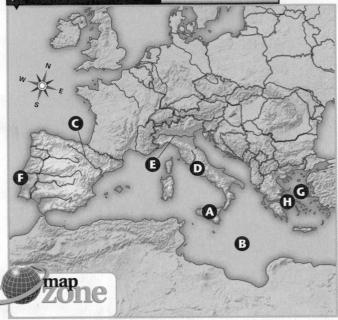

FOCUS ON READING AND WRITING

Asking Questions *Read the passage below. After you read it, answer the questions below to be sure you have understood what you read.*

> Spain is a democracy, but it has not always been. From 1939 to 1975, a dictator named Francisco Franco ruled the country. He came to power as a result of a bloody civil war and was unpopular with the Spanish people.

18. Who is this paragraph about?

19. What did the people in this passage do?

20. When did the events described take place?

21. Where did the events described take place?

22. Why did the events happen?

Writing Your News Report *Use your notes and the instructions below to help you create your news report.*

23. Select a topic for your news report. Create a plan for your report by answering these questions: What is the scene or setting of the event? Who is there? Why is it important enough to include in the news? What happened? Start your news report with a dateline, for example: Rome, May 5, 2009. Begin your first paragraph with an interesting observation or detail. Explain the event in two or three short paragraphs. Close with an important piece of information or interesting detail.

Standardized Test Prep

DIRECTIONS: Read questions 1 through 7 and write the letter of the best response. Then read question 8 and write your own well-constructed response.

1 In which country of Southern Europe is the Orthodox Church dominant?

A Portugal

B Spain

C Italy

D Greece

2 Two of the most common foods in Southern European cooking are

A grapes and olives.

B corn and barley.

C beans and squash.

D beef and pork.

3 The form of government for which ancient Greece is best known is

A monarchy.

B dictatorship.

C democracy.

D parliamentary monarchy.

4 The Moors were Muslims who conquered

A Spain.

B Greece.

C Crete.

D Italy.

5 Which of these cities is in Portugal?

A Rome

B Athens

C Lisbon

D Madrid

Spain and Portugal: Climates

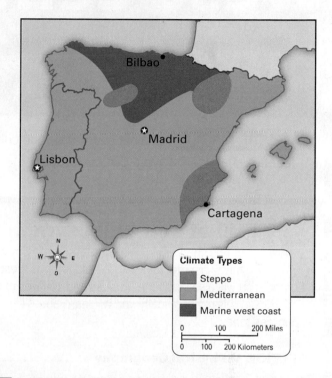

6 Based on the map above, which city in Spain lies in an area with a steppe climate?

A Bilbao

B Cartagena

C Lisbon

D Madrid

7 Based on the map on this page, which is the most common climate in Spain?

A Steppe

B Mediterranean

C Marine west coast

D Tropical

8 **Extended response** Climate influences many aspects of people's lives in Southern Europe. Write a short paragraph that describes the region's climate. At the end of the paragraph, list two ways in which climate affects how people live.

West-Central Europe

Essential Question What geographic and cultural features characterize West-Central Europe?

What You Will Learn...

In this chapter you will learn about the physical features, climate, and natural resources of West-Central Europe. You will also study the histories and cultures of the countries in this region. Finally, you will learn about life in these countries today.

FOCUS ON READING AND SPEAKING

Recognizing Word Origins Many of the words we use today came into English from other languages, such as Latin, French, or German. As you read this chapter, think about the origin, or sources, of words. Knowing a word's origin can help you remember the word's meaning. **See the lesson, Recognizing Word Origins, on page 224.**

Writing a Persuasive Speech As you read about West-Central Europe, you will discover some issues. Issues are topics that people disagree about. Think about which of the issues seem important to you. Later, you will take a stand on one of these issues by writing and presenting a persuasive speech.

History The Eiffel Tower in Paris, France, was completed in 1889. It was the world's tallest structure until 1930.

West-Central Europe: Political

North Sea

Kiel Canal

NETHERLANDS

Amsterdam ☆

• Rotterdam

• Hamburg

Elbe River

Weser River

Oder River

Berlin ☆

Neisse River

RUHR

• Antwerp

Lille •   • Brussels

BELGIUM

Rhine River

GERMANY

• Frankfurt

LUXEMBOURG
☆ Luxembourg

Seine River

• Paris
☆

River

Loire River

CZECH REPUBLIC

Danube River

Munich
•

Vienna ☆

FRANCE

LIECHTENSTEIN

Zurich •
☆ Bern

SWITZERLAND

Salzburg
•

• Innsbruck

AUSTRIA

HUNGARY

Lake Geneva

Geneva ☆
Lyon •

Rhône River

ITALY

Adriatic Sea

Marseille •

MONACO

Corsica (FRANCE)

Mediterranean Sea

10°E

20°E

map zone Geography Skills

Regions The countries of West-Central Europe are some of the most industrialized and richest countries in the world.

1. **Identify** Which countries make up this region?
2. **Make Inferences** Why do you think some of the countries in this region might want to join together to promote economic growth?

Geography The Netherlands is famous for its fields of brightly colored tulips.

Culture A German teen participates in a Bavarian cow festival.

Physical Geography

What You Will Learn...

Main Ideas

1. The physical features of West-Central Europe include plains, uplands, mountains, rivers, and seas.
2. West-Central Europe's mild climate and resources support agriculture, energy production, and tourism.

The Big Idea

West-Central Europe has a range of landscapes, a mild climate, and rich farmland.

Key Terms and Places

Northern European Plain, *p. 128*
North Sea, *p. 130*
English Channel, *p. 130*
Danube River, *p. 130*
Rhine River, *p. 130*
navigable river, *p. 130*

hmhsocialstudies.com
TAKING NOTES

Use the graphic organizer online to take notes on the physical geography of West-Central Europe.

If YOU lived there...

You are a photographer planning a book about the landscapes of West-Central Europe. You are trying to decide where to find the best pictures of rich farmland, forested plateaus, and rugged mountains. So far, you are planning to show the colorful tulip fields of the Netherlands, the hilly Black Forest region of Germany, and the snow-covered Alps in Switzerland.

What other places might you want to show?

BUILDING BACKGROUND The countries of West-Central Europe are among the most prosperous and powerful countries in the world. The reasons include their mild climates, good farmland, many rivers, market economies, and stable governments. In addition, most of these countries cooperate as members of the European Union.

Physical Features

From fields of tulips, to sunny beaches, to icy mountain peaks, West-Central Europe offers a wide range of landscapes. Even though the region is small, it includes three major types of landforms—plains, uplands, and mountains. These landforms extend in wide bands across the region.

Plains, Uplands, and Mountains

Look at the map at right. Picture West-Central Europe as an open fan with Italy as the handle. The outer edge of this imaginary fan is a broad coastal plain called the **Northern European Plain**. This plain stretches from the Atlantic coast into Eastern Europe.

Most of this plain is flat or rolling and lies less than 500 feet (150 m) above sea level. In the Netherlands, parts of the plain dip below sea level. There, people must build walls to hold back the sea. In Brittany in northwestern France, the land rises to form a plateau above the surrounding plain.

The Northern European Plain provides the region's best farmland. Many people live on the plain, and the region's largest cities are located there.

The Central Uplands extend across the center of our imaginary fan. This area has many rounded hills, small plateaus, and valleys. In France, the uplands include the <u>Massif</u> Central (ma-SEEF sahn-TRAHL), a plateau region, and the Jura Mountains.

This range is on the French-Swiss border. In Germany, uplands cover much of the southern two-thirds of the country. Dense woodlands, such as the Black Forest, blanket many of the hills in this area.

The Central Uplands have many productive coalfields. As a result, the area is important for mining and industry. Some valleys provide fertile soil for farming, but most of the area is too rocky to farm.

FOCUS ON READING

Look up the origin of *massif* in a dictionary. How does its origin relate to the description of the Massif Central?

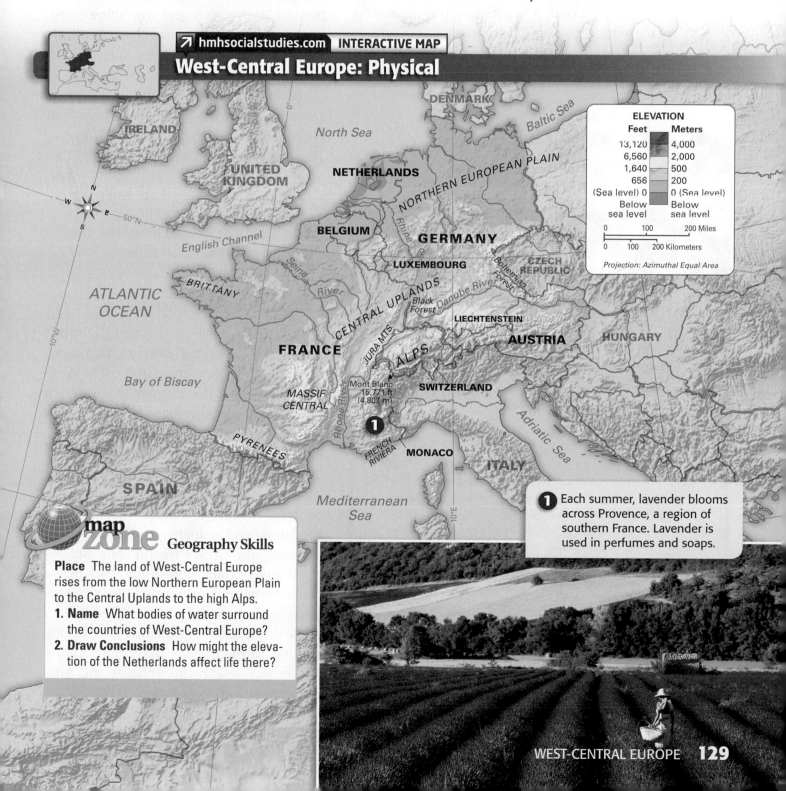

↗ hmhsocialstudies.com **INTERACTIVE MAP**

West-Central Europe: Physical

DENMARK

Baltic Sea

IRELAND

North Sea

NORTHERN EUROPEAN PLAIN

UNITED KINGDOM

NETHERLANDS

ELEVATION

Feet	Meters
13,120	4,000
6,560	2,000
1,640	500
656	200
(Sea level) 0	0 (Sea level)
Below sea level	Below sea level

0   100   200 Miles
0 100 200 Kilometers

Projection: Azimuthal Equal Area

BELGIUM

Rhine

GERMANY

LUXEMBOURG

CZECH REPUBLIC

English Channel

Seine River

ATLANTIC OCEAN

BRITTANY

CENTRAL UPLANDS

Bohemian Forest

Black Forest

Danube River

JURA MTS.

LIECHTENSTEIN

AUSTRIA

HUNGARY

FRANCE

ALPS

SWITZERLAND

Bay of Biscay

Mont Blanc 15,771 ft (4,807 m)

Rhone River

MASSIF CENTRAL

1

Adriatic Sea

PYRENEES

FRENCH RIVIERA

MONACO

ITALY

SPAIN

Mediterranean Sea

10°E

1 Each summer, lavender blooms across Provence, a region of southern France. Lavender is used in perfumes and soaps.

map Zone Geography Skills

Place The land of West-Central Europe rises from the low Northern European Plain to the Central Uplands to the high Alps.

1. **Name** What bodies of water surround the countries of West-Central Europe?

2. **Draw Conclusions** How might the elevation of the Netherlands affect life there?

Along the inner part of our imaginary fan, the land rises dramatically to form the alpine mountain system. This system includes the Alps and the Pyrenees, which you read about in the last chapter.

As you have read, the Alps are Europe's highest mountain range. They stretch from southern France to the Balkan Peninsula. Several of the jagged peaks in the Alps soar to more than 14,000 feet (4,270 m). The highest peak is Mont Blanc (mawn BLAHN), which rises to 15,771 feet (4,807 m) in France. Because of the height of the Alps, large snowfields coat some peaks.

Satellite View

High in the Swiss Alps, snow builds up to form glaciers like the one shown here.

The Swiss Alps

At high elevations in the Alps, snow does not melt. For this reason, the snow builds up over time. As the snow builds up, it turns to ice and eventually forms glaciers. A glacier is a large, slow–moving sheet or river of ice. The satellite image above shows glaciers in the Swiss Alps. The white regions are the glaciers, and the blue areas are alpine lakes.

The buildup of snow and ice in the Alps can cause avalanches at lower elevations. An avalanche is a large mass of snow or other material that suddenly rushes down a mountainside. Avalanches pose a serious danger to people.

Analyzing Why do glaciers sometimes form at higher elevations in the Alps?

Water Features

Several bodies of water are important to West-Central Europe's physical geography. The **North Sea** and **English Channel** lie to the north. The Bay of Biscay and Atlantic Ocean lie to the west. The Mediterranean Sea borders France to the south.

Several rivers cross the region as well. Look at the map on the previous page to identify them. Two important rivers are the **Danube** (DAN-yoob) and the **Rhine** (RYN). For centuries people and goods have traveled these rivers, and many cities, farms, and industrial areas line their banks.

Several of West-Central Europe's rivers are navigable. A **navigable river** is one that is deep and wide enough for ships to use. These rivers and a system of canals link the region's interior to the seas. These waterways are important for trade and travel.

READING CHECK **Finding Main Ideas** What are the region's three major landform areas?

Climate and Resources

A warm ocean current flows along Europe's northwestern coast. This current creates a marine west coast climate in most of West-Central Europe. This climate makes much of the area a pleasant place to live. Though winters can get cold, summers are mild. Rain and storms occur often, though.

At higher elevations, such as in the Alps, the climate is colder and wetter. In contrast, southern France has a warm Mediterranean climate. Summers are dry and hot, and winters are mild and wet.

West-Central Europe's mild climate is a valuable natural resource. Mild temperatures, plenty of rain, and rich soil have made the region's farmlands highly productive. Farm crops include grapes, grains, and vegetables. In the uplands and Alps, pastures and valleys support livestock.

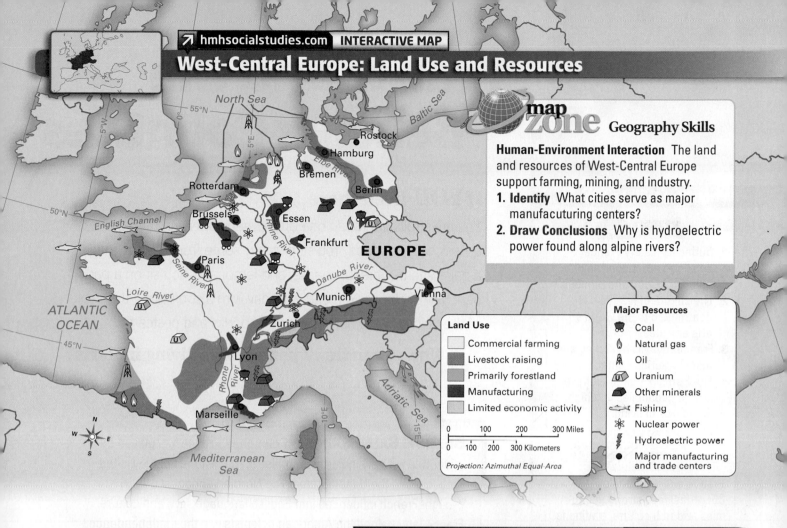

West-Central Europe: Land Use and Resources

map zone Geography Skills

Human-Environment Interaction The land and resources of West-Central Europe support farming, mining, and industry.
1. **Identify** What cities serve as major manufacuturing centers?
2. **Draw Conclusions** Why is hydroelectric power found along alpine rivers?

Land Use
- ☐ Commercial farming
- ☐ Livestock raising
- ☐ Primarily forestland
- ☐ Manufacturing
- ☐ Limited economic activity

0   100   200   300 Miles
0   100   200   300 Kilometers

Projection: Azimuthal Equal Area

Major Resources
- Coal
- Natural gas
- Oil
- Uranium
- Other minerals
- Fishing
- Nuclear power
- Hydroelectric power
- Major manufacturing and trade centers

Energy and mineral resources are not evenly distributed across the region, as the map shows. France has coal and iron ore, Germany also has coal, and the Netherlands has natural gas. Fast-flowing alpine rivers provide hydroelectric power. Even so, many countries must import fuels.

Another valuable natural resource is found in the breathtaking beauty of the Alps. Each year, tourists flock to the Alps to enjoy the scenery and to hike and ski.

READING CHECK **Summarizing** What natural resources contribute to the region's economy?

SUMMARY AND PREVIEW West-Central Europe includes low plains, uplands, and mountains. The climate is mild, and natural resources support farming, industry, and tourism. Next, you will read about France and the Benelux Countries.

Section 1 Assessment

↗ hmhsocialstudies.com
ONLINE QUIZ

Reviewing Ideas, Terms, and Places

1. **a. Describe** What are the main physical features of the **Northern European Plain**?
   b. Analyze How does having many **navigable** rivers benefit West-Central Europe?
2. **a. Recall** What is the region's main climate?
   b. Make Inferences How might an uneven distribution of mineral resources affect the region?

Critical Thinking

3. **Categorizing** Draw a fan like this one. Label each band with the landform area in West-Central Europe it represents. Using your notes, identify each area's physical features, climate, and resources.

FOCUS ON SPEAKING

4. **Noting the Physical Geography** What issues related to land use and resources can you think of? Could mining coal or importing fuel be an issue? Jot down ideas.

France and the Benelux Countries

What You Will Learn...

Main Ideas

1. During its history France has been a kingdom, empire, colonial power, and republic.
2. The culture of France has contributed to the world's arts and ideas.
3. France today is a farming and manufacturing center.
4. The Benelux Countries have strong economies and high standards of living.

The Big Idea

France and the Benelux Countries have strong economies and rich cultural traditions.

Key Terms and Places

Paris, *p. 135*
Amsterdam, *p. 137*
The Hague, *p. 137*
Brussels, *p. 137*
cosmopolitan, *p. 137*

↗ **hmhsocialstudies.com**
TAKING NOTES

Use the graphic organizer online to take notes on the Benelux countries.

If YOU lived there...

You are strolling through one of the many open-air markets in a Paris neighborhood. You stop to buy some fruit, then go into a bakery to buy bread, cheese, and lemonade. You sit on a park bench to eat lunch. You end your day with a stroll along the banks of the Seine River, where you look at books and postcards.

Why do you think people enjoy living in Paris?

BUILDING BACKGROUND For centuries, France has played a major role not only in Europe but also in the histories of the United Kingdom and the United States. The Norman Conquest in 1066 brought French influences into English language, law, and culture. France later helped the American colonists win their independence.

History of France

In southwest France, Lascaux (lah-SKOH) Cave holds a treasure from the past. Inside, prehistoric paintings of bulls run and jump along the stone walls. More than 15,000 years old, these paintings show how long people have lived in what is now France.

Early History

In ancient times, France was part of a region called Gaul (GAWL). Centuries ago, Celtic peoples from eastern Europe settled in Gaul. In the 50s BC, the Romans conquered the region. They introduced Roman law. The Romans also established a Latin-based language that in time developed into French.

Roman rule in Gaul lasted until the AD 400s. The Franks, a Germanic people, then conquered much of Gaul. It is from the Franks that France gets its name. The Franks' greatest ruler was Charlemagne (SHAHR-luh-mayn), who built a powerful Christian empire. After he had conquered much of the old Roman Empire, the pope crowned him Emperor of the Romans in 800.

After Charlemagne's death, many invaders attacked the Franks. One such group, the Normans, settled in northwestern France. This area is called Normandy.

In 1066 the Normans conquered England. William the Conqueror, the duke of Normandy, became king of England. He now ruled England as well as part of France. In the 1300s England's king tried to claim the French throne to gain control of the rest of France. This event led to the Hundred Years' War (1337–1453). The French eventually drove out the English.

Revolution and Empire

From the 1500s to the 1700s, France built a colonial empire. The French established colonies in the Americas, Africa, and Asia. At this time, most French people lived in poverty and had few rights. For these reasons, in 1789 the French people overthrew their king in the French Revolution.

A few years later a brilliant general named Napoleon took power. In time, he conquered much of Europe. Then in 1815 several European powers joined forces and defeated Napoleon. They exiled him and chose a new king to rule France.

Modern History

During both World War I and World War II, German forces invaded France. After each war, France worked to rebuild its economy. In the 1950s it experienced rapid growth.

During the 1950s and 1960s, many of of the French colonies gained their independence. Some people from these former colonies then moved to France.

France is now a republic with a parliament and an elected president. France still controls several overseas territories, such as Martinique in the West Indies.

READING CHECK **Summarizing** Which foreign groups have affected France's history?

France's History

During its long history, France has gone from strong kingdom to great empire, to colonial world power, to modern republic.

Early History

- Early Celtic peoples settle in Gaul.
- The Romans conquer Gaul and rule the region for hundreds of years.
- The Franks conquer Gaul. The ruler Charlemagne builds a powerful empire.
- Normans settle in northwestern France. In 1066 they conquer England and take the throne.
- France and England fight the Hundred Years' War.

Charlemagne

Revolution and Empire

- In the 1500s France begins to build a colonial empire.
- In 1789 the people rise up in the French Revolution.
- In 1799 Napoleon takes control. He soon conquers much of Europe.
- European powers unite to defeat Napoleon in 1815.

Arc de Triomphe

Modern History

- German forces invade France during World War I and World War II.
- Many French colonies declare independence in the 1950s and 1960s.
- Today France is a republic with a president and a democratic government.

WWII German occupation

The Culture of France

During their long history, the French have developed a strong cultural identity. Today French culture is admired worldwide.

FOCUS ON READING

Use a dictionary to find the origin of *cuisine*. How does the word's origin relate to the meaning of *cuisine* today?

Language and Religion

A common heritage unites the French. Most people speak French and are Catholic. At the same time, many immigrants have settled in France. These immigrants have their own languages, religions, and customs. For example, many Algerian Muslims have moved to France. This immigration is making France more culturally diverse.

Customs

The French have a phrase that describes their attitude toward life—*joie de vivre* (zhwah duh VEEV-ruh), meaning "enjoyment of life." The French enjoy good food, good company, and good conversation.

An enjoyment of food has helped make French cooking some of the best in the world. French chefs and cooking schools have worldwide reputations. The French have also contributed to the language of food. Terms such as *café*, *cuisine* (cooking), and *menu* all come from the French.

The French also enjoy their festivals. The major national festival is Bastille Day, held on July 14. On that date in 1789 a mob destroyed the Bastille, a Paris prison symbolizing the French king's harsh rule. The event began the French Revolution.

Ideas and the Arts

The French have made major contributions to the arts and ideas. In the Middle Ages, the French built majestic cathedrals in the Gothic style. This style has high pointed ceilings, stained-glass windows, and tall towers that reach heavenward. Notre Dame Cathedral in Paris is an example.

Close-up

Paris

Some 2,000 years old, Paris grew up along the banks of the Seine (SEN) River. Known as "the City of Light" for its gleaming beauty, Paris shines as one of Europe's most cultured cities. Wide tree-lined avenues, historic squares, and lovely gardens and parks grace the city center.

Notre Dame is France's most famous cathedral. It is a masterpiece of Gothic architecture.

The Seine River winds through the heart of Paris. Beautiful bridges cross the river, and in places booksellers line its banks.

In the 1700s France was a center of the Enlightenment, a period in which people used reason to improve society. French Enlightenment ideas about government inspired the American Revolution and the development of modern democracy.

In the 1800s France was the center of one of the most famous art movements of the modern age—impressionism. This style of painting uses rippling light to create an impression of a scene. During the same period, French authors wrote classics such as *The Three Musketeers* by Alexandre Dumas (doo-mah). Today France is known for art and its fashion and film industries.

READING CHECK **Summarizing** What are some main features of French culture?

France Today

France is now West-Central Europe's largest country. It plays a leading role in Europe and in the European Union (EU).

Today about 75 percent of the French live in cities. **Paris**, the capital, is by far the largest city, with about 10 million people.

Fashionable with a quick pace, Paris is a center of business, finance, learning, and culture. It boasts world-class museums, art galleries, and restaurants as well as famous landmarks such as the Eiffel Tower and Notre Dame Cathedral.

Other major cities include Marseille (mar-SAY), a Mediterranean seaport, and Lyon (LYAWN), located on the Rhone River. A modern system of highways, canals, and high-speed trains links France's cities.

France has a strong economy. It is the EU's top agricultural producer, and its major crops include wheat and grapes. French workers are also highly productive. Rich soil and efficient workers have made France a major exporter of goods, such as its famous perfumes and wines.

The Paris Métro, or subway, is known for its decorative wrought-iron entrances, built in the early 1900s.

Paris is known for its many sidewalk cafés, where people meet to eat, socialize, and relax.

ANALYSIS SKILL **ANALYZING VISUALS**
What examples do you see of the mixing of the new and the old in Paris?

Dutch Polders

More than 25 percent of the Netherlands lies below sea level. For centuries, the Dutch have reclaimed land from the sea. These reclaimed lands are called polders.

To create polders, the Dutch build dikes near the shoreline. They then use pumps to remove the water behind the dikes. A national system of dikes, dams, floodgates, and storm barriers now holds back the sea.

Unfortunately, creating polders has caused sinking lowlands and other environmental damage. The Dutch are working to address these problems. For example, they are considering restoring some of the polders to wetlands, lakes, and the seas.

Finding Main Ideas How have the Dutch modified their environment to live in a region that lies below sea level?

Tourism is also vital to the economy. Each year, millions of people visit Paris, the French Alps, and the sunny French Riviera, a resort area on the Mediterranean coast.

READING CHECK **Drawing Conclusions** Why do you think tourists might want to visit Paris?

The Benelux Countries

Belgium, the Netherlands, and Luxembourg are called the Benelux Countries. *Benelux* combines the first letters of each country's name. They are also called the Low Countries because of their elevation.

History

Many nations and empires dominated the Benelux region. In 1648 the Netherlands gained its independence. It ruled Belgium until 1830, and Luxembourg until 1867, when they gained independence.

In World War II, Germany occupied the Benelux Countries. After the war, they joined the North Atlantic Treaty Organization (NATO) for protection. NATO is an alliance of nations. In the 1950s the Benelux Countries joined the group of nations now known as the EU.

Today the Benelux Countries each have a parliament and ceremonial monarch. The tiny, densely populated countries lie between larger, stronger countries. This location has led to invasions but has also promoted trade. The Benelux Countries now have wealthy economies.

The Netherlands

Bordering the North Sea, the Netherlands is low and flat. Some of the land lies below sea level. The Netherlands includes the historical region of Holland and is sometimes called Holland. The people here are the Dutch, and the language they speak is also called Dutch.

Excellent harbors on the North Sea have made the Netherlands a center of international trade. The city of Rotterdam is one of the world's busiest seaports. It is also part of a highly industrial and urban, or city-based, area. This area includes **Amsterdam**, the capital, and **The Hague** (HAYG), the seat of government. Agriculture is also important to the Dutch economy, and Dutch cheese and tulips are world famous.

Belgium

Belgium is a highly urban country. More than 95 percent of the people of Belgium live in cities. The capital city, **Brussels**, serves as the headquarters for many international organizations, including the EU and NATO. The city of Brussels is as a result highly **cosmopolitan**, or characterized by many foreign influences.

Language divides Belgium. The coast and north are called Flanders. The people there speak Flemish. The southern interior is called Wallonia. The people there speak French and are called Walloons. These cultural differences have caused tensions.

Belgium is known for its cheeses, chocolate, cocoa, and lace. The city of Antwerp is a key port and diamond-cutting center.

Luxembourg

Luxembourg is a forested, hilly country. Although smaller than Rhode Island, it has one of the world's highest standards of living. Most of the people in Luxembourg are Roman Catholic and speak either French or German.

Luxembourg earns much of its income from services such as banking. The region also produces steel and chemicals. Its small cities are cosmopolitan centers of international business and government.

READING CHECK **Comparing** What do the Benelux Countries have in common?

SUMMARY AND PREVIEW As you have learned, France and the Benelux Countries are modern and urban with strong economies. Next, you will read about Germany and the Alpine Countries.

Section 2 Assessment

hmhsocialstudies.com
ONLINE QUIZ

Reviewing Ideas, Terms, and Places

1. **a. Identify** Who was Charlemagne?
   b. Explain Why is Napoleon considered a significant figure in French history?
   c. Develop Why might the French be proud of their long history?
2. **a. Define** What is impressionism?
   b. Summarize What are some major contributions of French culture?
   c. Elaborate How has immigration influenced French culture?
3. **a. Describe** Why is **Paris** an important city?
   b. Summarize What is the French economy like?
4. **a. Describe** How does language divide Belgium?
   b. Draw Conclusions Why might **Brussels** be such a **cosmopolitan** city?

Critical Thinking

5. **Categorizing** Draw a chart like the one here. Use your notes and enter information into each category. Within each category, organize the information by country.

FOCUS ON SPEAKING

6. **Describing France and the Benelux Countries** For each country, note one possible issue for your persuasive speech. For example, one issue might be language in Belgium. Should all Belgians have to speak the same language?

The European Union

How can smaller countries compete with larger ones? One way is by working together. Since the 1950s, countries across Europe have been working to build a united community. Today this organization is called the European Union (EU). It promotes political and economic cooperation among member nations. The chart on the next page shows how the EU has changed life in Europe.

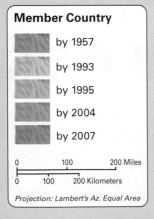

Member Country

- by 1957
- by 1993
- by 1995
- by 2004
- by 2007

```
0          100          200 Miles
0      100      200 Kilometers
```
Projection: Lambert's Az. Equal Area

SW

DENMARK

IRELAND

UNITED KINGDOM

NETHERLANDS

GERMANY

BELGIUM

LUXEMBOURG

C
REPU

FRANCE

AUSTR

SLO

ITA

PORTUGAL

SPAIN

FINLAND

ESTONIA

LATVIA

LITHUANIA

POLAND

SLOVAKIA

HUNGARY

ROMANIA

BULGARIA

TURKEY

GREECE

CYPRUS

Benefits of Membership in the European Union

Trade

Before	After
■ European countries had to pay customs duties, or taxes, on goods they traded with other European countries. ■ Many European countries' economies were small compared to those of larger nations such as the United States.	■ EU countries are part of a common market. They can trade freely with each other without paying duties. ■ EU countries create a combined economy that is one of the largest in the world.

Currency

Before	After
■ Each European country had its own separate currency, or form of money. ■ European countries and their citizens had to exchange currencies to buy goods from other European countries.	■ Most EU countries share one currency, the euro. ■ EU countries and their citizens can use the euro to buy goods and trade throughout the EU.

Work and Travel

Before	After
■ Europeans had to have passports or other special permits to travel from one European country to another. ■ Europeans had to obtain permission to live and work in other countries in Europe.	■ Citizens of EU countries do not need passports or special permits to travel throughout most of the EU. ■ Citizens of EU countries can live and work anywhere in the EU without having to obtain permission.

The Euro The front sides of euro coins all have the same image, but the backs feature a unique symbol for each country. Euro bills show symbols of unity.

ANALYSIS SKILL **ANALYZING VISUALS**

1. **Name** Which six countries were the first to unite?
2. **Make Inferences** How do you think democracy's spread in Eastern Europe has affected the EU?
3. **Interpreting Charts** Based on the chart above, what are two benefits of EU membership?

Germany and the Alpine Countries

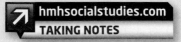

If YOU lived there...

You are walking with your grandfather through Berlin, Germany. He begins telling you about a time when Germany was divided into two countries—one democratic and one Communist. A large wall even divided the city of Berlin. Germans could not pass freely through the wall. You think of your friends who live in eastern Berlin. They would have been on the other side of the wall back then.

What do you think life in Berlin was like then?

BUILDING BACKGROUND Since the Middle Ages, Germany and France have been the dominant countries in West-Central Europe. Both are large and prosperous with hardworking people and good farmland. The two countries have often been at war, but today they are partners in building a cooperative European Union.

History of Germany

Some countries have had a strong influence on world events. Germany is one of these countries. From its location in the heart of Europe, Germany has shaped events across Europe and the world—for both good and bad.

Growth of a Nation

In ancient times, tribes from northern Europe settled in the land that is now Germany. The Romans called this region Germania, after the name of one of the tribes. Over time, many small German states developed in the region. Princes ruled these states. With the support of the Roman Catholic Church, these states became part of the Holy Roman Empire.

For hundreds of years, Germany remained a loose association of small states. Then in 1871, Prussia, the strongest state, united Germany into one nation. As a unified nation, Germany developed into an industrial and military world power.

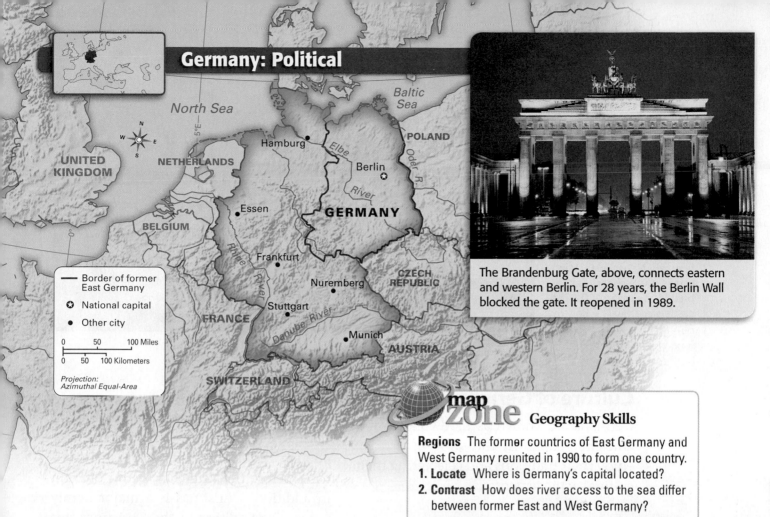

Germany: Political

North Sea

Baltic Sea

UNITED KINGDOM

NETHERLANDS

BELGIUM

FRANCE

SWITZERLAND

Hamburg

Berlin ✪

GERMANY

Essen

Frankfurt

Nuremberg

Stuttgart

Munich

POLAND

CZECH REPUBLIC

AUSTRIA

Elbe

Oder R.

River

Rhine River

Danube River

5°E

— Border of former East Germany
✪ National capital
• Other city

0   50   100 Miles
0   50   100 Kilometers

Projection:
Azimuthal Equal-Area

The Brandenburg Gate, above, connects eastern and western Berlin. For 28 years, the Berlin Wall blocked the gate. It reopened in 1989.

map zone Geography Skills

Regions The former countries of East Germany and West Germany reunited in 1990 to form one country.
1. **Locate** Where is Germany's capital located?
2. **Contrast** How does river access to the sea differ between former East and West Germany?

War and Division

In 1914–1918, Germany fought and lost World War I. Payments for war damages and a major depression severely hurt the German economy. Looking for a strong leader, Germans found Adolf Hitler and his Nazi Party. Hitler promised the Germans to restore their country to its former glory.

In 1939 Germany attacked Poland, starting World War II. Soon, Germany had conquered much of Europe. The Nazis also sought to kill all European Jews in what is called the Holocaust. Germany lost the war, though. By 1945 it lay in ruins, defeated.

After the war, British, French, and U.S. troops occupied West Germany. The Soviet Union's troops occupied East Germany. Over time, two countries emerged.

The city of **Berlin** was in Communist East Germany. Even so, West Germany kept control of the western part of the city.

In 1961 Communist leaders built the Berlin Wall. The Wall's **purpose** was to prevent East Germans from fleeing to West Berlin.

ACADEMIC VOCABULARY
purpose the reason something is done

A Reunited Germany

After World War II, U.S. aid helped West Germany rebuild rapidly. It soon became an economic power. East Germany rebuilt as well, but its economy lagged. In addition, its people had limited freedoms.

In 1989 movements for democracy swept through Eastern Europe. Communist governments began collapsing. Joyful East Germans tore down the Berlin Wall. In 1990 East and West Germany reunited.

READING CHECK **Finding Main Ideas** What major challenges has Germany overcome?

Germany's long history has enriched its culture. Historic castles dot the landscape, and long-held traditions continue. Blending with this history is a modern culture that includes a love of sports.

A Bavarian Castle King Ludwig II of Bavaria had the fairy-tale Neuschwanstein (noy-SHVAHN-shtyn) Castle built in the mid-1800s. The castle sits amid the Bavarian Alps in southern Germany.

Culture of Germany

Germans are known as hardworking and efficient people. At the same time, they enjoy their traditions and celebrating their cultural achievements.

People

Most Germans share a common heritage. About 90 percent are ethnic German, and most speak German. In recent years, significant numbers of immigrants have come to Germany to live and work as well. These immigrants include Turks, Italians, and refugees from Eastern Europe. Their influence is making German culture more diverse.

Religion

In 1517 Martin Luther, a German monk, helped start the Reformation. This religious reform movement led to the development of Protestant churches. Many Germanic states became Protestant; others remained Roman Catholic. Today in north and central Germany, most people are Protestant. In the south, most are Catholic. In eastern Germany, fewer Germans have religious ties, reflecting the area's Communist past.

Customs

Festivals and holidays tell us much about German culture. Religious festivals are very popular. For example, many areas hold festivals before the Christian season of Lent. In addition, Christmas is a major family event. The tradition of the Christmas tree even began in Germany.

Each region has local festivals as well. The best known is Oktoberfest in Bavaria, the region of southeast Germany. This festival is held each fall in Munich (MYOO-nik) to celebrate the region's food and drink.

The Arts and Sciences

Germany's contributions to the arts and sciences are widely admired. In music, Germany has produced famed classical composers, such as Johann Sebastian Bach and Ludwig van Beethoven. In literature, author Johann Wolfgang von Goethe (GOOH-tuh) ranks among Europe's most important writers. In science, Germans have made contributions in chemistry, engineering, medicine, and physics.

READING CHECK **Summarizing** What contributions have Germans made to world culture?

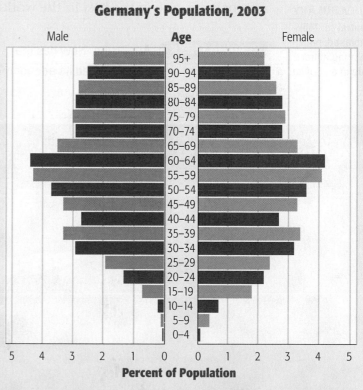

Soccer Fans
German soccer fans celebrate a victory. Soccer is the most popular sport in Germany. The country hosted the soccer World Cup in 2006.

Christmas Markets
German Christmas markets and fairs like this one have been popular for centuries. Booths sell trees, crafts, and food. Rides and music provide entertainment.

Germany Today

Despite a stormy history, Germany has endured. Today the country is a leading power in Europe and the world.

Government and Economy

Germany is a federal republic. A parliament chooses a **chancellor**, or prime minister, to run the government. The parliament also helps elect a president, whose duties are largely ceremonial. On the world stage, Germany belongs to the EU and NATO.

Germany's market economy has helped the country become an economic giant. It is Europe's largest economy, producing nearly one-fifth of all goods and services in the EU. The nation exports a wide range of products. You may be familiar with German cars, such as BMWs or Volkswagens.

The German economy is based on industry, such as chemicals, engineering, and steel. The main industrial district is the Ruhr, located in western Germany. Fewer Germans farm than in the past, but agriculture remains important. Major crops include grain, potatoes, and grapes. Timber is harvested in the south.

THE WORLD ALMANAC®
Facts about Countries

Germany's Population, 2003

Male — Age — Female

Age
95+
90–94
85–89
80–84
75–79
70–74
65–69
60–64
55–59
50–54
45–49
40–44
35–39
30–34
25–29
20–24
15–19
10–14
5–9
0–4

5 4 3 2 1 0   0 1 2 3 4 5
Percent of Population

Interpreting Graphs Germany's population is slowly aging because Germans are living longer and families are becoming smaller. Which age group in Germany is now the largest?

⬈ hmhsocialstudies.com

FOCUS ON
READING
Use a dictionary
to find the origin
of *lag.* How does
the word's origin
relate to its
meaning here?

Economic growth has slowed since East and West Germany reunited, however. The economy of former East Germany continues to lag. The region also suffers high unemployment. Germany's government is working to solve these problems.

Cities

Most Germans live in cities. The largest city is Berlin, the capital. During World War II, Berlin suffered major destruction. Today Germans have restored their capital to its former splendor. A historic city, it has wide boulevards and many parks.

Other major German cities include Hamburg, a key port city on the North Sea, and Munich, a cultural and manufacturing center. Like France, Germany has an excellent transportation system that links its cities. Germany's highway system, the Autobahn, is one of the best in the world.

ACADEMIC
VOCABULARY
neutral (p. 145)
unbiased, not
favoring either
side in a conflict

READING CHECK **Analyzing** How has the reunification of Germany affected its economy?

The Alpine Countries

The beauty of the Alps draws many tourists to Austria and Switzerland. These countries are called the Alpine Countries after the Alps, which cover much of them.

Austria and Switzerland have many similarities. Both are landlocked. Both are heavily influenced by German culture and were once part of the Holy Roman Empire. Yet, the countries have their differences.

Austria

Austria was once the center of one of the most powerful empires in Europe. The royal Habsburg family came to control this empire. At its height, the Habsburg line ruled the Netherlands, Spain, and much of Germany, Italy, and Eastern Europe.

In 1918, however, the Habsburgs were on the losing side of World War I. After the war, Austria became a republic. Since then, Austria has grown into a modern, industrialized nation. Today it is a federal republic and EU member.

The Alpine Countries

Austria and Switzerland draw millions of tourists each year. Above, tourists ride through Vienna, Austria, famous for its history and culture. At left, a mountain village shows the beauty of the Swiss Alps.

Most Austrians speak German and are Roman Catholic. The city of **Vienna** is Austria's capital and largest city. Located on the banks of the Danube, Vienna was once the center of Habsburg rule. Today historic palaces grace the city, which is a center of music and the fine arts.

Austria has a prosperous economy with little unemployment. Service industries, such as banking, are important and employ more than half of Austria's workforce. Tourism is important as well.

Switzerland

Since the 1600s Switzerland has been an independent country. Today it is a federal republic with 26 districts called **cantons**. Citizens are active in local government. In addition, all male citizens serve for a period in the militia, a citizen army.

Switzerland's location in the Alps has helped it remain **neutral** for centuries. To stay neutral, Switzerland has not joined the EU or NATO. The Swiss are active in international organizations, however.

As the map shows, the Swiss speak several languages. The main languages are German and French. Switzerland's capital, **Bern**, is centrally located to be near both German- and French-speaking regions.

Switzerland has one of the world's highest standards of living. It is famous for its banks, watches and other precision devices, and chocolate and cheese.

READING CHECK **Contrasting** How are the countries of Austria and Switzerland different?

SUMMARY AND PREVIEW You have read that Germany is an economic power with a rich culture, while the Alpine Countries are prosperous with beautiful mountain scenery. In the next chapter you will learn about Northern Europe.

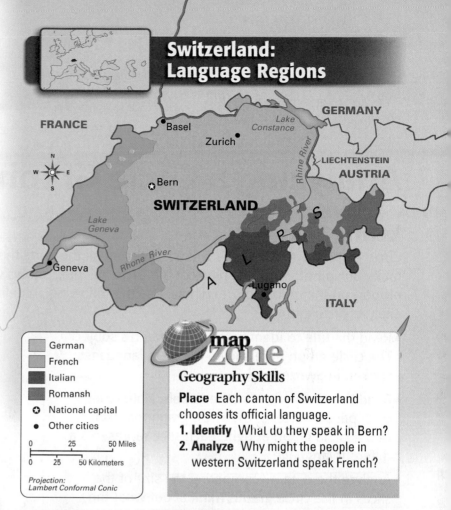

Switzerland: Language Regions

FRANCE — Basel, Zurich — GERMANY — Lake Constance — Rhine River — LIECHTENSTEIN — AUSTRIA — Bern — SWITZERLAND — Lake Geneva — A L P S — Rhone River — Geneva — Lugano — ITALY

- German
- French
- Italian
- Romansh
- ⊛ National capital
- • Other cities

0   25   50 Miles
0   25   50 Kilometers

Projection: Lambert Conformal Conic

mapzone

Geography Skills

Place Each canton of Switzerland chooses its official language.
1. **Identify** What do they speak in Bern?
2. **Analyze** Why might the people in western Switzerland speak French?

Section 3 Assessment

hmhsocialstudies.com
ONLINE QUIZ

Reviewing Ideas, Terms, and Places

1. a. **Identify** Why is Adolf Hitler significant in history?
   b. **Sequence** What events led to German reunification?
2. a. **Recall** What are some popular festivals in Germany?
   b. **Contrast** How does religion differ across Germany?
3. a. **Describe** What is the role of Germany's **chancellor**?
   b. **Explain** Why has Germany's economy slowed?
4. a. **Define** What are **cantons**, and where are they found?
   b. **Analyze** How are the Alps a valuable resource?

Critical Thinking

5. **Comparing and Contrasting** Draw a Venn diagram like this one. Use your notes to list the differences and similarities.

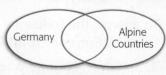

Germany — Alpine Countries

FOCUS ON SPEAKING

6. **Describing Germany and the Alpine Countries** For each country, note one issue for your speech. For example, you might argue that the Alps are the region's loveliest area.

Analyzing a Circle Graph

Learn

Circle graphs, also called pie charts, represent all the parts that make up something. Each piece of the circle, or "pie," shows what proportion that part is of the whole. Use the following guidelines to analyze circle graphs.

- Read the title to identify the circle graph's subject. The circle graph here shows the main languages spoken in Switzerland.

- Read the circle graph's other labels. Note what each part, or slice, of the circle graph represents. In the circle graph at right, each slice represents a different language.

- Analyze the data by comparing the size of the slices in the circle graph. Think about what the differences mean or imply.

Practice

❶ Based on the circle graph at right, what are the three main languages spoken in Switzerland?

❷ What language do less than 1 percent of the Swiss speak?

❸ What percentage of the Swiss speak other languages not listed individually?

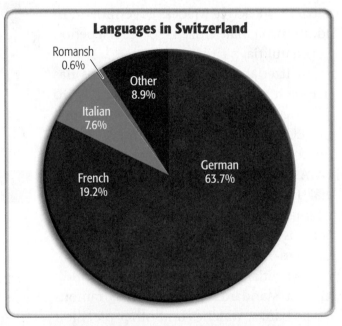

Languages in Switzerland

Romansh 0.6%
Other 8.9%
Italian 7.6%
French 19.2%
German 63.7%

Source: Central Intelligence Agency, *The World Factbook 2002*

Apply

To answer the following questions, use the circle graph titled France's Current Export Partners in the Standardized Test Practice.

1. To which country does France send the highest percentage of its exports?

2. How many of France's main export partners belong to the European Union?

3. What percentage of French exports go to the United States?

Chapter Review

Geography's Impact
video series
Review the video to answer the closing question:
Do you think proximity to the sea has been more beneficial or harmful to the Netherlands?

Visual Summary

Use the visual summary below to help you review the main ideas of the chapter.

QUICK FACTS

France is a leading European nation and cultural center. The Benelux Countries are small, densely populated, and rich.

Germany is an industrial powerhouse with a rich culture. The landlocked Alpine Countries have stunning mountains.

Reviewing Vocabulary, Terms, and Places

Match each "I" statement below with the person, place, or thing that might have made the statement.

a. Berlin
b. Brussels
c. canton
d. chancellor
e. cosmopolitan city
f. Danube River
g. dike
h. navigable river
i. North Sea
j. Paris

1. "I am the capital of France and a center of business, finance, learning, and culture."
2. "I am an important waterway in the region of West-Central Europe."
3. "I am a prime minister in Germany."
4. "I am an earthen wall used to hold back water."
5. "I am a type of river that is wide and deep enough for ships to use."
6. "I am a district in Switzerland."
7. "I am a city that has many foreign influences."
8. "I am an international city and the capital of Belgium."
9. "I am a large body of water located to the north of the Benelux Countries and Germany."
10. "I was divided into two parts after World War II and am now the capital of Germany."

Comprehension and Critical Thinking

SECTION 1 *(Pages 128–131)*

11. **a. Recall** From southeast to northwest, what are the major landforms in West-Central Europe?

b. Analyze How have geographic features supported trade and travel across the region of West-Central Europe?

c. Elaborate How does West-Central Europe's mild climate serve as a valuable resource and contribute to the economy?

SECTION 2 (Pages 132–137)

12. a. Identify Where is the busiest seaport in the Netherlands located?

b. Summarize What are some products and cultural features for which France is famous?

c. Develop How have geographic features helped the Benelux Countries become centers of trade and international business?

SECTION 3 (Pages 140–145)

13. a. Recall What are three major events in German history, and when did each one occur?

b. Analyze How is Switzerland's position in European affairs unique?

c. Elaborate How has the royal Habsburg family shaped Austria's history?

Social Studies Skills

Analyzing a Circle Graph *Use the circle graph titled Languages in Switzerland in the Social Studies Skills to answer the following questions.*

14. Based on the circle graph, what percentage of the Swiss speak German?

15. What percentage of the Swiss speak French and Italian?

16. What fourth language do the Swiss speak?

Using the Internet 21ST CENTURY

17. Activity: Researching Schools Imagine that your family is moving to Belgium or the Netherlands. In your new country you will be attending an international school. What kinds of classes will you have? What will your school day be like? What kinds of things might you see and do outside of school? Through your online textbook, research schools and daily life there. Then complete the online worksheet to record what you have learned. Finally, compare the schools you researched to the school you attend today.

⌐ hmhsocialstudies.com

Map Activity 21ST CENTURY

18. West-Central Europe On a separate sheet of paper, match the letters on the map with their correct labels.

Alps

Berlin, Germany

North Sea

Northern European Plain

Paris, France

Pyrenees

Vienna, Austria

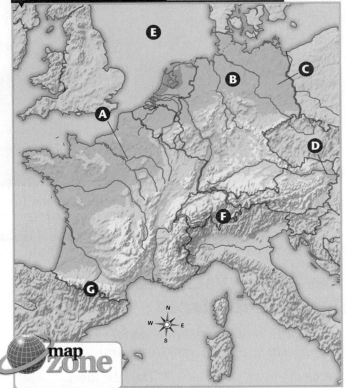

⌐ hmhsocialstudies.com **INTERACTIVE MAP**

map zone

FOCUS ON READING AND SPEAKING

19. Recognizing Word Origins Find the key term cosmopolitan in Section 2. Write the word's definition. Then use a good dictionary to research the word's origins. Explain how the word's origins relate to its definition.

20. Writing a Persuasive Speech Choose one of the issues you identified as you read the chapter. Write an opinion statement about the issue, such as "The Dutch polders should be restored to wetlands." Next, list three facts or examples that support your opinion. Use the chapter and other sources to find information. Then use the list to write your short persuasive speech. Practice delivering your speech using an assured tone of voice and a confident posture.

Standardized Test Prep

DIRECTIONS: Read questions 1 through 7 and write the letter of the best response. Then read question 8 and write your own well-constructed response.

1 The alpine mountain system includes the Alps and the

A Black Forest.

B Jura Mountains.

C Massif Central.

D Pyrenees.

2 What type of climate does *most* of West-Central Europe have?

A highland climate

B humid tropical climate

C marine west coast climate

D Mediterranean climate

3 Which three countries make up the Benelux Countries?

A Belgium, the Netherlands, and Luxembourg

B France, Belgium, and Luxembourg

C France, Germany, and Austria

D Germany, Austria, and Switzerland

4 Which French leader created a great empire only to be defeated in 1815?

A Adolf Hitler

B Charlemagne

C Napoleon

D William the Conqueror

5 What capital city in West-Central Europe was divided after World War II?

A Berlin

B Brussels

C Paris

D Vienna

France's Current Export Partners

Germany* 15%
Spain* 10%
Italy* 9%
United Kingdom* 9%
Belgium* 7%
United States 7%
Other 43%

*European Union Member

Source: Central Intelligence Agency, *The World Factbook 2005*

6 Based on the graph above, what percentage of French goods went to France's top two export partners?

A 10%

B 15%

C 25%

D 30%

7 What is the main language spoken in both of the Alpine Countries?

A Dutch

B French

C German

D Italian

8 **Extended Response** Examine the map of Germany in Section 3. Use the map to explain how the physical geography of former East and West Germany differed. Then analyze how you think each former country's physical geography affected its economy.

CHAPTER 6

Northern Europe

Essential Question How has location shaped the development of nations in Northern Europe?

What You Will Learn...

In this chapter you will discover Northern Europe's unique and varied physical geography. You will also study the history and culture of Northern Europe's two main regions—the British Isles and Scandinavia. Finally, you will learn about the British Isles and Scandinavia today.

FOCUS ON READING AND WRITING

Using Context Clues—Synonyms As you read, you may occasionally encounter a word or phrase that you do not know. When that happens, use the words and sentences around the unfamiliar word—context clues—to help you determine the word's meaning. As you read this chapter, look for words that are synonyms, or words that mean the same as the unfamiliar word. **See the lesson, Using Context Clues—Synonyms, on page 225.**

Writing a Letter Letters are a great way to stay in touch with friends and family. As you read this chapter, gather information about Northern Europe. Then imagine you are traveling through this region. Write a letter to your friends and family at home in which you describe what you have learned on your travels.

Geography Fertile plains like this one in Ireland provide Northern Europe with much of its farmland.

Northern Europe: Political

HISTORY Winston Churchill

↗ hmhsocialstudies.com **VIDEO**

70°N

ARCTIC OCEAN

Tromso

Arctic Circle

Norwegian Sea

10°E

20°E

FINLAND

SWEDEN

Gulf of Bothnia

RUSSIA

NORWAY

Bergen

Oslo

Helsinki

Gulf of Finland

North Sea

Stockholm

ESTONIA

Göteborg

Baltic Sea

LATVIA

DENMARK
Copenhagen

LITHUANIA

RUSSIA

BELARUS

NETHERLANDS

GERMANY

POLAND

map zone Geography Skills

Location Much of Northern Europe is separated from the rest of the continent by the English Channel and the North and Baltic seas.

1. Identify What countries extend north of the Arctic Circle?

2. Contrast How does Northern Europe differ physically from the rest of Europe?

History The Palace of Westminster in London has been home to the British Parliament for over 600 years.

Culture Skiing and other forms of outdoor recreation are popular throughout much of Scandinavia.

Physical Geography

What You Will Learn...

Main Ideas

1. The physical features of Northern Europe include low mountain ranges and jagged coastlines.
2. Northern Europe's natural resources include energy sources, soils, and seas.
3. The climates of Northern Europe range from a mild coastal climate to a freezing ice cap climate.

The Big Idea

Northern Europe is a region of unique physical features, rich resources, and diverse climates.

Key Terms and Places

British Isles, *p. 152*
Scandinavia, *p. 152*
fjord, *p. 153*
geothermal energy, *p. 154*
North Atlantic Drift, *p. 154*

hmhsocialstudies.com
TAKING NOTES

Use the graphic organizer online to take notes on the physical geography of Northern Europe.

If **YOU** lived there...

Your family is planning to visit friends in Tromso, Norway. It is a city on the Norwegian Sea located 200 miles north of the Arctic Circle. You imagine a landscape covered in snow and ice. When you arrive, however, you discover green hills and ice-free harbors.

What might explain the mild climate?

BUILDING BACKGROUND Although located at high latitudes, Norway and the rest of Northern Europe have surprisingly mild temperatures. All the countries of Northern Europe are located on seas and oceans. As a result, they benefit from ocean currents that bring warm water north and keep the climate reasonably warm.

Physical Features

From Ireland's gently rolling hills to Iceland's icy glaciers and fiery volcanoes, Northern Europe is a land of great variety. Because of this variety, the physical geography of Northern Europe changes greatly from one location to another.

Two regions—the British Isles and Scandinavia—make up Northern Europe. To the southwest lie the **British Isles**, a group of islands located across the English Channel from the rest of Europe. Northeast of the British Isles is **Scandinavia**, a region of islands and peninsulas in far northern Europe. The island of Iceland, to the west, is often considered part of Scandinavia.

Hills and Mountains Rough, rocky hills and low mountains cover much of Northern Europe. Rugged hills stretch across much of Iceland, northern Scotland, and Scandinavia. The jagged Kjolen (CHUH-luhn) Mountains on the Scandinavian Peninsula divide Norway from Sweden. The rocky soil and uneven terrain in these parts of Northern Europe make farming there difficult. As a result, fewer people live there than in the rest of Northern Europe.

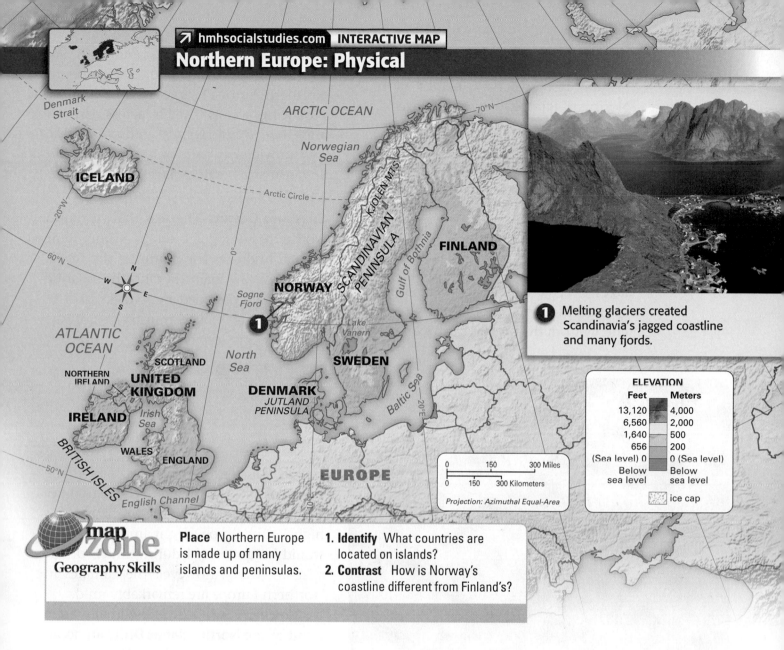

1 Melting glaciers created Scandinavia's jagged coastline and many fjords.

ELEVATION

Feet	Meters
13,120	4,000
6,560	2,000
1,640	500
656	200
(Sea level) 0	0 (Sea level)
Below sea level	Below sea level

ice cap

0   150   300 Miles
0   150   300 Kilometers
Projection: Azimuthal Equal-Area

map zone

Geography Skills

Place Northern Europe is made up of many islands and peninsulas.

1. **Identify** What countries are located on islands?
2. **Contrast** How is Norway's coastline different from Finland's?

Farmland and Plains Fertile farmland and flat plains stretch across the southern parts of the British Isles and Scandinavia. Ireland's rolling, green hills provide rich farmland. Wide valleys in England and Denmark also have plenty of fertile soil.

Effects of Glaciers Slow-moving sheets of ice, or glaciers, have left their mark on Northern Europe's coastlines and lakes. As you can see on the map above, Norway's western coastline is very jagged. Millions of years ago, glaciers cut deep valleys into Norway's coastal mountains. As the glaciers melted, these valleys filled with water, creating deep fjords. A **fjord** (fee-AWRD) is a narrow inlet of the sea set between high, rocky cliffs. Many fjords are very long and deep. Norway's Sogne (SAWNG-nuh) Fjord, for example, is over 100 miles (160 km) long and more than three-quarters of a mile (1.2 km) deep. Melting glaciers also carved thousands of lakes in Northern Europe. Sweden's Lake Vanern, along with many of the lakes in the British Isles, were carved by glaciers thousands of years ago.

READING CHECK **Summarizing** What are some physical features of Northern Europe?

Natural Resources

Natural resources have helped to make Northern Europe one of the wealthiest regions in the world. Northern Europe's **primary** resources are its energy resources, forests and soils, and surrounding seas.

Energy Northern Europe has a variety of energy resources. Norway and the United Kingdom benefit from oil and natural gas deposits under the North Sea. Hydroelectric energy is produced by the region's many lakes and rivers. In Iceland steam from hot springs produces **geothermal energy**, or energy from the heat of Earth's interior.

Forests and Soils Forests and soils are two other important natural resources in Northern Europe. Large areas of timber-producing forests stretch across Finland and the Scandinavian Peninsula. Fertile soils provide rich farmland for crops, such as wheat and potatoes. Livestock like sheep and dairy cattle are also common.

Seas and Oceans The seas that surround Northern Europe are another important natural resource. For centuries, the North Sea, the Norwegian Sea, and the Atlantic Ocean have provided rich stocks of fish. Today, fishing is a key industry in Norway, Denmark, and Iceland.

READING CHECK **Summarizing** What natural resources are found in Northern Europe?

Satellite View

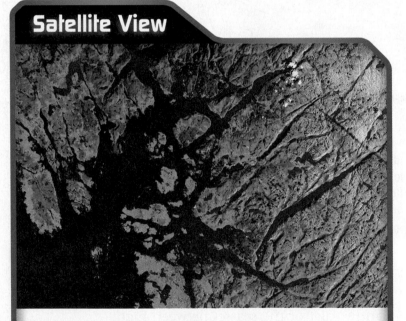

Norway's Fjords

Millions of years ago much of Norway was covered with glaciers. As the glaciers flowed slowly downhill, they carved long, winding channels, or fjords, into Norway's coastline.

As you can see in this satellite image, fjords cut many miles into Norway's interior, bringing warm waters from the North and Norwegian seas. As warm waters penetrate inland, they keep temperatures relatively mild. In fact, people have used these unfrozen fjords to travel during the winter when ice and snow made travel over land difficult.

Drawing Conclusions How do fjords benefit life in Norway?

Climates

Locate Northern Europe on a map of the world. Notice that much of the region lies near the Arctic Circle. Due to the region's high latitude, you might imagine that it would be quite cold during much of the year. In reality, however, the climates in Northern Europe are remarkably mild.

Northern Europe's mild climates are a result of the **North Atlantic Drift**, an ocean current that brings warm, moist air across the Atlantic Ocean. Warm waters from this ocean current keep most of the region warmer than other locations around the globe at similar latitudes.

Much of Northern Europe has a marine west coast climate. Denmark, the British Isles, and western Norway benefit from mild summers and frequent rainfall. Snow and frosts may occur in winter but do not usually last long.

Central Norway, Sweden, and southern Finland have a humid continental climate. This area has four true seasons with cold, snowy winters and mild summers.

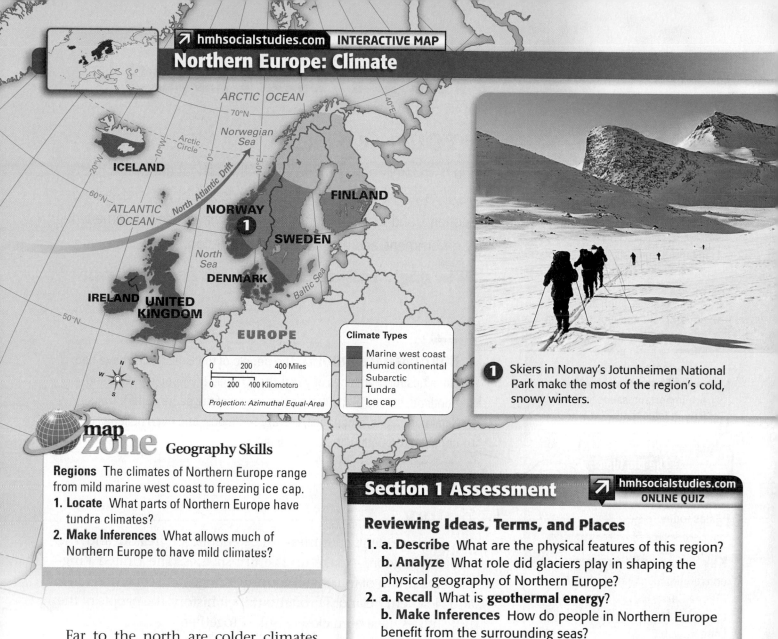

ARCTIC OCEAN
70°N
Arctic Circle
Norwegian Sea
ICELAND
ATLANTIC OCEAN
60°N
NORWAY ①
North Atlantic Drift
FINLAND
SWEDEN
North Sea
DENMARK
Baltic Sea
IRELAND
UNITED KINGDOM
50°N
EUROPE

Climate Types
- Marine west coast
- Humid continental
- Subarctic
- Tundra
- Ice cap

0   200   400 Miles
0   200   400 Kilometers
Projection: Azimuthal Equal-Area

① Skiers in Norway's Jotunheimen National Park make the most of the region's cold, snowy winters.

map zone Geography Skills

Regions The climates of Northern Europe range from mild marine west coast to freezing ice cap.
1. **Locate** What parts of Northern Europe have tundra climates?
2. **Make Inferences** What allows much of Northern Europe to have mild climates?

Far to the north are colder climates. Subarctic regions, like those in Northern Scandinavia, have long, cold winters and short summers. Iceland's tundra and ice cap climates produce extremely cold temperatures all year.

READING CHECK **Analyzing** How does the North Atlantic Drift keep climates mild?

SUMMARY AND PREVIEW Northern Europe has many different physical features, natural resources, and climates. Next, you will learn about the history and culture of the British Isles.

Section 1 Assessment

↗ hmhsocialstudies.com
ONLINE QUIZ

Reviewing Ideas, Terms, and Places

1. **a. Describe** What are the physical features of this region?
   b. Analyze What role did glaciers play in shaping the physical geography of Northern Europe?
2. **a. Recall** What is **geothermal energy**?
   b. Make Inferences How do people in Northern Europe benefit from the surrounding seas?
3. **a. Identify** What climates exist in Northern Europe?
   b. Predict How might the climates of Northern Europe be different without the **North Atlantic Drift**?

Critical Thinking

4. **Comparing and Contrasting** Using your notes and a chart like the one below, compare and contrast the physical geography of the British Isles and Scandinavia.

	British Isles	Scandinavia
Physical Features		
Resources		
Climates		

FOCUS ON WRITING

5. **Describing the Physical Geography** Take notes on the physical features, resources, and climates of Northern Europe. In what season might you visit the region?

The British Isles

If YOU lived there...

You have family and friends that live throughout the British Isles. On visits you have discovered that the people of England, Ireland, Scotland, and Wales share the same language, use the same type of government, and eat many of the same foods.

Why might culture in the British Isles be similar?

BUILDING BACKGROUND The people of the British Isles have had close ties for thousands of years. As a result, the people of England, Scotland, Ireland, and Wales share many of the same culture traits. Similar religions, languages, literary traditions, and even holidays are common throughout the British Isles.

History

Two independent countries—the Republic of Ireland and the United Kingdom—make up the British Isles. The United Kingdom is a union of four small countries: England, Scotland, Wales, and Northern Ireland. Throughout their history, the people of the British Isles have been closely linked together.

What You Will Learn...

Main Ideas

1. Invaders and a global empire have shaped the history of the British Isles.
2. British culture, such as government and music, has influenced much of the world.
3. Efforts to bring peace to Northern Ireland and maintain strong economies are important issues in the British Isles today.

The Big Idea

Close cultural and historical ties link the people of the British Isles today.

Key Terms and Places

constitutional monarchy, *p. 158*
Magna Carta, *p. 158*
disarm, *p. 159*
London, *p. 160*
Dublin, *p. 160*

hmhsocialstudies.com
TAKING NOTES

Use the graphic organizer online to take notes on the British Isles.

Time Line

History of the British Isles

1558–1603
England becomes a world power during the reign of Queen Elizabeth I.

3100 BC **1600**

3100 BC Ancient settlers in England build Stonehenge.

Early History

The history of the British Isles dates back thousands of years. Early settlers built Stonehenge, an ancient monument, some 5,000 years ago. Around 450 BC, the Celts (KELTS) arrived in the British Isles and settled Scotland, Wales, and Ireland. Britain was even part of the ancient Roman Empire.

In the Middle Ages a series of invaders ruled the British Isles. The Angles, Saxons, and Vikings all established small kingdoms in Britain. Finally, in 1066, the Normans from northern France conquered England and established a strong kingdom there.

Over time, England grew in strength and power. It soon overshadowed its neighbors in the British Isles. By the 1500s strong rulers like Queen Elizabeth I had turned England into a world power.

Rise of the British Empire

A strong economy and mighty navy helped England build a vast empire. Over time, England joined with Wales and Scotland to create the United Kingdom of Great Britain. Eventually, Ireland was annexed too. England also launched an overseas empire. By the 1800s Britain had colonies in the Americas, India, and Australia.

The United Kingdom's economy soared in the 1700s and 1800s, thanks to the Industrial Revolution. Industries like iron, steel, and textiles, or cloth products, helped make the United Kingdom one of the world's richest countries.

Not everyone benefited, however. In the 1840s a severe food shortage devastated Ireland. Lack of support from the English government during the famine increased tensions between the two countries.

BIOGRAPHY

Sir Winston Churchill
(1874–1965)

One of Britain's greatest leaders, Sir Winston Churchill, guided the United Kingdom through the dark days of World War II. Churchill was appointed prime minister shortly after the beginning of World War II. He inspired the British to continue fighting despite Germany's defeat of much of Europe. During the Battle of Britain, Churchill gave fiery speeches. He encouraged British citizens to "never surrender." His creation of an alliance with the Soviet Union and the United States led to Germany's eventual defeat. Churchill's determination helped the Allies win the war.

Evaluating Do you think Churchill was important to British history? Why or why not?

HISTORY

VIDEO
Winston Churchill

↗ hmhsocialstudies.com

FOCUS ON READING
What are *textiles*? How can you tell?

1730–1860
The Industrial Revolution brings great wealth to England.

1940
London is bombed during the Battle of Britain in World War II.

1700 · · · 1800 · · · 1900 · · · 2000

1858–1947
The British Empire controls India, its most valuable colony.

ANALYSIS SKILL   READING TIME LINES

About how many years ago was Stonehenge built?

By the late 1800s the British Empire spanned the globe. Africa, Asia, Australia, and the Americas were all home to British colonies. At its height, the British Empire was the largest empire in history.

Decline of Empire

In the 1900s the British Empire began to fall apart. Both World War I and the Great Depression hurt the British economy. Rebellions in Ireland forced Britain to grant self-rule to all but the northern part of Ireland. In 1949 the Republic of Ireland gained full independence. Movements for independence also emerged in Britain's overseas colonies. After World War II, Great Britain gave up most of its colonies. The British Empire was no more.

READING CHECK Sequencing What major events mark the history of the British Isles?

Culture

People in different regions of the British Isles hold fast to regional traditions and customs. Here, Scots proudly display two symbols of Scottish culture—bagpipes and kilts.

Culture

For years the British ruled much of the world. As a result, the government, people, and popular culture of the British Isles have influenced people all around the globe.

Government

The government of the United Kingdom is a **constitutional monarchy**, a type of democracy in which a king or queen serves as head of state but a legislature makes the laws. The English first limited the power of monarchs in the Middle Ages. A document known as **Magna Carta**, or Great Charter, limited the powers of kings. It also required everyone to obey the law. Today, a prime minister leads the British government. Most members of Britain's legislative body, known as Parliament, are elected.

The Republic of Ireland has a president as head of state. The president, who has limited powers, appoints a prime minister. Together with the Irish parliament, the prime minister runs the government.

People

For hundreds of years, the countries of the British Isles have had close ties. As a result, the countries share many culture traits. One similarity is their common heritage. Many people in the British Isles can trace their heritage to the region's early settlers, such as the Celts, Angles, and Saxons. Sports like soccer and rugby are another shared trait among the people of Britain.

Although people in the British Isles share many culture traits, each region still maintains its own unique identity. This is particularly true in Ireland and Scotland. Unlike the rest of the British Isles, most Irish are Roman Catholic. Irish Gaelic, a Celtic language, is one of the country's official languages. The people of Scotland have also maintained their unique culture.

It is not unusual in Scotland to see people wearing kilts and playing bagpipes on special occasions.

Immigrants from all corners of the world have settled in Britain. Many immigrants from former British colonies, such as India and Jamaica, add to the rich culture of the British Isles.

Popular Culture

British popular culture influences people all around the globe. For example, English is the language of business, education, and the Internet in many places. British music and literature are also popular. Millions of people around the globe listen to music by bands like Ireland's U2 and England's The Beatles and read works by British authors like William Shakespeare.

READING CHECK **Summarizing** What parts of British culture have spread around the world?

British Isles Today

The British Isles face some challenges. Efforts to bring peace to Northern Ireland and to maintain a powerful economy are key issues in the British Isles today.

Northern Ireland

One of the toughest problems facing the British Isles today is conflict in Northern Ireland. Disputes between the people of Northern Ireland have a long history.

In the 1500s Protestants from England and Scotland began settling in Northern Ireland. Over time, they outnumbered Irish Catholics in the area. When Ireland became a separate state, Northern Ireland's Protestant majority chose to remain part of the United Kingdom.

Since then, many Catholics in Northern Ireland believe they have not been treated fairly by Protestants. Some Catholics hope to unite with the Republic of Ireland. For years the two sides have waged a bitter and violent struggle. In the late 1990s peace talks between the two warring sides began. An **agreement** eventually led to a cease-fire and the creation of a national assembly in Northern Ireland. However, the refusal of some groups to **disarm**, or give up all weapons, stalled the peace talks. Recently, however, hopes are once again high that peaceful relations between the groups will bring about a long-lasting peace.

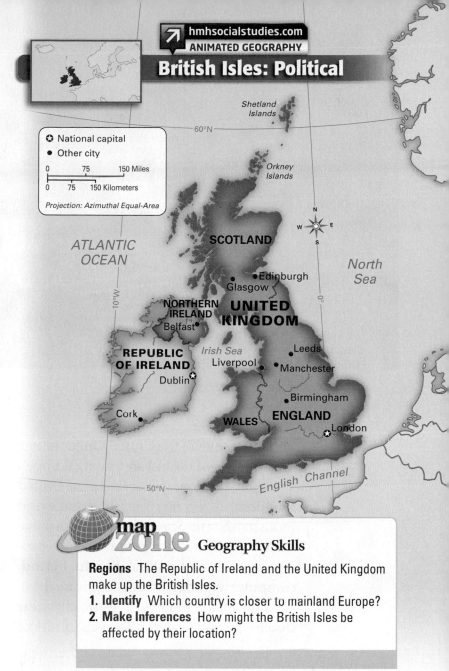

Shetland Islands
60°N
Orkney Islands

⊕ National capital
● Other city
0   75   150 Miles
0   75   150 Kilometers
Projection: Azimuthal Equal-Area

ATLANTIC OCEAN
SCOTLAND
North Sea
Edinburgh
Glasgow
NORTHERN IRELAND
UNITED KINGDOM
Belfast
REPUBLIC OF IRELAND
Irish Sea
Liverpool
Leeds
Manchester
Dublin
Birmingham
Cork
WALES
ENGLAND
London
English Channel
50°N

map zone **Geography Skills**

Regions The Republic of Ireland and the United Kingdom make up the British Isles.
1. **Identify** Which country is closer to mainland Europe?
2. **Make Inferences** How might the British Isles be affected by their location?

ACADEMIC VOCABULARY

agreement a decision reached by two or more people or groups

The largest city in the British Isles, London serves as one of Europe's major financial centers.

The Economy

The economies of the United Kingdom and the Republic of Ireland are among Europe's strongest. **London**, the capital of the United Kingdom, is a center for world trade and industry. North Sea energy reserves have made the United Kingdom a major producer of oil and natural gas. In Ireland, computer equipment and software have become major industries, especially near **Dublin**, Ireland's capital. The economies of the United Kingdom and the Republic of Ireland also rely on service industries like banking, tourism, and insurance.

READING CHECK **Summarizing** What has been the cause of conflict in Northern Ireland?

SUMMARY AND PREVIEW You have learned about the rich history and culture of the British Isles. Next, you will learn about the countries of Scandinavia.

Section 2 Assessment

Reviewing Ideas, Terms, and Places

1. **a. Identify** What peoples invaded the British Isles?
   b. Make Inferences How did the Industrial Revolution strengthen the British Empire?
2. **a. Describe** What elements of British culture are found around the world?
   b. Explain How did **Magna Carta** affect British government?
3. **a. Define** What does **disarm** mean?
   b. Analyze What are the central issues of the conflict in Northern Ireland?
   c. Elaborate Why do you think the economy of the British Isles is so strong?

Critical Thinking

4. **Summarizing** Using your notes and a graphic organizer like the one here, summarize the history and culture of the British Isles in your own words.

FOCUS ON WRITING

5. **Writing about the British Isles** What information about the British Isles do you think is most interesting? Take notes on what you could include in a letter to someone who has never visited the area.

Social Studies Skills

Writing to Learn

Learn

Writing is an important tool for learning new information. When you write about what you read, you can better understand and remember information. For example, when you write a list of items you need from the grocery store, the act of writing can help you remember what to buy. Use the steps below to write to learn.

• Read the text carefully. Look for the main idea and important details.

• Think about the information you just read. Then summarize in your own words what you learned.

• Write a personal response to what you read. What do you think about the information? What questions might you have? How does this information affect you?

Practice

Use the steps you just learned to practice writing to learn. Read the paragraph below carefully, then complete a chart like the one here.

Tromso, Norway, is one of Europe's northern-most cities. Because of Earth's tilt and Tromso's location north of the Arctic Circle, the city experiences unusual conditions in both summer and winter. During the summer, the sun stays above the horizon continuously from late May to late July. In winter, residents of Tromso do not see the sun from November to January.

What I Learned	Personal Response

Apply

Read the information in Section 3 carefully. Then create a chart similar to the one above. In the first column, summarize the key ideas from the section in your own words. Use the second column to write your personal reaction to the information you learned.

Scandinavia

If YOU lived there...

You live in Copenhagen, the picturesque capital of Denmark. One of your favorite walks is along the waterfront, which is lined with colorful medieval buildings. Sailing boats of all sizes are anchored here. A famous statue in the harbor shows the Little Mermaid. But your favorite place of all is the huge amusement park called Tivoli Gardens, where you can enjoy fun and good food.

What sights would you show to a visitor?

What You Will Learn...

Main Ideas

1. The history of Scandinavia dates back to the time of the Vikings.
2. Scandinavia today is known for its peaceful and prosperous countries.

The Big Idea

Scandinavia has developed into one of the most stable and prosperous regions in Europe.

Key Terms and Places

Vikings, *p. 162*
Stockholm, *p. 164*
neutral, *p. 164*
uninhabitable, *p. 165*
Oslo, *p. 165*
Helsinki, *p. 165*
geysers, *p. 166*

hmhsocialstudies.com
TAKING NOTES

Use the graphic organizer online to take notes on Scandinavia.

BUILDING BACKGROUND After a long and warlike history, the modern countries of Scandinavia are models of peace and prosperity for the rest of Europe. Their cultures are similar in several ways, but each country has its own personality.

History

Hundreds of years ago, Scandinavia was home to warlike Vikings. The **Vikings** were Scandinavian warriors who raided Europe and the Mediterranean in the early Middle Ages. Excellent sailors, the Vikings used quick and powerful longboats to attack villages along coasts or rivers. The Vikings conquered the British Isles, Finland, and parts of France, Germany, and Russia. They were some of the most feared warriors of their time.

The Vikings were also great explorers. They established the first settlements in Iceland in the 800s and in Greenland in the 900s. A short time later, Vikings led by Leif Eriksson became the first Europeans to reach North America. The ruins of a Viking colony have been found in present-day Newfoundland, off the southeast coast of Canada.

In the 1100s the Viking raids ended. Powerful Scandinavian chiefs instead concentrated on strengthening their kingdoms. During the Middle Ages three kingdoms—Norway, Sweden, and Denmark—competed for power in the region.

Denmark was the first to gain the upper hand. By the late 1300s Denmark ruled a union of all the Scandinavian kingdoms and territories. Eventually, Sweden challenged Denmark's power.

In time, Sweden left the Danish-led union, taking Finland with it. Many years later, Sweden won control of Norway as well.

By the 1900s Scandinavian countries wanted their independence. Norway won its independence from Sweden in the early 1900s. Soon after, Finland became independent after centuries of foreign <u>domination</u>, or control, by Sweden and later by Russia. Iceland, then a Danish territory, declared its independence in 1944. To this day, however, Greenland remains a part of Denmark as a self-ruling territory.

READING CHECK **Analyzing** What historical ties do the countries of Scandinavia have?

FOCUS ON READING

What other word has the same meaning as *domination*? How can you tell?

Close-up

Viking Raids

The Vikings of Scandinavia launched raids on many European settlements in the early Middle Ages. Using powerful longships, Viking warriors attacked towns and villages near coasts and rivers. Vikings even sailed as far as North America in their longships.

A large woolen sail helped increase the ship's speed.

Sometimes as many as 30 oars spanned each side of a longship.

Viking longships were designed the same at each end. As a result, warriors did not have to turn the ship around to make a quick escape.

The longship's shallow design made river travel possible and allowed Viking raiders to sail their ships ashore.

ANALYSIS SKILL **ANALYZING VISUALS**

What aspects of Viking longships might have frightened Europeans who saw them approaching?

Scandinavia Today

Today the countries of Scandinavia have much in common. Similar political views, languages, and religion unite the region. The countries of Scandinavia have large, wealthy cities, strong economies, and well-educated workers. Scandinavians enjoy some of the world's highest standards of living. Each country provides its citizens with excellent social programs and services, such as free health care. Sweden, Denmark, Greenland, Norway, Finland, and Iceland are among the world's most peaceful, stable, and prosperous nations.

Sweden

Sweden is Scandinavia's largest and most populous country. Most Swedes live in the southern part of the country in large towns and cities. In fact, more than 84 percent of Swedes live in urban areas. **Stockholm**, Sweden's capital and largest city, is located on the east coast near the Baltic Sea. Often called a floating city, Stockholm is built on 14 islands and part of the mainland.

For almost 200 years, Sweden has been a neutral country. **Neutral** means that it has chosen not to take sides in an international conflict. Sweden does, however, play an active role in the United Nations as well as the European Union.

Denmark

Denmark, once the most powerful country in Scandinavia, is also the smallest. It is Scandinavia's most densely populated country, with some 336 people per square mile (130 per square km).

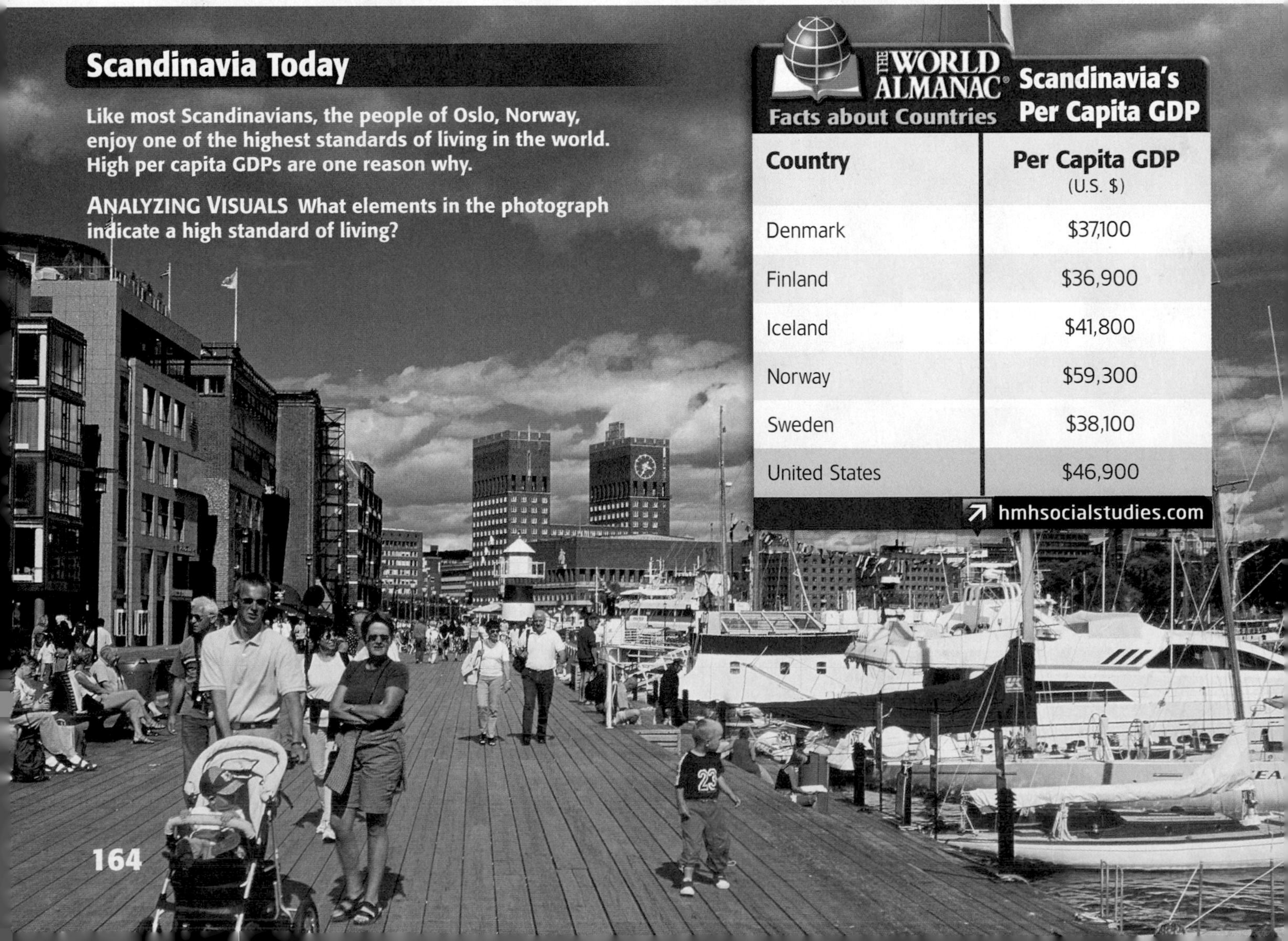

Scandinavia Today

Like most Scandinavians, the people of Oslo, Norway, enjoy one of the highest standards of living in the world. High per capita GDPs are one reason why.

ANALYZING VISUALS What elements in the photograph indicate a high standard of living?

THE WORLD ALMANAC Facts about Countries — Scandinavia's Per Capita GDP

Country	Per Capita GDP (U.S. $)
Denmark	$37,100
Finland	$36,900
Iceland	$41,800
Norway	$59,300
Sweden	$38,100
United States	$46,900

↗ hmhsocialstudies.com

About 50 percent of Denmark's land is good for farming. Farm goods, especially meat and dairy products, are important Danish exports. Denmark also has modern industries, including iron, steel, textiles, and electronics industries.

Greenland

The island of Greenland is geographically part of North America. However, it is a territory of Denmark. A thick ice sheet covers about 80 percent of the island. Because of this, much of Greenland is **uninhabitable**, or not able to support human settlement. Most people live on the island's southwest coast where the climate is warmest.

Recently, a movement for complete independence from Denmark has gained popularity. However, economic problems make independence unlikely, as Greenland relies heavily on imports and economic aid from Denmark.

Norway

With one of the longest coastlines in the world, Norway takes advantage of its access to the sea. Fjords shelter Norway's many harbors. Its fishing and shipping fleets are among the largest in the world. **Oslo**, Norway's capital, is the country's leading seaport as well as its industrial center.

Norway has other valuable resources as well. Oil and natural gas provide Norway with the highest per capita GDP in Scandinavia. However, North Sea oil fields are expected to run dry over the next century. Despite strong economic ties to the rest of Europe, Norway's citizens have refused to join the European Union.

Finland

Finland is Scandinavia's easternmost country. It lies between Sweden and Russia. The capital and largest city is **Helsinki**, which is located on the southern coast.

The Sami

The Sami (SAH-mee) people are a unique culture group that lives in far northern Norway, Sweden, Finland, and parts of Russia. They are descendants of Scandinavia's earliest settlers. Traditionally, Sami have earned a living herding reindeer, farming, and fishing. While today's Sami often work and live in modern cities and towns, they try to preserve many traditional Sami culture traits. The Sami language is taught in public schools, traditional reindeer grazing land is protected, and organizations promote Sami customs.

Making Inferences Why do you think the Sami are trying to preserve their traditions and customs?

As with other countries in the region, trade is important to Finland. Paper and other forest products are major exports. Shipbuilding and electronics are also important industries in Finland.

Iceland

Iceland is much greener than its name implies. Fertile farmland along the island's coast produces potatoes and vegetables and supports cattle and sheep.

Icelanders also make good use of their other natural resources. Fish from the rich waters of the Atlantic Ocean account for about 70 percent of Iceland's exports.

Iceland

Iceland's geysers and hot springs produce great amounts of energy. Geothermal plants like this one near the Blue Lagoon hot spring provide heat for buildings and homes throughout the country.

In addition, steam from hot springs and geysers produces geothermal energy. **Geysers** are springs that shoot hot water and steam into the air. Geothermal energy heats many of Iceland's buildings. Each year thousands of tourists flock to see Iceland's many geysers, volcanoes, and glaciers.

READING CHECK **Comparing and Contrasting** In what ways are the countries of Scandinavia similar and different?

SUMMARY AND PREVIEW Scandinavia today is a region of relative peace and stability. A common history and culture link the people of the region. Today, Scandinavia is one of the wealthiest regions in Europe and in the world. In the next chapter, you will learn about the unique geography, history, and culture of another European region—Eastern Europe.

Section 3 Assessment

hmhsocialstudies.com
ONLINE QUIZ

Reviewing Ideas, Terms, and Places

1. **a. Identify** Who were the **Vikings**?
   b. Analyze What effect did the Vikings have on Scandinavian history?
   c. Evaluate Do you think the Vikings helped or hurt the future of Scandinavia? Explain your answer.

2. **a. Define** What does the term **neutral** mean?
   b. Compare What features do the countries of Scandinavia have in common today?
   c. Elaborate In which Scandinavian country would you prefer to live? Why?

Critical Thinking

3. **Finding Main Ideas** Use your notes and this chart to identify two main ideas about Scandinavia's history and two about its culture today.

History	Today

Focus on Writing

4. **Writing about Scandinavia** Where would you travel and what would you see in Scandinavia? Take notes on the details you might include in your letter.

Chapter Review

Geography's Impact
video series
Review the video to answer the closing question:
How have Icelanders made good use of their island's volcanoes?

Visual Summary

Use the visual summary below to help you review the main ideas of the chapter.

QUICK FACTS

Low mountains and plentiful resources are key features of Northern Europe's physical geography.

The British Isles are known around the world for their rich history, vibrant culture, and healthy economies.

The countries of Scandinavia are among the most peaceful and prosperous in the world.

Reviewing Vocabulary, Terms, and Places

Write each word defined below, and circle each letter marked by a star. Then write the word these letters spell.

1. _ _ * _ _ _—to give up all weapons

2. _ _ _ _ _ _ _ _ _ *—a decision reached by two or more people or groups

3. _ _ * _ _—a narrow inlet of the sea set between high, rocky cliffs

4. _ * _ _ _ _ _ _ _ _ _ _ _—a region in far Northern Europe that crosses the Arctic Circle

5. _ _ * _ _ _ _—warriors from Northern Europe who raided much of Europe and the Mediterranean during the early Middle Ages

6. _ _ _ _ * _ _ _ _ _ _ _ _ _—unable to support human settlement

7. _ _ * _ _ _ _ _ _ _ energy—energy produced by the heat of the planet's interior

8. _ _ _ * _ _ _—the capital of the Republic of Ireland

9. _ _ _ * _ _ _—main or most important

Comprehension and Critical Thinking

SECTION 1 *(Pages 152–155)*

10. **a. Identify** What are the major resources found in Northern Europe?

    b. Analyze Explain how the North Atlantic Drift is responsible for the relatively mild climates in Northern Europe.

    c. Elaborate In which region of Northern Europe would you prefer to live—the British Isles or Scandinavia? Why?

SECTION 2 *(Pages 156–160)*

11. **a. Describe** What culture traits do the people of the British Isles share in common?

    b. Make Inferences Why did the people of Ireland want to break away from the British Empire?

    c. Predict How might the conflict in Northern Ireland affect the future of the United Kingdom?

12. a. Recall What countries make up Scandinavia?

b. Compare and Contrast In what ways are the countries of Scandinavia similar and different?

c. Elaborate Why do you think Scandinavian countries today are so prosperous and stable?

Social Studies Skills

13. Writing to Learn Read the paragraph below carefully, then summarize it in your own words. Finally, write a personal response to what you learned in the paragraph.

In the mid-1800s Ireland was devastated by a severe famine. For many Irish, the potato was a key part of their diet. When a disease infected potato crops around the country, millions were left without enough to eat. About 1.5 million Irish died as a result of the Irish Potato Famine.

Map Activity

14. Northern Europe On a separate sheet of paper, match the letters on the map with their correct labels.

Dublin	Oslo
English Channel	Reykjavik
Helsinki	Scandinavian Peninsula
London	Stockholm

hmhsocialstudies.com INTERACTIVE MAP

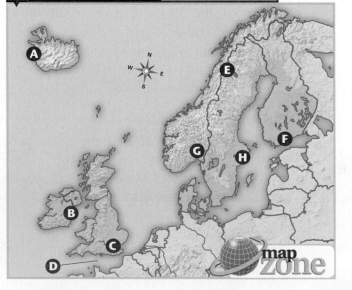

Using the Internet 21st CENTURY

15. Activity: Creating a Poster What does a medieval king have to do with modern democracy? Magna Carta was signed in 1215 by King John I of England. It established the principle that no one, including the king, is above the law. It also opened the door to a more democratic government in England. Centuries later, emerging democracies in the United States and France looked to Magna Carta for guidance. Through your online textbook, learn more about Magna Carta and its relationship with modern democracy. Then create a poster to display some of the ways this document has influenced modern governments.

hmhsocialstudies.com

FOCUS ON READING AND WRITING

Using Context Clues—Synonyms *Use context clues to determine the meaning of the underlined words in the sentences below.*

16. Wealthy in part because of its many natural resources, Scandinavia is one of the most <u>affluent</u> regions in Europe.

17. Thanks to the North Atlantic Drift, the British Isles are rarely affected by <u>inclement</u>, or harsh, weather.

18. <u>Dissent</u>, or disagreement, between Catholics and Protestants has caused years of conflict in Northern Ireland.

Writing a Letter *Use your notes from the chapter and the directions below to write a letter.*

19. Tell your friends and family members what you have seen on your travels in the British Isles and Scandinavia. You may want to organize the information by country. For example, you could start with a flight into London and end in Iceland. Include descriptions of fascinating physical features as well as any cities or cultural activities that are unusual or interesting.

DIRECTIONS: Read questions 1 through 7 and write the letter of the best response. Then read question 8 and write your own well-constructed response.

1 **What group of people from Northern Europe raided Europe between 800 and 1100?**

A Anglo-Saxons

B Celts

C Sami

D Vikings

2 **Which of the following accounts for the relatively mild climate throughout much of Northern Europe?**

A Arctic Ocean

B few mountains or hills

C North Atlantic Drift

D seasonal monsoons

3 **Which Northern European city is a major European economic center?**

A Dublin

B Helsinki

C London

D Stockholm

4 **What important energy source does Iceland use to heat buildings?**

A geothermal energy

B hydroelectric energy

C natural gas

D solar energy

5 **Since the early 1900s, disputes and even violence have disrupted life in**

A Finland.

B Greenland.

C Northern Ireland.

D Scotland.

Scandinavia: Population Density

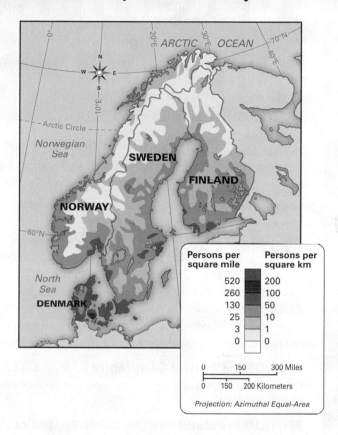

6 **According to the map above, which part of Scandinavia is *least* densely populated?**

A Northern Scandinavia

B Southern Scandinavia

C Eastern Scandinavia

D Western Scandinavia

7 **Which of the following characteristics do the countries of Scandinavia have in common?**

A high standards of living

B membership in the European Union

C status as neutral nations

D high unemployment rates

8 **Extended Response Question** Use the climate map in Section 1 and the map above to write a paragraph explaining how climate might affect settlement patterns in Scandinavia.

Eastern Europe

Essential Question What challenges has Eastern Europe faced since the breakup of the Soviet Union?

What You Will Learn...

In this chapter you will learn about the countries of Eastern Europe. Once dominated by the Soviet Union, these countries have experienced major changes since the early 1990s. In some cases, those changes have been peaceful and have led to great economic success. In other places, the changes resulted in war, economic hardship, and political problems.

FOCUS ON READING AND VIEWING

Understanding Problems and Solutions Writers sometimes organize information by stating a problem and then explaining the solution taken to solve it. To understand this type of writing, you need to identify both problems and solutions. **See the lesson, Understanding Problems and Solutions, on page 226.**

Making a Presentation After you read this chapter, you will present an oral report about one Eastern European country. You will also create a poster showing important features of the country. Finally, you will view and critique your classmates' reports and posters.

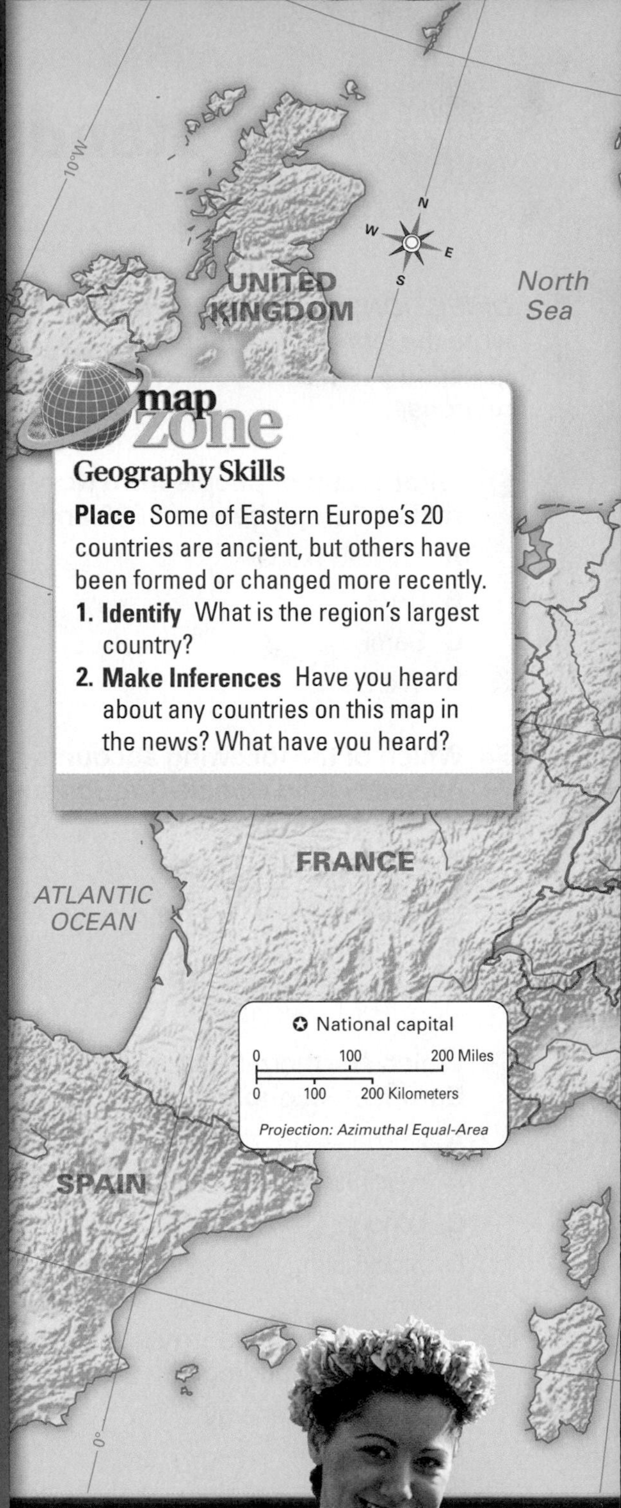

---

map zone
Geography Skills

Place Some of Eastern Europe's 20 countries are ancient, but others have been formed or changed more recently.
1. **Identify** What is the region's largest country?
2. **Make Inferences** Have you heard about any countries on this map in the news? What have you heard?

UNITED KINGDOM

North Sea

FRANCE

ATLANTIC OCEAN

⊙ National capital

0   100   200 Miles
0   100   200 Kilometers

Projection: Azimuthal Equal-Area

SPAIN

Culture Eastern Europe is home to dozens of cultures, each with its own unique customs.

H HISTORY Chernobyl

↗ hmhsocialstudies.com **VIDEO**

Tallinn
ESTONIA

Baltic Sea

Riga
LATVIA

LITHUANIA
Vilnius

RUSSIA

Minsk

BELARUS

RUSSIA

GERMANY

POLAND
Warsaw

Kiev

Prague
CZECH REPUBLIC

UKRAINE

SLOVAKIA
Bratislava

AUSTRIA

Budapest

HUNGARY

MOLDOVA

Chișinău

SLOVENIA
Ljubljana

Zagreb

CROATIA

ROMANIA

BOSNIA AND HERZEGOVINA
Sarajevo

Belgrade

SERBIA

Bucharest

Danube River

Black Sea

ITALY

Adriatic Sea

MONTENEGRO
Podgorica

KOSOVO
Pristina

Skopje

BULGARIA

Sofia

Tirana
MACEDONIA

ALBANIA

TURKEY

GREECE

Aegean Sea

20°E   50°N   30°E   40°E

History Buildings in cities like Prague, Czech Republic, are symbols of Eastern Europe's long history.

Geography Like the Danube River shown here, many rivers flow through the mountains and plains of Eastern Europe.

171

Physical Geography

What You Will Learn...

Main Ideas

1. The physical features of Eastern Europe include wide open plains, rugged mountain ranges, and many rivers.
2. The climate and vegetation of Eastern Europe differ widely in the north and the south.

The Big Idea

The physical geography of Eastern Europe varies greatly from place to place.

Key Places

Carpathians, *p. 172*
Balkan Peninsula, *p. 173*
Danube, *p. 174*
Chernobyl, *p. 175*

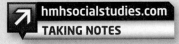
hmhsocialstudies.com
TAKING NOTES

Use the graphic organizer online to take notes on the physical geography of Eastern Europe.

If YOU lived there...

You are traveling on a boat down the Danube River, one of the longest in Europe. As you float downstream, you pass through dozens of towns and cities. Outside of the cities, the banks are lined with huge castles, soaring churches, and busy farms. From time to time, other boats pass you, some loaded with passengers and some with goods.

Why do you think the Danube is so busy?

BUILDING BACKGROUND The physical geography of Eastern Europe varies widely from north to south. Many of the landforms you learned about in earlier chapters, including the Northern European Plain and the Alps, extend into this region.

Physical Features

Eastern Europe is a land of amazing contrasts. The northern parts of the region lie along the cold, often stormy shores of the Baltic Sea. In the south, however, are warm, sunny beaches along the Adriatic and Black seas. Jagged mountain peaks jut high into the sky in some places, while wildflowers dot the gently rolling hills of other parts of the region. These contrasts stem from the region's wide variety of landforms, water features, and climates.

Landforms

As you can see on the map, the landforms of Eastern Europe are arranged in a series of broad bands. In the north is the Northern European Plain. As you have already learned, this large plain stretches across most of Northern Europe.

South of the Northern European Plain is a low mountain range called the **Carpathians** (kahr-PAY-thee-uhnz). These rugged mountains are an extension of the Alps of West-Central Europe. They stretch in a long arc from the Alps to the Black Sea area.

South and west of the Carpathians is another plain, the Great Hungarian Plain. As its name suggests, this fertile area is located mostly within Hungary.

South of the plain are more mountains, the Dinaric (duh-NAR-ik) Alps and Balkan Mountains. These two ranges together cover most of the **Balkan Peninsula**, one of the largest peninsulas in Europe. It extends south into the Mediterranean Sea.

Water Features

Like the rest of the continent, Eastern Europe has many bodies of water that affect how people live. To the southwest is the Adriatic Sea, an important route for transportation and trade. To the east, the Black Sea serves the same **function**. In the far north is the Baltic Sea. It is another important trade route, though parts of the sea freeze over in the winter.

ACADEMIC VOCABULARY

function
use or purpose

↗ hmhsocialstudies.com **INTERACTIVE MAP**

Eastern Europe: Physical

ELEVATION

Feet		Meters
13,120		4,000
6,560		2,000
1,640		500
656		200
(Sea level) 0		0 (Sea level)
Below sea level		Below sea level

0   150   300 Miles
0   150   300 Kilometers

Projection: Azimuthal Equal-Area

1 The Carpathian Mountains run through the center of Eastern Europe.

2 Many rivers flow across the plains of Eastern Europe. The Vistula, shown here, is one of them.

map zone
Geography Skills

Place The physical features of Eastern Europe are arranged in alternating bands of rugged mountains and fertile plains.

1. **Locate** What large river flows through the southern part of the region?
2. **Interpret** Where do you think most of Eastern Europe's large cities are? Why?

In addition to these seas, Eastern Europe has several rivers that are vital paths for transportation and trade. The longest of these rivers, the **Danube** (DAN-yoob), begins in Germany and flows east across the Great Hungarian Plain. The river winds its way through nine countries before it finally empties into the Black Sea.

Primary Source

BOOK
The Plains of Ukraine

One of Russia's greatest novelists, Nikolai Gogol (gaw-guhl), was actually born in what is now Ukraine. Very fond of his homeland, he frequently wrote about its great beauty. In this passage from the short story "Taras Bulba," he describes a man's passage across the wide open fields of Ukraine.

❝No plough had ever passed over the immeasurable waves of wild growth; horses alone, hidden in it as in a forest, trod it down. Nothing in nature could be finer. The whole surface resembled a golden-green ocean, upon which were sprinkled millions of different flowers. Through the tall, slender stems of the grass peeped light-blue, dark-blue, and lilac star-thistles; the yellow broom thrust up its pyramidal head; the parasol-shaped white flower of the false flax shimmered on high. A wheat-ear, brought God knows whence, was filling out to ripening. Amongst the roots of this luxuriant vegetation ran partridges with outstretched necks. The air was filled with the notes of a thousand different birds.❞

—from "Taras Bulba," by Nikolai Gogol

ANALYSIS SKILL **ANALYZING PRIMARY SOURCES**

What features does Gogol describe on the plains of Ukraine?

As you might expect, the Danube is central to the Eastern European economy. Some of the region's largest cities lie on the Danube's banks. Thousands of ships travel up and down the river every year, loaded with both goods and people. In addition, dams on the western parts of the river generate much of the region's electricity. Unfortunately, the high level of activity on the Danube has left it heavily polluted.

READING CHECK **Finding Main Ideas** What are the main bodies of water in Eastern Europe?

Climate and Vegetation

Like its landforms, the climates and natural vegetation of Eastern Europe vary widely. In fact, the climates and landscapes found across Eastern Europe determine which plants will grow there.

The Baltic Coast
The shores of the Baltic Sea are the coldest location in Eastern Europe. Winters there are long, cold, and harsh. This northern part of Eastern Europe receives less rain than other areas, but fog is common. In fact, some parts of the area have as few as 30 sunny days each year. The climate allows huge forests to grow there.

The Interior Plains
The interior plains of Eastern Europe are much milder than the far north. Winters there can be very cold, but summers are generally pleasant and mild. The western parts of these plains receive much more rain than those areas farther east.

Because of this variation in climate, the plains of Eastern Europe have many types of vegetation. Huge forests cover much of the north. South of these forests are open grassy plains. In the spring, these plains erupt with colorful wildflowers.

Radiation Cleanup

A nuclear accident in 1986 leaked dangerous amounts of radiation into Eastern Europe's soil. Ukraine's government and scientists are still working to repair the damage.

Unfortunately, Eastern Europe's forests were greatly damaged by a terrible accident in 1986. A faulty reactor at the **Chernobyl** (chuhr-NOH-buhl) nuclear power plant in Ukraine exploded, releasing huge amounts of radiation into the air. This radiation poisoned millions of acres of forest and ruined soil across much of the region.

The Balkan Coast

Along the Adriatic Sea, the Balkan coast has a Mediterranean climate, with warm summers and mild winters. As a result, its beaches are popular tourist destinations.

Because a Mediterranean climate does not bring much rain, the Balkan coast does not have many forests. Instead, the land there is covered by shrubs and hardy trees that do not need much water.

READING CHECK **Contrasting** How do the climates and vegetation of Eastern Europe vary?

FOCUS ON READING

What problems did the Chernobyl accident cause for Eastern Europe?

SUMMARY AND PREVIEW The landforms of Eastern Europe vary widely, as do its cultures. Next you will study the cultures of the northernmost parts of the region.

Section 1 Assessment

hmhsocialstudies.com
ONLINE QUIZ

Reviewing Ideas, Terms, and Places

1. **a. Identify** What are the major mountain ranges of Eastern Europe?
   b. Make Inferences How do you think the physical features of Eastern Europe influence where people live?
   c. Elaborate Why is the **Danube** so important to the people of Eastern Europe?
2. **a. Describe** What is the climate of the **Balkan Peninsula** like?
   b. Explain Why are there few trees in the far southern areas of Eastern Europe?
   c. Predict How do you think the lingering effects of the **Chernobyl** accident affect the plant life of Eastern Europe?

Critical Thinking

3. **Categorizing** Draw a chart like the one shown here. In each column, identify the landforms, climates, and vegetation of each area in Eastern Europe.

	Landforms	Climates	Vegetation
Baltic coast			
Interior plains			
Balkan coast			

Focus on Viewing

4. **Presenting Physical Geography** Until you decide what country you will report on, take notes about all of them. Make a list of the countries of Eastern Europe and the physical features found in each.

Poland and the Baltic Republics

What You Will Learn...

Main Ideas

1. History ties Poland and the Baltic Republics together.
2. The cultures of Poland and the Baltic Republics differ in language and religion but share common customs.
3. Economic growth is a major issue in the region today.

The Big Idea

The histories of Poland and the Baltic Republics, both as free states and as areas dominated by the Soviet Union, still shape life there.

Key Terms and Places

infrastructure, *p. 179*
Warsaw, *p. 179*

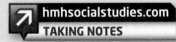
hmhsocialstudies.com
TAKING NOTES

Use the graphic organizer online to take notes on Poland and the Baltic Republics.

If YOU lived there...

You live in the beautiful and historic city of Krakow, Poland. Over the centuries, terrible wars have damaged many Polish cities, but Krakow is filled with cobblestone streets, romantic castles, and elaborate churches. The city is home to one of Europe's oldest shopping malls, the 500-year-old Cloth Hall. Glorious old Catholic churches also rise high above many parts of the city.

What does the city suggest about Polish history?

BUILDING BACKGROUND Located on the Northern European Plain, Poland and the Baltic Republics are caught between east and west. As a result, the region has often been a battlefield. On the other hand, this location at a cultural crossroads has helped each country develop its own distinctive culture, traditions, and customs.

History

The area around the Baltic Sea was settled in ancient times by many different groups. In time, these groups developed into the people who live in the region today. One group became the Estonians, one became the Latvians and Lithuanians, and one became the Polish. Each of these groups had its own language and culture. Over the centuries, however, shared historical events have helped tie all these people together.

Early History

By the Middle Ages, the people of the Baltics had formed many independent kingdoms. The kingdoms of Lithuania and Poland were large and strong. Together they ruled much of Eastern and Northern Europe. The smaller kingdoms of Latvia and Estonia, on the other hand, were not strong. In fact, they were often invaded by their more powerful neighbors. These invasions continued through the 1800s.

Eastern Europe under Soviet Influence, 1988

Extent of
Soviet
influence

0   100   200 Miles
0 100 200 Kilometers

Projection: Azimuthal Equal-Area

map zone

Geography Skills

Place From World War II until 1989, politics in Eastern Europe was dominated by the Soviet Union.

1. **Identify** Which modern countries were part of the Soviet Union?
2. **Name** What other countries have changed since 1988?

BIOGRAPHY

Pope John Paul II
(1920–2005)

Karol Wojtyla, later called Pope John Paul II, was born in Poland. Raised a Roman Catholic, he became a priest shortly after the Soviets took over the country. After becoming pope in 1978, he encouraged the Polish people to protest against their Communist government. Largely because of his efforts, Poland broke away from the Soviet Union in 1989.

The World Wars

Both World War I and World War II were devastating for the Baltic people. Much of the fighting in World War I took place in Poland. As a result, millions of Poles—both soldiers and civilians—died. Thousands more were killed in the Baltic countries.

World War II began when the Germans invaded Poland from the west. As the Germans pushed through Poland from the west, the army of the Soviet Union invaded Poland from the east. Once again, Poland suffered tremendously. Millions of people were killed, and property all over Poland was destroyed. Estonia, Latvia, and Lithuania also suffered. All three countries were occupied by the Soviet army.

Soviet Domination

As the map shows, the Soviet Union totally dominated Eastern Europe after World War II. Estonia, Latvia, and Lithuania became parts of the Soviet Union. Poland remained free, but the Soviets forced the Poles to accept a Communist government.

Many Eastern Europeans opposed Communist rule, and the Communist governments in the region eventually fell. Poland rejected Communism and elected new leaders in 1989. The Baltic Republics broke away from the Soviet Union in 1991 and became independent once more.

READING CHECK Analyzing How did the Soviet Union influence the region's history?

FOCUS ON READING

What problems were created in the Baltic region after World War II?

Culture

In some ways, the cultures of Poland and the Baltic Republics are very different from each other. For example, people in the area speak different languages and practice different religions. In other ways, however, their cultures are actually quite similar. Because the four countries lie near each other, common customs have taken root in all of them. People cook similar foods and enjoy the same types of entertainment.

CONNECTING TO the Arts

Baltic Embroidery

One of the crafts for which the people of the Baltic region are best known is embroidery. This type of decorative sewing lets people create beautiful designs. They use these designs on their clothing, tablecloths, and other cloth goods.

For centuries, people in the Baltic countries—both men and women—have embroidered the clothing they wear on special occasions, such as weddings. They use many colors of thread to sew intricate patterns of flowers, hearts, and geometric designs. Because the embroidery is done by hand, it can take hours of work to create a single garment.

Drawing Conclusions Why do you think people embroider only clothing for special occasions?

Cultural Differences

The most obvious differences between the cultures of the Baltic countries are their languages and religions. Because the countries were first settled by different groups, each has its own language today. Of these languages, only Latvian and Lithuanian are similar to each other. Polish is related to the languages of countries farther south. Estonian is similar to Finnish.

Trade patterns and invasions have affected religion in the area. Poland and Lithuania traded mostly with Roman Catholic countries, and so most people there are Catholic. Latvia and Estonia, on the other hand, were ruled for a long time by Sweden. Because the Swedish are mostly Lutheran, most people in Latvia and Estonia are Lutheran as well.

Cultural Similarities

Unlike language and religion, many of the customs practiced in the Baltic countries cross national boundaries. For example, people in these countries eat many of the same types of foods. Potatoes and sausage are very popular, as is seafood.

Other shared customs tie the Baltic countries together as well. For example, people in all three countries practice many of the same crafts. Among these crafts are pottery, painting, and embroidery.

Also common to the countries of the Baltic Sea area is a love of music and dance. For centuries, people of the Baltics have been famous for their musical abilities. Frédéric Chopin (1810–1849), for example, was a famous Polish pianist and composer. Today, people throughout Poland and the Baltic Republics gather at music festivals to hear popular and traditional tunes.

READING CHECK **Comparing** How are the cultures of the Baltic countries similar?

The Region Today

Estonia, Latvia, Lithuania, and Poland all still feel the effects of decades of Soviet rule. The economies of all four countries suffered because the Soviets did not build a decent infrastructure. An **infrastructure** is the set of resources, like roads, airports, and factories, that a country needs in order to support economic activities. The many factories built by the Soviets in Poland and the Baltics could not produce as many goods as those in Western Europe.

Today Poland and the Baltic Republics are working to rebuild and strengthen their economies. They are replacing the old and outdated factories built by the Soviets with new ones that take advantage of modern technology. As a result, cities like **Warsaw**, the capital of Poland, have become major industrial centers.

To further their economic growth, the countries of this region are also seeking new sources of income. One area in which they have found some success is tourism. Since the collapse of the Soviet Union in 1991, many Americans and Western Europeans have begun visiting. Polish cities like Warsaw and Krakow have long attracted tourists with their rich history and famous sites. Vilnius, Lithuania; Tallinn, Estonia; and Riga, Latvia, have also become tourist attractions. People are drawn to these cities by their fascinating cultures, cool summer climates, and historic sites.

READING CHECK **Generalizing** How has the region changed in recent years?

SUMMARY AND PREVIEW Poland and the Baltic Republics are still feeling the effects of decades of Soviet rule. In the next section, you will learn about more countries that feel the same effects.

Tourism in the Baltics

Baltic cities such as Tallinn, Estonia, draw many tourists each year. These tourists are attracted to the cities' many churches and cultural sites.

Section 2 Assessment

hmhsocialstudies.com
ONLINE QUIZ

Reviewing Ideas, Terms, and Places

1. a. **Identify** What country ran the area after World War II?
   b. **Draw Conclusions** How do you think the two world wars affected the people of Poland?
2. a. **Describe** How do the languages spoken in Poland and the Baltic Republics reflect the region's history?
   b. **Elaborate** Why do you think that people across the region practice many of the same customs?
3. a. **Recall** What is one industry that has grown in the region since the fall of the Soviet Union?
   b. **Explain** How did Soviet rule hurt the area's economy?

Critical Thinking

4. **Identifying Cause and Effect** Draw a chart like the one shown here. In each box on the right, explain how the event affected the cultures or economies of the region.

Event	Effect
Soviet rule	
Breakup of the Soviet Union	
Growth of tourism	

FOCUS ON VIEWING

5. **Considering Poland and the Baltics** If you were to give your report about Poland or one of the Baltic Republics, what details would you include? Write down some ideas.

Inland Eastern Europe

Main Ideas

1. The histories and cultures of inland Eastern Europe vary from country to country.
2. Most of inland Eastern Europe today has stable governments, strong economies, and influential cities.

The Big Idea

The countries of inland Eastern Europe have varied histories and cultures but face many of the same issues today.

Key Terms and Places

Prague, *p. 181*
Kiev, *p. 181*
Commonwealth of Independent States, *p. 182*
Budapest, *p. 183*

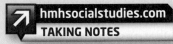

hmhsocialstudies.com
TAKING NOTES

Use the graphic organizer online to take notes on inland Eastern Europe.

If YOU lived there...

You are a tourist visiting Budapest, the capital of Hungary. Early one morning, you stand on a bridge over the glittering water of the Danube River. You read in your guidebook that the two banks of the river were once separate cities. On the bank to your right, you see huge castles and churches standing on a tall hill. To your left is the Parliament building, obviously a much newer building.

What might have brought the cities together?

BUILDING BACKGROUND The city of Budapest, like many of the cities of inland Eastern Europe, has a long, colorful history. Various parts of the city reflect wildly different eras in its past. Medieval churches, for example, stand near huge imperial fortresses and Soviet-built warehouses, all relics of the region's history.

History and Culture

Located on the Northern European and Hungarian plains, inland Eastern Europe consists of six countries. They are the Czech (CHEK) Republic, Slovakia, Hungary, Ukraine, Belarus, and Moldova. Throughout history, many different peoples ruled these countries. Each ruling group influenced the culture and customs of the area.

Czech Republic and Slovakia

The area that now includes the Czech Republic and Slovakia was once home to many small kingdoms. People called the Slavs founded these kingdoms. The Slavs were people from Asia who moved into Europe by AD 1000. Eventually, strong neighbors such as Austria conquered the Slavic kingdoms.

After World War I, the victorious Allies took land away from Austria to form a new nation, Czechoslovakia. About fifty years later, in 1993, it split into the Czech Republic and Slovakia.

Because of their location, these two countries have long had ties with Western Europe. As a result, Western influences are common. For example, many people in the two countries are Roman Catholic. The architecture of cities like **Prague** (PRAHG), the capital of the Czech Republic, also reflects Western influences.

Hungary

In the 900s, a group of fierce invaders called the Magyars swept into what is now Hungary. Although they were conquered by the Austrians, the Magyars continued to shape Hungarian culture. The Hungarian language is based on the language spoken by the Magyars. In fact, people in Hungary today still refer to themselves as Magyars.

Ukraine, Belarus, and Moldova

The Slavs also settled Ukraine, Belarus, and Moldova. Later other groups, including the Vikings of Scandinavia, invaded and conquered the Slavs.

A group called the Rus (RUHS) built a settlement in what is now **Kiev**, Ukraine, in the 800s. The rulers of Kiev eventually created a huge empire.

In the late 1700s, that empire became part of Russia. When the Soviet Union was formed in 1922, Ukraine and Belarus were made Soviet republics. Moldova became a republic two years later. They did not become independent until the breakup of the Soviet Union in 1991.

The long history of Russian influence in the region is reflected in the countries' cultures. For example, most people in these countries are Orthodox Christians, like the people of Russia. In addition, Ukrainian and Belarusian languages are written in the Cyrillic, or Russian, alphabet.

READING CHECK **Analyzing** Which groups have influenced the history of the region?

The Kievan Empire

Kiev, now the capital of Ukraine, was once the capital of a large and powerful empire. At its height, the Kievan Empire stretched across much of Eastern Europe and Central Asia.

Kiev

According to an old legend, the city of Kiev was built by three brothers and their sister. This monument built in the 1980s honors the city's legendary founders.

The people of Kiev built Saint Sophia Cathedral in the 1000s. By that time, nearly everyone who lived in the Kievan Empire was Orthodox Christian.

Budapest

Budapest, Hungary, is one of the largest cities of Eastern Europe. The city's two parts, Buda and Pest, are separated by the Danube River.

Once the poorer half of the city, Pest has grown quickly. Hungary's Parliament meets here.

Only a few bridges link the two halves of Budapest.

Inland Eastern Europe Today

FOCUS ON READING

How might the CIS help solve problems in this region?

All of the countries of inland Eastern Europe were either part of the Soviet Union or run by Soviet-influenced governments. Since the end of Soviet domination, the people of inland Eastern Europe have largely overcome the problems created by the Soviets. Still, a few issues remain for the region's governments and economies.

Government

During the Soviet era, the countries of inland Eastern Europe had Communist governments. Under the Communists, people had few freedoms. In addition, the Soviets were poor economic planners, and their policies caused many hardships.

Since the collapse of the Soviet Union, the governments of inland Eastern Europe have changed. Hungary, Slovakia, the Czech Republic, Ukraine, and Moldova are now republics in which the people elect their leaders. Belarus also claims to be a republic, but it is really a dictatorship.

The countries of inland Eastern Europe belong to several international alliances. One such alliance, the **Commonwealth of Independent States**, or CIS, meets to discuss issues such as trade and immigration that affect former Soviet republics. The CIS is based in Minsk, the capital of Belarus. Ukraine and Moldova are also members, as are many countries in Asia.

The Czech Republic, Slovakia, Hungary, Romania, and Bulgaria are not part of the CIS. They have sought closer ties to the West than to the former Soviet Union. As a result, all five belong to the EU.

Economy

Economic development has been a major challenge for these countries since the collapse of the Soviet Union. The Czech Republic, Slovakia, Hungary, and Ukraine have been most successful. All four are thriving industrial centers. Ukraine, with rich, productive farmlands, grows grains, potatoes, and sugar beets.

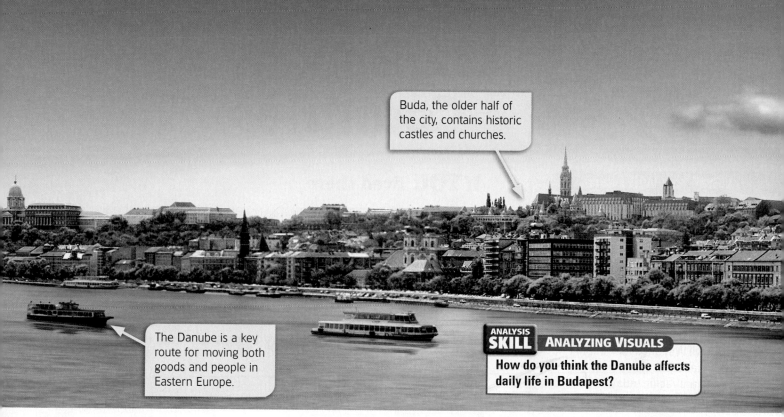

Buda, the older half of the city, contains historic castles and churches.

The Danube is a key route for moving both goods and people in Eastern Europe.

ANALYSIS SKILL **ANALYZING VISUALS**

How do you think the Danube affects daily life in Budapest?

Cities

Life in inland Eastern Europe is centered around cities, especially national capitals. In each country, the capital is both a key economic center and a cultural one.

Three cities in the region are especially important—Prague, Kiev, and **Budapest**, the capital of Hungary. They are the most prosperous cities in the region and home to influential leaders and universities. In addition, the cities are popular tourist destinations. People from all over the world visit Eastern Europe to see these cities' architectural and cultural sites.

READING CHECK **Generalizing** What are the countries of inland Eastern Europe like today?

SUMMARY AND PREVIEW Inland Eastern Europe has been successful in facing the challenges left by Soviet influence. Next, you will learn about a region that has faced more challenges, the Balkans.

Section 3 Assessment

hmhsocialstudies.com
ONLINE QUIZ

Reviewing Ideas, Terms, and Places

1. **a. Recall** In what country is **Prague** located?
   b. Sequence List the groups that ruled **Kiev** and the surrounding area in chronological order.
   c. Elaborate How has Hungary's history helped set it apart from other countries in inland Eastern Europe?
2. **a. Identify** What is the **Commonwealth of Independent States**? Which countries in this region are members?
   b. Draw Conclusions How have the economies of the region changed since the collapse of the Soviet Union?
   c. Develop Why do you think life is largely centered around cities in inland Eastern Europe?

Critical Thinking

3. **Generalizing** Draw a diagram like the one shown here. In the left oval, describe the government and economy of inland Eastern Europe under the Soviet Union. In the right oval, describe them since the Soviet Union's collapse.

Russia Today

FOCUS ON VIEWING

4. **Picturing Inland Eastern Europe** Which country sounds most interesting to you? Write down some details about it. Make a list of pictures you could use on your poster.

EASTERN EUROPE **183**

The Balkan Countries

What You Will Learn...

Main Ideas

1. The history of the Balkan countries is one of conquest and conflict.
2. The cultures of the Balkan countries are shaped by the many ethnic groups who live there.
3. Civil War and weak economies are major challenges to the region today.

The Big Idea

Life in the Balkans reflects the region's troubled past and its varied ethnic makeup.

Key Terms

ethnic cleansing, *p. 186*

hmhsocialstudies.com
TAKING NOTES

Use the graphic organizer online to take notes on the Balkan countries.

If YOU lived there...

As part of your summer vacation, you are hiking across the Balkan Peninsula. As you hike through villages in the rugged mountains, you are amazed at the different churches you see. There are small Roman Catholic churches, huge Orthodox churches with onion-shaped domes, and Muslim mosques with tall minarets.

Why are there so many types of churches here?

BUILDING BACKGROUND The Balkan countries are possibly the most diverse area in Europe. In addition to practicing many religions, the people there speak many languages and have different customs. At times, the area's diversity has led to serious problems.

History

Like the rest of Eastern Europe, the Balkan Peninsula has been conquered and ruled by many different groups. The presence of these many groups continues to shape life in the area today.

Early History

By the 600s BC the ancient Greeks had founded colonies on the northern Black Sea coast. The area they settled is now part of Bulgaria and Romania. Later, the Romans conquered most of the area from the Adriatic Sea to the Danube River.

When the Roman Empire divided into west and east in the late AD 300s, the Balkan Peninsula became part of the Eastern, or Byzantine, Empire. Under Byzantine rule, many people of the Balkans became Orthodox Christians. More than 1,000 years later, Muslim Ottoman Turks conquered the Byzantine Empire. Under the Ottomans, many people became Muslims.

The Ottomans ruled the Balkan Peninsula until the 1800s. At that time, the people of the region rose up and drove the Ottomans out. They then created their own kingdoms.

World War I and After

Trouble between the Balkan kingdoms and their neighbors led to World War I. In the late 1800s the Austro-Hungarian Empire, which lay north of the Balkans, took over part of the peninsula. In protest, a man from Serbia shot the heir to the Austro-Hungarian throne, sparking the war.

After World War I, the Balkans changed dramatically. Europe's leaders divided the peninsula into new countries. Among these new countries was Yugoslavia, which combined many formerly independent countries under one government.

The nation of Yugoslavia lasted until the 1990s. The country eventually broke up, however, because of conflict between ethnic and religious groups.

READING CHECK **Summarizing** How did World War I affect the Balkan Peninsula?

Culture

Culturally, the Balkans are the most diverse area of Europe. This diversity is reflected in the large number of religions practiced and languages spoken there.

Religion

Most of the people of the Balkans, like most Europeans, are Christian. However, three types of Christianity are practiced in the area. Most Balkan Christians belong to the Orthodox Church. In the western part of the peninsula, there are many Roman Catholics. In addition, many countries also have large Protestant communities.

Christianity is not the only religion in the Balkans. Because of the Ottomans' long rule, Islam is also common. In fact, Albania is the only country in Europe in which most people are Muslims.

Religion in the Balkans

Buildings from many religions can be found around the Balkans. This Orthodox church is in Bulgaria.

THE WORLD ALMANAC
Facts about the World

Major Religions in the Balkans

Analyzing Graphs What is the largest religion in the Balkans?

↗ hmhsocialstudies.com

185

Language

People in the Balkans speak languages from three major groups. Most languages in the region belong to the Slavic family and are related to Russian. In Romania, though, people speak a language that developed from Latin. It is more closely related to French, Italian, and Spanish than to Slavic languages. In addition, some people in Romania speak Germanic languages.

Some languages of the Balkans are not related to these groups. For example, Albanian is unlike any other language in the world. In addition, a group called the Roma have a language of their own.

ACADEMIC VOCABULARY

implications
consequences

READING CHECK **Drawing Conclusions** Why is Balkan culture so diverse?

FOCUS ON CULTURE

The Roma

The Roma are a nomadic people. For centuries, they have roamed from place to place in horse-drawn wagons, working as blacksmiths, animal trainers, and musicians. Although Roma live all over the world, the largest concentration of them is in southeastern Europe.

For centuries, many other Europeans did not trust the Roma. They were suspicious of the Roma's nomadic lifestyle and could not understand their language. As a result, many Roma have been subject to prejudice and discrimination.

Summarizing What is traditional Roma life like?

The Balkans Today

The countries of the Balkan Peninsula, like most of Eastern Europe, were once run by Communist governments. Weak economic planning has left most of them poor and struggling to improve their economies. This area is still the poorest in Europe today.

Relations among religious and ethnic groups have had serious **implications** for the Balkans. When Yugoslavia broke apart, violence broke out among groups in some of the newly formed countries. Members of the largest religious or ethnic group in each country tried to get rid of all other groups who lived there. They threatened those who refused to leave with punishments or death. This kind of effort to remove all members of a group from a country or region is called **ethnic cleansing**.

The violence in the former Yugoslavia was so terrible that other countries stepped in to put an end to it. In 1995 countries around the world sent troops to Bosnia and Herzegovina to help bring an end to the fighting. The fighting between groups eventually ended and, in 2008, ten countries shared the Balkan Peninsula:

Albania The poorest country in Europe, Albania has struggled since the end of the Soviet period. High unemployment and crime rates have prevented the country's economy from improving.

Macedonia Once a part of Yugoslavia, Macedonia broke away in 1991. It was the first country to do so peacefully.

Slovenia Slovenia also broke from Yugoslavia in 1991. In 2004 it became the first Balkan country to join the EU.

Croatia When Croatia broke away from Yugoslavia, fighting broke out within the country. Ethnic Croats and Serbs fought over land for many years. In the end, many Serbs left Croatia, and peace was restored.

Mostar

Fighting between ethnic groups left the city of Mostar in Bosnia and Herzegovina in ruins. After the war, the people of Mostar had to rebuild their city.

ANALYZING VISUALS What does this photo suggest about life in Mostar today?

Bosnia and Herzegovina Since the end of ethnic and religious violence, peace has returned to Bosnia and Herzegovina. The people there are working to rebuild.

Serbia Serbia is the largest nation to emerge from the former Yugoslavia. Like other Balkan countries, Serbia has seen fighting among ethnic groups.

Kosovo Formerly a province of Serbia, Kosovo declared independence in 2008. Its population is mostly ethnic Albanian.

Montenegro The mountainous country of Montenegro separated peacefully from Serbia in June 2006.

Romania Romania, the largest of the Balkan states, is working to recover from years of bad government. Poor leaders have left its government and economy in ruins.

Bulgaria Since the fall of the Soviet Union, Bulgaria has changed dramatically. People there are working to develop a capitalist economy based on industry and tourism.

READING CHECK **Generalizing** What issues does the Balkan region face today?

FOCUS ON READING
What solutions are Bulgaria's leaders seeking to their economic problems?

SUMMARY AND PREVIEW The Soviet Union had a huge effect on Eastern Europe. Next, you will read about the Soviet Union and Russia.

Section 4 Assessment

hmhsocialstudies.com
ONLINE QUIZ

Reviewing Ideas, Terms, and Places

1. **a. Describe** What was Yugoslavia? When did it break apart?
   b. Explain What role did the Balkan countries play in starting World War I?
2. **a. Identify** What are the four most common religions in the Balkans?
   b. Analyze Why are so many different languages spoken in the Balkans?
3. **a. Define** What is **ethnic cleansing**?
   b. Elaborate Why do you think other countries sent troops to Bosnia and Herzegovina? How has the country changed since the war ended?

Critical Thinking

4. **Summarizing** Draw a chart like this one. Use your notes to write a sentence about how each topic listed in the left column affected life in the Balkans after the breakup of Yugoslavia.

The Balkans Today	
Soviet influence	
Ethnic diversity	
Religion	

Focus on Viewing

5. **Choosing a Country** Now that you have studied all of Eastern Europe, choose your topic. What information and pictures will you include?

The Breakup of Yugoslavia

Essential Elements

The World in Spatial Terms
Places and Regions
Physical Systems
Human Systems
Environment and Society
The Uses of Geography

Background A school playground has a limited amount of space. If many students want to use the playground at the same time, they have to work together and consider each other's feelings. Otherwise, conflict could break out.

Space on Earth is also limited. As a result, people are sometimes forced to live near people with whom they disagree. Like students on a playground, they must learn to work together to live in peace.

Yugoslavia The country of Yugoslavia was created after World War I. As a result, people from many ethnic groups—Serbs, Montenegrins, Bosnians, Croats, Slovenes, and Macedonians—lived together in one country. Each group had its own republic, or self-governed area, in the new country.

For decades, the republics of Yugoslavia worked together peacefully. People from various ethnic groups mixed within each republic. Then in 1991 Croatia, Macedonia, and Slovenia declared independence. The republic of Bosnia and Herzegovina did the same a year later. These republics were afraid Serbia wanted to take over Yugoslavia.

It appeared that they were right. Serbia's leader, Slobodan Milosevic (sloh-BOH-dahn mee-LOH-suh-vich), wanted to increase Serbia's power. He took land from other ethnic groups. He also called on Serbs who lived in other republics to vote to give Serbia more influence in the country.

Refugees Violence between ethnic groups led many people in Yugoslavia to leave their homes. The people in this photo are fleeing Bosnia to seek refuge in a safer area.

The Former Yugoslavia, 2000

map zone

Yugoslavia, 1991

Zagreb
Belgrade
Sarajevo
YUGOSLAVIA
Adriatic Sea

N

SLOVENIA
Zagreb
CROATIA
BOSNIA AND HERZEGOVINA
Belgrade
Sarajevo
SERBIA AND MONTENEGRO
Adriatic Sea
MACEDONIA

Ethnic Groups
- Albanian
- Croat
- Macedonian
- Montenegrin
- Bosnian
- Serb
- Slovene
- Other or no majority

When the other republics broke away from Yugoslavia, Milosevic called on Serbs who lived there to rise up and demand that they rejoin the country. He also provided aid to Serbian military groups in these republics. In Bosnia and Herzegovina, Serbian rebels fought for three years against the Bosnian army in a destructive civil war.

Milosevic's actions caused other ethnic groups in Yugoslavia to resent the Serbs. As a result, additional violence broke out. In Croatia, for example, the army violently expelled all Serbs from their country. War raged in the area until 1995, when a peace accord was signed. As a result of that accord, Yugoslavia was dissolved. In its place were five countries that had once been Yugoslav republics.

What It Means The violent breakup of Yugoslavia has taught other countries some valuable lessons. First, it reinforced the idea that national borders are not permanent. Borders can and do change.

More importantly, however, the struggles in Yugoslavia have made some countries more aware of their people's needs. People want to feel that they have some say in their lives. When they feel as though another group is trying to take that say from them, as many in Yugoslavia felt the Serbs were doing, then trouble will often follow.

Geography for Life Activity

1. What led to the breakup of Yugoslavia?

2. Look at the maps on this page. How did the pattern of ethnic groups in Yugoslavia change between 1991 and 2000? Why do you think this is so?

3. **Investigating Ethnic Relationships** Yugoslavia is not the only country in which multiple ethnic groups lived together. Research another country in which multiple groups live together, such as Switzerland or Indonesia. How do the groups who live there live together?

Analyzing Benefits and Costs

Learn

Decisions can be tough to make. A seemingly simple choice can have both positive effects, or benefits, and negative effects, or costs. Before you make a decision, it can be helpful to analyze all the possible benefits and costs that will result.

One way to analyze benefits and costs is to create a chart like the one below. On one side, list all the benefits that will result from your decision. On the other side, list the costs. Not all costs involve money. You must also consider opportunity costs, or the things that you might lose as a result of your decision. For example, going to a movie might mean that you have to miss a baseball game.

Practice

The chart to the right could have been written by an official considering whether to develop a tourism industry in Croatia. Decide whether each of the numbered items listed here should be added to the benefits column or the costs column. Once you have determined that, use the chart to decide whether the benefits of tourism outweigh the costs. Write a short paragraph to support your decision.

❶ Would mean that tourist areas were not available for farming or industry

❷ Would improve Croatia's image to people in other parts of the world

Tourism in Dalmatia, Croatia

Benefits	Costs
■ Would create much-needed income for towns in the region	■ Would require building of hotels, airports, and roads
■ Would not require much new investment, since tourists are drawn to region's beaches and climate	■ Increase in tourism could lead to damaging of local environments
■	■
■	■

Apply

Imagine that city leaders in your area are trying to decide whether to build a new school. They cannot make a decision and have asked you to help analyze the benefits and costs of building the school. Create a chart like the one above to list those benefits and costs. Then write a brief paragraph stating whether the benefits of the plan outweigh its costs.

Chapter Review

Geography's Impact
video series
Review the video to answer the closing question:
How have the changing political borders in the Balkans affected people's lives?

Visual Summary

Use the visual summary below to help you review the main ideas of the chapter.

QUICK FACTS

Poland and the Baltics
The history of Poland and the Baltic Republics still shapes their culture, government, and economy.

Inland Eastern Europe
Once Communist, the countries of inland Eastern Europe have stable governments and strong economies.

The Balkans
Since the breakup of Yugoslavia, the Balkans have been faced with conflict and economic challenges.

Reviewing Vocabulary, Terms, and Places

Unscramble each group of letters below to spell a term that matches the given definition.

1. **arwswa**—the capital of Poland

2. **neicht glncaenis**—the effort to remove all members of a group from a country or region

3. **ebndua**—the major river that flows through Eastern Europe, one of the longest on the continent

4. **ageurp**—the capital and largest city of the Czech Republic

5. **ncimlaitpiso**—consequences

6. **laknab**—the peninsula on which much of Eastern Europe is located

7. **ufrnrtriuacste**—the set of resources, like roads and factories, that a country needs to support economic activities

8. **nrhatcapias**—a mountain range in Eastern Europe

Comprehension and Critical Thinking

SECTION 1 *(Pages 172–175)*

9. **a. Identify** Name two major bodies of water that border Eastern Europe.

   b. Explain How do the Danube and other rivers affect life for people in Eastern Europe?

   c. Evaluate If you could live in any region of Eastern Europe, where would it be? Why?

SECTION 2 *(Pages 176–179)*

10. **a. Identify** What are the three Baltic Republics? Why are they called that?

   b. Compare and Contrast What are two cultural features that Poland and the Baltic Republics have in common? What are two features that are different in those countries?

   c. Elaborate How did the collapse of the Soviet Union affect people in Poland and the Baltic Republics?

SECTION 3 (Pages 180–183)

11. a. Describe What is the government of Belarus like? What type of government do the other countries of inland Eastern Europe have?

b. Draw Conclusions Why do you think that some countries in inland Eastern Europe have stronger economies than others?

c. Elaborate How has its location influenced the culture of the Czech Republic?

SECTION 4 (Pages 184–187)

12. a. Identify What religions are common in the Balkan countries?

b. Explain Why did countries from around the world send troops to Kosovo?

c. Predict How do you think peace will affect life in the Balkans?

Map Activity

13. Eastern Europe On a separate sheet of paper, match the letters on the map with their correct labels.

Great Hungarian Plain	Kiev, Ukraine
Latvia	Warsaw, Poland
Albania	Danube River

Using the Internet

14. Activity: Writing a Report For centuries the Balkans have been an arena of conflict. Through your online textbook, learn about the history and cultures of the Balkans and investigate recent conflicts there. Write a report on what you find.

hmhsocialstudies.com

Social Studies Skills

15. Analyzing Costs and Benefits Imagine that you are a government official in Ukraine. Your country cannot produce enough energy to meet its needs and has to buy energy from Russia. A company in Kiev has expressed interest in building nuclear power plants, but many people are leery of nuclear power since the Chernobyl incident. Make a list of the costs and benefits of nuclear power. Then write a statement that either supports or argues against the plan.

FOCUS ON READING AND VIEWING

16. Understanding Problems and Solutions Re-read the first paragraph under the heading The Region Today in Section 2. Then write a short paragraph that explains the main problem facing Poland and the Baltics today. End your paragraph by suggesting a solution their governments might use to address the problem.

17. Making a Presentation Write a brief report about a country in Eastern Europe and prepare a poster that illustrates your main ideas. Find pictures of major features of your chosen country and arrange them on a poster board. Write a short caption that explains what each picture is. Present your report to the class. As you discuss each main idea, point out the pictures that illustrate it on your poster. Speak clearly and keep eye contact with your audience. Then, listen as your peers present their reports and posters. Note whether they speak clearly and maintain eye contact. Do their posters illustrate the main ideas in their reports?

CHAPTER 7

Standardized Test Prep

DIRECTIONS: Read questions 1 through 7 and write the letter of the best response. Then read question 8 and write your own well-constructed response.

1 The country *most* influential in Eastern Europe after World War II was

A the United States.

B the Soviet Union.

C France.

D Germany.

2 Which of the following countries violently broke apart in the 1990s?

A Poland

B Romania

C Czechoslovakia

D Yugoslavia

3 The major river of Eastern Europe is the

A Baltic River.

B Carpathian River.

C Danube River.

D Hungarian River.

4 Which of these countries is located on the Balkan Peninsula?

A Croatia

B Poland

C Belarus

D Estonia

5 Which of these statements about religion in Eastern Europe is correct?

A Nearly everyone in the region is Muslim.

B Nearly everyone in the region is Catholic.

C Nearly everyone in the region is Orthodox Christian.

D People in the region practice many different religions.

Hungary

For those in search of the heart and soul of Europe, there's nowhere better. Hungarians, who call themselves Magyars, speak a language and revel in a culture unlike any other. Away from the cosmopolitan charms of Budapest, life in the provinces is more redolent of times past—simpler, slower, often friendlier. There are endless opportunities for those with special interests—from horse riding and cycling to bird-watching and "taking the waters" at the country's many thermal spas.

–from *Lonely Planet World Guide Online*

6 Read the passage above from a travel guide to Hungary. According to this passage, what do people from Hungary call themselves?

A Hungarians

B Magyars

C Budapestians

D Europeans

7 Based on the above passage, which of the following statements is true?

A Hungarian culture is similar to many others in Europe.

B There are few things to do in Hungary.

C People outside of Budapest live simpler and slower lives than people in the city.

D Hungary is the largest country in Europe.

8 **Extended Response** Life in Eastern Europe is still influenced by the Soviet era, even though the Soviet Union collapsed many years ago. Consider what you have read in this chapter and write a paragraph in which you explain how Soviet influence is still felt in the region.

CHAPTER **8**

Russia and the Caucasus

Essential Question What cultural and geographic features help define Russia and the Caucasus?

What You Will Learn...

In this chapter you will learn about the physical features, climate, and natural resources of Russia and the Caucasus. You will also study the histories and cultures of these countries. Finally, you will learn about life in each of the countries today.

FOCUS ON READING AND WRITING

Making Generalizations A generalization is a broad, general idea drawn from new information combined with what you already know. As you read this chapter, stop now and then to make a generalization. It will help you pull the pieces of information together and make sense of them. **See the lesson, Making Generalizations, on page 227.**

Creating a Real Estate Ad As you read this chapter, imagine you work for a real estate agency in Russia or the Caucasus. You are trying to sell a piece of property there. In order to sell the property, you must write an ad to be published in the newspaper and on the Internet. As you read, decide where your property would be located and what its characteristics would be.

Geography A volcano created Crater Bay in the Kuril Islands off the east coast of Russia. The islands have several active volcanoes.

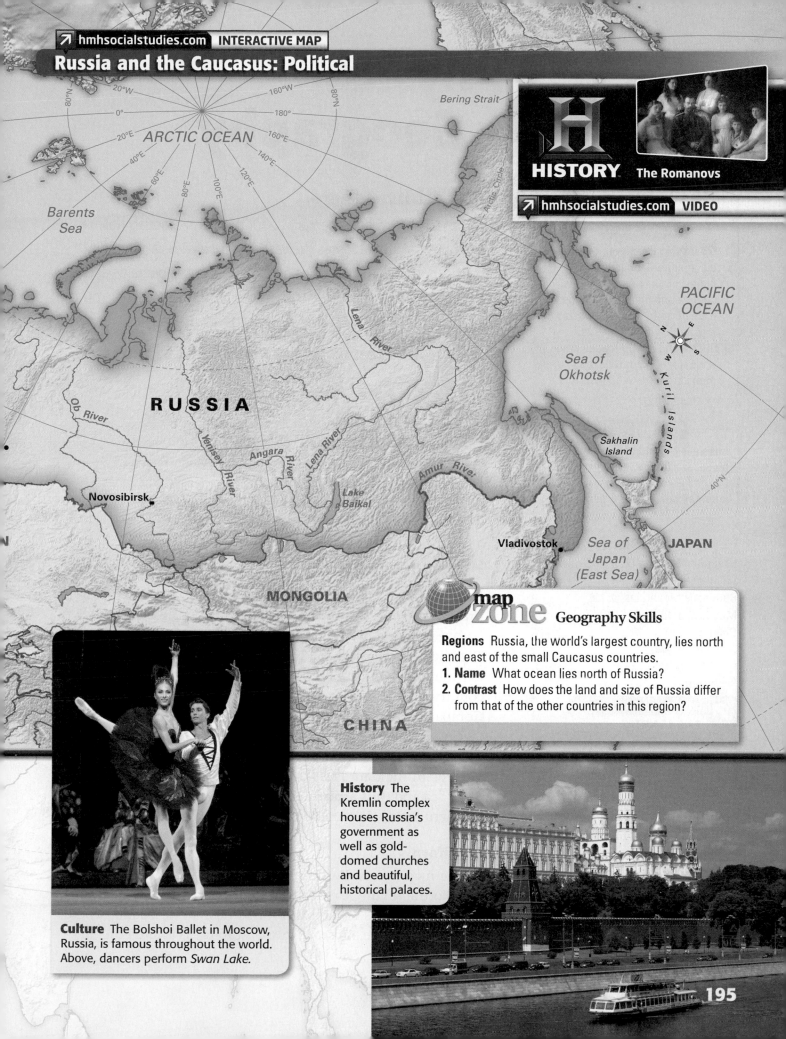

20°W · 0° · 20°E · 160°W · 180° · 160°E · 80°N · 80°N

ARCTIC OCEAN

40°E · 60°E · 80°E · 100°E · 120°E · 140°E

Bering Strait

HISTORY The Romanovs

↗ hmhsocialstudies.com **VIDEO**

Barents
Sea

Arctic Circle

PACIFIC
OCEAN

Lena River

Sea of
Okhotsk

R U S S I A

Kuril Islands

Ob River

Yenisey River

Angara River

Lena River

Amur River

Sakhalin
Island

40°N

Novosibirsk

Lake
Baikal

Vladivostok

Sea of
Japan
(East Sea)

JAPAN

MONGOLIA

map zone Geography Skills

Regions Russia, the world's largest country, lies north and east of the small Caucasus countries.
1. **Name** What ocean lies north of Russia?
2. **Contrast** How does the land and size of Russia differ from that of the other countries in this region?

CHINA

History The Kremlin complex houses Russia's government as well as gold-domed churches and beautiful, historical palaces.

Culture The Bolshoi Ballet in Moscow, Russia, is famous throughout the world. Above, dancers perform *Swan Lake*.

Physical Geography

What You Will Learn...

Main Ideas

1. The physical features of Russia and the Caucasus include plains, mountains, and rivers.
2. Climate and plant life change from north to south in Russia and vary in the Caucasus.
3. Russia and the Caucasus have a wealth of resources, but many are hard to access.

The Big Idea

Russia is big and cold with vast plains and forests; whereas the Caucasus countries are small, mountainous, and warmer.

Key Terms and Places

Ural Mountains, *p. 196*
Caspian Sea, *p. 196*
Caucasus Mountains, *p. 196*
Moscow, *p. 196*
Siberia, *p. 197*
Volga River, *p. 198*
taiga, *p. 199*

hmhsocialstudies.com
TAKING NOTES

Use the graphic organizer online to take notes on the physical geography of Russia and the Caucasus.

If YOU lived there...

You are making a documentary about the Trans–Siberian Railroad, a famous train that crosses the vast country of Russia. The train travels more than 5,700 miles across plains and mountains and through thick forests. As the train leaves the city of Moscow, you look out the window and see wheat fields and white birch trees.

What scenes might you include in your film?

BUILDING BACKGROUND Look at a globe, and you will see that Russia extends nearly halfway around the world. Russia is the world's largest country. It is so vast that it spans 11 time zones. While huge, much of Russia consists of flat or rolling plains.

Physical Features

Have you ever stood on two continents at once? In Russia's **Ural** (YOOHR-uhl) **Mountains**, you can. There, the continents of Europe and Asia meet. Europe lies to the west; Asia to the east. Together, Europe and Asia form the large landmass of Eurasia. On the map, you can see that a large chunk of Eurasia is the country of Russia. In fact, Russia is the world's largest country. Compared to the United States, Russia is almost twice as big.

South of Russia are three much smaller countries—Georgia, Armenia (ahr-MEE-nee-uh), and Azerbaijan (a-zuhr-by-JAHN). They lie in the Caucasus (KAW-kuh-suhs), the area between the Black Sea and the **Caspian Sea**. This area, which includes part of southern Russia, is named for the **Caucasus Mountains**.

Landforms

As the map shows, Russia's landforms vary from west to east. The Northern European Plain stretches across western, or European, Russia. This fertile plain forms Russia's heartland, where most Russians live. **Moscow**, Russia's capital, is located there.

Russia and the Caucasus: Physical

ARCTIC
OCEAN

Bering
Sea

North
Sea

Barents
Sea

PACIFIC
OCEAN

KOLYMA MTS.

KAMCHATKA
PENINSULA

Baltic Sea

TAYMYR
PENINSULA

CHERSKIY
RANGE

NORTHERN EUROPEAN PLAIN

S I B E R I A

Sea of
Okhotsk

EUROPE

WEST
SIBERIAN
PLAIN

CENTRAL SIBERIAN
PLATEAU

Lena R.

Sakhalin
Island

Kuril Islands

Ob River

R U S S I A

Lena River

STANOVOY MTS.

Don R.

URAL MOUNTAINS

KUZNETSK
BASIN

Lake
Baikal

Amur R.

Black Sea

Volga R.

YABLONOVY
RANGE

Sea of
Japan
(East Sea)

GEORGIA
Mt. Elbrus
18,510 ft (5,642 m)

CAUCASUS MTS.

SAYAN MTS.

ARMENIA

Caspian Sea

**EAST
ASIA**

AZERBAIJAN

**SOUTHWEST
ASIA**

map zone Geography Skills

Regions The Caucasus Mountains separate Russia from the three Caucasus countries to the south.
1. **Locate** What part of Russia is called Siberia?
2. **Interpret** What is the land like in the Caucasus countries?

ELEVATION

Feet	Meters
13,120	4,000
6,560	2,000
1,640	500
656	200
(Sea level) 0	0 (Sea level)
Below sea level	Below sea level

0   500   1,000 Miles
0 500 1,000 Kilometers

Projection: Two-Point Equidistant

To the east, the plain rises to form the Ural Mountains. These low mountains are worn down and rounded from erosion.

The vast area between the Urals and the Pacific Ocean is **Siberia**. This area includes several landforms, shown on the map. The West Siberian Plain is a flat, marshy area. It is one of the largest plains in the world.

East of this plain is an upland called the Central Siberian Plateau. Mountain ranges run through southern and eastern Siberia.

Eastern Siberia is called the Russian Far East. This area includes the Kamchatka (kuhm-CHAHT-kuh) Peninsula and several islands. The Russian Far East is part of the Ring of Fire, the area circling the Pacific.

1 The Kamchatka Peninsula on Russia's east coast has many old and active volcanoes.

The Ring of Fire is known for its volcanoes and earthquakes, and the Russian Far East is no exception. It has several active volcanoes, and earthquakes can occur. In some areas, steam from within Earth breaks free to form geysers and hot springs.

South of Russia, the Caucasus countries consist largely of rugged uplands. The Caucasus Mountains cover much of Georgia and extend into Armenia and Azerbaijan.

These soaring mountains include Mount Elbrus (el-BROOS). At 18,510 feet (5,642 m), it is the highest peak in Europe. South of the mountains, a plateau covers much of Armenia. Gorges cut through this plateau, and earthquakes are common there. Lowlands lie along the Black and Caspian seas.

Bodies of Water

Some of the longest rivers in the world flow through the region of Russia and the Caucasus. One of the most important is the **Volga** (VAHL-guh) **River** in western Russia. The longest river in Europe, the Volga winds southward to the Caspian Sea. The Volga has long formed the core of Russia's river network. Canals link the Volga to the nearby Don River and to the Baltic Sea.

Even longer rivers than the Volga flow through Siberia in the Asian part of Russia. The Ob (AWB), Yenisey (yi-ni-SAY), and Lena rivers flow northward to the Arctic Ocean. Like many of Russia's rivers, they are frozen for much of the year. The ice often hinders shipping and trade and closes some of Russia's ports for part of the year.

In addition to its rivers, Russia has some 200,000 lakes. Lake Baikal (by-KAHL), in south-central Siberia, is the world's deepest lake. Although not that large in surface area, Lake Baikal is deep enough to hold all the water in all five of the Great Lakes. Because of its beauty, Lake Baikal is called the Jewel of Siberia. Logging and factories have polluted the water, but Russians are now working to clean up the lake.

In the southwest part of the region, the Black and Caspian Seas border Russia and the Caucasus. The Black Sea connects to the Mediterranean Sea and is important for trade. The Caspian Sea holds saltwater and is the world's largest inland sea.

READING CHECK **Summarizing** What are the major landforms in Russia and the Caucasus?

Russia's Climate and Plant Life

In the top photo, Russians bundled up in furs hurry through the snow and cold of Moscow, the capital. In the lower photo, evergreen forest called taiga blankets a Russian plain. In the distance, the low Ural Mountains mark the division between Europe and Asia.

Climate and Plant Life

Russians sometimes joke that winter lasts for 12 months and then summer begins. Russia is a cold country. The reason is its northern location partly within the Arctic Circle. In general, Russia has short summers and long, snowy winters. The climate is milder west of the Urals and grows colder and harsher as one goes north and east.

Russia's northern coast is tundra. Winters are dark and bitterly cold, and the brief summers are cool. Much of the ground is permafrost, or permanently frozen soil. Only small plants such as mosses grow.

South of the tundra is a vast forest of evergreen trees called **taiga** (TY-guh). This huge forest covers about half of Russia. In Siberia, snow covers the taiga much of the year. South of the taiga is a flat grassland called the steppe (STEP). With rich, black soil and a warmer climate, the steppe is Russia's most important farming area.

Farther south, the Caucasus countries are warmer than Russia in general. Climate in the Caucasus ranges from warm and wet along the Black Sea to cooler in the uplands to hot and dry in much of Azerbaijan.

READING CHECK Finding Main Ideas How does Russia's location affect its climate?

Natural Resources

Russia and the Caucasus have a wealth of resources. The Northern European Plain and the steppe provide fertile soil for farming. The taiga provides wood for building and paper products. Metals, such as copper and gold, and precious gems such as diamonds provide useful raw materials.

The region's main energy resources are coal, hydroelectricity, natural gas, and oil. Both Russia and Azerbaijan have large oil and gas fields. Oil also lies beneath the Caspian Sea.

The region's natural resources have been poorly managed, however. Until the early 1990s this region was part of the Soviet Union. The Soviet government put more importance on industry than on managing its resources. In Russia, many of the resources that were easy to access are gone. For example, most of the timber in western Russia has been cut down. Many remaining resources are in remote Siberia.

READING CHECK Analyzing Why are some of Russia's natural resources difficult to obtain?

SUMMARY AND PREVIEW Russia is big and cold, with vast plains and forests. The Caucasus countries are small, mountainous, and warmer. The region also has many natural resources. Next, you will read about Russia's history and culture.

FOCUS ON READING

What general idea can you draw from the text about natural resources? What facts or details support that idea?

Section 1 Assessment

hmhsocialstudies.com
ONLINE QUIZ

Reviewing Ideas, Terms, and Places

1. **a. Describe** Why are the **Ural Mountains** significant?
   b. Draw Conclusions Why might the Russian Far East be a dangerous place to live?
2. **a. Describe** What are winters like in much of Russia?
   b. Analyze How does climate affect Russia's plant life?
3. **a. Recall** What valuable resource is in the **Caspian Sea**?
   b. Make Inferences Why might resources located in remote, cold areas be difficult to use?

Critical Thinking

4. **Generalizing** Draw a chart like the one here. Use your notes and enter one general idea for each topic in the chart.

Physical Features	
Climate and Plants	
Natural Resources	

FOCUS ON WRITING

5. **Describing the Physical Geography** Now that you know the physical geography of the region, make a list of possible locations for the house or land you are selling.

History and Culture of Russia

What You Will Learn...

Main Ideas

1. The Russian Empire grew under powerful leaders, but unrest and war led to its end.
2. The Soviet Union emerged as a Communist superpower with rigid government control.
3. Russia's history and diversity have influenced its culture.

The Big Idea

Strict rule, unrest, and ethnic diversity have shaped Russia's history and culture.

Key Terms and Places

Kiev, *p. 200*
Cyrillic, *p. 200*
czar, *p. 201*
Bolsheviks, *p. 201*
gulags, *p. 202*

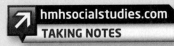
hmhsocialstudies.com
TAKING NOTES

Use the graphic organizer online to take notes on the history and culture of Russia.

If YOU lived there...

It is 1992, an exciting time in your home town of Moscow. At the end of 1991 the Soviet Union fell apart. Russia became independent. You watched on TV as people pulled down the red Soviet flag and knocked down statues of former leaders. Everyone is talking about new freedoms and a new kind of government.

What new freedoms do you hope to have?

BUILDING BACKGROUND The fall of the Soviet Union was not the first time Russia had experienced change. For centuries Russia was part of a great empire. Then in the early 1900s Communists overthrew the empire. The Soviet Union was born. Today it too is gone.

The Russian Empire

Russia's roots lie in the grassy, windswept plains of the steppe. For thousands of years, people from Asia moved across the steppe. These groups of people included the Slavs. As you read in the last chapter, the Slavs settled in Eastern Europe, including what is now Ukraine and western Russia.

Early History and Empire

The Slavs developed towns and began trading with people from other areas. In the AD 800s, Viking traders from Scandinavia invaded the Slavs. These Vikings were called Rus (ROOS), and the word *Russia* probably comes from their name. The Vikings shaped the first Russian state among the Slavs. This Russian state, called Kievan (KEE-e-fuhn) Rus, centered around the city of **Kiev**. This city is now the capital of Ukraine.

Over time, missionaries introduced the Orthodox Christian faith to Kiev. In addition, the missionaries introduced a form of the Greek alphabet called **Cyrillic** (suh-RI-lik). The Russians adopted this Cyrillic alphabet and still use it today.

Baltic
republics:
independent
1918–1940
and 1991

Finland:
Russian
territory
1809–1918

Poland:
Russian
territory
1815–1918

ARCTIC
OCEAN

Bering
Sea

St.
Petersburg

☆ Moscow

Sea of
Okhotsk

Black Sea

Caspian Sea

Sea of
Japan
(East Sea)

Russian
territory
1871–1881

	Russia, 1462–1533
Territory gained	
	by 1689
	by 1725
	by 1801
	by 1945
	Russian boundary, 1993

0   250   500 Miles
0 250 500 Kilometers

*Projection:
Two-Point Equidistant*

map zone Geography Skills

Location The colors in the map show the growth of the Russian Empire and of the Soviet Union over time.
1. **Name** What city is located in territory gained by 1725?
2. **Interpret** When was the period of greatest expansion?

In the 1200s, fierce Mongol invaders called Tatars (TAH-ters) swept out of Central Asia and conquered Kiev. The Mongols allowed Russian princes to rule over local states. In time, Muscovy became the strongest state. Its main city was Moscow.

After about 200 years Muscovy's prince, Ivan III, seized control from the Mongols. In the 1540s his grandson, Ivan IV, crowned himself **czar** (ZAHR), or emperor. *Czar* is Russian for "caesar." As czar, Ivan IV had total power. A cruel and savage ruler, he became known as Ivan the Terrible.

In time, Muscovy developed into the country of Russia. Strong czars such as Peter the Great (1682–1725) and Catherine the Great (1762–1796) built Russia into a huge empire and a world power. This empire included many conquered peoples.

In spite of its growth, Russia remained largely a country of poor farmers, while the czars and nobles had most of the wealth. In the early 1900s Russians began demanding improvements. The czar agreed to some changes, but unrest continued to grow.

War and Revolution

In 1914 Russia entered World War I. The country suffered huge losses in the war. In addition, the Russian people experienced severe shortages of food. When the czar seemed to ignore the people's hardship, they rose up against him. He was forced to give up his throne in 1917.

Later that year the **Bolsheviks**, a radical Russian Communist group, seized power in the Russian Revolution. They then killed the czar and his family. In 1922 the Bolsheviks formed a new country, the Union of Soviet Socialist Republics (USSR), or the Soviet Union. It soon included 15 republics, the strongest of which was Russia. The first leader was Vladimir Lenin.

HISTORY

VIDEO
The
Romanovs

↗ hmhsocialstudies.com

READING CHECK **Sequencing** What series of events led to the creation of the Soviet Union?

The Soviet Union

The Soviet Union, led by Lenin, became a Communist country. In this political system, the government owns all property and controls all aspects of life. In 1924 Lenin died. Joseph Stalin took power, ruling as a brutal and paranoid dictator.

The Soviet Union under Stalin

FOCUS ON READING
Based on the Soviet Union's economy, what generalization might you make about command economies?

Under Stalin, the Soviet Union set up a command economy. In this system, the government owns all businesses and farms and makes all decisions. People were told what to make and how much to charge. Without competition, though, efficiency and the quality of goods fell over time.

The Soviet Union strictly controlled its people as well as its economy. Stalin had anyone who spoke out against the government jailed, exiled, or killed. Millions of people were sent to **gulags**, harsh Soviet labor camps often located in Siberia.

Cold War and Collapse

During World War II, the Soviet Union fought with the Allies against Germany. Millions of Soviet citizens died in the war. Stalin's <u>reaction</u> to the war was to build a buffer around the Soviet Union to protect it from invasion. To do so, he set up Communist governments in Eastern Europe.

ACADEMIC VOCABULARY
reaction
a response to something

The United States opposed communism and saw its spread as a threat to democracy. This opposition led to the Cold War, a period of tense rivalry between the Soviet Union and the United States. The two rival countries became superpowers as they competed to have superior weapons.

In part because of the high costs of weapons, the Soviet economy was near collapse by the 1980s. Mikhail Gorbachev (GAWR-buh-chawf), the Soviet leader, began making changes. He reduced government control and introduced some democracy.

Despite his actions, the Soviet republics began pushing for independence. In 1991 the Soviet Union collapsed. It broke apart into 15 independent countries, including Russia. The Soviet Union was no more.

READING CHECK **Analyzing** How did the Cold War help lead to the Soviet Union's collapse?

Culture

In the Soviet Union, the government had controlled culture just like everything else. Today, however, Russian culture is once again alive and vibrant.

People and Religion

Russia is big and diverse, with more than 140 million people. About 80 percent are ethnic Russians, or Slavs, but Russia also has many other ethnic groups. The largest are the Tatars and Ukrainians. Russia's many ethnic groups are once again taking great pride in their cultures.

Like ethnic culture, religious worship has seen a revival. The Soviet government opposed religion and closed many houses of worship. Today many have reopened, including historic Russian cathedrals with their onion-shaped domes. The main faith is Russian Orthodox Christian. Other religions include Islam, Buddhism, and other forms of Christianity.

Customs

Russian history has shaped its customs, such as holidays. Religious holidays, like Easter and Christmas, are popular. The main family holiday is New Year's Eve. To celebrate this holiday, families decorate a tree where, according to Russian folklore, Grandfather Frost and his helper the Snow Maiden leave gifts. A newer holiday is Russian Independence Day, which marks the end of the Soviet Union on June 12.

Close-up

St. Basil's Cathedral

Colorful St. Basil's Cathedral, in Moscow's Red Square, has become a symbol of Russia. Czar Ivan IV had the cathedral built between 1555 and 1561 in honor of Russian military victories. According to legend, Ivan had the architects blinded so they could never design anything else as magnificent.

Steeply sloped towers, called tent roofs, and onion-shaped domes easily shed snow.

Onion-shaped domes, based on Byzantine designs, decorate many early Russian churches.

St. Basil's Cathedral houses nine small, separate chapels.

In 1588 a chapel was added for the tomb of St. Basil the Blessed, a popular saint in Russia. In time, his name became linked to the cathedral.

ANALYSIS SKILL **ANALYZING VISUALS**

Besides onion domes, what other shapes and patterns are visible on the cathedral?

Communist-era Poster

The Soviet Union used posters as propaganda. Propaganda is information designed to promote a specific cause or idea by influencing people's thoughts and beliefs. For example, Soviet posters often promoted the greatness and power of the Soviet state, its leaders, and their Communist policies.

The message of this 1924 poster reads, "Long live the Young Communist League! The young are taking over the older generation's torch!"

The color red in this poster symbolizes communism and the Russian Revolution.

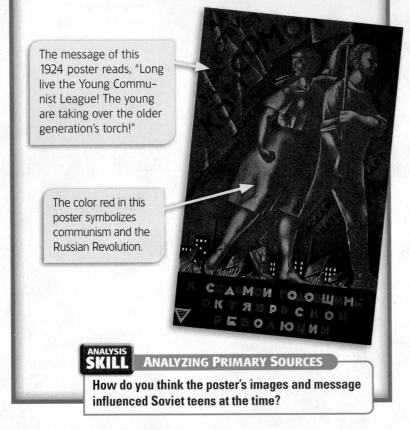

ANALYSIS SKILL **ANALYZING PRIMARY SOURCES**

How do you think the poster's images and message influenced Soviet teens at the time?

The Arts and Sciences

Russia has made great contributions in the arts and sciences. In the performing arts, Russia's ballet companies are world famous for their skill. In music, Peter Tchaikovsky (chy-KAWF-skee) is Russia's most famous composer. His many works include *The Nutcracker* ballet and the *1812 Overture*.

In the material arts, Russia's Fabergé eggs are priceless. Gifts for the czars, these eggs are made of precious metals and covered with gems such as emeralds and rubies. Each egg opens to reveal a tiny surprise.

In the sciences, Russia has contributed to space research. In 1957 the Soviet Union launched Sputnik, the first artificial satellite in space. Russian scientists now help work on the International Space Station.

READING CHECK **Generalizing** How did the end of the Soviet Union affect Russian culture?

SUMMARY AND PREVIEW The history of Russia, from a great empire to a Communist superpower to a new nation, has shaped its rich culture. Next, you will read about life in Russia today.

Section 2 Assessment

hmhsocialstudies.com
ONLINE QUIZ

Reviewing Ideas, Terms, and Places

1. a. **Define** Who were the **czars**?
   b. **Analyze** What role did the city of **Kiev** play in Russian history?
   c. **Elaborate** What problems and events caused the Russian Empire to decline?
2. a. **Identify** Why are Vladimir Lenin and Joseph Stalin significant in Russian history?
   b. **Evaluate** Do you think life in the Soviet Union was an improvement over life in the Russian empire? Why, or why not?
3. a. **Recall** What is the main religion in Russia?
   b. **Summarize** How has Russian culture changed since the collapse of the Soviet Union in 1991?

Critical Thinking

4. **Sequencing** Draw a chart like the one here. Use your notes to list the order of the major events leading up to the collapse of the Soviet Union.

Focus on Writing

5. **Considering Russia's History and Culture** Look at the locations you listed for Section 1. For the Russian locations, make notes about historical or cultural details you could include in your ad.

Social Studies Skills

Interpreting a Population Map

Learn

Population maps give you a snapshot of the distribution of people in a region or country. Each color on a population map represents an average number of people living within a square mile or square kilometer. Sometimes symbols identify the cities with populations of a certain size. The map's legend identifies what the colors and symbols in the map mean.

Practice

① Based on the map below, in which region of Russia do most of the country's people live?

② Which two cities in Russia have the largest population?

③ How many Russian cities have more than 1 million people?

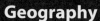

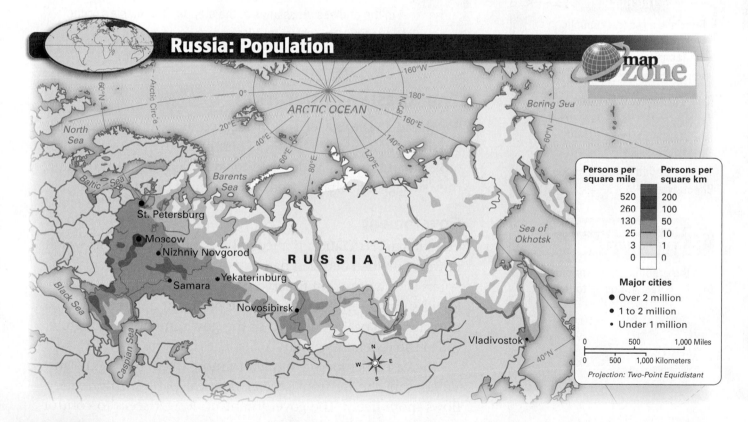

Russia: Population

Persons per square mile	Persons per square km
520	200
260	100
130	50
25	10
3	1
0	0

Major cities
● Over 2 million
● 1 to 2 million
• Under 1 million

Projection: Two-Point Equidistant

Apply

Use an atlas to locate a current population map of the United States. Using the map, identify where the most and the least populated regions of the United States are. Then identify the number of U.S. cities or metropolitan areas with more than 2 million people.

Russia Today

What You Will Learn...

Main Ideas

1. The Russian Federation is working to develop democracy and a market economy.
2. Russia's physical geography, cities, and economy define its many culture regions.
3. Russia faces a number of serious challenges.

The Big Idea

Russia is a federal republic with a growing market economy but faces tough challenges.

Key Terms and Places

dachas, *p. 207*
St. Petersburg, *p. 208*
smelters, *p. 209*
Trans-Siberian Railroad, *p. 209*
Chechnya, *p. 210*

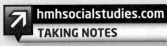
hmhsocialstudies.com
TAKING NOTES

Use the graphic organizer online to take notes on Russia today.

If YOU lived there...

You live in St. Petersburg, a city of beautiful palaces and canals. You are looking forward to the end of school, when your family will go to their dacha, a cottage in the country. In midsummer, when the nights are long and the sun never really sets, you will go to concerts and other celebrations of the "White Nights" in your city.

What do you like about living in St. Petersburg?

BUILDING BACKGROUND Russians have always had a special feeling for the countryside, from the wheat fields and birch forests in the west to the endless grasslands of the steppe. But Russia's great cities are exciting, too, with many shops, museums, and events.

The Russian Federation

For decades, the Soviet Union reigned as a superpower, with Russia as its strongest republic. Then in 1991 the Soviet Union broke apart. Russia's leaders had to create a new government as they struggled to change from communism to democracy.

Government

The Russian Federation is a federal republic, a system in which power is divided between national and local governments. The voters elect a president to serve as the country's chief executive, Russia's most powerful official. The president appoints a prime minister to serve as the head of the government. A legislature, called the Federal Assembly, makes the country's laws.

Increased democracy has led to more freedom for Russians. Voters can choose from several political parties. Information flows more freely. The government no longer seeks to control every aspect of life. In addition, the move toward democracy has improved relations between Russia and Western nations.

Changing to a democratic system has been difficult, though. Problems such as government corruption, or dishonesty, have slowed the development of a free society in Russia. Time will tell whether Russia will continue to grow as a democracy.

Economy

With the move to democracy, Russia also began shifting to a market economy. This type of economy is based on free trade and competition. Today the Russian government has greatly reduced its control of the economy, and most businesses and farms are now privately owned. These changes have led to economic growth. At the same time, most of Russia's wealth is now in the hands of a small number of people.

Today Russia produces and exports oil, natural gas, timber, metals, and chemicals. Heavy industry, such as machinery, is still important. However, light industry, such as clothing and electronics, has grown. Furthermore, service industries now make up the largest part of Russia's economy.

In agriculture, Russia is now a major grower and exporter of grains. Other major crops are fruits, potatoes, and sugar beets.

City and Rural Life

The changes sweeping Russia are visible in its cities. More restaurants and shopping centers are available. Stores offer a wider range of consumer goods, such as TVs. Some Russians have become wealthy and can afford luxuries. In fact, in 2005 Russia had more billionaires than any other European country. Nevertheless, the average Russian's standard of living remains low.

About 75 percent of all Russians live in cities. Most of these people live in small apartments in high-rise buildings. In rural areas, more people live in houses.

Although most Russians live in cities, they still have access to nature. Cities often have large parks and wooded areas in and around them. Many richer Russians own **dachas**, or Russian country houses, where they can garden and enjoy the fresh air.

READING CHECK **Summarizing** How has Russia changed since it became independent?

Kaliningrad

The small region of Kaliningrad—only slightly bigger than Connecticut—is more than 200 miles (320 km) from the rest of Russia. So why would Russia want this area? The reason has to do with the country's cold climate. Kaliningrad is Russia's only Baltic seaport that is free of ice all year. This important port provides Russia with year-round access to profitable European markets and trade. Railroads connect the port to Russia's major cities, as the map below shows.

Drawing Conclusions How do you think Russia's economy benefits from a Baltic seaport that is free of ice all year?

Culture Regions

You have learned that Russia is vast and diverse. For this reason, we divide Russia into several culture regions, as the map on the next page shows. These regions differ in **features** such as population, natural resources, and economic activity.

The four western culture regions make up Russia's heartland. This area is home to the vast majority of Russia's people as well as to the country's capital and largest cities. In addition, the fertile plains of Russia's heartland are the country's most productive farming area.

ACADEMIC VOCABULARY
features
characteristics

Russia: Culture Regions

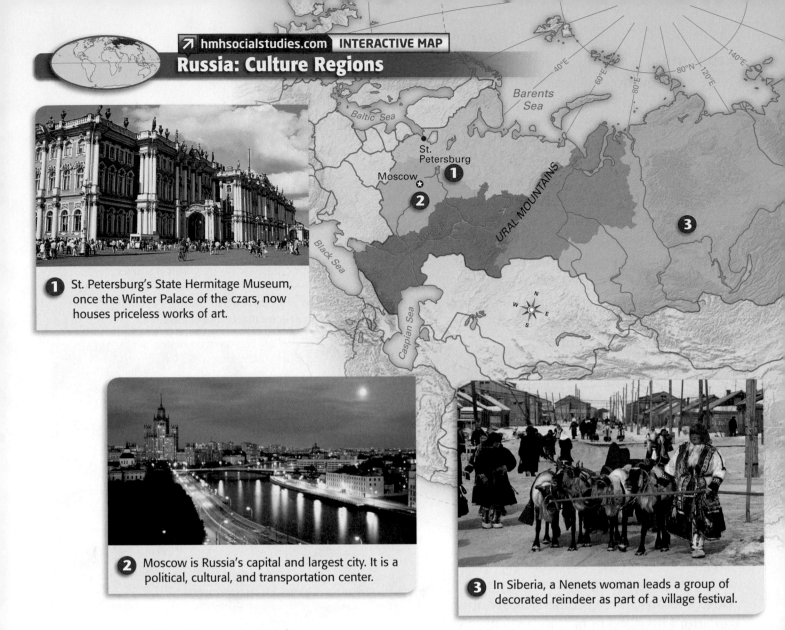

1 St. Petersburg's State Hermitage Museum, once the Winter Palace of the czars, now houses priceless works of art.

2 Moscow is Russia's capital and largest city. It is a political, cultural, and transportation center.

3 In Siberia, a Nenets woman leads a group of decorated reindeer as part of a village festival.

The Moscow Region

Moscow is Russia's capital and largest city. The sprawling, modern city has wide boulevards and large public squares. Its many cultural attractions include the world-famous Bolshoi Ballet and Moscow Circus.

At Moscow's heart is the Kremlin, the center of Russia's government. In Russian, *kremlin* means "fortress." The Kremlin consists of several buildings surrounded by a wall and towers. The buildings include not only government offices but also palaces, museums, and gold-domed churches.

Next to the Kremlin is Red Square, an immense plaza. It is lined by many famous landmarks, such as St. Basil's Cathedral.

The Moscow region is Russia's most important economic area, and its factories produce a wide range of goods. The city is also a transportation center and links by road, rail, and plane to all parts of Russia.

The St. Petersburg Region

St. Petersburg reflects Russians' desire for Western ways. Peter the Great founded the city and styled it after those of Western Europe. For some 200 years, St. Petersburg served as Russia's capital and home to the czars. It features wide avenues, grand palaces, and numerous canals. Theaters and museums enrich the city's cultural life.

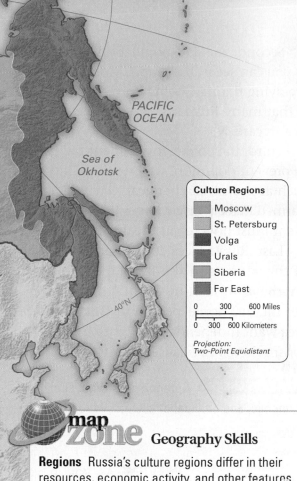

Sea of
Okhotsk

PACIFIC
OCEAN

40°N

Culture Regions

- Moscow
- St. Petersburg
- Volga
- Urals
- Siberia
- Far East

0   300   600 Miles

0   300   600 Kilometers

Projection:
Two-Point Equidistant

map zone Geography Skills

Regions Russia's culture regions differ in their resources, economic activity, and other features.
1. **Identify** What are the six culture regions?
2. **Interpret** What is the major defining feature in each of the four western culture regions?

St. Petersburg's location on the Gulf of Finland has made the city a major port and trade center. This northern location also produces "White Nights," a period during summer when it never gets totally dark.

The Volga and Urals Regions

The Volga River and Ural Mountains are the third and fourth culture regions. The broad Volga is a major shipping route. Dams along its course form lakes and provide hydroelectric power. Factories in the area process oil and gas. In addition, a site on the Caspian Sea provides fish called sturgeon. The eggs of this fish are called black caviar, which is a costly delicacy, or rare and valued food.

The Ural Mountains are an important mining region and produce nearly every major mineral. **Smelters**, factories that process metal ores, process copper and iron. The Urals region is also known for gems and semiprecious stones.

Siberia

East of the Urals lies the vast expanse of Siberia. In the Tatar language, *Siberia* means "Sleeping Land." Siberian winters are long and severe. As you have read, much of the land lies frozen or buried under snow for most or all of the year. The remote region has many valuable resources, but accessing them in the harsh climate is difficult.

Siberia's main industries are lumber, mining, and oil production. Large coal deposits are mined in southwest Siberia. Rivers produce hydroelectric power. The southern steppes, where the weather is warmer, are Siberia's main farmlands.

Because of Siberia's harsh climate, jobs there pay high wages. Even so, few people choose to live in Siberia. Most towns and cities are in the western and southern parts of the region. These cities tend to follow the **Trans-Siberian Railroad**. This rail line runs from Moscow to Vladivostok on the east coast, and is the longest single rail line in the world.

The Russian Far East

Russia has a long coastline on the Pacific Ocean. There, in the Russian Far East, much land remains heavily forested. In the few cities, factories process forest and mineral resources. Farming occurs in the Amur River valley. The city of Vladivostok is a naval base and the area's main seaport. Islands off the coast provide oil, minerals, and commercial fishing.

READING CHECK **Finding Main Ideas** What areas make up Russia's culture regions?

FOCUS ON READING

Based on this description of Siberia, what generalization about human settlement can you make?

⬈ hmhsocialstudies.com

ANIMATED GEOGRAPHY

Trans-Siberian Railroad

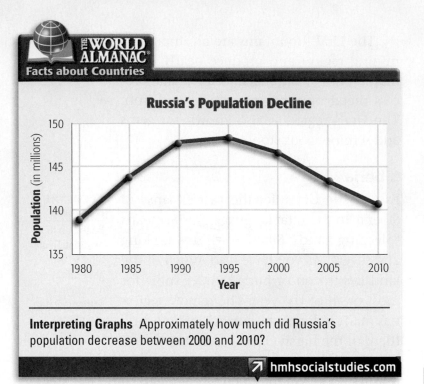

Facts about Countries
THE WORLD ALMANAC®

Russia's Population Decline

Population (in millions)

| 150 |
| 145 |
| 140 |
| 135 |

1980 1985 1990 1995 2000 2005 2010
Year

Interpreting Graphs Approximately how much did Russia's population decrease between 2000 and 2010?

↗ hmhsocialstudies.com

Russia's Challenges

Although Russia has made great progress since 1991, challenges remain. First, Russia's shift to a market economy has not been without problems. For example, prices and unemployment have risen, and the gap between rich and poor has widened.

Second, Russia's population is falling, as you can see in the graph. More Russians are dying than are being born. One reason is that many Russians cannot afford good health care.

Third, the Soviet government did little to prevent pollution. As a result pollution, such as industrial chemicals, has seriously harmed Russia's environment. The government must now repair the damage.

Last, Russia faces ethnic conflicts. One of the worst is in the Russian republic of **Chechnya** (CHECH-nyah) in the Caucasus Mountains. Some people in this Muslim area want independence. Fighting and terrorism there have caused many deaths.

READING CHECK **Categorizing** What social, economic, and political challenges face Russia?

SUMMARY AND PREVIEW As you have read, Russia is a federal republic working to build a market economy. The west is Russia's heartland, but Siberia has many valuable resources. In the next section, you will read about the Caucasus.

Section 3 Assessment

↗ hmhsocialstudies.com
ONLINE QUIZ

Reviewing Ideas, Terms, and Places

1. **a. Recall** What type of government does Russia now have?
   b. Explain How is Russia's economy changing?
2. **a. Recall** From west to east, what are Russia's major culture regions?
   b. Draw Conclusions Why do you think most Siberian towns and cities are located along the **Trans-Siberian Railroad**?
   c. Rate Which of Russia's culture regions would you most want to live in, and why?
3. **a. Identify** What are the main challenges that face Russia today?
   b. Elaborate What difficulties does **Chechnya** pose for Russia's leaders?

Critical Thinking

4. **Categorizing** Draw a concept web like the one shown. Use your notes to list facts about each Russian culture region.

Russia's Culture Regions

FOCUS ON WRITING

5. **Collecting Details about Russia Today** Based on conditions in Russia today, what location would you choose for your property? Review your notes from Section 2 and this section. Then choose one location in Russia for the property you are selling.

from
The Endless Steppe

by Esther Hautzig

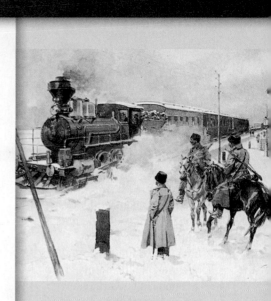

About the Reading *In* The Endless Steppe, *an autobiographical novel, Esther Hautzig writes about her own experiences as a teenage girl. In the novel, the girl Esther is from a wealthy Jewish family in Poland. In 1941 her family is deported to a labor camp in Siberia. In the excerpt below, Esther and her family are on the train to Siberia. She is dreading their destination.*

AS YOU READ Think about what Esther feels as she watches the passing landscape. What ideas does she already have about life in Siberia?

The flatness of this land was awesome. There wasn't a hill in sight; it was an enormous, unrippled sea of parched and lifeless grass.

"Tata, why is the earth so flat here?"

"These must be steppes, Esther."

"Steppes? But steppes are in Siberia."

"This is Siberia," he said quietly.

If I had been told that I had been transported to the moon, I could not have been more stunned.

"Siberia?" My voice trembled. "But Siberia is full of snow."

"It will be," my father said. ❶

Siberia! Siberia was the end of the world, a point of no return. Siberia was for criminals and political enemies, where the punishment was unbelievably cruel, and where people died like flies. ❷ Summer or no summer—and who had ever talked about hot Siberia?—Siberia was the tundra and mountainous drifts of snow. Siberia was *wolves*.

Connecting Literature to Geography

1. **Analyzing** Russian soldiers took Esther's family from their home in Poland to work in Siberia. How do you think this fact affects Esther's feelings as she views the landscape of Siberia from the train?

2. **Drawing Inferences** Why do you think Siberia was chosen as a place of exile? What made it a punishment to live there?

The Caucasus

What You Will Learn...

Main Ideas

1. Many groups have ruled and influenced the Caucasus during its long history.
2. Today the Caucasus republics are working to improve their economies but struggle with ethnic unrest and conflict.

The Big Idea

In an area long ruled by outside groups, the Caucasus republics are struggling to strengthen their economies and to deal with ethnic unrest.

Key Places

Tbilisi, *p. 213*
Yerevan, *p. 213*
Baku, *p. 214*

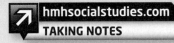
hmhsocialstudies.com
TAKING NOTES

Use the graphic organizer online to take notes on the Caucasus.

If YOU lived there...

You live in Tbilisi, the capital of the country of Georgia. Several years ago, your sister and her college friends joined the Rose Revolution, a political protest that forced a corrupt president to resign. The protestors' symbol was a red rose. Since the protest, you have become more interested in politics.

What kind of government do you want?

BUILDING BACKGROUND Georgia is one of three republics in the area called the Caucasus. In 1991, when the Soviet Union ended, the Caucasus republics gained independence. Since then, the republics have struggled to become democracies with market economies.

History

The Caucasus lies in the rugged Caucasus Mountains between the Black and Caspian seas. Located where Europe blends into Asia, the Caucasus reflects a range of cultural influences. At one time or another, Persians, Greeks, Romans, Arabs, Turks, and Mongols have all ruled or invaded the area. The Russians took control of much of the Caucasus in the early 1800s.

Russian control in the Caucasus did not include what is now western Armenia. The Ottoman Turks held this area. Over time, the Turks grew to distrust the Armenians, however; and in the late 1800s began abusing and killing them. During World War I (1914–1918), the Turks forced all Armenians to leave. Hundreds of thousands of Armenians died during this ethnic cleansing, or attempt to remove an ethnic group. The Turks lost World War I, though, and had to give up western Armenia.

After World War I, Armenia, Azerbaijan, and Georgia gained independence—but not for long. By the early 1920s they were part of the vast Soviet Union. Finally in 1991, when the Soviet Union fell, the Caucasus republics achieved true independence.

READING CHECK Finding Main Ideas Why do the countries in the Caucasus reflect a range of cultural influences?

The snow-capped peaks of the Caucasus Mountains rise above a mountain village and the remains of a fortress built in the 900s.

The Caucasus: Political

National capital

Mount Elbrus
18,510 ft
(5,642 m)

RUSSIA

CAUCASUS MOUNTAINS

Black Sea

GEORGIA

Tbilisi

TURKEY

ARMENIA

Lake Sevan

Yerevan

AZERBAIJAN

Baku

Kura River

Aras River

Caspian Sea

IRAN

map
zone   **Geography Skills**

Location South of western Russia, the Caucasus is located where Europe blends into Asia.
1. **Name** What two seas border the Caucasus?
2. **Contrast** Based on the map, how does Armenia differ from Azerbaijan and Georgia?

The Caucasus Today

The Caucasus may have a long history, but the Caucasus countries do not. Like other former Soviet republics, these young countries have had to create new governments and economies. Meanwhile, ethnic unrest and conflicts have slowed progress.

The Caucasus republics have similar governments. An elected president governs each nation, and an appointed prime minister runs each government. An elected parliament, or legislature, makes the laws.

Georgia

The country of Georgia lies in the Caucasus Mountains east of the Black Sea. **Tbilisi** is the capital. About 70 percent of the people are ethnic Georgians, and most belong to the Georgian Orthodox Church. The official language is Georgian, a unique language with its own alphabet. However, many other languages are also spoken.

Since 1991 Georgia has struggled with unrest and civil war. In 2003 Georgians forced out their president in the peaceful Rose Revolution. Meanwhile, ethnic groups in northern Georgia were fighting for independence. Because these groups now hold parts of northern Georgia, division and unrest continues.

Although unrest has hurt Georgia's economy, international aid is helping it improve. Georgia's economy is based on services and farming. Major crops include citrus fruits, grapes, and tea. In addition, Georgia produces steel and mines copper and manganese. Georgia is also famous for its wines. The Black Sea is a resort area, and tourism contributes to the economy, too.

Armenia

South of Georgia is the small, landlocked country of Armenia. The tiny country is slightly larger than the state of Maryland. **Yerevan** (yer-uh-VAHN) is the capital. Almost all the people are ethnic Armenian. Armenia prides itself as being the first country to adopt Christianity, and most people belong to the Armenian Orthodox Church.

Baku

Located on the Caspian Sea, the city of Baku is the capital and chief port of Azerbaijan.

FOCUS ON READING

What general statements can you make about the Caucasus as a whole?

In the early 1990s, Armenia fought a bitter war with its neighbor Azerbaijan. The war involved an area of Azerbaijan where most people are ethnic Armenian. Armenia wanted this area to become part of its country. Although a cease-fire stopped the fighting in 1994, Armenian armed forces still control the area. The issue remained unsettled as of the early 2000s.

This conflict has greatly hurt Armenia's economy. However, international aid is helping Armenia's economy recover and expand. For example, diamond processing is now a growing industry in Armenia.

Azerbaijan

East of Armenia is Azerbaijan. In contrast to the other Caucasus republics, Azerbaijan is largely Muslim. The Azeri (uh-ZE-ree) make up 90 percent of the population.

Azerbaijan's economy is based on oil, found along and under the Caspian Sea. **Baku**, the capital, is the center of a large oil-refining industry. This industry has led to strong economic growth. Corruption is high, though; and many people are poor. In addition, Azerbaijan has many refugees as a result of its conflict with Armenia.

READING CHECK **Summarizing** What challenges do the Caucasus republics face?

SUMMARY The Caucasus republics face challenges but are working to develop democracy and build their economies.

Section 4 Assessment

hmhsocialstudies.com
ONLINE QUIZ

Reviewing Ideas, Terms, and Places

1. a. **Identify** Which country controlled much of the Caucasus for most of the 1800s?
   b. **Identify Cause and Effect** How did Turkish rule affect Armenians in the Ottoman Empire?
   c. **Elaborate** How has location affected the history and culture of the Caucasus area?

2. a. **Recall** How does **Baku** contribute to the economy of Azerbaijan?
   b. **Compare and Contrast** How is religion in Georgia and Armenia similar? How does religion in these countries differ from that in Azerbaijan?
   c. **Elaborate** How has the war that occurred between Armenia and Azerbaijan affected each country?

Critical Thinking

3. **Comparing and Contrasting** Draw a Venn diagram like the one here. Use your notes to identify the ways in which Georgia, Armenia, and Azerbaijan are similar and different.

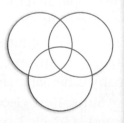

FOCUS ON WRITING

4. **Collecting Details about the Caucasus** You have narrowed Russian locations to one possibility. What features do the Caucasus countries have that might be attractive to potential buyers? Identify one Caucasus location you might use in your ad.

Chapter Review

Geography's Impact
video series
Review the video to answer the closing question:
Why was the Soviet Union so determined to become a major industrial power?

Visual Summary

Use the visual summary below to help you review the main ideas of the chapter.

QUICK FACTS

Russia is an immense, cold country with plains, mountains, and forest. The Caucasus is a small, mountainous area.

With a long history and a rich culture, Russia ranges from large modern cities to the vast plains and forests of Siberia.

The three small Caucasus republics lie between the Black and Caspian seas, and face ethnic unrest and conflict.

Reviewing Vocabulary, Terms, and Places

For each statement below, write T if it is true and F if it is false. If the statement is false, replace the boldfaced term with one that makes the sentence a true statement.

1. The **Caucasus Mountains** separate European Russia from Asian Russia.

2. Russia's capital and largest city is **St. Petersburg**.

3. The Caucasus is bordered by the Black Sea to the west and **Lake Baikal** to the east.

4. Under the rule of the **Bolsheviks**, the Russian Empire expanded in size and power.

5. Much of the country of Georgia is located in the high, rugged **Ural Mountains**.

6. Many wealthier Russians have country houses, which are called **gulags**.

7. Russia's main government buildings are located in the **Kremlin** in Moscow.

8. Russia's culture regions differ in **features** such as cities, natural resources, and economic activity.

9. **Moscow** is a major port and was once home to Russia's czars.

10. The capital city of Armenia is **Yerevan**.

Comprehension and Critical Thinking

SECTION 1 *(Pages 196–199)*

11. **a. Recall** What is Russia's most important river, and to what major bodies of water does it link?

   b. Identify Cause and Effect How does Russia's location affect its climate?

   c. Elaborate Why might developing the many natural resources in Siberia be difficult?

SECTION 2 *(Pages 200–204)*

12. **a. Identify** Who was Joseph Stalin?

   b. Summarize How has Russia contributed to world culture?

   c. Elaborate How was the end of the Soviet Union similar to the end of the Russian Empire?

SECTION 3 (Pages 206–210)

13. a. Identify What four culture regions make up the Russian heartland?

b. Compare and Contrast How are Moscow and St. Petersburg similar and different?

c. Elaborate How might Siberia help make Russia an economic success?

SECTION 4 (Pages 212–214)

14. a. Recall What is the capital of each of the Caucasus republics?

b. Compare What do the three Caucasus countries have in common?

c. Elaborate What issues and challenges do the Caucasus countries need to address to improve their economies?

Using the Internet

15. Activity: Making a Map The Trans-Siberian Railroad is the longest single rail line in the world. Climb aboard in Moscow and travel all the way across Russia. Through your online textbook, research the people, places, and history along the railroad's route. Then create an illustrated map of your journey. On the map, show the train's route, indicate the places where you stopped, and include images and descriptions about what you saw.

↗ hmhsocialstudies.com

Social Studies Skills

Interpreting a Population Map *Use a good atlas to find a population map of Europe. The map does not need to include Russia. Use the map to answer the following questions. Do not include the country of Russia when answering the questions.*

16. Not including the cities of Russia, how many cities or metropolitan areas in Europe have more than 2 million people?

17. Not including Russia, which regions of Europe are the most populated? Which regions of Europe are the least populated?

Map Activity

18. Russia and the Caucasus On a separate sheet of paper, match the letters on the map with their correct labels.

Caucasus Mountains	Ural Mountains
Caspian Sea	Vladivostok, Russia
Kamchatka Peninsula	Volga River
Moscow, Russia	West Siberian Plain
St. Petersburg, Russia	

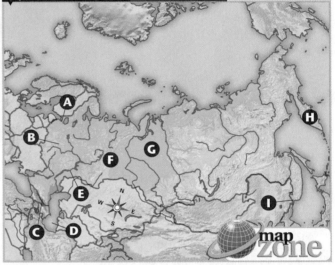

↗ hmhsocialstudies.com **INTERACTIVE MAP**

FOCUS ON READING AND WRITING

19. Making Generalizations Examine the information in Section 3 about the four culture regions that make up Russia's heartland. Based on the specific information about these regions, make two generalizations about western Russia.

20. Creating a Real Estate Ad Review your notes about locations in Russia and the Caucasus. Choose one location for the real estate you are selling. What are its best features? How would you describe the land and climate? What are the benefits of living there? If it is a building, what does it look like? What is nearby? Answer these questions in your real estate ad. Remember to include details that will make the property attractive to possible buyers.

Standardized Test Prep

DIRECTIONS: Read questions 1 through 7 and write the letter of the best response. Then read question 8 and write your own well-constructed response.

1 Which word below *best* describes Russia's overall climate?

A Cold

B Dry

C Hot

D Wet

2 What is the name of the vast forest that covers much of Russia?

A Siberia

B Steppe

C Taiga

D Tundra

3 What was the name of the second Soviet leader, who ruled as a brutal dictator?

A Ivan III

B Ivan the Terrible

C Vladimir Lenin

D Joseph Stalin

4 The majority of Russians are descended from the

A Bolsheviks.

B Slavs.

C Tatars.

D Ukrainians.

5 What are the Caucasus countries?

A Armenia, Moscow, and St. Petersburg

B Azerbaijan, Georgia, and Russia

C Azerbaijan, Armenia, and Georgia

D Georgia, Moscow, and Russia

The Caucasus: Climate

6 Based on the map above, which of the following climates is found along part of the coast of the Black Sea?

A Humid subtropical

B Mediterranean

C Steppe

D Tropical Savanna

7 What year did the Soviet Union collapse and break apart into 15 independent republics?

A 1990

B 1991

C 2000

D 2001

8 **Extended Response** Examine the Section 3 map of Russia's culture regions. Based on the map, describe how the physical geography in three of the culture regions contributes to the economic activity in those regions.

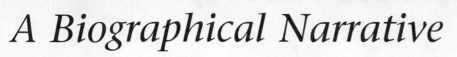

A Biographical Narrative

People have shaped the world. Who are the important people in history? What were the critical events in their lives? How did geography or location affect those events? These are questions we ask as we try to understand our world.

Assignment

Write a biographical narrative about a significant event in the life of a historical figure such as Queen Isabella, Martin Luther, Napoleon, or Mikhail Gorbachev.

1. Prewrite

Choose a Topic

- Choose a person who affected European or Russian history in some way.
- Choose a specific event or incident in the person's life. For example, you might choose Napoleon at the Battle of Waterloo.

TIP To choose the event, think about the person's importance or significance. Choose an event that will help you make that point.

Gather and Organize Information

- Look for information about your topic in the library or on the Internet. Book-length biographies about the person are a good source.
- Identify the parts of the event. Organize them in chonological, or time, order. Note details about people, actions, and the location of the event.

2. Write

Use a Writer's Framework

A Writer's Framework

Introduction
- Introduce the person and the event.
- Identify the importance of the event.

Body
- Write at least one paragraph for each major part of the event. Include specific details.
- Use chronological, or time, order to organize the parts of the event.

Conclusion
- Summarize the importance of the person and event in the final paragraph.

3. Evaluate and Revise

Review and Improve Your Paper

- Read your first draft at least twice, and then use the questions below to evaluate your paper.
- Make the changes needed to improve your paper.

Evaluation Questions for a Biographical Narrative

1. Do you introduce the person and event and identify the importance of each?
2. Do you have one paragraph for each major part of the event?
3. Do you include specific details about people, actions, and location?
4. Do you use chronological order, the order in time, to organize the parts of the event?
5. Do you end the paper with a summary of the importance of the person and event?

4. Proofread and Publish

Give Your Explanation the Finishing Touch

- Make sure your transitional phrases—such as then, next, later, or finally—help clarify the order of the actions that took place.
- Make sure you capitalized all proper names.
- You can share your biographical narrative by reading it aloud in class or adding it to a class collection of biographies.

5. Practice and Apply

Use the steps and strategies outlined in this workshop to write your biographical narrative. Share your work with others, comparing and contrasting the importance of the people and events.

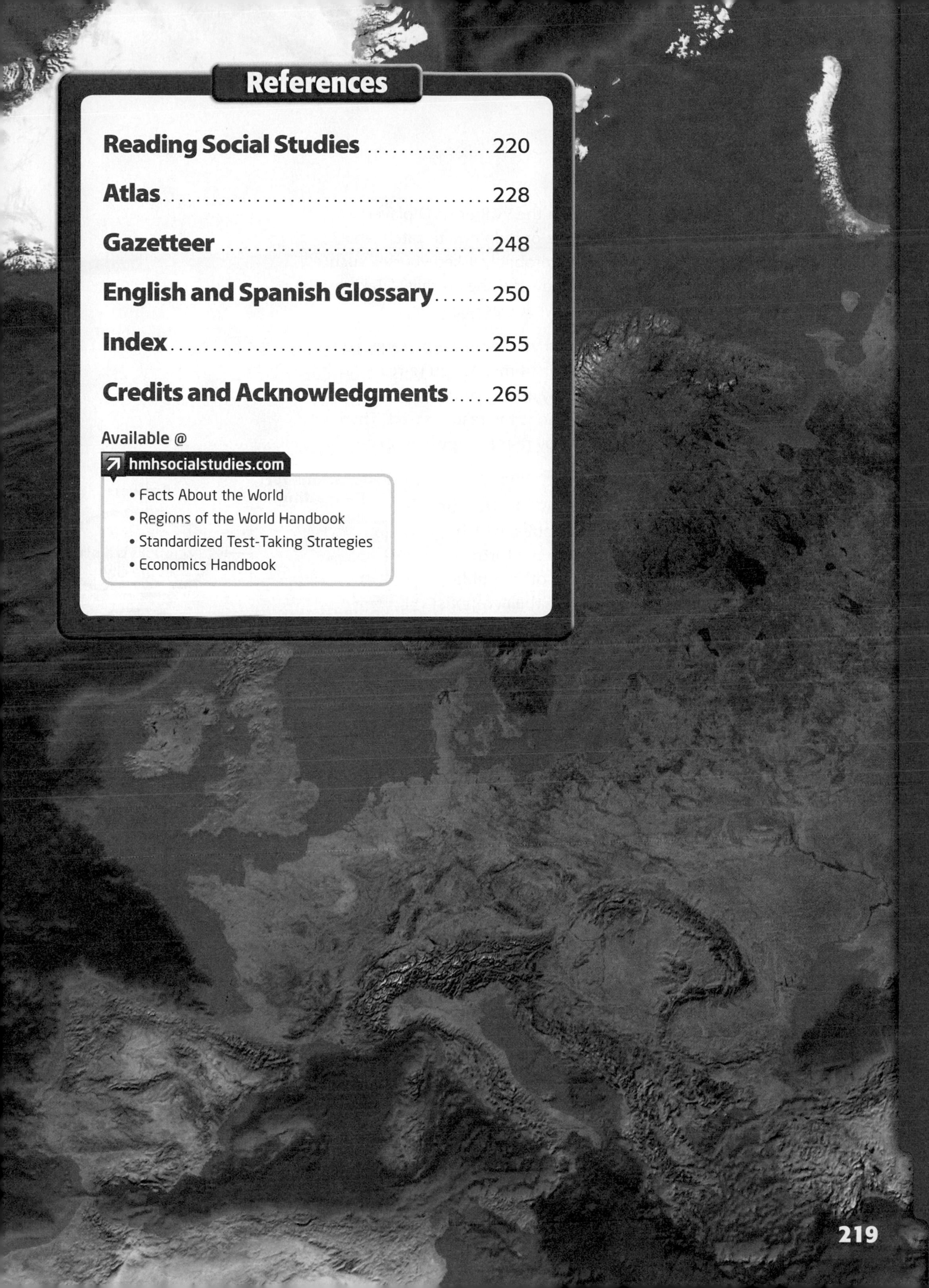

References

Available @

↗ **hmhsocialstudies.com**

- Facts About the World
- Regions of the World Handbook
- Standardized Test-Taking Strategies
- Economics Handbook

Re-reading

FOCUS ON READING

Have you ever hit the rewind button on the VCR or DVD player because you missed an important scene or didn't quite catch what a character said? As you rewound, you probably asked yourself such questions as, "What did he say?" or "How did she do that?" Taking a second look helped you understand what was going on.

The same idea is true for reading. When you re-read a passage, you can catch details you didn't catch the first time. As you re-read, go slowly and check your understanding by asking yourself questions. In the example below, notice the questions the reader asked. Then see how the questions were answered by re-reading the passage.

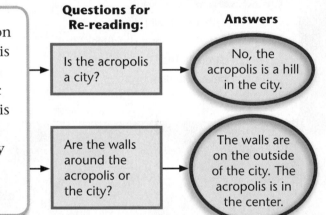

In the center of most city-states was a fortress on a hill. This hill was called the acropolis, which is Greek for "top city." In addition to the fortress, many city-states built temples and other public buildings on the acropolis. Around the acropolis was the rest of the city, including houses and markets. High walls usually surrounded the city for protection.

From Section 1, Ancient Greece

Questions for Re-reading:

Is the acropolis a city?

Are the walls around the acropolis or the city?

Answers

No, the acropolis is a hill in the city.

The walls are on the outside of the city. The acropolis is in the center.

YOU TRY IT!

Read the following passage, and then develop two questions you can answer as you re-read the passage. Write down the questions and the answers.

When historians talk about the past, they often divide it into three long periods. The first period is the ancient world, the time of the world's earliest civilizations, such as Egypt, China, Greece, and Rome. The last period historians call the modern world, the world since about 1500. Since that time, new ideas and contacts between civilizations changed the world completely. What happened between ancient and modern times? We call this period, which lasted from about 500 until about 1500, the Middle Ages.

From Section 3, The Middle Ages

Understanding Chronological Order

FOCUS ON READING

History is full of fascinating events. Some of them happen quickly, while others take decades to unfold. Many events overlap. Sometimes it may be challenging to keep the sequence of events straight. One helpful strategy is to identify chronological order or the order in which events happened. Writers use dates or clue words such as *first*, *next*, *before*, *meanwhile*, and *then* to describe the order of events. Notice the words in the following passage that help show the sequence of events.

> In **1812** Napoleon led an invasion of Russia. The invasion was a disaster. Bitterly cold weather and smart Russian tactics forced Napoleon's army to retreat. Many French soldiers died. Great Britain, Prussia, and Russia **then** joined forces and in **1814** defeated Napoleon's weakened army. He returned **a year later** with a new army, but was again defeated. The British **then** exiled him to an island, where he died in **1821**.
>
> *From Section 3, Political Change in Europe*

Time Markers/Dates
1812
1814
1821

Clue Words
then
a year later

| First Event: Napoleon invades Russia. | → | Second Event: Countries join forces and defeat Napoleon. | → | Third Event: Napoleon returns with a new army. | → | Fourth Event: Napoleon exiled to an island and dies. |

YOU TRY IT!

Read the passage below. Identify the three main events the passage describes and their chronological order. List the clue words or time markers that signal the order of the events.

> In 1642 England's power struggle erupted in civil war. Supporters of Parliament forced King Charles I from power. . . A new government then formed, but it was unstable. By 1660 many of the English were tired of instability. They wanted to restore the monarchy. They asked the former king's son to rule England as Charles II.
>
> *From Section 3, Political Change in Europe*

Using Context Clues—Contrast

FOCUS ON READING

Maybe you played this game as a young child: "Which of these things is not like the others?" This same game can help you understand new words as you read. Sometimes the words or sentences around a new word will show contrast, or how the word is not like something else. These contrast clues can help you figure out the new word's meaning. Look at how the following passage indicates that *persevered* means something different from *give in*.

> The German air force repeatedly attacked British cities and military targets. Hitler hoped the British would surrender. Rather than give in, however, the British *persevered*.
>
> *From Section 2, World War II*

Contrast Clues:

1. Look for words or sentences that signal contrast.
Words that signal contrast include *however, rather than, instead of,* and *not*. In this paragraph, the words *rather than* signal the contrast clues for the unfamiliar word *persevered*.

2. Check the definition by substituting a word or phrase that fits.
Persevere likely means to keep on trying. *Rather than give in, however, the British kept on trying.*

YOU TRY IT!

Read the following paragraph, and then use the steps listed above to develop a definition for the word *compete.*

> Some people believed that creating a feeling of community in Europe would make countries less likely to go to war. Leaders like Great Britain's Winston Churchill believed the countries of Europe should cooperate rather than *compete*.
>
> *From Section 3, Europe since 1945*

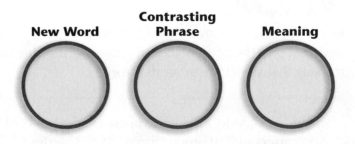

New Word   Contrasting Phrase   Meaning

Asking Questions

FOCUS ON READING

Reading is one place where asking questions will never get you in trouble. The five W questions – who, what, when, where, and why – can help you be sure you understand the material you read. After you read a section, ask yourself the 5 Ws: **Who** was this section about? **What** did they do? **When** and **where** did they live? **Why** did they do what they did? See the example below to learn how this reading strategy can help you identify the main points of a passage.

> Many Greeks were not happy under Turkish rule. They wanted to be free of foreign influences. In the early 1800s, they rose up against the Turks. The rebellion seemed likely to fail, but the Greeks received help from other European countries and drove the Turks out. After the rebellion, Greece became a monarchy.
>
> *From Section 2, Greece*

The 5 Ws

Who? Greeks

What? Led rebellion to become independent from Turks

Where? Greece

When? Early 1800s

Why? Wanted to be free of foreign influences

YOU TRY IT!

Read the following passage and answer the 5 Ws to check your understanding of it.

> Italy remained divided into small states until the mid-1800s. At that time, a rise in nationalism, or strong patriotic feelings for a country, led people across Italy to fight for unification. As a result of their efforts, Italy became a unified kingdom in 1861.
>
> *From Section 3, Italy*

Recognizing Word Origins

READING SOCIAL STUDIES

FOCUS ON READING

English is a language that loves to borrow words from other languages and cultures. From the French, we took *faceon* and changed it to *fashion*. From the German, we took *strollen* and changed it to *stroll*. From the Dutch, we took *koekje* and changed it to *cookie*. Below is a list of examples of other words that come from other languages.

English Words from French	English Words from German	English Words from Latin
conquer	muffin	culture
brilliant	dollar	defeat
restaurant	rocket	general
republic	kindergarten	forces
fashion	hamburger	join
parliament	noodle	president
several	pretzel	elect
power	snorkel	control
exiled	hex	territory

YOU TRY IT!

Read the following sentences. Refer to the above word lists and make a list of the words in the passage below that originally came from other languages. After each word, list the original language.

A few years later a brilliant general named Napoleon took power. In time, he conquered much of Europe. Then in 1815 several European powers joined forces and defeated Napoleon. They exiled him and chose a new king to rule France.

France is now a republic with a parliament and an elected president. France still controls several overseas territories, such as Martinique in the West Indies.

From Section 2, France and the Benelux Countries

Using Context Clues— Synonyms

FOCUS ON READING

You have probably discovered that geography is a subject with many new words and terms. What if you don't remember or don't know what a word means? You may be able to use context clues to determine its meaning. Context clues are words near the unfamiliar word that indicate its meaning.

One helpful context clue is the synonym—words or phrases that mean the same as the new word. Look for synonyms in the words and sentences surrounding an unfamiliar term. Synonyms can help you understand the meaning of the new word. They may come in the same sentence or in the sentence following the words they define. Notice how the following passage uses synonyms to define the word *urban*.

Most Swedes live in the southern part of the country in large towns and cities. In fact, more than 80 percent of Swedes live in *urban* areas. Stockholm, Sweden's capital and largest city, is located on the east coast near the Baltic Sea.

From Section 3, Scandinavia

---

1. Look for words or phrases that mean the same thing.
The first sentence uses the phrase large towns and cities to describe where most Swedes live.

2. Substitute the synonym for the new word to confirm its meaning.
More than 80 percent of Swedes live in large towns and cities.

YOU TRY IT!

As you read the following sentences, look for synonyms that mean the same as the italicized words. Then use a graphic organizer like the one below to define each italicized word.

Slow-moving sheets of ice, or *glaciers*, have left their mark on Northern Europe's coastlines and lakes.

As the glaciers flowed slowly downhill, they carved long, winding channels, or *fjords*, into Norway's coastline.

From Section 1, Physical Geography

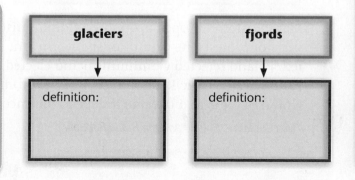

READING SOCIAL STUDIES

Understanding Problems and Solutions

FOCUS ON READING

Throughout history, people have faced problems and found solutions to them. As a result, writers who describe historical events often structure their writing by identifying a problem and then describing its solution. The ability to identify this pattern of writing will help you understand what you read. Notice how the following passage presents one problem with a two-pronged solution.

> Estonia, Latvia, Lithuania, and Poland all still suffer from decades of Soviet rule. Under the Soviets, the economies of all four countries suffered.
>
> Today, Poland and the Baltic Republics are working to rebuild and strengthen their economies. They are replacing the old and outdated factories built by the Soviets with new ones that take advantage of modern technology.
>
> To further their economic growth, the countries of this region are also seeking new sources of income. One area in which they have found success is tourism.
>
> *From Section 2, Poland and the Baltic Republics*

Problem:
Poor economies from Soviet rule

Solution #1:
Building new factories

Solution #2:
New source of income through tourism

YOU TRY IT!

Read the following passage, and then use the process shown above to identify the problems and solutions the writer presents. Create as many boxes as you need.

> Many Eastern Europeans opposed Communist rule. After years of protest, the Communist government in the region fell. Poland rejected Communism and elected new leaders in 1989. The Baltic Republics broke away from the Soviet Union in 1991 and became independent once more.
>
> *From Section 2, Poland and the Baltic Republics*

Making Generalizations

FOCUS ON READING

As you read about different people and cultures, you probably realize that people share some similarities. Seeing those similarities may lead you to make a generalization. A generalization is a broad, general idea drawn from new information combined with what you already know, such as your own experience. Notice how this process works with the following passage.

> Russians sometimes joke that winter lasts for 12 months and then summer begins. Russia is a cold country. The reason is its northern location partly within the Arctic Circle. In general, Russia has short summers and long, snowy winters. The climate is milder west of the Urals and grows colder and harsher as one goes north and east.
>
> *From Section 1, Physical Geography*

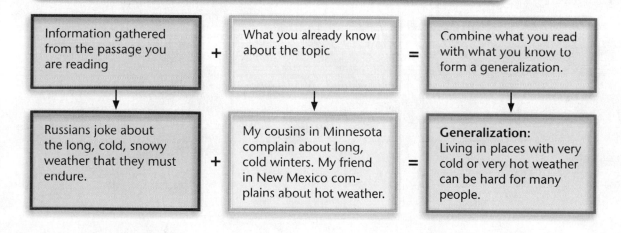

Information gathered from the passage you are reading	+	What you already know about the topic	=	Combine what you read with what you know to form a generalization.
Russians joke about the long, cold, snowy weather that they must endure.	+	My cousins in Minnesota complain about long, cold winters. My friend in New Mexico complains about hot weather.	=	**Generalization:** Living in places with very cold or very hot weather can be hard for many people.

YOU TRY IT!

Read the following passage. Using the process described above, form a general idea about holidays. Write your generalization in one sentence.

> Russian history has shaped its customs, such as holidays. Religious holidays, like Easter and Christmas, are popular. The main family holiday is New Year's Eve. To celebrate this holiday, families decorate a tree where, according to Russian folklore, Grandfather Frost and his helper the Snow Maiden leave gifts. A newer holiday is Russian Independence Day, which marks the end of the Soviet Union on June 12.
>
> *From Section 2, History and Culture of Russia*

ATLAS

Strait of Juan de Fuca

Puget Sound

Mount Rainier
14,410 ft
(4,392 m)

Franklin D. Roosevelt Lake

Pend Oreille River

Flathead Lake

Milk River

Missouri River

Fort Peck Lake

Lake Sakakawea

COAST RANGES

CASCADE RANGE

Willamette River

Columbia River

Bitterroot Range

ROCKY

Lewis Range

CONTINENTAL

Yellowstone River

Lake Oahe

Klamath River

Goose Lake

Columbia Plateau

Salmon River

Salmon River Mts.

Sawtooth Mts.

Snake River

Grand Tetons

Yellowstone Lake

Bighorn Mts.

Bighorn River

Powder River

Black Hills

Cheyenne River

White River

Cape Mendocino

Shasta Lake

Pyramid Lake

Great Salt Lake

Gannett Peak
13,804 ft
(4,207 m)

Wind River Range

MOUNTAINS

Niobrara River

San Francisco Bay

Sacramento River

Central Valley

SIERRA NEVADA

Lake Tahoe

GREAT BASIN

Utah Lake

Uinta Mts.

Wasatch Range

DIVIDE

Front Range

South Platte River

North Platte River

Platte River

Republican River

Monterey Bay

San Joaquin River

Coast Ranges

Mount Whitney
14,494 ft
(4,419 m)

Death Valley

Green River

Colorado River

Lake Powell

COLORADO

Mount Elbert
14,433 ft
(4,400 m)

Pikes Peak
14,110 ft
(4,301 m)

Smoky Hill River

PACIFIC OCEAN

Channel Islands

Mojave Desert

Lake Mead

Grand Canyon

Colorado River

Painted Desert

PLATEAU

San Juan River

San Luis Valley

Sangre De Cristo Mts.

GREAT   INTER   PLAINS

Salton Sea

Imperial Valley

DIVIDE

Rio Grande

Canadian River

Gila River

Sonoran Desert

CONTINENTAL

Gulf of California

Pecos River

Colorado

Amistad Reservoir

Rio Grande

MEXICO

Nueces R.

To understand the relative locations of Alaska and Hawaii, as well as the vast distances separating them from the rest of the United States, see the world map.

Kauai

Niihau

Oahu

HAWAII

Molokai

PACIFIC OCEAN

Lanai

Maui

Kahoolawe

Mauna Kea
13,796 ft
(4,206 m)

Hawaii

0   75   150 Miles
0   75   150 Kilometers
Projection: Mercator

ARCTIC OCEAN

RUSSIA

Bering Strait

Arctic Circle

BROOKS RANGE

Yukon River

Tanana River

CANADA

St. Lawrence Island

St. Matthew Island

Nunivak Island

Kuskokwim River

ALASKA RANGE

Mount McKinley
20,320 ft
(6,194 m)

Bering Sea

Attu Island

ALEUTIAN ISLANDS

PACIFIC OCEAN

Gulf of Alaska

Kodiak Island

Alexander Archipelago

0   250   500 Miles
0   250   500 Kilometers
Projection: Albers Equal Area

CANADA

Isle Royale
Mesabi Range
Lake Superior

Minnesota River
Mississippi River
Wisconsin River

Des Moines River
Missouri River
Lake Michigan
Lake Huron

Illinois River
Wabash River
Scioto River
Lake Erie

P L A I N S

Ohio River

Lake of the Ozarks
OZARK PLATEAU

Keystone Lake
Arkansas River
White River

Ouachita Mts.

Lake Barkley
Kentucky Lake
Cumberland River
Tennessee River

Coosa River

Red River
Saline River

Toledo Bend Reservoir

Trinity River

G U L F   C O A S T A L

Chandeleur Islands
Mississippi Delta
Pearl River
Tombigbee River
Alabama R.

P L A I N

Chattahoochee River

Mississippi

St. Lawrence River
St. Lawrence Seaway

Penobscot River
St. John River
Longfellow Mts.

Lake Champlain
Adirondack Mts.
Green Mts.
White Mts.
Connecticut River

Lake Ontario

ALLEGHENY   PLATEAU

Catskill Mts.
Susquehanna River

Allegheny R.
Monongahela R.
Kanawha River
Potomac River

A P P A L A C H I A N   M O U N T A I N S

Cape Cod
Long Island Sound
Long Island
Delaware River
Delaware Bay

Chesapeake Bay

James River

B L U E   R I D G E   M O U N T A I N S

P I E D M O N T

Cumberland Plateau
Great Smoky Mts.

Roanoke River

Pamlico Sound
Cape Hatteras

Oconee River
Savannah River

Altamaha River

Sea Islands

Okefenokee Swamp

F L O R I D A   P E N I N S U L A

Cape Canaveral

Lake Okeechobee

The Everglades

Cape Sable
Florida Keys

Gulf of Mexico

Straits of Florida

BAHAMAS

ATLANTIC OCEAN

40°N
70°W
35°N
25°N
80°W
85°W
90°W
95°W
75°W

N
W   E
S

ELEVATION

Feet	Meters
13,120	4,000
6,560	2,000
1,640	500
656	200
(Sea level) 0	0 (Sea level)
Below sea level	Below sea level

0   100   200 Miles
0   100   200 Kilometers

Projection: Albers Equal Area

ATLAS

Strait of
Juan de Fuca

Puget Sound
Seattle
Tacoma
Olympia
45°N

Portland
★Salem

Eugene

OREGON

Cape
Mendocino
40°N

Goose
Lake

Shasta
Lake

Pyramid
Lake

Reno
Carson City
Lake Tahoe

NEVADA

Berkeley
Oakland
San Francisco
San Francisco Bay
San Jose

Sacramento

Sacramento River

San Joaquin River

Monterey
Bay

Fresno

CALIFORNIA

35°N

PACIFIC
OCEAN

Santa Barbara
Ventura
Los
Angeles
Long
Beach
Anaheim
Santa Ana
San Diego

Channel
Islands

Riverside
Palm Springs

Salton
Sea

Las
Vegas

WASHINGTON

Spokane

Pend
Oreille

Columbia River

IDAHO

Boise

Sun Valley

Snake
River

Pocatello

Flathead
Lake

Great Falls

Helena ★

MONTANA

Billings

Yellowstone River

Yellowstone
Lake

WYOMING

Ogden
Great
Salt
Lake
Salt Lake City
Provo

Utah
Lake

UTAH

Green River

Lake
Powell

Colorado River

Lake
Mead

Flagstaff

ARIZONA

Phoenix ★

Gila   River

Casa Grande

Tucson

Missouri River

NORTH DAKOTA

Lake
Sakakawea

Bismarck

Lake
Oahe

SOUTH DAKOTA

Pierre

Rapid City

Cheyenne
★

NEBRASKA

Platte River

Boulder
Vail
Aspen ★Denver
Colorado
Springs
COLORADO
Pueblo

Arkansas River

KANS.

Taos

Santa Fe ★

Albuquerque

NEW MEXICO

Las Cruces

El Paso

OKLAHOMA

Canadian River

Oklahoma

Amarillo

Law

Lubbock

Brazos River

Abilene

Fort W

Midland

Odessa

TEXAS

Colorado R

Pecos River

Amistad
Reservoir

Aust

San Antonio

Rio Grande

Corpus Chr

Laredo

MEXICO

To understand the relative locations of Alaska and
Hawaii, as well as the vast distances separating them
from the rest of the United States, see the world map.

Gulf of
California

Kauai
Niihau
Oahu
HAWAII
Honolulu
PACIFIC
OCEAN
Molokai
Lanai
Maui
Kahoolawe
Hilo
Hawaii

22°N
-155°W
N
W   E
S
19°N

0   75   150 Miles
0   75   150 Kilometers
Projection: Mercator

160°W
170°W
180°
170°E
55°N
50°N

PACIFIC
OCEAN

ARCTIC OCEAN

Arctic Circle

Bering Strait

RUSSIA

Nome

Yukon River

St. Lawrence
Island

St. Matthew
Island

Nunivak
Island

Bering Sea

Attu Island

ALEUTIAN
ISLANDS

N
W   E
S

Fairbanks

ALASKA

Anchorage
Valdez

Gulf of Alaska

Kodiak Island

CANADA

Skagway

Juneau

Alexander
Archipelago

55°N

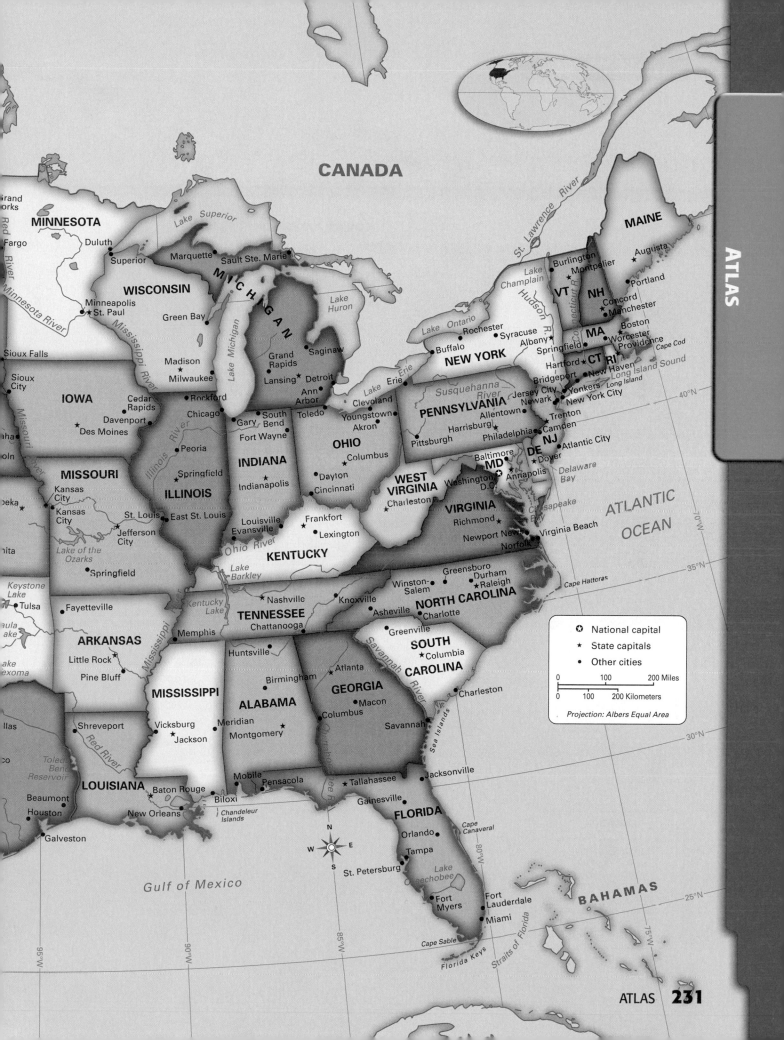

CANADA

MINNESOTA
Grand
Forks
Fargo
Duluth
Superior
Red River
Minnesota River
Sioux Falls
Minneapolis
St. Paul

Lake Superior

Marquette
Sault Ste. Marie

MICHIGAN

WISCONSIN
Green Bay
Madison
Milwaukee

Lake Michigan

Lake Huron

Grand Rapids
Saginaw
Lansing
Detroit
Ann Arbor

MAINE
Augusta
Portland

Lake Champlain
Burlington
Montpelier
VT
NH
Concord
Manchester
Boston
Worcester
Providence
MA
RI
Hartford
CT
New Haven
Bridgeport
Yonkers
Long Island Sound
Long Island
Cape Cod

Hudson River
Connecticut R.
St. Lawrence River

Lake Ontario
Rochester
Syracuse
Albany
Springfield
Buffalo
NEW YORK

Lake Erie
Erie

IOWA
Sioux City
Cedar Rapids
Davenport
Des Moines
Rockford
Chicago
Peoria

Mississippi River

Rockford
South Bend
Gary
Fort Wayne

Cleveland
Toledo
Youngstown
Akron
OHIO
Columbus
Dayton
Cincinnati

PENNSYLVANIA
Allentown
Harrisburg
Pittsburgh
Philadelphia

Susquehanna River

Trenton
Camden
NJ
Atlantic City
Newark
Jersey City
New York City
40°N

MISSOURI
Kansas City
Kansas City
St. Louis
East St. Louis
Jefferson City
Lake of the Ozarks
Springfield

ILLINOIS
Springfield
Indianapolis
INDIANA

Illinois River

Louisville
Evansville
Frankfort
Lexington

KENTUCKY
Lake Barkley
Kentucky Lake

Ohio River

WEST VIRGINIA
Charleston

VIRGINIA
Richmond
Newport News
Norfolk
Virginia Beach

Baltimore
MD
Washington, D.C.
Annapolis
Dover
DE
Delaware Bay
Chesapeake Bay

70°W

ATLANTIC OCEAN

35°N
Cape Hatteras

Keystone Lake
Tulsa
Lake Eufaula
Oklahoma

ARKANSAS
Fayetteville
Little Rock
Pine Bluff

Memphis

Nashville
TENNESSEE
Chattanooga
Knoxville
Asheville
Charlotte
Greenville

Winston-Salem
Greensboro
Durham
Raleigh
NORTH CAROLINA

SOUTH CAROLINA
Columbia
Charleston

MISSISSIPPI
Vicksburg
Jackson

ALABAMA
Birmingham
Meridian
Montgomery

Huntsville

GEORGIA
Atlanta
Columbus
Macon
Savannah

Savannah River
Chattahoochee R.
Sea Islands

30°N

Shreveport
Red River
Toledo Bend Reservoir

Dallas
Beaumont
Houston
Galveston

LOUISIANA
Baton Rouge
New Orleans
Biloxi
Chandeleur Islands

Mobile
Pensacola
Tallahassee
Jacksonville
Gainesville

FLORIDA
Orlando
Tampa
St. Petersburg
Lake Okeechobee
Cape Canaveral

80°W

N
W
E
S

Gulf of Mexico

Fort Myers
Fort Lauderdale
Miami

BAHAMAS

25°N

85°W
90°W
95°W
75°W

Cape Sable
Florida Keys
Straits of Florida

○ National capital
★ State capitals
• Other cities

0   100   200 Miles
0   100   200 Kilometers

Projection: Albers Equal Area

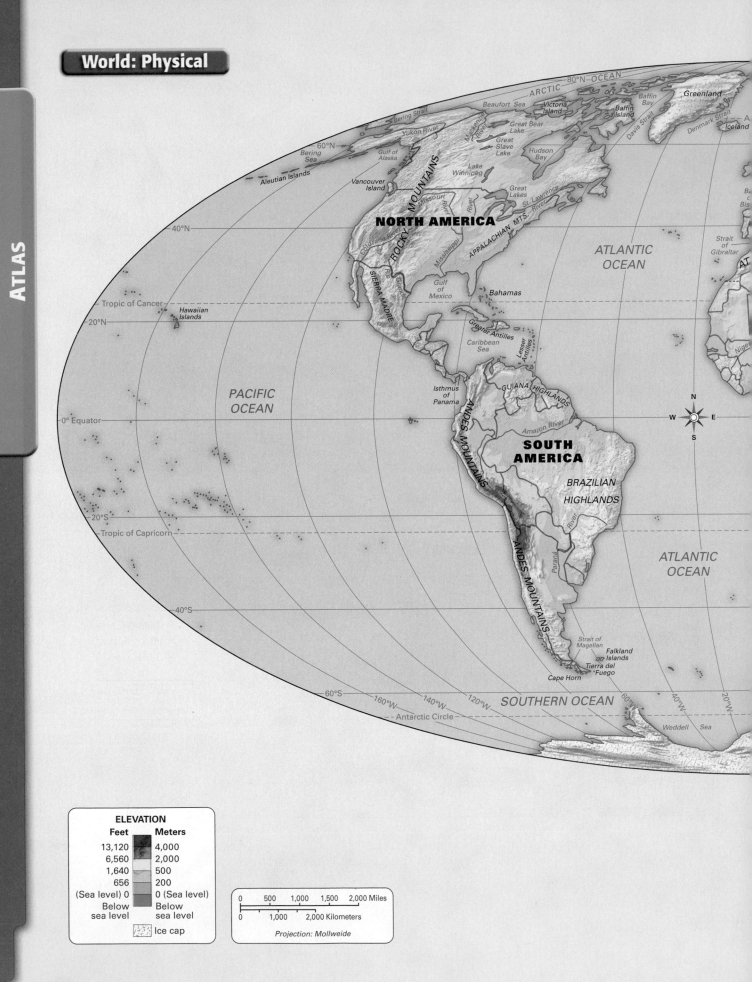

World: Physical

NORTH AMERICA

SOUTH AMERICA

ARCTIC OCEAN
80°N

Beaufort Sea
Victoria Island
Baffin Island
Baffin Bay
Greenland
Davis Strait
Denmark Strait
Iceland

Bering Strait
Yukon River
Mackenzie River
Great Bear Lake
Great Slave Lake
Hudson Bay

60°N
Bering Sea
Gulf of Alaska
Lake Winnipeg
Great Lakes
St. Lawrence River

Aleutian Islands
Vancouver Island
ROCKY MOUNTAINS
Missouri River
APPALACHIAN MTS.

40°N
ATLANTIC OCEAN
Strait of Gibraltar

Colorado River
Mississippi River
SIERRA MADRE
Rio Grande
Gulf of Mexico
Bahamas

Tropic of Cancer
Hawaiian Islands

20°N
Greater Antilles
Caribbean Sea
Lesser Antilles

Niger

PACIFIC OCEAN
Isthmus of Panama
GUIANA HIGHLANDS
ANDES MOUNTAINS
Amazon River

N
W   E
S

0° Equator

BRAZILIAN HIGHLANDS

20°S
Tropic of Capricorn
Paraná River
ATLANTIC OCEAN

ANDES MOUNTAINS

40°S
Paraná

Strait of Magellan
Falkland Islands
Tierra del Fuego
Cape Horn

60°S   160°W   140°W   120°W   SOUTHERN OCEAN   60°
40°W   20°W

Antarctic Circle
Weddell Sea

ELEVATION

Feet		Meters
13,120		4,000
6,560		2,000
1,640		500
656		200
(Sea level) 0		0 (Sea level)
Below sea level		Below sea level

Ice cap

0   500   1,000   1,500   2,000 Miles
0   1,000   2,000 Kilometers

Projection: Mollweide

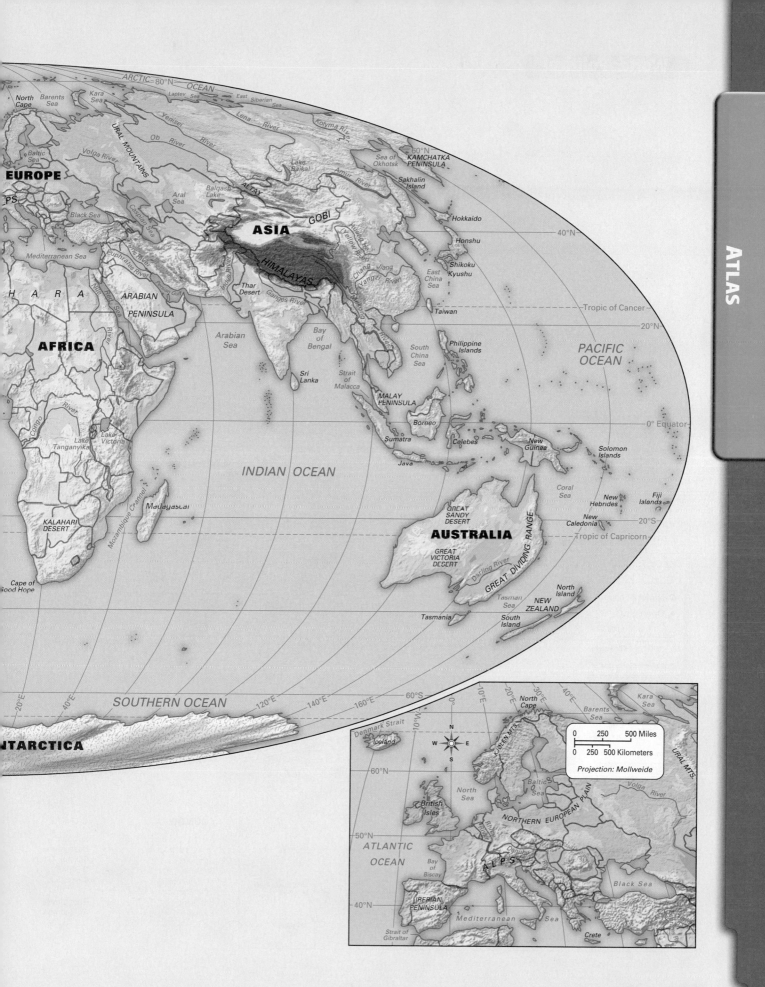

ARCTIC 80°N OCEAN
North Cape
Barents Sea
Kara Sea
Laptev Sea
East Siberian Sea
Yenisei River
Ob River
Lena River
Kolyma River
60°N
Sea of Okhotsk
KAMCHATKA PENINSULA
URAL MOUNTAINS
Volga River
Baltic Sea
Black Sea
EUROPE
PS
Mediterranean Sea
Aral Sea
Balqash Lake
Caspian Sea
Lake Baikal
ALTAY
Amur River
Sakhalin Island
40°N
Hokkaido
Honshu
GOBI
ASIA
Euphrates River
Tigris River
HIMALAYAS
Huang He
Yellow River
Jiang
Chang
Yangzi River
Shikoku
Kyushu
East China Sea
SAHARA
ARABIAN PENINSULA
Nile River
Persian Gulf
Indus River
Thar Desert
Ganges River
Mekong River
Taiwan
Tropic of Cancer
AFRICA
Arabian Sea
Bay of Bengal
South China Sea
Philippine Islands
20°N
PACIFIC OCEAN
River
Congo River
Lake Victoria
Lake Tanganyika
Sri Lanka
Strait of Malacca
MALAY PENINSULA
Sumatra
Borneo
Celebes
New Guinea
0° Equator
Java
Solomon Islands
INDIAN OCEAN
Madagascar
Mozambique Channel
Coral Sea
New Hebrides
New Caledonia
Fiji Islands
20°S
KALAHARI DESERT
GREAT SANDY DESERT
AUSTRALIA
GREAT VICTORIA DESERT
Darling River
GREAT DIVIDING RANGE
Tropic of Capricorn
Cape of Good Hope
North Island
Tasman Sea
NEW ZEALAND
South Island
Tasmania
SOUTHERN OCEAN
120°E
140°E
160°E
60°S
NTARCTICA
20°E
40°E

Denmark Strait
Iceland
60°N
North Cape
Barents Sea
Kara Sea
10°W
0°
10°E
20°E
30°E
40°E
KJOLEN MTS.
URAL MTS.
0 250 500 Miles
0 250 500 Kilometers
Projection: Mollweide
N
W E
S
North Sea
British Isles
Baltic Sea
50°N
ATLANTIC OCEAN
NORTHERN EUROPEAN PLAIN
Volga River
Bay of Biscay
Danube River
ALPS
Black Sea
IBERIAN PENINSULA
40°N
Strait of Gibraltar
Mediterranean Sea
Crete

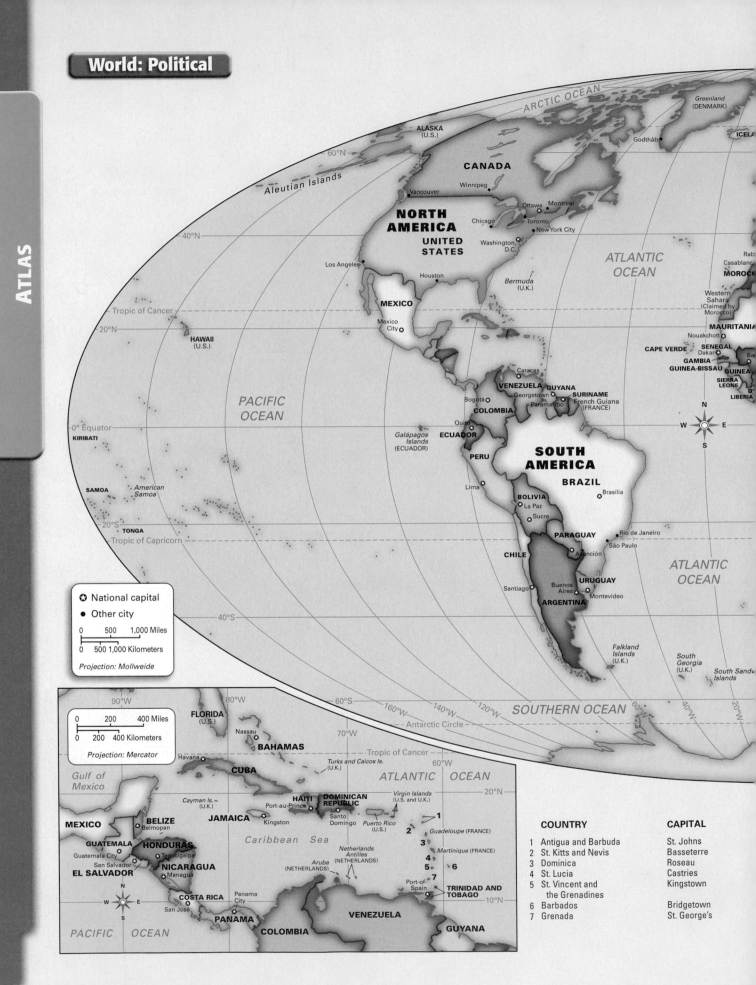

World: Political

ATLAS

ARCTIC OCEAN

Greenland
(DENMARK)

ALASKA
(U.S.)

60°N

CANADA

Godthåb

ICELA

Aleutian Islands

Vancouver   Winnipeg

Ottawa   Montreal

NORTH
AMERICA

Chicago   Toronto

40°N

UNITED
STATES

New York City

Washington,
D.C.

ATLANTIC
OCEAN

Rab

Casablanc

MOROC

Los Angeles

Houston

Bermuda
(U.K.)

Western
Sahara
(Claimed by
Morocco)

MEXICO

Tropic of Cancer

MAURITANIA

Nouakchott

20°N

Mexico
City

HAWAII
(U.S.)

CAPE VERDE   SENEGAL

Dakar   Ba

GAMBIA
GUINEA-BISSAU   GUINEA

Caracas

SIERRA
LEONE

PACIFIC
OCEAN

VENEZUELA GUYANA

LIBERIA

Bogotá

Georgetown   SURINAME
Paramaribo   French Guiana
(FRANCE)

N

W   E

COLOMBIA

Quito

S

0° Equator

Galápagos
Islands
(ECUADOR)

ECUADOR

KIRIBATI

PERU

SOUTH
AMERICA

BRAZIL

Lima

Brasília

SAMOA

American
Samoa

BOLIVIA

La Paz

20°S

Sucre

TONGA

Rio de Janeiro

Tropic of Capricorn

PARAGUAY

São Paulo

CHILE

Asunción

ATLANTIC
OCEAN

URUGUAY

Santiago

Buenos
Aires

Montevideo

National capital

ARGENTINA

Other city

0   500   1,000 Miles

40°S

0   500 1,000 Kilometers

Falkland
Islands
(U.K.)

South
Georgia
(U.K.)

Projection: Mollweide

South Sandy
Islands

60°S

SOUTHERN OCEAN

160°W   140°W   120°W

90°W   80°W

FLORIDA
(U.S.)

70°W

Antarctic Circle

60°W   40°W   20°W

0   200   400 Miles

Nassau

Tropic of Cancer

0   200   400 Kilometers

BAHAMAS

60°W

Projection: Mercator

Havana

Turks and Caicos Is.
(U.K.)

ATLANTIC OCEAN

20°N

Gulf of
Mexico

CUBA

Cayman Is.
(U.K.)

HAITI   DOMINICAN
REPUBLIC

Virgin Islands
(U.S. and U.K.)

1

MEXICO

BELIZE

Port-au-Prince

Santo
Domingo

Guadeloupe (FRANCE)

2

Belmopan

JAMAICA

Kingston

Puerto Rico
(U.S.)

3

Caribbean Sea

Martinique (FRANCE)

GUATEMALA   HONDURAS

Netherlands
Antilles
(NETHERLANDS)

4

Guatemala City   Tegucigalpa

San Salvador   NICARAGUA

Aruba
(NETHERLANDS)

5   6

EL SALVADOR

Managua

7

N

Port-of-
Spain

TRINIDAD AND
TOBAGO

W   E

COSTA RICA

Panama
City

S

San José

PANAMA

VENEZUELA

10°N

PACIFIC   OCEAN

COLOMBIA

GUYANA

COUNTRY	CAPITAL
1 Antigua and Barbuda	St. Johns
2 St. Kitts and Nevis	Basseterre
3 Dominica	Roseau
4 St. Lucia	Castries
5 St. Vincent and the Grenadines	Kingstown
6 Barbados	Bridgetown
7 Grenada	St. George's

234 ATLAS

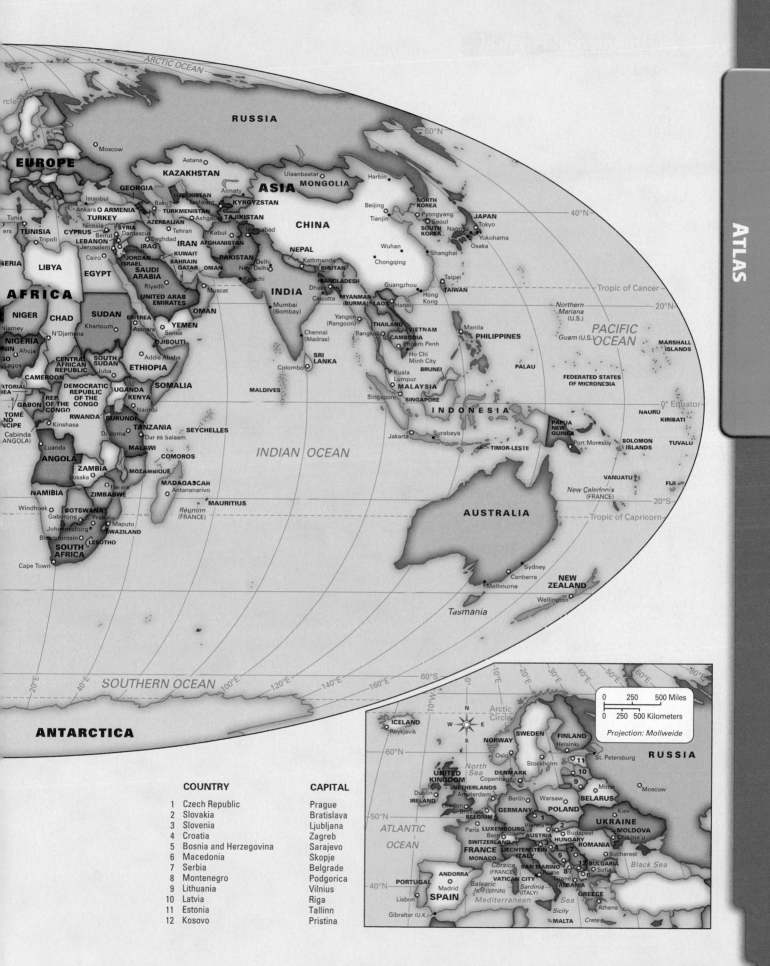

ARCTIC OCEAN

RUSSIA

EUROPE

Moscow

Astana

KAZAKHSTAN

ASIA

MONGOLIA

Ulaanbaatar

Harbin

NORTH KOREA

JAPAN

GEORGIA

UZBEKISTAN

KYRGYZSTAN

Almaty

Beijing

Pyongyang

Seoul

Nagoya

Tokyo

Istanbul

Ankara

ARMENIA

TURKMENISTAN

TAJIKISTAN

Tianjin

SOUTH KOREA

Yokohama

TURKEY

AZERBAIJAN

Baku

Ashgabat

Kabul

CHINA

Osaka

CYPRUS

Nicosia

SYRIA

Tehran

Islamabad

Wuhan

Beirut

Damascus

IRAN

AFGHANISTAN

Shanghai

LEBANON

Baghdad

Chongqing

Jerusalem

IRAQ

KUWAIT

PAKISTAN

Delhi

NEPAL

Kathmandu

Taipei

Amman

JORDAN

BAHRAIN

New Delhi

BHUTAN

Guangzhou

TAIWAN

Tropic of Cancer

ISRAEL

SAUDI ARABIA

QATAR

Karachi

Hong Kong

Cairo

EGYPT

Riyadh

OMAN

Muscat

INDIA

BANGLADESH

Calcutta

MYANMAR (BURMA)

LAOS

Hanoi

Northern Mariana (U.S.)

20°N

PACIFIC OCEAN

AFRICA

UNITED ARAB EMIRATES

Dhaka

Mumbai (Bombay)

Chennai (Madras)

Yangon (Rangoon)

THAILAND

VIETNAM

Manila

Guam (U.S.)

NIGER

CHAD

SUDAN

ERITREA

Asmara

YEMEN

Sanaa

OMAN

Khartoum

Bangkok

CAMBODIA

Phnom Penh

PHILIPPINES

MARSHALL ISLANDS

Niamey

N'Djamena

DJIBOUTI

SRI LANKA

Ho Chi Minh City

PALAU

NIGERIA

Abuja

CENTRAL AFRICAN REPUBLIC

SOUTH SUDAN

Juba

ETHIOPIA

Addis Ababa

Colombo

MALDIVES

Kuala Lumpur

BRUNEI

FEDERATED STATES OF MICRONESIA

Lagos

CAMEROON

DEMOCRATIC REPUBLIC OF THE CONGO

UGANDA

KENYA

SOMALIA

MALAYSIA

Singapore

SINGAPORE

NAURU

KIRIBATI

GABON

REP. OF THE CONGO

RWANDA

BURUNDI

Nairobi

INDONESIA

PAPUA NEW GUINEA

TOMÉ

ANGOLA (Cabinda)

Kinshasa

TANZANIA

Dodoma

Dar es Salaam

SEYCHELLES

Port Moresby

SOLOMON ISLANDS

TUVALU

Luanda

ANGOLA

ZAMBIA

MALAWI

COMOROS

INDIAN OCEAN

TIMOR-LESTE

Jakarta

Surabaya

Lusaka

MOZAMBIQUE

MADAGASCAR

Antananarivo

VANUATU

FIJI

NAMIBIA

ZIMBABWE

Windhoek

BOTSWANA

Gaborone

Pretoria

Maputo

MAURITIUS

Réunion (FRANCE)

AUSTRALIA

New Caledonia (FRANCE)

20°S

Tropic of Capricorn

Johannesburg

SWAZILAND

Bloemfontein

LESOTHO

SOUTH AFRICA

Cape Town

Sydney

Canberra

Melbourne

NEW ZEALAND

Wellington

20°E

40°E

SOUTHERN OCEAN

100°E

120°E

140°E

160°E

60°S

Tasmania

ANTARCTICA

	COUNTRY	CAPITAL
1	Czech Republic	Prague
2	Slovakia	Bratislava
3	Slovenia	Ljubljana
4	Croatia	Zagreb
5	Bosnia and Herzegovina	Sarajevo
6	Macedonia	Skopje
7	Serbia	Belgrade
8	Montenegro	Podgorica
9	Lithuania	Vilnius
10	Latvia	Riga
11	Estonia	Tallinn
12	Kosovo	Pristina

0 250 500 Miles

0 250 500 Kilometers

Projection: Mollweide

ICELAND

Reykjavik

Arctic Circle

SWEDEN

FINLAND

Helsinki

NORWAY

Oslo

Stockholm

St. Petersburg

RUSSIA

60°N

UNITED KINGDOM

North Sea

DENMARK

Copenhagen

11

10

Minsk

Moscow

Dublin

IRELAND

NETHERLANDS

Amsterdam

Berlin

Warsaw

BELARUS

9

London

Brussels

GERMANY

POLAND

Kiev

50°N

BELGIUM

Paris

LUXEMBOURG

Vienna

UKRAINE

ATLANTIC OCEAN

FRANCE

SWITZERLAND

Bern

LIECHTENSTEIN

AUSTRIA

Budapest

HUNGARY

ROMANIA

MOLDOVA

Chișinău

MONACO

ITALY

Bucharest

ANDORRA

Corsica (FRANCE)

SAN MARINO

Rome

BULGARIA

Sofia

Black Sea

PORTUGAL

VATICAN CITY

Balearic Is. (SPAIN)

Sardinia (ITALY)

ALBANIA

40°N

Madrid

GREECE

Lisbon

SPAIN

Mediterranean Sea

Athens

Gibraltar (U.K.)

Sicily

MALTA

Crete

ATLAS **235**

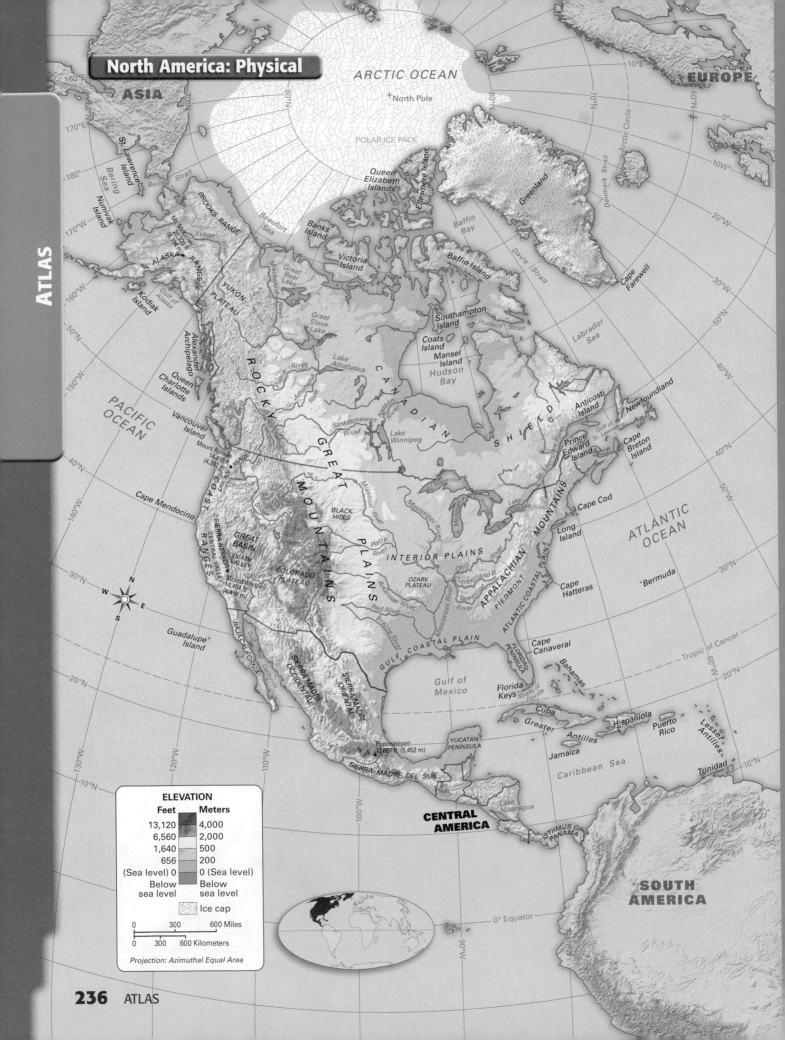

North America: Physical

ASIA

ARCTIC OCEAN

+North Pole

EUROPE

POLAR ICE PACK

St. Lawrence Island

Bering Sea

Nunivak Island

BROOKS RANGE

Mt. McKinley 20,320 ft. (6,194 m)

ALASKA RANGE

Yukon River

Queen Elizabeth Islands

Ellesmere Island

Greenland

Kodiak Island

Gulf of Alaska

YUKON PLATEAU

Beaufort Sea

Banks Island

Victoria Island

Great Bear Lake

Baffin Island

Baffin Bay

Cape Farewell

Denmark Strait

Arctic Circle

Alexander Archipelago

Queen Charlotte Islands

ROCKY

Mackenzie River

Great Slave Lake

Southampton Island

Hudson Strait

Davis Strait

Labrador Sea

Vancouver Island

PACIFIC OCEAN

Peace River

GREAT

Lake Athabasca

CANADIAN

Coats Island

Mansel Island

Hudson Bay

SHIELD

Anticosti Island

Newfoundland

Cape Mendocino

Mount Rainier 14,410 ft. (4,392 m)

CASCADE RANGE

Columbia River

COAST RANGES

SIERRA NEVADA

CENTRAL VALLEY

DEATH VALLEY

Mount Whitney 14,494 ft (4,419 m)

Snake River

GREAT BASIN

Great Salt Lake

COLORADO PLATEAU

Colorado River

MOUNTAINS

Saskatchewan River

Nelson River

Lake Winnipeg

PLAINS

Missouri River

BLACK HILLS

Platte River

Mississippi River

INTERIOR PLAINS

OZARK PLATEAU

Arkansas River

L. Superior

L. Michigan

Lake Huron

Lake Ontario

Lake Erie

Ohio River

St. Lawrence River

Prince Edward Island

Gulf of St. Lawrence

Cape Breton Island

APPALACHIAN MOUNTAINS

Cape Cod

Long Island

ATLANTIC OCEAN

Guadalupe Island

BAJA CALIFORNIA

Gulf of California

SIERRA MADRE OCCIDENTAL

Rio Grande

Red River

Brazos River

Cumberland R.

Tennessee River

PIEDMONT

ATLANTIC COASTAL PLAIN

Cape Hatteras

Bermuda

Tropic of Cancer

SIERRA MADRE ORIENTAL

Popocatépetl 17,887 ft (5,452 m)

GULF COASTAL PLAIN

Gulf of Mexico

YUCATÁN PENINSULA

FLORIDA PENINSULA

Cape Canaveral

Florida Keys

Straits of Florida

Bahamas

Cuba

Greater Antilles

Jamaica

Hispaniola

Puerto Rico

Lesser Antilles

SIERRA MADRE DEL SUR

CENTRAL AMERICA

Lake Nicaragua

ISTHMUS OF PANAMA

Caribbean Sea

Trinidad

SOUTH AMERICA

0° Equator

ELEVATION

Feet		Meters
13,120		4,000
6,560		2,000
1,640		500
656		200
(Sea level) 0		0 (Sea level)
Below sea level		Below sea level

Ice cap

0   300   600 Miles

0   300   600 Kilometers

Projection: Azimuthal Equal Area

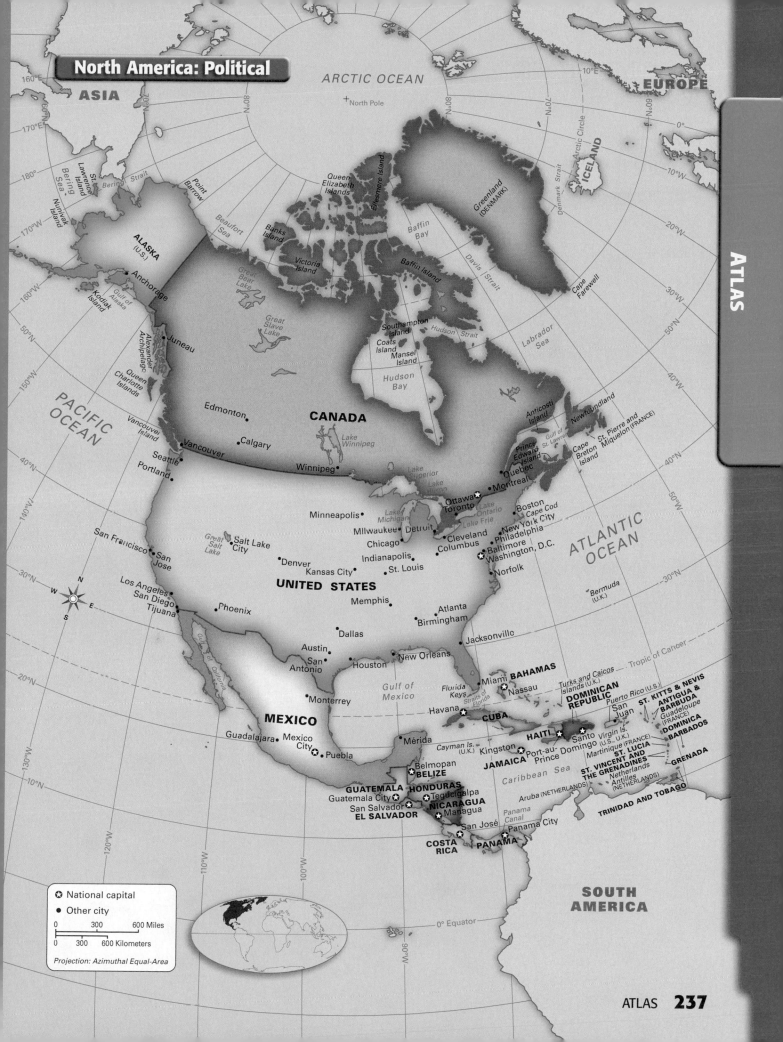

North America: Political

ASIA

ARCTIC OCEAN

EUROPE

North Pole

160°E

170°E

180°

170°W

160°W

10°E

10°W

20°W

30°W

40°W

50°W

60°N

70°N

80°N

Arctic Circle

ICELAND

Denmark Strait

Bering Strait

St. Lawrence Island

Nunivak Island

Bering Sea

Point Barrow

Beaufort Sea

Banks Island

Queen Elizabeth Islands

Ellesmere Island

Baffin Bay

Greenland (DENMARK)

Victoria Island

Baffin Island

Cape Farewell

ALASKA (U.S.)

Anchorage

Gulf of Alaska

Kodiak Island

Great Bear Lake

Great Slave Lake

Hudson Strait

Davis Strait

Labrador Sea

50°N

Juneau

Alexander Archipelago

Queen Charlotte Islands

Southampton Island

Coats Island

Mansel Island

PACIFIC OCEAN

Vancouver Island

Edmonton

Hudson Bay

Anticosti Island

Newfoundland

St. Pierre and Miquelon (FRANCE)

CANADA

Lake Winnipeg

Prince Edward Island

Cape Breton Island

Gulf of St. Lawrence

Vancouver

Calgary

40°N

Seattle

Winnipeg

Lake Superior

Lake Huron

Quebec

Montreal

Portland

Ottawa

Toronto

Lake Ontario

Boston

Cape Cod

Minneapolis

Lake Michigan

Detroit

Lake Erie

New York City

Milwaukee

Cleveland

Philadelphia

ATLANTIC OCEAN

San Francisco

Great Salt Lake

Salt Lake City

Chicago

Columbus

Baltimore

Washington, D.C.

San Jose

Denver

Indianapolis

St. Louis

Norfolk

Kansas City

UNITED STATES

30°N

Los Angeles

Memphis

Bermuda (U.K.)

San Diego

Tijuana

Phoenix

Atlanta

Birmingham

30°N

Dallas

Jacksonville

Austin

San Antonio

Houston

New Orleans

Tropic of Cancer

Monterrey

Gulf of Mexico

Florida Keys

Miami

BAHAMAS

Turks and Caicos Islands (U.K.)

Nassau

MEXICO

Havana

CUBA

DOMINICAN REPUBLIC

Puerto Rico (U.S.)

San Juan

ST. KITTS & NEVIS

ANTIGUA & BARBUDA

Guadeloupe (FRANCE)

Guadalajara

Mexico City

Mérida

Cayman Is. (U.K.)

Straits of Florida

HAITI

Santo Domingo

Virgin Is. (U.S. & U.K.)

DOMINICA

Puebla

Kingston

Port-au-Prince

Martinique (FRANCE)

BARBADOS

JAMAICA

ST. LUCIA

GRENADA

Belmopan

BELIZE

Caribbean Sea

ST. VINCENT AND THE GRENADINES

Netherlands Antilles (NETHERLANDS)

GUATEMALA

HONDURAS

20°N

Guatemala City

Tegucigalpa

Panama Canal

TRINIDAD AND TOBAGO

San Salvador

NICARAGUA

Aruba (NETHERLANDS)

EL SALVADOR

Managua

10°N

San José

Panama City

COSTA RICA

PANAMA

SOUTH AMERICA

130°W

120°W

110°W

100°W

90°W

0° Equator

⊕ National capital

• Other city

0   300   600 Miles

0   300   600 Kilometers

Projection: Azimuthal Equal-Area

South America: Physical

CENTRAL AMERICA

Caribbean Sea

Panama Canal

Gulf of Panama

Malpelo Island

Margarita Island

Tobago

Trinidad

Orinoco River Delta

LLANOS

Lake Maracaibo

Orinoco River

Meta River

Cauca River

Magdalena River

Angel Falls

GUIANA HIGHLANDS

Devil's Island
Cape Orange

▲ Mount Tolima
18,425 ft
(5,616 m)

Orinoco River

Caquetá River

Rio Negro

Amazon River Delta

ATLANTIC OCEAN

Japurá River

AMAZON BASIN

Amazon River

▲ Mount Chimborazo
20,561 ft
(6,267 m)

Galápagos Islands

Gulf of Guayaquil

Marañón River

Amazon River

Juruá River

Purus

Madeira River

Tapajós River

Xingu River

Tocantins River

Parnaíba River

River

ANDES

BRAZILIAN HIGHLANDS

▲ Mount Huascarán
22,205 ft
(6,768 m)

Ucayali River

Beni River

Mamoré River

MATO GROSSO PLATEAU

Araguaia River

São Francisco River

PACIFIC OCEAN

Ancohuma Peak
20,958 ft
(6,388 m)

Lake Titicaca

Desaguadero River

Lake Poopó

CHACO

Paraguay River

BRAZILIAN PLATEAU

ATACAMA DESERT

ANDES

Salado

Paraná River

Uruguay River

San Ambrosio Island

San Félix Island

Juan Fernández Islands

▲ Mount Aconcagua
22,834 ft
(6,960 m)

Salado River

PAMPAS

Rio de la Plata

ATLANTIC OCEAN

Colorado River

PATAGONIA

Gulf of San Matías

Chiloé Island

Chonos Archipelago

Gulf of San Jorge

Cape Tres Puntas

Bahía Grande

Strait of Magellan

Falkland Islands

Tierra del Fuego

Cape Horn

South Georgia Islands

N
W   E
S

ELEVATION

Feet	Meters
13,120	4,000
6,560	2,000
1,640	500
656	200
(Sea level) 0	0 (Sea level)
Below sea level	Below sea level

0   250   500 Miles

0   250   500 Kilometers

Projection: Azimuthal Equal Area

South America: Political

CENTRAL AMERICA

Caribbean Sea

Barranquilla
Cartagena
Caracas

Lake Maracaibo

VENEZUELA

Georgetown
Paramaribo
Cayenne

Medellín

Bogotá

GUYANA

Malpelo Island (COLOMBIA)

COLOMBIA

Cali

SURINAME

French Guiana (FRANCE)

Quito

ECUADOR

Guayaquil

0° Equator

Belém

Galápagos Islands (ECUADOR)

PERU

Trujillo

BRAZIL

Recife

Callao Lima

PACIFIC OCEAN

Lake Titicaca

Arequipa

La Paz

Lake Poopó

Brasília

Salvador

BOLIVIA

Sucre

Belo Horizonte

PARAGUAY

Campinas
São Paulo

Rio de Janeiro

Asunción

Tropic of Capricorn

San Ambrosio Island (CHILE)

San Félix Island (CHILE)

Curitiba

CHILE

Pôrto Alegre

Juan Fernández Islands (CHILE)

Córdoba

Valparaíso
Santiago

Rosario

URUGUAY

Buenos Aires

Montevideo

ATLANTIC OCEAN

ARGENTINA

ATLANTIC OCEAN

⊕ National capital
• Other city

0   250   500 Miles
0   250   500 Kilometers

Projection: Azimuthal Equal-Area

Strait of Magellan

Falkland Islands (U.K.)

Tierra del Fuego

South Georgia Island (U.K.)

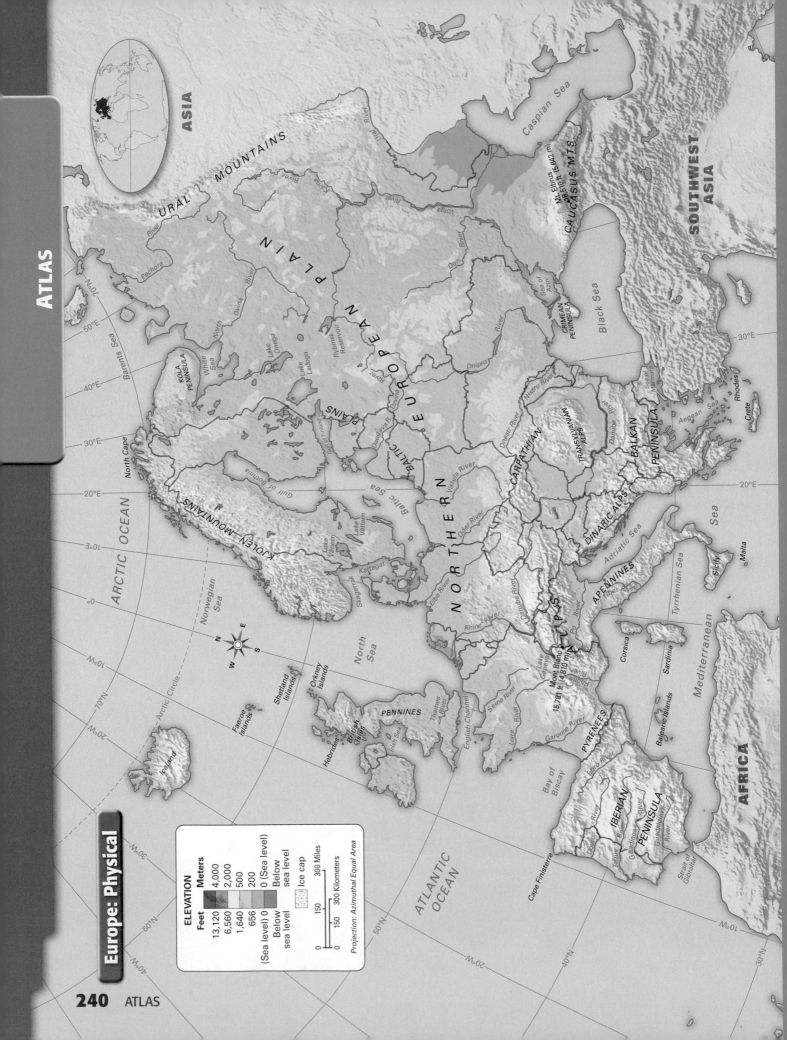

ASIA

URAL MOUNTAINS

SOUTHWEST ASIA

Caspian Sea

Mt. Elbrus 18,510 ft (5,642 m)

CAUCASUS MTS.

Ural River

Kama River

Pechora River

NORTHERN EUROPEAN PLAIN

Don River

Volga River

Sea of Azov

CRIMEAN PENINSULA

Black Sea

Dnipro River

Rybinsk Reservoir

Northern Dvina River

White Sea

KOLA PENINSULA

Lake Onega

Lake Ladoga

BALTIC PLAINS

Gulf of Finland

Barents Sea

North Cape

ARCTIC OCEAN

KJÖLEN MOUNTAINS

Norwegian Sea

Daugava R.

BALTIC

Vistula River

Dniester River

Nistru River

TRANSYLVANIAN ALPS

CARPATHIAN

Danube

Tisza River

BALKAN PENINSULA

DINARIC ALPS

Aegean Sea

Rhodes

Crete

Sea of Marmara

Gulf of Bothnia

Lake Vänern

Lake Vättern

Baltic Sea

Oder River

Elbe River

Danube River

Rhine River

ALPS

APENNINES

Tiber River

Adriatic Sea

Tyrrhenian Sea

Sicily

Malta

Kattegat

Skagerrak

North Sea

Orkney Islands

Shetland Islands

Faeroe Islands

Iceland

PENNINES

British Isles

Hebrides

Irish Sea

Thames River

English Channel

Seine River

Loire River

Bay of Biscay

Mont Blanc 15,781 ft (4,810 m)

Lake Geneva

Rhône River

Po River

Corsica

Sardinia

Balearic Islands

Mediterranean Sea

AFRICA

PYRENEES

Garonne River

Ebro River

IBERIAN PENINSULA

Duero River

Tagus River

Guadiana River

Guadalquivir River

Cape Finisterre

Strait of Gibraltar

ATLANTIC OCEAN

Arctic Circle

ATLAS

N
W E
S

70°N

60°N

50°N

40°N

30°N

40°E

30°E

20°E

10°E

0°

10°W

20°W

30°W

40°W

50°N

40°N

30°N

70°N

60°N

30°E

20°E

Europe: Physical

ELEVATION

Feet	Meters
13,120	4,000
6,560	2,000
1,640	500
656	200
(Sea level) 0	0 (Sea level)
Below sea level	Below sea level

Ice cap

0   150   300 Miles
0   150   300 Kilometers

Projection: Azimuthal Equal Area

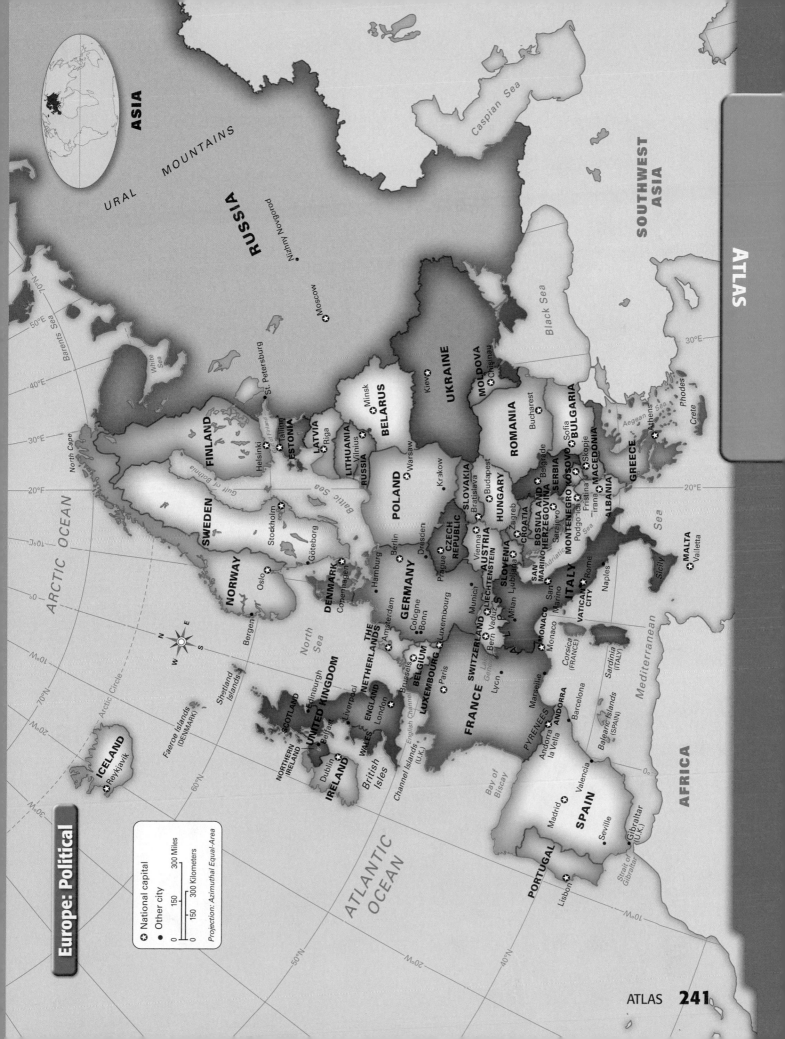

Europe: Political

Legend

⬙ National capital
• Other city

300 Miles
0   150   300 Kilometers

Projection: Azimuthal Equal-Area

ASIA

URAL MOUNTAINS

RUSSIA

Nizhny Novgorod

Moscow

Caspian Sea

SOUTHWEST ASIA

Black Sea

Barents Sea

White Sea

St. Petersburg

UKRAINE

Kiev

MOLDOVA
Chişinău

ROMANIA
Bucharest

BULGARIA
Sofia

Rhodes

Crete

Aegean Sea

Athens

GREECE

North Cape

FINLAND
Helsinki

ESTONIA
Tallinn

LATVIA
Riga

LITHUANIA
Vilnius

RUSSIA

Minsk

BELARUS

Warsaw

Kraków

POLAND

SLOVAKIA
Bratislava

Budapest

HUNGARY

SERBIA
Belgrade

KOSOVO
Priština

Skopje

MACEDONIA

ALBANIA
Tirana

Gulf of Bothnia

Baltic Sea

SWEDEN
Stockholm
Göteborg

NORWAY
Oslo

Bergen

DENMARK
Copenhagen

Hamburg

Berlin

Dresden

GERMANY

Prague

CZECH REPUBLIC

AUSTRIA
Vienna

Zagreb

CROATIA

SLOVENIA
Ljubljana

BOSNIA AND HERZEGOVINA
Sarajevo

MONTENEGRO
Podgorica

SAN MARINO
San Marino

Adriatic Sea

ITALY
Rome

Naples

VATICAN CITY

Sicily

MALTA
Valletta

Mediterranean Sea

ARCTIC OCEAN

ALPS

Munich

LIECHTENSTEIN
Vaduz

SWITZERLAND
Bern

Lake Geneva

Milan

MONACO
Monaco

Corsica (FRANCE)

Sardinia (ITALY)

Amsterdam

THE NETHERLANDS

Cologne
Bonn

LUXEMBOURG
Luxembourg

BELGIUM
Brussels

Paris

FRANCE

Lyon

Marseille

ANDORRA
Andorra la Vella

PYRENEES

Barcelona

Balearic Islands (SPAIN)

Valencia

Madrid

SPAIN

Seville

Gibraltar (U.K.)

Strait of Gibraltar

AFRICA

North Sea

Shetland Islands

Faeroe Islands (DENMARK)

ICELAND
Reykjavík

SCOTLAND
Edinburgh

UNITED KINGDOM

Liverpool

ENGLAND
London

WALES

NORTHERN IRELAND
Belfast

IRELAND
Dublin

British Isles

Channel Islands (U.K.)

English Channel

Bay of Biscay

PORTUGAL
Lisbon

ATLANTIC OCEAN

Arctic Circle

N E W S

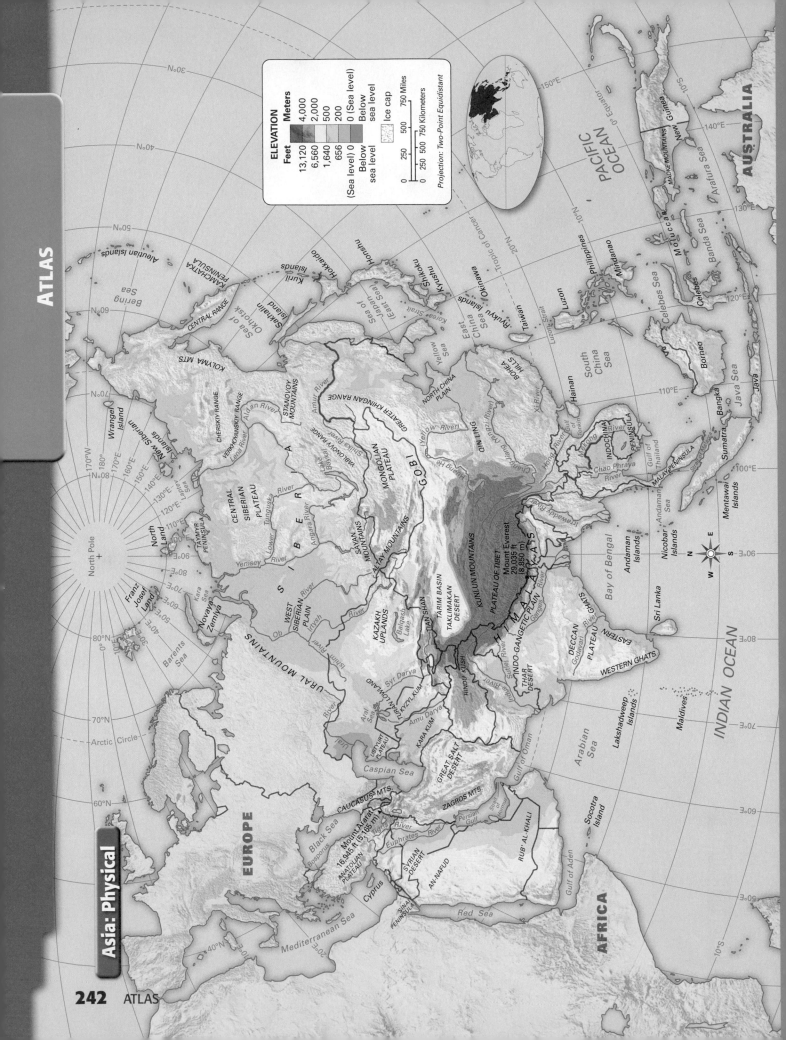

Asia: Physical

ELEVATION

Feet	Meters
13,120	4,000
6,560	2,000
1,640	500
656	200
0 (Sea level)	0 (Sea level)
Below sea level	Below sea level

Ice cap

750 Miles
750 Kilometers
0   250   500
0   250   500

Projection: Two-Point Equidistant

EUROPE

AFRICA

AUSTRALIA

PACIFIC OCEAN

INDIAN OCEAN

North Pole

Wrangel Island
New Siberian Islands
Aleutian Islands
KAMCHATKA PENINSULA
Bering Sea
Sea of Okhotsk
Sakhalin Island
Kuril Islands
Hokkaido
Honshu
Sea of Japan (East Sea)
Korea Strait
Shikoku
Kyushu
Okinawa
Ryukyu Islands
Taiwan
Luzon Strait
Luzon
Philippines
Mindanao
Celebes Sea
Celebes
Molucca Sea
Banda Sea
New Guinea
MAOKE MOUNTAINS
Arafura Sea

CENTRAL RANGE
KOLYMA MTS.
CHERSKY RANGE
VERKHOYANSKY RANGE
STANOVOY MOUNTAINS
YABLONOVY RANGE
Aldan River
Yana River
Lena River
Lake Baykal
Amur River
Shilka River
GREATER KHINGAN RANGE
MONGOLIAN PLATEAU
GOBI
Yellow (Huang He) River
NORTH CHINA PLAIN
BOHEA HILLS
Yellow Sea
East China Sea
QIN LING
South China Sea
Hainan
Xi River
Gulf of Tonkin
Hong River
INDOCHINA PENINSULA
Mekong River
Chao Phraya River
Gulf of Thailand
MALAY PENINSULA
Strait of Malacca
Sumatra
Bangka
Java Sea
Java
Borneo
Mentawai Islands

SIBERIA
CENTRAL SIBERIAN PLATEAU
Lower Tunguska River
Angara River
Yenisey River
SAYAN MOUNTAINS
ALTAY MOUNTAINS
TIAN SHAN
TARIM BASIN
TAKLIMAKAN DESERT
KUNLUN MOUNTAINS
PLATEAU OF TIBET
Mount Everest 29,035 ft (8,850 m)
HIMALAYAS
INDO-GANGETIC PLAIN
Ganges River
Brahmaputra River
Irrawaddy River
Bay of Bengal
Andaman Islands
Nicobar Islands
Andaman Sea

TAYMYR PENINSULA
North Land
Novaya Zemlya
Kara Sea
Ob River
WEST SIBERIAN PLAIN
Irtysh River
Ishim River
KAZAKH UPLANDS
Balqash Lake
Syr Darya
TURAN LOWLAND
KYZYL KUM
Aral Sea
Amu Darya
KARA KUM
HINDU KUSH
THAR DESERT
DECCAN PLATEAU
Godavari River
EASTERN GHATS
WESTERN GHATS
Sri Lanka
Lakshadweep Islands
Maldives

Franz Josef Land
Barents Sea
URAL MOUNTAINS
Ural River
USTYURT PLATEAU
Caspian Sea
GREAT SALT DESERT
ZAGROS MTS.
Persian Gulf
Strait of Hormuz
Gulf of Oman
Arabian Sea
Socotra Island
Gulf of Aden

Arctic Circle
North Pole

EUROPE
Black Sea
Bosporus
CAUCASUS MTS.
Mount Ararat 16,945 ft (5,165 m)
ANATOLIAN PLATEAU
Cyprus
Mediterranean Sea
Tigris River
Euphrates River
SYRIAN DESERT
AN-NAFUD
SINAI PENINSULA
Red Sea
RUB' AL-KHALI

30°N 40°N 50°N 60°N 70°N 80°N
170°W 180° 170°E 160°E 150°E 140°E 130°E 120°E 110°E 100°E 90°E 80°E 70°E 60°E 50°E 40°E 30°E 20°E 0°
150°E 140°E 130°E 120°E 110°E 100°E
Tropic of Cancer
Equator
10°S
20°N 10°N 30°N 60°N 70°N 80°N 90°N

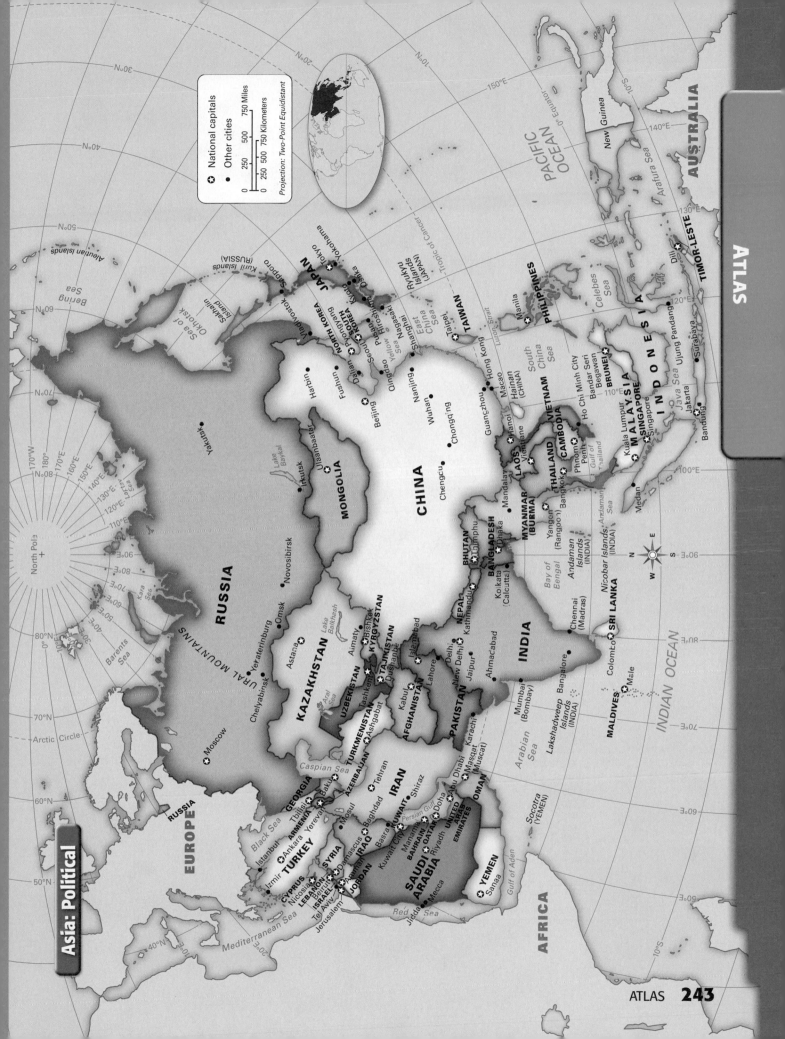

Asia: Political

National capitals
Other cities

750 Miles
0 250 500 750 Kilometers

Projection: Two-Point Equidistant

AUSTRALIA

New Guinea

PACIFIC OCEAN

Arafura Sea

TIMOR-LESTE

Dili

PHILIPPINES

Manila

Celebes Sea

Luzon Strait

INDONESIA

Ujung Pandang

Surabaya

Java Sea

Jakarta

Bandung

BRUNEI
Bandar Seri Begawan

Kuala Lumpur

MALAYSIA

SINGAPORE
Singapore

Macao

Hainan (CHINA)

Hong Kong

Guangzhou

South China Sea

VIETNAM

Ho Chi Minh City

Hanoi

Vientiane

LAOS

CAMBODIA

Phnom Penh

Gulf of Thailand

THAILAND

Bangkok

Medan

Andaman Sea

Andaman Islands (INDIA)

Nicobar Islands (INDIA)

Aleutian Islands

Bering Sea

Sea of Okhotsk

Sakhalin Island

Kuril Islands (RUSSIA)

JAPAN

Sapporo

Vladivostok

Tokyo

Yokohama

Osaka

Hiroshima

Nagasaki

NORTH KOREA

Pyongyang

SOUTH KOREA

Seoul

Pusan

East China Sea

Yellow Sea

Tropic of Cancer

Qingdao

Shanghai

TAIWAN

Taipei

Harbin

Fushun

Dalian

Beijing

Nanjing

Wuhan

Chongqing

CHINA

Chengdu

Yakutsk

Lake Baykal

Irkutsk

Ulaanbaatar

MONGOLIA

MYANMAR (BURMA)

Yangon (Rangoon)

Mandalay

BHUTAN

Thimphu

BANGLADESH

Dhaka

NEPAL

Kathmandu

Kolkata (Calcutta)

Bay of Bengal

Chennai (Madras)

SRI LANKA

Colombo

Bangalore

Mumbai (Bombay)

Lakshadweep Islands (INDIA)

MALDIVES

Male

Arabian Sea

INDIAN OCEAN

RUSSIA

Moscow

Novosibirsk

Omsk

Yekaterinburg

Chelyabinsk

URAL MOUNTAINS

Astana

KAZAKHSTAN

Lake Balkhash

Aral Sea

Almaty

Bishkek

KYRGYZSTAN

Tashkent

UZBEKISTAN

TAJIKISTAN

Dushanbe

TURKMENISTAN

Ashgabat

Islamabad

AFGHANISTAN

Kabul

PAKISTAN

Lahore

Karachi

Delhi

New Delhi

Jaipur

Ahmadabad

INDIA

Caspian Sea

GEORGIA

Tbilisi

ARMENIA

Yerevan

AZERBAIJAN

Baku

Tehran

IRAN

Shiraz

Mosul

Baghdad

Basra

KUWAIT

Kuwait City

Abu Dhabi

Masqat (Muscat)

UNITED ARAB EMIRATES

OMAN

Socotra (YEMEN)

EUROPE

RUSSIA

Black Sea

Istanbul

Ankara

TURKEY

Izmir

CYPRUS

Nicosia

LEBANON

Beirut

ISRAEL

Tel Aviv

Jerusalem

SYRIA

Damascus

Amman

JORDAN

IRAQ

BAHRAIN

Manama

QATAR

Doha

Riyadh

SAUDI ARABIA

Mecca

Jidda

Red Sea

YEMEN

Sanaa

Gulf of Aden

AFRICA

Mediterranean Sea

North Pole

Arctic Circle

Barents Sea

Kara Sea

Persian Gulf

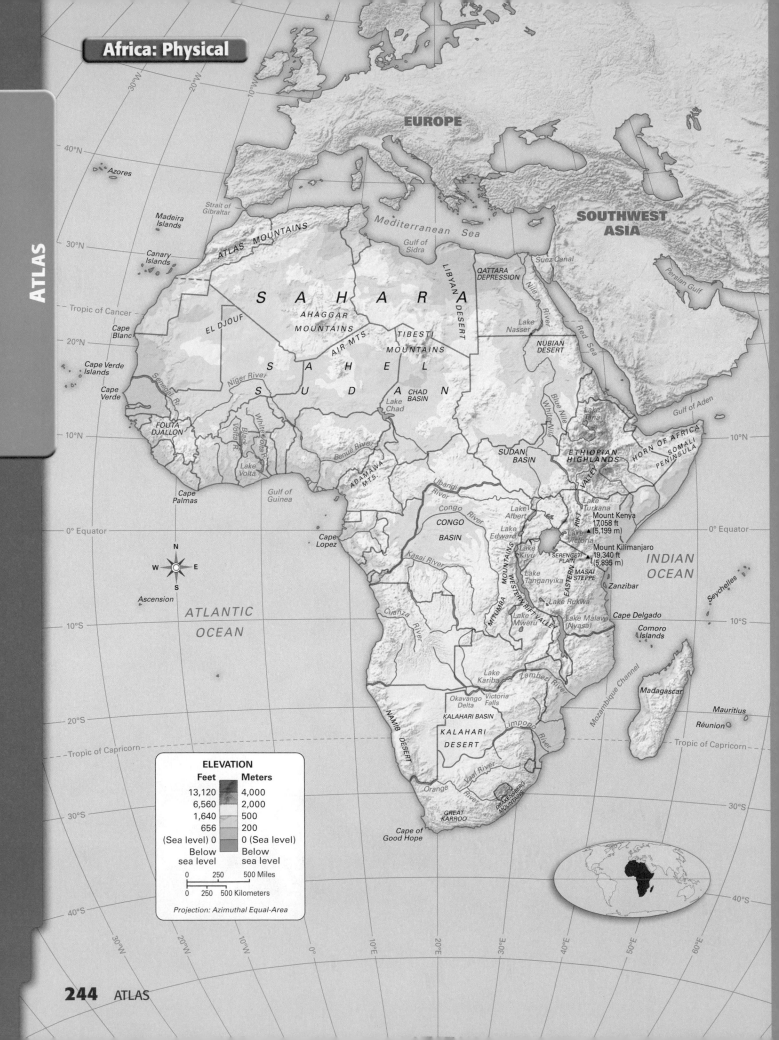

Africa: Physical

EUROPE

SOUTHWEST ASIA

Azores

Madeira Islands

Strait of Gibraltar

ATLAS MOUNTAINS

Mediterranean Sea

Gulf of Sidra

Canary Islands

Tropic of Cancer

Cape Blanc

EL DJOUF

S A H A R A

AHAGGAR MOUNTAINS

AIR MTS.

TIBESTI MOUNTAINS

LIBYAN DESERT

QATTARA DEPRESSION

Suez Canal

Nile River

Lake Nasser

NUBIAN DESERT

Red Sea

Persian Gulf

Cape Verde Islands

S A H E L

Cape Verde

Senegal R.

Niger River

S U D A N

CHAD BASIN

Lake Chad

Persian Gulf

FOUTA DJALLON

White Volta R.

Black Volta R.

Benue River

Lake Volta

Cape Palmas

Gulf of Guinea

ADAMAWA MTS.

Ubangi River

Congo River

SUDAN BASIN

Blue Nile

White Nile

Lake Tana

ETHIOPIAN HIGHLANDS

HORN OF AFRICA

Gulf of Aden

SOMALI PENINSULA

Cape Lopez

CONGO BASIN

Lake Albert

Lake Edward

Lake Turkana

Mount Kenya 17,058 ft (5,199 m)

Equator

Kasai River

Lake Kivu

Lake Victoria

Serengeti Plain

MASAI STEPPE

Mount Kilimanjaro 19,340 ft (5,895 m)

INDIAN OCEAN

Seychelles

Cuanza River

MITUMBA MOUNTAINS

Lake Tanganyika

WESTERN RIFT VALLEY

EASTERN RIFT VALLEY

Lake Rukwa

Zanzibar

Ascension

ATLANTIC OCEAN

Lake Mweru

Lake Malawi (Nyasa)

Cape Delgado

Comoro Islands

Madagascar

Lake Kariba

Zambezi River

Mozambique Channel

Mauritius

Okavango Delta

Victoria Falls

Réunion

NAMIB DESERT

KALAHARI BASIN

KALAHARI DESERT

Limpopo River

Tropic of Capricorn

Vaal River

Orange River

DRAKENSBERG MOUNTAINS

GREAT KARROO

Cape of Good Hope

ELEVATION

Feet	Meters
13,120	4,000
6,560	2,000
1,640	500
656	200
(Sea level) 0	0 (Sea level)
Below sea level	Below sea level

0   250   500 Miles

0   250   500 Kilometers

Projection: Azimuthal Equal-Area

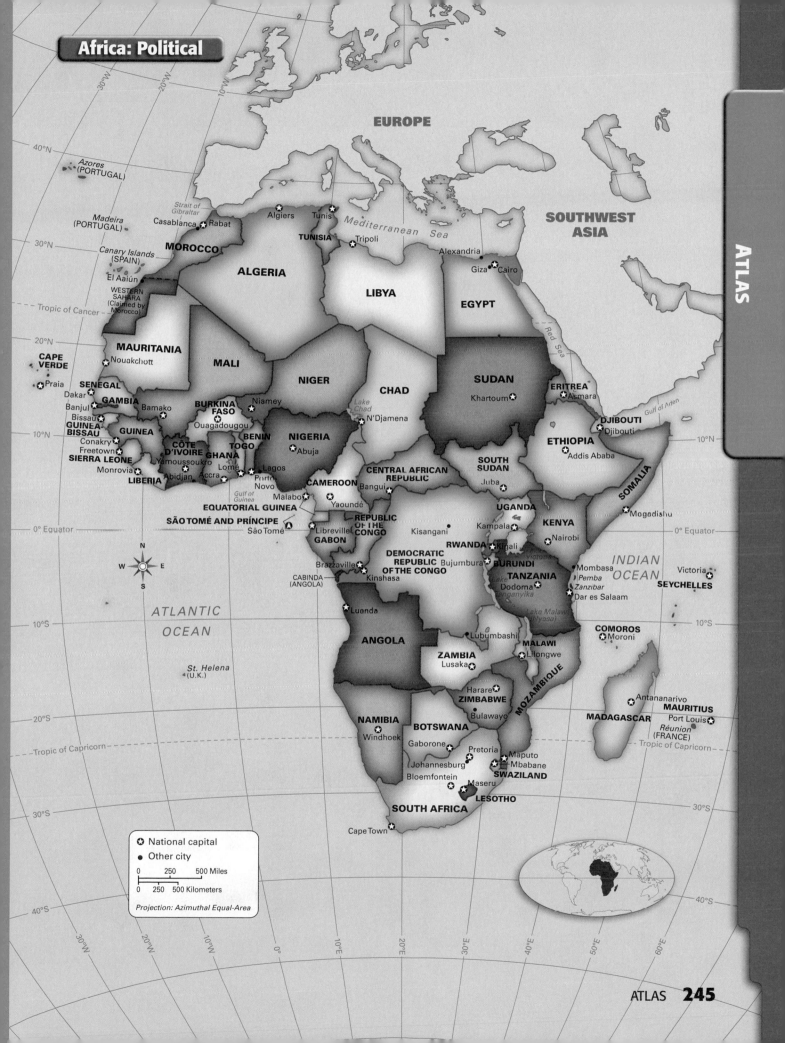

Africa: Political

EUROPE

SOUTHWEST ASIA

Mediterranean Sea

Strait of Gibraltar

Azores (PORTUGAL)

Madeira (PORTUGAL)

Canary Islands (SPAIN)

MOROCCO
Casablanca • Rabat

Algiers • Tunis **TUNISIA** • Tripoli

Alexandria
Giza • Cairo

ALGERIA

LIBYA

EGYPT

El Aaiún

WESTERN SAHARA (Claimed by Morocco)

Tropic of Cancer

Red Sea

MAURITANIA
• Nouakchott

MALI

NIGER

CHAD

SUDAN
• Khartoum

ERITREA
• Asmara

Gulf of Aden

CAPE VERDE

• Praia

SENEGAL
Dakar •
• Banjul
GAMBIA

Bamako •

Niamey •

Lake Chad

N'Djamena •

DJIBOUTI
• Djibouti

Bissau •
GUINEA-BISSAU

GUINEA
Conakry •

BURKINA FASO
Ouagadougou •

BENIN
NIGERIA
• Abuja

CENTRAL AFRICAN REPUBLIC

SOUTH SUDAN
• Juba

ETHIOPIA
• Addis Ababa

Freetown •
SIERRA LEONE
Monrovia •

CÔTE D'IVOIRE
Yamoussoukro •
GHANA
Abidjan • Accra •

TOGO
Lomé •
Lagos •
Porto Novo •

CAMEROON
Bangui •

Malabo •
LIBERIA

Gulf of Guinea

SOMALIA
• Mogadishu

EQUATORIAL GUINEA
Yaoundé •

UGANDA
Kampala •

KENYA
• Nairobi

SÃO TOMÉ AND PRÍNCIPE
São Tomé •

0° Equator

Libreville •
GABON

REPUBLIC OF THE CONGO

Kisangani •

RWANDA
• Kigali

0° Equator

Brazzaville •

CABINDA (ANGOLA)

DEMOCRATIC REPUBLIC OF THE CONGO
Bujumbura •
BURUNDI

Lake Victoria

Mombasa •

INDIAN OCEAN

Victoria •

Kinshasa •

TANZANIA
Dodoma •
Lake Tanganyika

• Pemba
Zanzibar •
Dar es Salaam •

SEYCHELLES

ATLANTIC OCEAN

• Luanda

Lake Malawi (Nyasa)

COMOROS
• Moroni

ANGOLA

Lubumbashi •

MALAWI
• Lilongwe

St. Helena • (U.K.)

ZAMBIA
Lusaka •

Harare •
ZIMBABWE

Bulawayo •

MOZAMBIQUE

Antananarivo •
MADAGASCAR

MAURITIUS
Port Louis •

Réunion (FRANCE)

NAMIBIA
Windhoek •

BOTSWANA
Gaborone •

Pretoria •
Johannesburg •

Maputo •
Mbabane •
SWAZILAND

Tropic of Capricorn

Bloemfontein •

Maseru •
LESOTHO

SOUTH AFRICA

Cape Town •

Legend

✪ National capital
• Other city

0   250   500 Miles
0   250   500 Kilometers

Projection: Azimuthal Equal-Area

NORTH AMERICA

ASIA

The Pacific: Political

NORTH PACIFIC OCEAN

SOUTH PACIFIC OCEAN

INDIAN OCEAN

National capital
Other city

1,000 Miles
1,000 Kilometers

Projection: Azimuthal Equal-Area

Tropic of Cancer

Equator

Tropic of Capricorn

International Date Line

30°N
15°N
0°
15°S
30°S
45°S

120°W
135°W
150°W
165°W
180°
165°E
150°E
135°E
120°E

15°N
0°
15°S
30°S
45°S

Hawaiian Islands
Hawaii (U.S.)

Midway Island (U.S.)

Johnston Island (U.S.)

Kingman Reef (U.S.)
Palmyra Island (U.S.)
Fanning Island (U.S.)

Washington Island (U.S.)

Jarvis I. (U.S.)

Howland I. (U.S.)
Baker I. (U.S.)

McKean I.
Gardner I.
Phoenix Islands

Starbuck Island

KIRIBATI

Marquesas Islands (FRANCE)

Tuamotu Archipelago (FRANCE)

Rapa Island (FRANCE)

French Polynesia

P O L Y N E S I A

Society Islands (FRANCE)
Tahiti (FRANCE)
Papeete

Tubuai Islands (FRANCE)

Manihiki Island

Cook Islands (NEW ZEALAND)
Rarotonga Island

Niue (N.Z.)

Pitcairn (U.K.)
Pitcairn Island
Ducie Island

Easter Island (CHILE)

Tokelau (N.Z.)
American Samoa
Pago Pago
SAMOA
Apia

TONGA
Nuku'alofa

Wallis & Futuna (FR.)

TUVALU
Funafuti

FIJI
Suva

Tarawa

MARSHALL ISLANDS
Kwajalein Island
Eniwetok I.
Majuro

Gilbert Islands

NAURU

SOLOMON ISLANDS

M E L A N E S I A

Honiara

Guadalcanal I.

Espiritu Santo I.
Malekula I.
VANUATU
Port-Vila

New Caledonia (FRANCE)
Nouméa
Loyalty Islands (FRANCE)

Kermadec Islands (N.Z.)

Norfolk Island (AUSTRALIA)

Chatham Islands (N.Z.)

Auckland
Wellington
Christchurch
NEW ZEALAND
North Island
South Island

Bounty Islands (N.Z.)

Auckland Islands (NEW ZEALAND)

Wake Island (U.S.)

M I C R O N E S I A

Palikir

Truk Is.

Bismarck Archipelago

PAPUA NEW GUINEA
Port Moresby

New Guinea

FEDERATED STATES OF MICRONESIA

Bonin Islands (JAPAN)

Volcano Islands (JAPAN)

Northern Marianas (U.S.)

Guam (U.S.)
Agana

PALAU
Koror

Coral Sea

Arafura Sea

Timor Sea

Philippine Sea

South China Sea

Christmas Island (AUSTRALIA)

Darwin

Brisbane
Sydney
Canberra

Adelaide
Melbourne

Perth

Hobart

Tasman Sea

AUSTRALIA

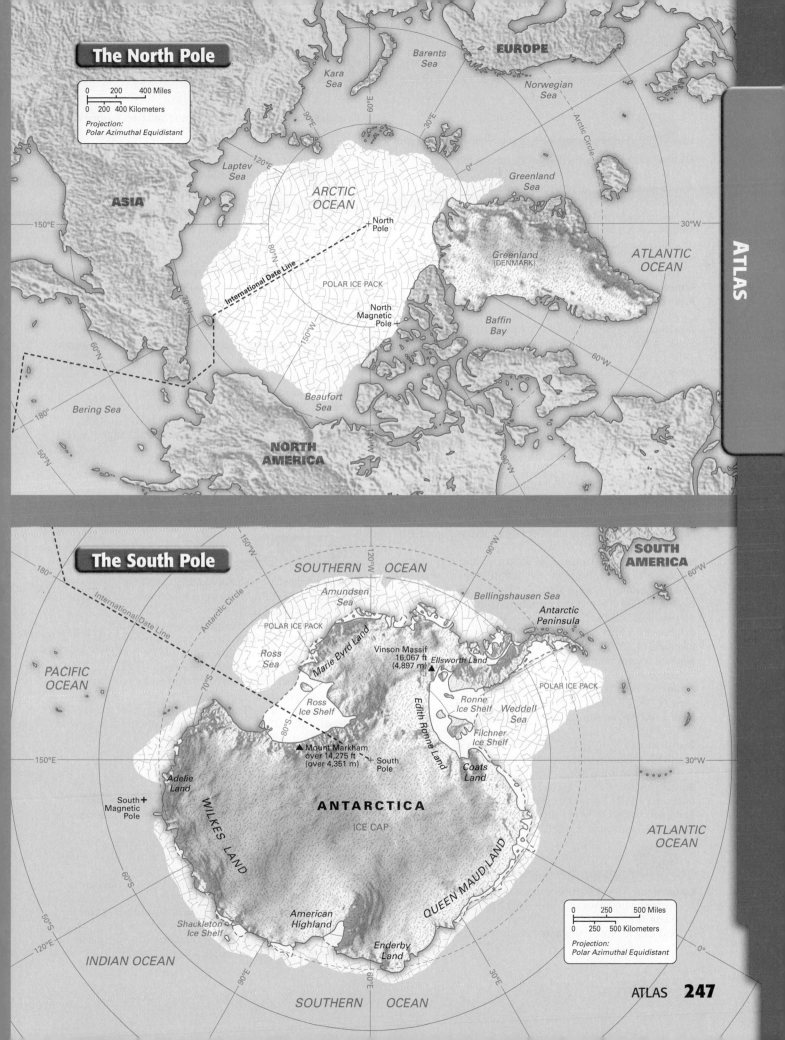

The North Pole

0   200   400 Miles
0   200   400 Kilometers

Projection:
Polar Azimuthal Equidistant

ASIA

EUROPE

Kara
Sea

Barents
Sea

Laptev
Sea

Norwegian
Sea

Arctic Circle

ARCTIC
OCEAN

Greenland
Sea

+ North
Pole

International Date Line

POLAR ICE PACK

Greenland
(DENMARK)

ATLANTIC
OCEAN

North
Magnetic
Pole +

Baffin
Bay

Bering Sea

Beaufort
Sea

NORTH
AMERICA

150°E
90°E
60°E
30°E
0°
30°W
60°W
80°N
70°N
60°N
50°N
180°
150°W
120°W
90°W

The South Pole

SOUTH
AMERICA

International Date Line

Antarctic Circle

SOUTHERN   OCEAN

Amundsen
Sea

Bellingshausen Sea

Antarctic
Peninsula

POLAR ICE PACK

PACIFIC
OCEAN

Ross
Sea

Marie Byrd Land

Vinson Massif
16,067 ft
(4,897 m) ▲

Ellsworth Land

POLAR ICE PACK

Ross
Ice Shelf

Ronne
Ice Shelf

Weddell
Sea

Edith Ronne Land

Filchner
Ice Shelf

▲ Mount Markham
over 14,275 ft
(over 4,351 m)

+ South
Pole

Coats
Land

South +
Magnetic
Pole

Adelie
Land

WILKES LAND

ANTARCTICA

ICE CAP

QUEEN MAUD LAND

ATLANTIC
OCEAN

Shackleton
Ice Shelf

American
Highland

Enderby
Land

0   250   500 Miles
0   250   500 Kilometers

Projection:
Polar Azimuthal Equidistant

INDIAN OCEAN

SOUTHERN   OCEAN

180°
150°W
120°W
90°W
60°W
30°W
0°
30°E
60°E
90°E
120°E
150°E
60°S
70°S
80°S
50°S

Gazetteer

A

Albania a country on the Balkan Peninsula in southeastern Europe (p. 171)

Alps a great mountain system in central Europe (p. 105)

Amsterdam (52°N, 5°E) the capital and largest city of the Netherlands (p. 127)

Amur River a river in Asia that forms part of the Russia-China border (p. 195)

Apennines (A-puh-nynz) the major mountain range on the Italian Peninsula (p. 105)

Armenia a country in the Caucasus Mountains (p. 213)

Asia the world's largest continent; located between Europe and the Pacific Ocean (p. 242)

Asia Minor a large peninsula in Southwest Asia between the Black Sea and the Mediterranean Sea, forming most of Turkey (p. 15)

Athens (38°N, 24°E) an ancient city and the modern capital of Greece (p. 112)

Atlantic Ocean the ocean between North and South America and Europe and Africa (pp. 232–233)

Austria a country in West-Central Europe (p. 127)

Azerbaijan (a-zuhr-by-JAHN) a country in the Caucasus Mountains (p. 213)

B

Baku (40°N, 48°E) the capital of Azerbaijan (p. 213)

Baltic Sea a shallow arm of the Atlantic Ocean in northern Europe (p. 153)

Balkan Peninsula a peninsula in Southern Europe (p. 240)

Barcelona (41°N, 2°E) a large port city in Spain on the Mediterranean Sea (p. 120)

Bavaria a state and region in southern Germany (p. 142)

Belarus a country in Eastern Europe (p. 171)

Belgium a country in West-Central Europe (p. 127)

Belgrade (45°N, 21°E) the capital of Serbia (p. 189)

Benelux a term that refers to Belgium, the Netherlands, and Luxembourg (p. 136)

Berlin (53°N, 13°E) the capital of Germany (p. 141)

Bern (47°N, 7°E) the capital of Switzerland (p. 127)

Bosnia and Herzegovina a country on the Balkan Peninsula (p. 171)

Bratislava (48°N, 17°E) the capital of Slovakia (p. 171)

British Isles a group of islands off the northwestern coast of Europe including Britain and Ireland (p. 153)

Brussels (51°N, 4°E) the capital of Belgium (p. 127)

Bucharest (44°N, 26°E) the capital of Romania (p. 171)

Budapest (48°N, 19°E) the capital of Hungary (p. 171)

Bulgaria a country in the Balkans (p. 171)

C

Carpathians (kahr-PAY-thee-uhnz) a major mountain chain in central and eastern Europe (p. 173)

Carthage (KAHR-thij) (37°N, 10°E) an ancient Phoenician port city in North Africa in modern Tunisia (p. 25)

Caspian Sea a large inland sea located between Europe and Asia (p. 194)

Caucasus Mountains a mountain system in southeastern Europe between the Black Sea and Caspian Sea (p. 196)

Central Uplands an area of hills, plateaus, and valleys in central Europe (p. 129)

Chechnya (CHECH-nyuh) a republic in Russia that is fighting a violent struggle for independence (p. 218)

Chernobyl (51°N, 30°E) a city in Ukraine; the world's worst nuclear reactor accident occurred there in 1986 (p. 175)

Chişinau (47°N, 29°E) the capital of Moldova (p. 171)

Copenhagen (56°N, 13°E) the capital of Denmark (p. 151)

Croatia a country in the Balkans (p. 171)

Czech Republic a country in Eastern Europe (p. 171)

D, E

Danube (DAN-yoob) the second-longest river in Europe; it flows from Germany east to the Black Sea (p. 129)

Denmark a country in Northern Europe (p. 151)

Dublin (53°N, 6°W) the capital of Ireland (p. 159)

Edinburgh (56°N, 3°W) the capital of Scotland (p. 159)

England a part of the United Kingdom occupying most of the island of Great Britain (p. 159)

English Channel a strait of the Atlantic Ocean between England and France (p. 159)

Estonia a Baltic country in Eastern Europe (p. 171)

Europe the continent between the Ural Mountains and the Atlantic Ocean (p. 240)

F, G, H

Finland a country in Northern Europe (p. 151)

Florence (44°N, 11°E) a city in Italy that was a major center of the Renaissance (p. 47)

France a country in West-Central Europe (p. 127)

Georgia a country in the Caucasus Mountains (p. 213)

Germany a country in West-Central Europe (p. 127)

Greece a country in Southern Europe (p. 15)

Greenland a large island in North America controlled by Denmark (p. 232)

The Hague the Netherlands' seat of government (p. 137)

Helsinki (60°N, 25°E) the capital of Finland (p. 151)

Holland a region in the Netherlands (p. 136)

Hungary a country in central Europe (p. 171)

I, J, K

Iberian Peninsula a large peninsula in Southern Europe; Spain and Portugal are located there (p. 105)

Iceland an island country in Northern Europe (p. 150)

Ireland a country west of Britain in the British Isles (p. 150)

Italy a country in Southern Europe (p. 103)

Jura Mountains a mountain range in West-Central Europe in Switzerland and France (p. 129)

Kaliningrad (55°N, 21°E) a strategic city and port controlled by Russia (p. 207)

Kamchatka Peninsula a large, mountainous peninsula in eastern Russia on the Pacific Ocean (p. 197)

Kiev (50°N, 31°E) the capital of Ukraine (p. 171)

Kjølen Mountains a mountain range in Scandinavia along the Norway-Sweden border (p. 153)

Lake Baikal a huge freshwater lake in Russia; it is the deepest lake in the world (p. 197)

Latvia a Baltic country in Eastern Europe (p. 171)

Lena River a long river in central Russia that flows north to the Arctic Sea (p. 197)

Lisbon (39°N, 9°W) the capital of Portugal (p. 102)

Lithuania a Baltic country in Eastern Europe (p. 171)

Ljubljana (46°N, 15°E) the capital of Slovenia (p. 171)

London (51°N, 1°W) the capital of England and the United Kingdom (p. 159)

Luxembourg a country in West-Central Europe (p. 127)

Luxembourg City (45°N 6°E) capital of Luxembourg (p. 127)

Macedonia a country on the Balkan Peninsula in southeastern Europe (p. 189)

Madrid (40°N 4°W) the capital of Spain (p. 102)

Marseille (mar-SAY) (43°N, 5°E) a port city in France on the Mediterranean Sea (p. 127)

Massif Central (ma-SEEF sahn-TRAHL) an upland region in south-central France (p. 129)

Mediterranean Sea a sea between Europe and Africa (p. 105)

Moldova a country in Eastern Europe (p. 171)

Monaco a small country in West-Central Europe (p. 127)

Mont Blanc (mawn BLAHN) (46°N, 7°E) a mountain peak in France; highest of the Alps (p. 129)

Montenegro (43°N 19°E) a country in the Balkans (p. 171)

Mount Elbrus (el-BROOS) the highest peak of the Caucasus Mountains (p. 197)

Moscow (56°N, 38°E) the capital of Russia (p. 194)

Netherlands a country in West-Central Europe (p. 127)

Normandy a region in northwestern France (p. 90)

Northern European Plain a large plain across central and northern Europe (p. 129)

Northern Ireland a part of the United Kingdom occupying the northeastern portion of the island of Ireland (p. 159)

North Sea a shallow arm of the Atlantic Ocean in Northern Europe (p. 129)

Norway a country in Northern Europe (p. 151)

Ob River a long river in central Russia (p. 197)

Oslo (60°N, 11°E) the capital of Norway (p. 151)

Paris (46°N, 0°) the capital of France (p. 127)

Po River a major river in northern Italy (p. 105)

Podgorica (43°N, 19°E) capital of Montenegro (p. 171)

Poland a country in Eastern Europe (p. 171)

Portugal a country in Southern Europe on the Iberian Peninsula (p. 102)

Prague (50°N, 14°E) capital of the Czech Republic (p. 171)

Pyrenees (PIR-uh-neez) a high mountain range between Spain and France (p. 105)

Reykjavik (64°N, 22°W) the capital of Iceland (p. 150)

Rhine a major river in Europe; it begins in Switzerland and flows north to the North Sea (p. 129)

Riga (57°N, 24°E) the capital of Latvia (p. 171)

Romania a country in Eastern Europe (p. 171)

Rome (42°N, 13°E) the capital of Italy; it was the capital of the ancient Roman Empire (p. 103)

Ruhr a major industrial region in Germany (p. 143)

Russia a huge country that extends from Eastern Europe to the Pacific Ocean (p. 197)

Sarajevo (44°N, 18°E) the capital of Bosnia and Herzegovina (p. 189)

Scandinavian Peninsula a large peninsula in Northern Europe that includes Norway and Sweden (p. 153)

Scotland a part of the United Kingdom located in the northern part of Great Britain (p. 150)

Serbia a country in the Balkans (p. 171)

Siberia a huge region in eastern Russia (p. 197)

Slovakia a country in Eastern Europe (p. 171)

Slovenia a country in Eastern Europe (p. 171)

Sofia (43°N, 23°E) the capital of Bulgaria (p. 171)

Spain a country in Southern Europe on the Iberian Peninsula (p. 102)

Sparta (37°N, 22°E) an ancient city-state in Greece (p. 20)

Stockholm (59°N, 18°E) the capital of Sweden (p. 151)

Sweden a country in Northern Europe (p. 151)

Switzerland a country in West-Central Europe (p. 127)

Tallinn (59°N, 25°E) the capital of Estonia (p. 171)

Tbilisi (42°N, 45°E) the capital of Georgia (p. 213)

Tirana (41°N, 20°E) the capital of Albania (p. 171)

Ukraine a country in Eastern Europe (p. 171)

United Kingdom a country in the British Isles that includes England, Wales, Scotland, and Northern Ireland (p. 159)

Ural Mountains (YOOHR-uhl) a mountain range in Russia that separates Europe and Asia (p. 197)

Vatican City (42°N, 12°E) a small country in Rome that is the head of the Roman Catholic Church (p. 103)

Vienna (45°N, 12°E) the capital of Austria (p. 127)

Vilnius (55°N, 25°E) the capital of Lithuania (p. 171)

Volga (VAHL-guh) the longest river in Europe and Russia's most important commercial river (p. 197)

Wales a part of the United Kingdom located west of England on the island of Great Britain (p. 153)

Warsaw (52°N, 21°E) the capital of Poland (p. 171)

Yenisey River a long river in central Russia that flows north to the Arctic Ocean (p. 197)

Yerevan (40°N, 45°E) the capital of Armenia (p. 213)

Yugoslavia a former country in the Balkans that broke apart in the 1990s (p. 188)

Zagreb (46°N, 16°E) the capital of Croatia (p. 189)

Zurich (47°N, 9°E) a city in Switzerland (p. 127)

English and Spanish Glossary

MARK	AS IN	RESPELLING	EXAMPLE
a	alphabet	a	*AL-fuh-bet
ā	Asia	ay	AY-zhuh
ä	cart, top	ah	KAHRT, TAHP
e	let, ten	e	LET, TEN
ē	even, leaf	ee	EE-vuhn, LEEF
i	it, tip, British	i	IT, TIP, BRIT-ish
ī	site, buy, Ohio	y	SYT, BY, oh-HY-oh
	iris	eye	EYE-ris
k	card	k	KAHRD
kw	quest	kw	KWEST
ō	over, rainbow	oh	OH-vuhr, RAYN-boh
ů	book, wood	ooh	BOOHK, WOOHD
ò	all, orchid	aw	AWL, AWR-kid
òi	foil, coin	oy	FOYL, KOYN
àů	out	ow	OWT
ə	cup, butter	uh	KUHP, BUHT-uhr
ü	rule, food	oo	ROOL, FOOD
yü	few	yoo	FYOO
zh	vision	zh	VIZH-uhn

*A syllable printed in small capital letters receives heavier emphasis than the other syllable(s) in a word.

Phonetic Respelling and Pronunciation Guide

Many of the key terms in this textbook have been respelled to help you pronounce them. The letter combinations used in the respelling throughout the narrative are explained in this phonetic respelling and pronunciation guide. The guide is adapted from Merriam-Webster's Collegiate Dictionary, Eleventh Edition; Merriam-Webster's Geographical Dictionary; and Merriam-Webster's Biographical Dictionary.

agrarian a society that is organized around farming (p. 214)
agraria sociedad organizada en torno a la agricultura (pág. 214)
alliance an agreement to work together (p. 81)
alianza acuerdo de colaboración (pág. 81)
Allies Great Britain, France, the Soviet Union, and the United States; they joined together in World War II against Germany, Italy, and Japan (p. 89)
Aliados Gran Bretaña, Francia, la Unión Soviética y Estados Unidos; se unieron durante la Segunda Guerra Mundial contra Alemania, Italia y Japón (pág. 89)
aqueduct a human-made raised channel that carries water from distant places (p. 26)
acueducto canal elevado hecho por el ser humano que trae agua desde lugares lejanos (pág. 26)
arms race a competition between countries to build superior weapons (p. 94)
carrera armamentista competencia entre países para construir armas mejores (pág. 94)

Axis Powers the name for the alliance formed by Germany, Italy, and Japan during World War II (p. 89)
Potencias del Eje nombre de la alianza formada por Alemania, Italia y Japón durante la Segunda Guerra Mundial (pág. 89)

Bolsheviks a radical Russian Communist group that seized power in 1917 (p. 201)
bolcheviques grupo comunista ruso radical que obtuvo el poder en 1917 (pág. 201)

canton one of 26 districts in the republic of Switzerland (p. 145)
cantón uno de los 26 distritos de la república de Suiza (pág. 145)

capitalism an economic system in which individuals and private businesses run most industries (p. 72)
capitalismo sistema económico en el que los individuos y las empresas privadas controlan la mayoría de las industrias (pág. 72)

Catholic Reformation the effort of the late 1500s and 1600s to reform the Catholic Church from within; also called the Counter-Reformation (p. 53)
Reforma católica iniciativa para reformar la Iglesia católica desde dentro a finales del siglo XVI y en el XVII; también conocida como la Contrarreforma (pág. 53)

chancellor a German prime minister (p. 143)
canciller primer ministro alemán (pág. 143)

circumnavigate to go all the way around (p. 59)
circunnavegar dar una vuelta completa (pág. 59)

citizen a person who has the right to take part in government (p. 23)
ciudadano persona que tiene el derecho de participar en el gobierno (pág. 23)

city-state a political unit consisting of a city and its surrounding countryside (p. 14)
ciudad estado unidad política formada por una ciudad y los campos que la rodean (pág. 14)

Cold War a period of distrust between the United States and Soviet Union after World War II, when there was a tense rivalry between the two superpowers but no direct fighting (p. 92)
Guerra Fría período de desconfianza entre Estados Unidos y la Unión Soviética que siguió a la Segunda Guerra Mundial; existía una rivalidad tensa entre las dos superpotencias, pero no se llegó a la lucha directa (pág. 92)

common market a group of nations that cooperates to make trade among members easier (p. 96)
mercado común grupo de naciones que cooperan para facilitar el comercio entre los miembros (pág. 96)

Commonwealth of Independent States (CIS) a union of former Soviet republics that meets about issues such as trade and immigration (p. 182)
Comunidad de Estados Independientes (CEI) unión de ex repúblicas soviéticas que se reúne para tratar temas como el comercio y la inmigración (pág. 182)

Communism an economic and political system in which the government owns all businesses and controls the economy (p. 84)
comunismo sistema económico y político en el que el gobierno es dueño de todos los negocios y controla la economía (pág. 84)

constitutional monarchy a type of democracy in which a monarch serves as head of state, but a legislature makes the laws (p. 158)

monarquía constitucional tipo de democracia en la cual un monarca sirve como jefe de estado, pero una asamblea legislativa hace las leyes (pág. 158)

cosmopolitan characterized by many foreign influences (p. 137)
cosmopolita caracterizado por muchas influencias extranjeras (pág. 137)

Crusades a long series of wars between Christians and Muslims in Southwest Asia fought for control of the Holy Land; took place from 1096 to 1291 (p. 33)
cruzadas larga serie de guerras entre cristianos y musulmanes en el suroeste de Asia para conseguir el control de la Tierra Santa; tuvieron lugar entre 1096 y 1291 (pág. 33)

Cyrillic (suh-RIHL-ihk) a form of the Greek alphabet (p. 200)
cirílico forma del alfabeto griego (pág. 200)

czar (ZAHR) a Russian emperor (p. 201)
zar emperador ruso (pág. 201)

dachas Russian country houses (p. 207)
dachas casas de campo rusas (pág. 207)

Declaration of Independence a document written in 1776 that declared the American colonies' independence from British rule (p. 65)
Declaración de Independencia documento escrito en 1776 que declaró la independencia de las colonias de América del Norte del dominio británico (pág. 65)

Declaration of the Rights of Man and of the Citizen a document written in France in 1789 that guaranteed specific freedoms for French citizens (p. 66)
Declaración de los Derechos del Hombre y del Ciudadano documento escrito en Francia en 1789 que garantizaba libertades específicas para los ciudadanos franceses (pág. 66)

dictator a ruler who has almost absolute power (p. 87)
dictador gobernante que tiene poder casi absoluto (pág. 87)

disarm to give up all weapons (p. 159)
desarmarse renunciar a todas las armas (pág. 159)

E

empire land with different territories and peoples under a single rule (p. 24)
imperio zona con distintos territorios y grupos de personas bajo un mismo gobierno (pág. 24)

English Bill of Rights a document approved in 1689 that listed rights for Parliament and the English people and drew on the principles of Magna Carta (p. 64)

Declaración de Derechos inglesa documento aprobado en 1689 que enumeraba los derechos del Parlamento y del pueblo de Inglaterra, inspirada en los principios de la Carta Magna (pág. 64)

Enlightenment a period during the 1600s and 1700s when reason was used to guide people's thoughts about society, politics, and philosophy (p. 62)

Ilustración período durante los siglos XVII y XVIII en el que la razón guiaba las ideas de las personas acerca de la sociedad, la política y la filosofía (pág. 62)

ethnic cleansing the effort to remove all members of an ethnic group from a country or region (p. 186)

limpieza étnica esfuerzo por eliminar a todos los miembros de un grupo étnico de un país o región (pág. 186)

European Union (EU) an organization that promotes political and economic cooperation in Europe (p. 96)

Unión Europea (UE) organización que promueve la cooperación política y económica en Europa (pág. 96)

feudal system the system of obligations that governed the relationships between lords and vassals in medieval Europe (p. 35)

sistema feudal sistema de obligaciones que gobernaba las relaciones entre los señores feudales y los vasallos en la Europa medieval (pág. 35)

fjord (fyawrd) a narrow inlet of the sea set between high, rocky cliffs (p. 153)

fiordo entrada estrecha del mar entre acantilados altos y rocosos (pág. 153)

G

geothermal energy energy produced from the heat of Earth's interior (p. 154)

energía geotérmica energía producida a partir del calor del interior de la Tierra (pág. 154)

geyser a spring that shoots hot water and steam into the air (p. 166)

géiser manantial que lanza agua caliente y vapor al aire (pág. 166)

golden age a period in a society's history marked by great achievements (p. 16)

edad dorada período de la historia de una sociedad marcado por grandes logros (pág. 16)

Gothic architecture a style of architecture in Europe known for its high pointed ceilings, tall towers, and stained glass windows (p. 34)

arquitectura gótica estilo de arquitectura europea que se conoce por los techos altos en punta, las torres altas y los vitrales de colores (pág. 34)

Great Depression a global economic crisis that struck countries around the world in the 1930s (p. 86)

Gran Depresión crisis económica global que afectó a países de todo el mundo en la década de 1930 (pág. 86)

gulag a soviet labor camp (p. 202)

gulag campo soviético de trabajos forzados (pág. 202)

 H

Hellenistic Greek-like; heavily influenced by Greek ideas (p. 20)

helenístico al estilo griego; muy influenciado por las ideas de la Grecia clásica (pág. 20)

Holocaust the Nazis' effort to wipe out the Jewish people in World War II, when 6 million Jews throughout Europe were killed (p. 89)

Holocausto intento de los nazis de eliminar al pueblo judío durante la Segunda Guerra Mundial, en el que se mató a 6 millones de judíos en toda Europa (pág. 89)

humanism the study of history, literature, public speaking, and art that led to a new way of thinking in Europe in the late 1300s (p. 49)

humanismo estudio de la historia, la literatura, la oratoria y el arte que produjo una nueva forma de pensar en Europa a finales del siglo XIV (pág. 49)

 I

Industrial Revolution the period of rapid growth in machine-made goods that changed the way people across Europe worked and lived; it began in Britain in the 1700s (p. 70)

Revolución Industrial período de rápido aumento de los bienes producidos con máquinas que cambió la forma de vivir y trabajar en toda Europa; comenzó en Gran Bretaña a comienzos del siglo XVIII (pág. 70)

infrastructure the set of resources, like roads and factories, that a country needs to support economic activities (p. 179)

infraestructura conjunto de recursos, como carreteras o fábricas, que necesita un país para sostener su actividad económica (pág. 179)

ENGLISH AND SPANISH GLOSSARY

manor a large estate owned by a knight or lord (p. 36)

> **feudo** gran finca perteneciente a un caballero o señor feudal (pág. 36)

Mediterranean climate the type of climate found across Southern Europe; it features warm and sunny summer days, mild evenings, and cooler, rainy winters (p. 106)

> **clima mediterráneo** tipo de clima de todo el sur europeo; se caracteriza por días de verano cálidos y soleados, noches templadas e inviernos lluviosos y más frescos (pág. 106)

Magna Carta a document signed in 1215 by King John of England that required the king to honor certain rights (pág. 158)

> **Carta Magna** documento firmado por el rey Juan de Inglaterra en 1215 que exigía que el rey respetara ciertos derechos (pág. 158)

Middle Ages a period that lasted from about 500 to 1500 in Europe (p. 32)

> **Edad Media** período que duró aproximadamente desde el año 500 hasta el 1500 en Europa (pág. 32)

N

nationalism a devotion and loyalty to one's country; develops among people with a common language, religion, or history (p. 80)

> **nacionalismo** sentimiento de lealtad al país de uno; se desarrolla entre personas con un idioma, religión o historia en común (pág. 80)

nation-state a country united under a single strong government; made up of people with a common cultural background (p. 39)

> **nación-estado** país unido bajo un solo gobierno fuerte; formado de personas con una cultura común (pág. 39)

navigable river a river that is deep and wide enough for ships to use (p. 130)

> **río navegable** río que tiene la profundidad y el ancho necesarios para que pasen los barcos (pág. 130)

neutral not taking sides in an international conflict (p. 164)

> **neutral** que no toma partido en un conflicto internacional (pág. 164)

New World a term used by Europeans to describe the Americas after the voyages of Christopher Columbus; the Americas were a "New World" to Europeans, who did not know they existed until Columbus's voyages (p. 59)

> **Nuevo Mundo** término usado por los europeos para describir las Américas tras los viajes de Cristóbal Colón; las Américas eran un "Nuevo Mundo" para los europeos, que no sabían de su existencia hasta los viajes de Colón (pág. 59)

North Atlantic Drift a warm ocean current that brings warm, moist air across the Atlantic Ocean to Northern Europe (p. 154)

> **Corriente del Atlántico Norte** corriente oceánica cálida que trae aire cálido y húmedo a través del océano Atlántico al norte de Europa (pág. 154)

O

Orthodox Church a branch of Christianity that dates to the Byzantine Empire (p. 111)

> **Iglesia ortodoxa** rama del cristianismo que data del Imperio bizantino (pág. 111)

P

parliamentary monarchy a type of government in which a king shares power with an elected parliament and a prime minister (p. 122)

> **monarquía parlamentaria** tipo de gobierno en el que un rey rige conjuntamente con un parlamento elegido por votación y un primer ministro (pág. 122)

pope the spiritual head of the Roman Catholic Church (pp. 33, 116)

> **papa** jefe espiritual de la Iglesia Católica Romana (pág. 33, 116)

Protestant a Christian who protested against the Catholic Church (p. 53)

> **protestante** cristiano que protestaba en contra de la Iglesia católica (pág. 53)

R

Reformation (re-fuhr-MAY-shuhn) a reform movement against the Roman Catholic Church that began in 1517; it resulted in the creation of Protestant churches (p. 52)

> **Reforma** movimiento de reforma contra la Iglesia Católica Romana que comenzó en 1517; resultó en la creación de las iglesias protestantes (pág. 52)

Reign of Terror a bloody period of the French Revolution during which the government executed thousands of its opponents and others at the guillotine (p. 66)

  Reino del Terror período sangriento de la Revolución Francesa durante el cual el gobierno ejecutó a miles de personas, oponentes y otros, en la guillotina (pág. 66)

Renaissance (REN-uh-sahns) the period of "rebirth" and creativity that followed Europe's Middle Ages (p. 48)

  Renacimiento período de "volver a nacer" y creatividad que siguió a la Edad Media en Europa (pág. 48)

republic a political system in which people elect leaders to govern them (p. 23)

  república sistema politico en el que el pueblo elige a los líderes que lo gobernarán (pág. 23)

Scientific Revolution a series of events that led to the birth of modern science; it lasted from about 1540 to 1700 (p. 55)

  Revolución Científica serie de sucesos que produjeron el nacimiento de la ciencia moderna; duró desde alrededor de 1540 hasta 1700 (pág. 55)

Senate a council of rich and powerful Romans who helped run the city (p. 23)

  Senado consejo de romanos ricos y poderosos que ayudaban a dirigir la ciudad (pág. 23)

smelters factories that process metal ores (p. 209)

  fundiciones fábricas que tratan menas de metal (pág. 209)

suffragettes women who campaigned to gain the right to vote (p. 74)

  sufragistas mujeres que hicieron campaña para obtener el derecho a votar (pág. 74)

superpower a strong and influential country (p. 92)

  superpotencia país poderoso e influyente (pág. 92)

taiga (TY-guh) a forest of mainly evergreen trees covering much of Russia (p. 199)

  taiga bosque de árboles de hoja perenne principalmente que cubre gran parte de Rusia (pág. 199)

textile a cloth product (p. 72)

  textil producto de tela (pág. 72)

Trans-Siberian Railroad a rail line in Russia that extends about 5,800 miles (9,330 km) from Moscow to Vladivostok; it is the longest single rail line in the world (p. 209)

  Ferrocarril Transiberiano línea de ferrocarril rusa de 5,800 millas (9,330 km) de largo, desde Moscú hasta Vladivostok; es la vía de ferrocarril más larga del mundo (pág. 209)

Treaty of Versailles the final peace settlement of World War I (p. 83)

  Tratado de Versalles acuerdo de paz final de la Primera Guerra Mundial (pág. 83)

trench warfare a style of fighting common in World War I in which each side fights from deep ditches, or trenches, dug into the ground (p. 82)

  guerra de trincheras forma de guerra comúnmente usada en la Primera Guerra Mundial, en la cual ambos bandos luchan desde profundas zanjas, o trincheras, cavadas en el suelo (pág. 82)

uninhabitable unable to support human settlement (p. 165)

  inhabitable que no puede sustentar asentamientos humanos (pág. 165)

Vikings Scandinavian warriors who raided Europe in the early Middle Ages (p. 162)

  vikingos guerreros escandinavos que atacaron Europa al principio de la Edad Media (pág. 162)

Index

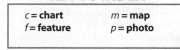

1487–1580, 58–59m; voyages around world, 58–59; voyages to America, 58–59; voyages to the East, 57–58

factory: factory system, 72; Industrial Revolution, 72; textile industry, 72
fados, 121
famine, 157
farming. *See* agriculture
Federal Republic of Germany, 93
Ferdinand, Archduke Francis, 81
feudal system, 35; end of, 39
Finland, 165. *See also* Scandinavia; after World War I, 84; climate of, 154, 155; in European Union, 96c; facts about, 8c; history of, 162–63; per capita GDP, 164c; physical geography of, 152–53, 153m; trade, 165
First Estate, 65
fishing: Iceland, 165; Norway, 165
five themes of geography, H12–H13
fjord, 153, 153p, 154p, 165
flamenco, 121
Flanders, 137
flat-plane projection, H5
Florence, 118; Renaissance and, 48–49, 49p
food/eating habits: Baltic Republics and Poland, 178; France, 134; Greece, 111; Italy, 116
forests: Chernobyl and, 175; defined, H10; in Northern Europe, 154; Russia and the Caucasus, 198p, 199; taiga, 198p, 199
forum: Roman Republic, 23, 23f
France, 132–136; agriculture, 135; Central Uplands, 129, 129m; Charlemagne, 132, 133p; climate, 130; colonization in Americas, 61; culture of, 134–35; customs, 134; in European Union, 96, 96c; facts about, 8c; formation of nation-state, 39; French Republic, 66; French Revolution, 65–66, 65p, 133; Great Fear, 66; history of, 132–33, 133c; Hundred Years' War, 39, 133; ideas and arts, 134–35; language and religion of, 134; mountains in, 130; Napoleon Bonaparte, 67–68, 133; Napoleonic Code, 67; Napoleonic Empire, 1812, 67m; National Assembly, 66; Northern European Plain, 128, 129m; Paris, 134–35f; Reign of Terror, 66; social classes in, 65; today, 135–36; tourism, 136; in World War I, 81–83, 133; in World War II, 88–91, 133
Franks, 132
French Republic, 66
French Revolution, 47m, 65–66, 65p, 66p, 133

Gaelic, 158
Galician, 120
Galileo, 55
Gama, Vasco da, 58
Garibaldi, Giuseppe, 115c, 115p
Gaul, 132
Genoa, 117
Geographic Dictionary, H10–H11
Geography and History: The Black Death, 40–41f; The European Union, 138–39f; Roman Roads, 30–31f
Geography and Map Skills Handbook: Geographic Dictionary, H10–H11; Geography Themes and Elements, H12–H13; Map Essentials, H6–H7; Mapmaking, H4–H5; Mapping the Earth, H2–H3; Working with Maps, H8–H9
Geography Skills: Interpreting a Historical Map, 42; Interpreting a Population Map, 205; Reading a Climate Map, 108
Georgia, 213; climate of, 199; economy of, 213; facts about, 9c; history of, 212
geothermal energy, 154; in Iceland, 166, 166p
German Democratic Republic, 93
Germania, 140
Germany, 140–144; arts, 142; Central Uplands, 129, 129m; cities in, 144; culture, 142–43, 142–43f; customs, 142; division of, after World War II, 93, 141; economy of, 143–44; in European Union, 96, 96c; facts about, 9c; fall of communism, 94, 141; government, 143; growth of nation, 140; history of, 140–41; Hitler, 87–90, 141; Holocaust, 89–90, 141; Holy Roman Empire, 140; industry and agriculture, 143; language, 142; Nazi Party, 87, 141; peace agreement after World War I, 83; people of, 142; political map of, 141m; population, 142, 143c; Reformation, 52–53; religion, 142; reunification, 94–95, 141; rise of Hitler before World War I, 87; science, 142; today, 143–44; transportation, 144; in World War I, 81–83, 141; in World War II, 88–91, 141
geysers, 166, 166p
glaciers: defined, H11; Northern Europe and, 153; in Swiss Alps, 130p
globe, H2
Goethe, Johann Wolfgang von, 142
gold: Spanish colonization in Americas and, 60
golden age, 16; of ancient Greece, 16–19
Gorbachev, Mikhail, 94, 202
Gothic architecture, 34, 34p

government: Austria, 144; Benelux countries, 136; British Isles, 158; chancellor, 143; city-state in ancient Greece, 14–15; communism in Russia after World War I, 84; constitutional monarchy, 158; democracy in ancient Greece, 18; Enlightenment and, 63; Germany, 143; Greece, 110; Inland Eastern Europe, 182; Ireland, 158; Magna Carta in England, 38; nation-state, 39; parliamentary monarchy, 122; problems in Roman Empire government, 28–29; rise of dictators before World War I, 87; Roman government as model for United States, 26; Roman Republic, 23–24; Russia, 206; Spain, 122; Switzerland, 145; United Kingdom, 158
graphs. *See* charts and graphs
Great Britain. *See also* British Isles; England: Churchill and, 157; Industrial Revolution, 71–72, 73f; Napoleon's defeat, 67–68; suffragettes, 74, 74p; in World War I, 81–83; in World War II, 88–91, 157
Great Depression, 86, 158
Great Fear, 66
Great Hungarian Plain, 173, 173m
Greece: agriculture, 112, 113; Byzantine Empire, 110; climate and resources of, 106–7; culture, 111; customs, 111; economy of, 113; in European Union, 96c; facts about, 9c; government of, 110; history of, 109–10; independent, 110; language, 111; Orthodox Church, 111, 111p; Ottoman Turks, 110; Per Capita GDP of Greece, 1999–2004, 113c; physical geography of, 104–6, 105m; religion, 111; resources, 113; Roman Empire, 110; shipping, 113; today, 112–13; tourism, 113; urban and rural, 112
Ancient Greece, 14–21; acropolis, 15; Alexander the Great's Empire, c. 323 BC, 20–21m; architecture, 16–17f, 18–19, 109, 110; art, 12p, 17–19, 19p, 109; Athenian culture, 17; Athenian democracy, 18; city-states, 14–15; culture of, 14–15; decline of city-states, 19; empire of Alexander, 20–21m; golden age of Greece, 16–19; Greek City-States and Colonies, c. 600 BC, 15m; growth of Greek power, 16–17; HISTORY Multimedia Connections, 45 MC1–45 MC2; mathematics, 110; Parthenon, 16–17f; science, philosophy and literature, 19; victory over Persians, 16–17; voting, 14, 18
Greenland, 152, 165; independence of, 163
grid, H2
gulags, 202
gulf: defined, H10
Gutenberg, Johann, 51

Credits and Acknowledgments

HISTORY Unless otherwise indicated below, all video reference screens are © 2010 A&E Television Networks, LLC. All rights reserved.

For permission to reproduce copyrighted material, grateful acknowledgment is made to the following sources:

Doubleday, a division of Random House, Inc.: From *The Diary of a Young Girl, The Definitive Edition* by Anne Frank, edited by Otto H. Frank and Mirjam Pressler, translated by Susan Massotty. Copyright © 1995 by Doubleday, a division of Random House, Inc.

HarperCollins Publishers: The Endless Steppe by Esther Hautzig. Copyright © 1968 by Esther Hautzig.

Lonely Planet: From "Hungary" from the *Lonely Planet WorldGuide Online* Web site. Copyright © 2005 by Lonely Planet. Accessed at http://www.lonelyplanet.com/worldguide/ destinations/europe/hungary/.

Estate of Erich Maria Remarque: From *All Quiet on the Western Front* by Erich Maria Remarque. Copyright 1929, 1930 by Little, Brown and Company; copyright renewed © 1957, 1958 by Erich Maria Remarque. All rights reserved. "Im Westen Nichts Neues" copyright 1928 by Ullstein A. G.; copyright renewed © 1956 by Erich Maria Remarque.

Sources used by The World Almanac® for charts and graphs:

Geographical Extremes: Europe and Russia: *The World Almanac and Book of Facts, 2005; The World Factbook, 2005;* U.S. Bureau of the Census; Europe and Russia: The World Factbook, 2005; U.S. Bureau of the Census, International Database; United Nations Statistical Yearbook; World's Highest Per Capita GDPs: *The World Factbook, 2005;* Densely Populated Countries in Europe: *The World Factbook, 2005;* U.S. Bureau of the Census, International Database; The European Union: European Union, International Programs Center; U.S. Bureau of the Census, International Database; Per Capita GDP of Greece: *The World Factbook, 2005;* Scandinavia's Per Capita GDP: *The World Factbook, 2005;* U.S. Bureau of the Census, International Database; United Nations Statistical Yearbook; Major Religions in the Balkans: World Christian Database; Russia's Population Decline: U.S. Census Bureau, International Programs Center; State Statistical Committee of Russia

Illustrations and Photo Credits

Cover: (l), Rubberball Productions/Getty Images; (r), Harald Sund/Getty Images.

Front Matter: iv (b), Christopher Groenhout/ Lonely Planet Images; v (tr), The Granger Collection, New York; v (b), Bettmann/Corbis; vi (tl), Charles O'Rear/Corbis; vii (br), Kurt Scholz/ SuperStock; viii (br), WorldSat; H16 (t), Earth Satellite Corporation/Photo Researchers, Inc.; H16 (tc), Frans Lemmens/Getty Images; H16 (c), London Aerial Photo Library/Corbis; H16 (bc), Harvey Schwartz/Index Stock Imagery/ Fotosearch; H16 (b), Tom Nebbia/Corbis.

Introduction: A, Peter Turnley/Corbis; B (bkgd), Planetary Visions; B (bc), SIME, s.a.s./eStock Photo; B (t), Travel Ink/Getty Images; 1 (tl), blickwinkel/Alamy.

Chapter 1: 12 (br), HIP/Art Resource, NY; 13 (tr), 2010 A&E Television Networks, LLC. All rights reserved; 13 (br), Guglielmo De Micheli/Time Life Pictures/Getty Images; 13 (bl), Christopher Groenhout/Lonely Planet Images; 18 (cl), Gjon Mill/Time & Life Pictures/Getty Images; 19 (br), Alinari/Art Resource, NY; 26 (cl), Comstock/ Jupiter Images; 28 (tr), Richard T. Nowitz/National Geographic Image Collection; 31 (br), SEF/Art Resource, NY; 34 (tl), John Lamb/Getty Images; 38 (tl), Dept. of the Environment, London, UK/ Bridgeman Art Library; 43 (tc), Jupiter Images; 43 (tl), Alinari/Art Resource, NY; 45 MC1-MC2, GoodShoot/Jupiter Images/Getty Images.

Chapter 2: 46 (br), AKG-Images; 47 (tr), 2010 A&E Television Networks, LLC. All rights reserved; 47 (br), Ali Meyer/Corbis; 47 (bl), The Granger Collection, New York; 49 (bl), age fotostock/ SuperStock; 49 (br), Yann Arthus-Bertrand/ Corbis; 50 (tr), Giraudon/Art Resource, NY; 50 (tl), Rabatti-Domingie/AKG-Images; 51 (br), Bettmann/Corbis; 51 (tr), The Granger Collection, New York; 51 (cl), The Granger Collection, New York; 51 (cl), Historical Picture Archive/Corbis; 51 (tl), National Portrait Gallery/ SuperStock; 54 (br), HIP/Art Resource, NY; 55 (bl), Réunion des Musées Nationaux/Art Resource, NY; 55 (tr), Royal Society, London, UK/Bridgeman Art Library; 61 (tr), Archivo Iconografico, S.A./ Corbis; 63 (t), Rèunion des Musèes Nationaux/ Art Resource, NY; 64 (br), Custody of the House of Lords Record Office/Parliamentary Archives; 64 (cl), The Granger Collection, New York; 64 (bl), Dept. of the Environment, London, UK/ Bridgeman Art Library; 64 (cl), Bettmann/Corbis; 65 (br), Document conserve au Centre Historique des Archives Nationales a Paris/Centre Historique des Archives Nationales (CHAN); 65 (cl), Réunion des Musées Nationaux/Art Resource, NY; 65 (bl), Joseph Sohm/Visions of America/Corbis; 65 (cl), Bettmann/Corbis; 66 (bl), Gianni Dagli Orti/ Corbis, 67 (t), Erich Lessing/Art Resource, NY; 71 (br), Hulton Archive/Getty Images; 71 (bl), The Granger Collection, New York; 74 (tl), Hulton Archive/Getty Images; 75 (cr), Gianni Dagli Orti/ Corbis; 75 (cl), HIP/Art Resource, NY; 75 (tl), Rabatti-Dominigie/AKG-Images.

Chapter 3: 78, (br), Hulton Archive/Getty Images; 79 (tr), 2010 A&E Television Networks, LLC. All rights reserved; 79 (br), Thomas Kienzle/AP/Wide World Photos; 79 (bl), Hugo Jaeger/Timepix/Time Life Pictures/Getty Images; 84 (tl), The Granger Collection, New York; 85 (tr), Hulton Archive/ Getty Images; 87 (br), Hulton-Deutsch Collection/ Corbis; 87 (b), The Granger Collection, New York; 89 (br), AKG-Images; 90 (tr), Hulton Archive/ Getty Images; 90 (cl), Hulton-Deutsch Collection/ Corbis; 90 (cl), Hulton Archive/Getty Images; 91 (tl), Bettmann/Corbis; 91 (tr), Margaret Bourke-White/Time Life Pictures/Getty Images; 91 (tc), Bettmann/Corbis; 94 (bl), Peter Turnley/Corbis; 95 (tr), David Turnley/Corbis; 95 (tl), Robert Maas/Corbis; 97 (tr), Alain Nogues/Corbis; 98 (c), Library of Congress; 99 (bl), Robert Maas/Corbis; 99 (cl), Hulton-Deutsch Collection/Corbis; 100 (bl), *The Tide Comes In*, 1944, by John Collins. M965.199.4595. McCord Museum of Canadian History, Montreal; 101 MC1-MC2, Bettmann/ Corbis.

Chapter 4: 102 (br), Richard Klune/Corbis; 103 (tr), 2010 A&E Television Networks, LLC. All rights reserved; 103 (bl), Carlos Cazalis/Corbis; 103 (br), Digital Vision/Robert Harding; 105 (br), Dmitry Kovyazin/Alamy; 106 (cl), Jeremy Lightfoot/ Robert Harding; 106 (tl), Charles O'Rear/Corbis; 107 (tr), SIME s.a.s./eStock Photo; 107 (cl), IT Stock Free/eStock Photo; 109, Erich Lessing/Art Resource, NY; 110 (cl), Vega/Taxi/Getty Images;

111 (b), Roberto Meazza/IML Image Group; 112 (cl), Sylvain Grandadam/Robert Harding; 112 (cr), Mark Henley/Photolibrary; 115 (tc), Gianni Dagli Orti/Corbis; 115 (tr), Bildarchiv Preussischer Kulturbesitz/Art Resource, NY; 116(br), Giuseppe Cacace/Getty Images; 117 (br), Martin Moos/ Lonely Planet Images; 117 (bl), Steve Vidler/ SuperStock; 118 (tl), WorldSat; 119 (b), Digital Vision/Getty Images; 120 (tr), AFP/Getty Images; 121 (br), Latin Focus/HRW; 122 (tl), Nigel Francis Photography; 123 (tr), Latin Focus/HRW; 123 (tc), Steve Vidler/SuperStock; 123 (tl), Roberto Meazza/ IML Image Group.

Chapter 5: 126 (br), William Manning/Corbis; 127 (br), Elfi Kluck/Index Stock Imagery/PictureQuest/ Jupiter Images; 127 (bl), Brian Lawrence/Image State; 129 (br), Chad Ehlers/Alamy; 130 (cl), WorldSat; 133 (br), Corbis; 133 (tr), SuperStock; 133 (cl), Vince Streano/Corbis; 136 (tl), Goos van der Veen/Hollandse Hoogte/ Pictures; 138 (br), PhotoDisc Collection/Getty Images; 139 (br), AFP/Getty Images; 141 Walter Bibikow/Taxi/ Getty Images; 142 (tl), SuperStock RF/Superstock; 142-143 (tc), Sean Gallup/Getty Images; 143 (tr), Sean Gallup/Getty Images; 144 (br), Free Agents Limited/Corbis; 144 (bl), Ray Juno/Corbis; 147 (tl), Vince Streano/Corbis; 147 (tr), SuperStock RF/Superstock.

Chapter 6: 150 (br), Paul Harris/Stone/Getty Images; 151 (tr), 2010 A&E Television Networks, LLC. All rights reserved; 151 (br), Fredrik Naumann/Samfoto; 151 (bl), Steve Vidler/Image State; 153 (tr), Stefan Auth/Photolibrary; 154 (cl), WorldSat; 155 (tr), Espen Bratlie/Samfoto; 156 (cl), National Portrait Gallery/SuperStock; 156 (b), Steve Vidler/Image State; 157 (br), Hulton-Deutsch Collection/Corbis; 157 (bl), Hulton Archive/Getty Images; 157 (tr), Time Life Images/Getty Images; 158 (bl), SuperStock; 160 (tl), Michael Duerinckx/Image State; 164 (b), Jon Arnold/DanitaDelimont.com; 165 (cl), Dave Houser/Image State; 166 (tl), Hans Strand/ Corbis; 166 (tr), Hans Strand/Corbis; 167 (tr), Jon Arnold/DanitaDelimont.com; 167 (tc), Michael Duerinckx/Image State; 167 (tl), Stefan Auth/ Photolibrary.

Chapter 7: 170 (br), Gregory Wrona/Alamy; 171 (tr), 2010 A&E Television Networks, LLC. All rights reserved; 171 (bl), Adam Woolfitt/Corbis; 171 (br), Paul Springett 09/Alamy; 173 (br), M. ou Me. Desjeux, Bernard/Corbis; 173 (cl), Liba Taylor/Corbis; 174 (bl), Fred Bruemmer/ Photolibrary; 175 (tl), Reuters/Corbis; 177 (cl), Bettmann/Corbis; 178 (bl), Wally McNamee/ Corbis; 179 (tr), Jon Arnold/DanitaDelimont. com; 181 (cl), John Farrar; 181 (br), Age Fotostock/SuperStock; 185 (b), Ethel Davies/ Image State; 186 (bl), Barry Lewis/Corbis; 187 (t), AP Photo/Amel Emric; 188 (bl), David Turnley/ Corbis; 191 (tr), David Turnley/Corbis; 191 (tl), Jon Arnold/DanitaDelimont.com.

Chapter 8: 194 (br), Michael Yamashita/Corbis; 195 (tr), 2010 A&E Television Networks, LLC. All rights reserved; 195 (bl), Robbie Jack/Corbis; 195 (br), Steve Vidler/Image State; 197 Mikhail V. Propp/Peter Arnold Images/Photolibrary; 198 (cl), Maxim Marmur/Getty Images; 198 (bl), Oxford Scientific/PictureQuest/Jupiter Images; 203, Kurt Scholz/SuperStock; 204 (tl), The Granger Collection, New York; 208 (cl), Maria Stenzel/ National Geographic Image Collection; 208 (tl), Yogi, Inc./Corbis; 208 (cl), Harald Sund/The Image Bank/Getty Images; 211 (tr), Time Life Pictures/ Getty Images; 213 (tl), Marc Garanger/Corbis; 214 (tl), Jeremy Horner/Corbis; 215 (tr), Marc Garanger/Corbis; 215 (tc), Kurt Scholz/SuperStock; 215 (tl), Maxim Marmur/Getty Images.

Staff Credits

The people who contributed to **Holt McDougal: Europe and Russia** are listed below. They represent editorial, design, production, emedia, and permissions.

Melanie Baccus, Angela Beckmann, Julie Beckman-Key, Genick Blaise, Ed Blake, Jennifer Campbell, Henry Clark, Grant Davidson, Nina Degollado, Rose Degollado, Christine Devall, Michelle Dike, Lydia Doty, Chase Edmond, Mescal Evler, Susan Franques, Stephanie Friedman, Bob Fullilove, Matthew Gierhart, Bill Gillis, Ann Gorbett, Janet Harrington, Betsy Harris, Wendy Hodge, Tim Hovde, Cathy Jenevein, Carrie Jones, Kadonna Knape, Laura Lasley, Sarah Lee, Sean McCormick, Joe Melomo, Richard Metzger, Andrew Miles, Debra O'Shields, Jarred Prejean, Paul Provence, Shelly Ramos, Curtis Riker, Michelle Rimsa, Michael Rinella, Jennifer Rockwood, Carole Rollins, Beth Sample, Annette Saunders, Jenny Schaeffer, Kay Selke, Chris Smith, Jeremy Strykul, Jeannie Taylor, Terri Taylor, Joni Wackwitz, Mary Wages, Diana Holman Walker, Nadyne Wood, Robin Zaback

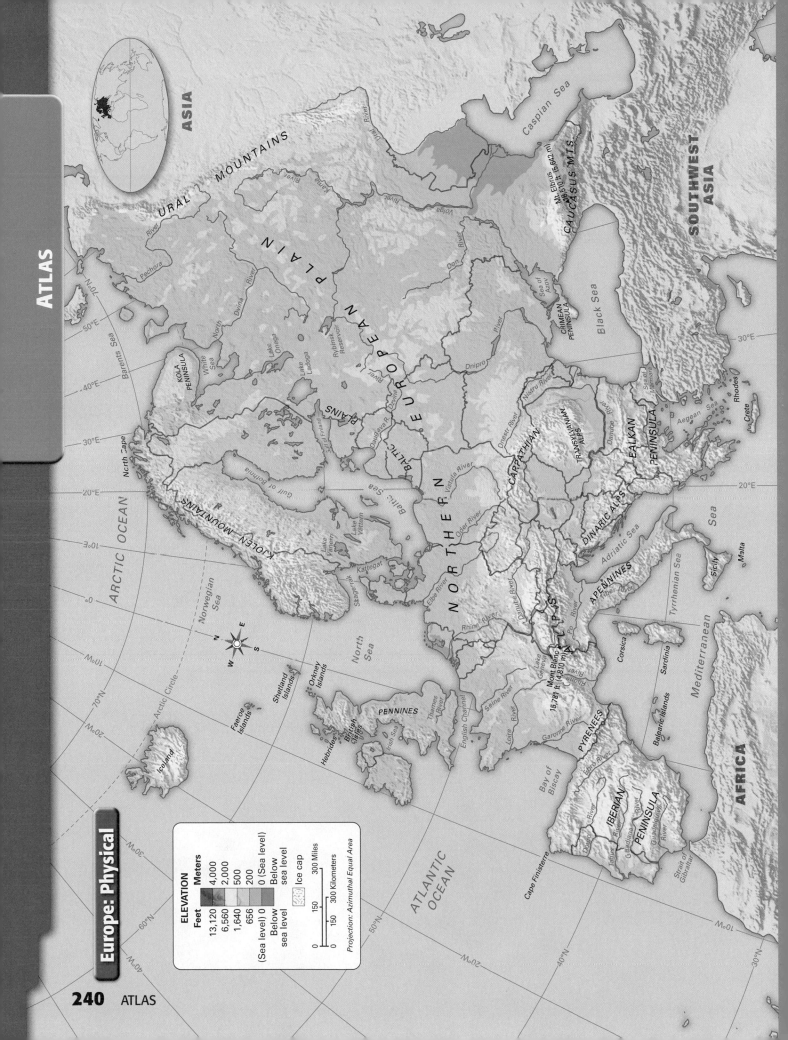

ASIA

SOUTHWEST
ASIA

AFRICA

URAL MOUNTAINS

River

Pechora

Kama River

Volga River

Ob River

Ural River

Caspian Sea

Mt. Elbrus (5,642 m)
18,510 ft
CAUCASUS MTS.

NORTHERN EUROPEAN PLAIN

Don River

Dnipro River

Sea of Azov

Black Sea

CRIMEAN PENINSULA

Rybinsk Reservoir

Lake Onega

Lake Ladoga

KOLA PENINSULA

White Sea

North Dvina River

BALTIC PLAINS

Daugava R.

Gulf of Finland

Dniester River

Nistru River

CARPATHIAN

TRANSYLVANIAN ALPS

Danube River

DINARIC ALPS

BALKAN PENINSULA

Sea of Marmara

Aegean Sea

Rhodes

Crete

Barents Sea

North Cape

70°N

60°E

50°E

40°E

30°E

20°E

30°E

ARCTIC OCEAN

North Cape

Arctic Circle

KJØLEN MOUNTAINS

Norwegian Sea

Lake Vänern

Lake Vättern

Kattegat

Skagerrak

Baltic Sea

Gulf of Bothnia

Vistula River

Oder River

Elbe River

Danube River

Rhine River

ALPS

Mont Blanc 15,781 ft (4,810 m)

Lake Geneva

APENNINES

Tiber River

Po River

Adriatic Sea

Tyrrhenian Sea

Corsica

Sardinia

Sicily

Malta

Mediterranean Sea

N
E
W
S

Shetland Islands

Orkney Islands

Faeroe Islands

Iceland

Hebrides

British Isles

PENNINES

Irish Sea

North Sea

Thames River

English Channel

Seine River

Loire River

Bay of Biscay

Garonne River

PYRENEES

Ebro River

IBERIAN PENINSULA

Duero River

Tagus River

Guadiana River

Guadalquivir River

Cape Finisterre

Strait of Gibraltar

ATLANTIC OCEAN

60°N

50°N

40°N

70°N

30°W

20°W

10°W

0°

10°W

20°W

30°W

40°W

Europe: Physical

ELEVATION
Feet	Meters
13,120	4,000
6,560	2,000
1,640	500
656	200
(Sea level) 0	0 (Sea level)
Below sea level	Below sea level

Ice cap

0   150   300 Miles
0   150   300 Kilometers

Projection: Azimuthal Equal Area

South America: Political

CENTRAL AMERICA

Caribbean Sea

Barranquilla
Cartagena
Caracas

Lake Maracaibo

VENEZUELA

Georgetown
Paramaribo
Cayenne

GUYANA

SURINAME
French Guiana (FRANCE)

Medellín

Bogotá

COLOMBIA

Cali

ATLANTIC OCEAN

Malpelo Island (COLOMBIA)

Quito

ECUADOR

Guayaquil

0° Equator

Galápagos Islands (ECUADOR)

Belém

PERU

Trujillo

BRAZIL

Recife

Callao ⊙ Lima

PACIFIC OCEAN

Lake Titicaca

Arequipa

La Paz

Lake Poopó

BOLIVIA

Sucre

Brasília

Salvador

Belo Horizonte

PARAGUAY

20°S

Campinas
São Paulo

Asunción

Rio de Janeiro

Tropic of Capricorn

San Ambrosio Island (CHILE)

San Félix Island (CHILE)

Curitiba

CHILE

Pôrto Alegre

Juan Fernández Islands (CHILE)

Córdoba

Valparaíso
Santiago

Rosario

URUGUAY

30°S

Buenos Aires

Montevideo

ATLANTIC OCEAN

ARGENTINA

⊙ National capital
● Other city

0   250   500 Miles
0   250   500 Kilometers

Projection: Azimuthal Equal-Area

Strait of Magellan

Falkland Islands (U.K.)

Tierra del Fuego

South Georgia Island (U.K.)

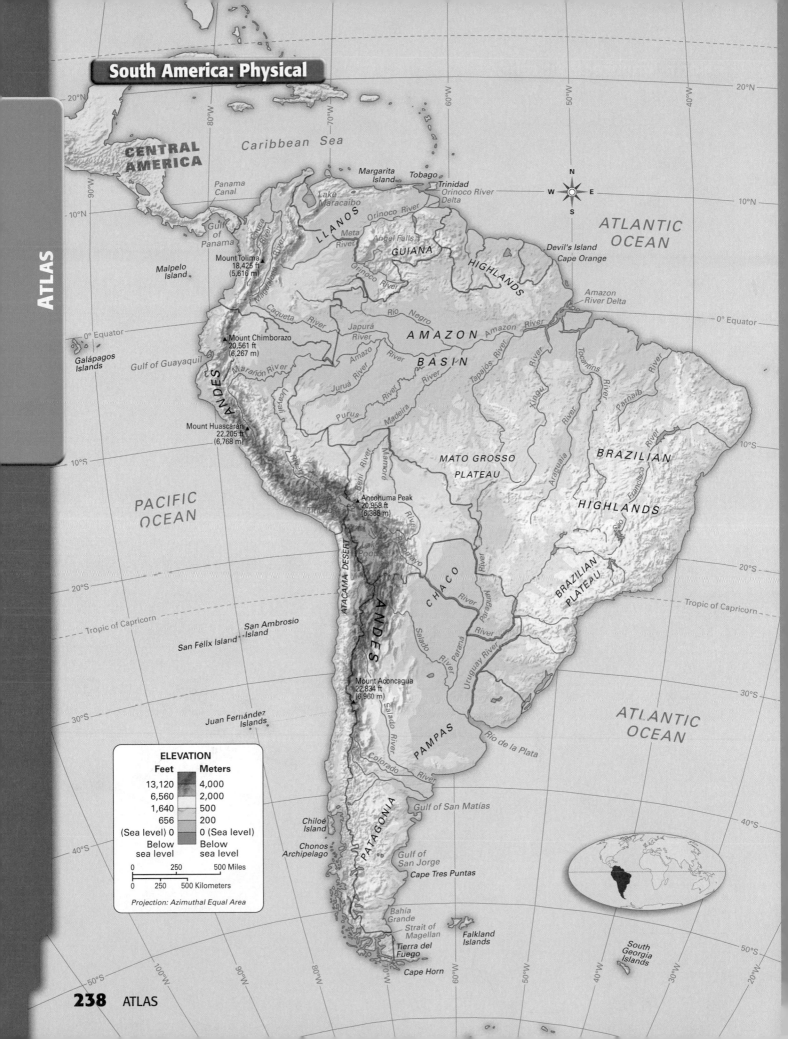

South America: Physical

CENTRAL AMERICA

Caribbean Sea

Panama Canal

Gulf of Panama

Malpelo Island

Margarita Island   Tobago
Trinidad
Lake Maracaibo   Orinoco River Delta

LLANOS
Meta River   Orinoco River
GUIANA HIGHLANDS
Angel Falls
Devil's Island
Cape Orange

Cauca River
Magdalena River
Mount Tolima 18,425 ft (5,616 m)

Orinoco River

Caquetá River
Rio Negro
Japurá River   Amazon River
AMAZON BASIN

Amazon River Delta

ATLANTIC OCEAN

Galápagos Islands

Gulf of Guayaquil

Mount Chimborazo 20,561 ft (6,267 m)

Marañón River
Amazon River
Juruá River
Ucayali River
Purus River

Madeira River
Tapajós River
Xingu River
Tocantins River
Parnaíba River

BRAZILIAN HIGHLANDS

ANDES
Mount Huascarán 22,205 ft (6,768 m)

PACIFIC OCEAN

Beni River
Mamoré River
MATO GROSSO PLATEAU
Araguaia River
São Francisco River

Ancohuma Peak 20,958 ft (6,388 m)
Lake Titicaca
Lake Poopó
Pilcomayo River

ATACAMA DESERT

CHACO
Paraguay River

BRAZILIAN PLATEAU

San Ambrosio Island
San Félix Island

Tropic of Capricorn

ANDES
Salado River
Paraná River
Uruguay River

Juan Fernández Islands

Mount Aconcagua 22,834 ft (6,960 m)
Salado River

PAMPAS
Colorado River
Rio de la Plata

ATLANTIC OCEAN

Gulf of San Matías

Chiloé Island
Chonos Archipelago
PATAGONIA
Gulf of San Jorge
Cape Tres Puntas

Bahía Grande
Strait of Magellan
Falkland Islands
Tierra del Fuego
Cape Horn

South Georgia Islands

ELEVATION

Feet	Meters
13,120	4,000
6,560	2,000
1,640	500
656	200
(Sea level) 0	0 (Sea level)
Below sea level	Below sea level

0   250   500 Miles
0   250   500 Kilometers

Projection: Azimuthal Equal Area

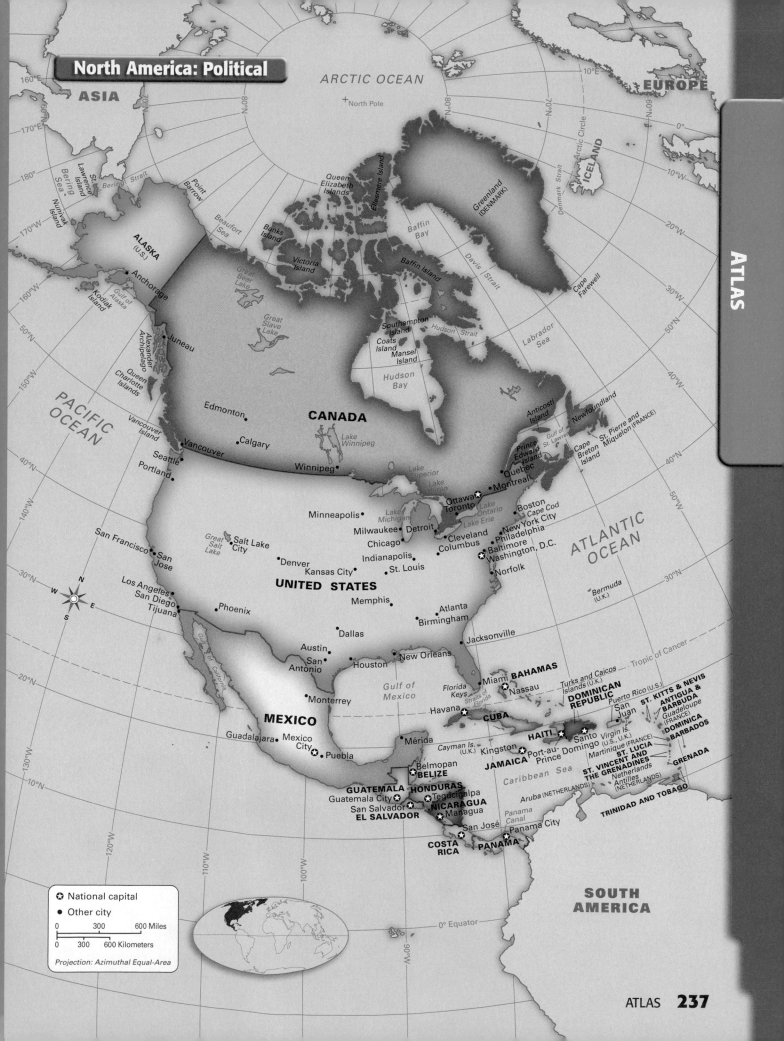

North America: Political

ASIA

ARCTIC OCEAN

+ North Pole

EUROPE

ICELAND

ATLAS

Bering
Sea

St.
Lawrence
Island

Nunivak
Island

Bering Strait

Point
Barrow

Beaufort
Sea

Banks
Island

Queen
Elizabeth
Islands

Ellesmere Island

Greenland
(DENMARK)

Arctic Circle

Denmark Strait

ALASKA
(U.S.)

Anchorage

Kodiak
Island

Gulf of
Alaska

Victoria
Island

Baffin
Bay

Davis Strait

Cape
Farewell

Great Bear
Lake

Baffin Island

Alexander
Archipelago

Juneau

Great
Slave
Lake

Southampton
Island

Coats
Island

Mansel
Island

Hudson
Strait

Labrador
Sea

Queen
Charlotte
Islands

PACIFIC
OCEAN

Vancouver
Island

Edmonton

CANADA

Hudson
Bay

Anticosti
Island

Newfoundland

Vancouver

Calgary

Lake
Winnipeg

Quebec

Gulf of
St. Lawrence

Prince
Edward
Island

Cape
Breton
Island

St. Pierre and
Miquelon (FRANCE)

Seattle

Winnipeg

Lake
Superior

Montreal

Portland

Minneapolis

Lake
Michigan

Lake
Huron

Ottawa

Toronto

Lake
Ontario

Lake Erie

Boston

Cape Cod

San Francisco

Salt Lake
City

Great
Salt
Lake

Milwaukee

Detroit

Cleveland

New York City

San
Jose

Chicago

Columbus

Philadelphia

Baltimore

ATLANTIC
OCEAN

Denver

Indianapolis

Washington, D.C.

Los Angeles

San Diego

Kansas City

St. Louis

Norfolk

UNITED STATES

Tijuana

Phoenix

Memphis

Atlanta

Bermuda
(U.K.)

Birmingham

Dallas

Jacksonville

Tropic of Cancer

Austin

San
Antonio

Houston

New Orleans

Gulf of
California

Gulf of
Mexico

Florida
Keys

Miami

BAHAMAS

Turks and Caicos
Islands (U.K.)

Puerto Rico (U.S.)

ST. KITTS & NEVIS

Nassau

DOMINICAN
REPUBLIC

San
Juan

ANTIGUA &
BARBUDA

Monterrey

Guadeloupe
(FRANCE)

MEXICO

Havana

CUBA

HAITI

Santo
Domingo

Virgin Is.
(U.S. & U.K.)

DOMINICA

Guadalajara

Mexico
City

Mérida

Cayman Is.
(U.K.)

Kingston

JAMAICA

Port-au-
Prince

Martinique (FRANCE)

ST. LUCIA

BARBADOS

Puebla

Belmopan

BELIZE

ST. VINCENT AND
THE GRENADINES

Netherlands
Antilles
(NETHERLANDS)

GRENADA

GUATEMALA

HONDURAS

Caribbean Sea

Guatemala City

Tegucigalpa

Aruba (NETHERLANDS)

TRINIDAD AND TOBAGO

San Salvador

NICARAGUA

Managua

Panama
Canal

EL SALVADOR

San José

Panama City

COSTA
RICA

PANAMA

SOUTH
AMERICA

0° Equator